ROUTLEDGE LIBRARY EDITIONS: COLONIALISM AND IMPERIALISM

Volume 28

THE GAMBIA COLONY AND PROTECTORATE

THE GAMBIA COLONY AND PROTECTORATE

An Official Handbook

FRANCIS BISSET ARCHER

LONDON AND NEW YORK

First published in 1906

This edition first published in 2023
by Routledge
4 Park Square, Milton Park, Abingdon, Oxon OX14 4RN

and by Routledge
605 Third Avenue, New York, NY 10158

Routledge is an imprint of the Taylor & Francis Group, an informa business

Second impression published in 1967 by Frank Cass & Co. Ltd.

British Library Cataloguing in Publication Data
A catalogue record for this book is available from the British Library

ISBN: 978-1-032-41054-8 (Set)
ISBN: 978-1-032-42173-5 (Volume 28) (hbk)
ISBN: 978-1-032-42174-2 (Volume 28) (pbk)
ISBN: 978-1-003-36151-0 (Volume 28) (ebk)

DOI: 10.4324/9781003361510

Publisher's Note
The publisher has gone to great lengths to ensure the quality of this reprint but points out that some imperfections in the original copies may be apparent.

Disclaimer
The publisher has made every effort to trace copyright holders and would welcome correspondence from those they have been unable to trace.

Elliott & Fry Photo — Emery Walker Ph. Sc.

George C. Druce

THE GAMBIA COLONY AND PROTECTORATE

AN OFFICIAL HANDBOOK

FRANCIS BISSET ARCHER

With a New Introduction by
J. M. GRAY

FRANK CASS & CO. LTD.
1967

Published by
FRANK CASS AND COMPANY LIMITED
67 Great Russell Street, London WC1

First edition	1906
New impression	1967

Printed in Great Britain by
Thomas Nelson (Printers) Ltd., London and Edinburgh

RESPECTFULLY DEDICATED TO
HIS EXCELLENCY
SIR GEORGE CHARDIN DENTON,
KNIGHT COMMANDER OF THE MOST DISTINGUISHED
ORDER OF ST. MICHAEL AND ST. GEORGE,
GOVERNOR AND COMMANDER-IN-CHIEF
OF THE COLONY OF
THE GAMBIA.

INTRODUCTION
TO THE 1967 REPRINT

All that we know about Francis Bisset Archer's career is what he tells about himself in *The Gambia Colony and Protectorate—An Official Handbook*. He began his West African career in March, 1894, as Principal Clerk in the Colonial Secretary's Office, Gold Coast, and became Chief Clerk, 1896. In 1896 he became Clerk of the Council. During his service in the Gold Coast he held a commission in Gold Coast Rifle Volunteers. In June 1897 he transferred to Lagos as Assistant Colonial Secretary and in that capacity compiled the *Lagos Official Handbook*. On 1 January, 1903, he transferred to the Gambia as Colonial Treasurer. On two occasions he acted as Colonial Secretary and from March to May, 1905, acted as Deputy Governor. In 1905 he produced the present handbook of *The Gambia Colony and Protectorate*.

This handbook must be left largely to speak for itself. It has been criticised by the late Sir Thomas Southorn, a former Governor of the Gambia, as being "too much an official record of contemporary conditions with a historical introduction". That criticism is to some extent true, but Archer, like Francis Moore, who sojourned in the Gambia more than a century and a half before him, could well have written that he "had not attempted to embellish the Work, since I am persuaded that Readers, will rather chose to read real facts, told in the plainest way than beautiful works of imagination. If I had had the conveniency of books in Africa, they would have taught me to have made such enquiries as would have enabled me to give a much better account than I can now possibly do."

As Archer says in his Introduction he has been confronted with "the half mythological character of ancient records and their disagreement. It has been no part of my purpose to reconcile conflicting authorities. I have, rather, steered clear of them with the intention of compressing into limited space a broad view of the history of the Gambia." With this object in view he has made free use of Robert Brown's *Story of Africa and its Explorers*. Much has been written about the history of the Gambia derived from sources of information which were unknown to Robert Brown, and the present writer has annexed hereto a list of the more important corrigenda in regard thereto.

CORRIGENDA REGARDING ARCHER'S STATEMENTS IN REGARD TO THE HISTORY OF THE GAMBIA

p. 6—The first European to reach the River Gambia was Nuno Christão who with most of his crew met his death at the river's mouth in 1546. The survivors of his party were a clerk, a seaman, and two boys, who returned in a boat without sighting any land until they made their landfall only twenty leagues from their destination. (Erik Axelson, "Prince Henry and the Discovery of the Sea Route to India", *Geographical Journal*, CXXVII, 148–9).

p. 12—Jobson made a further attempt to explore the upper reaches of the Gambia after the publication of *The Golden Trade*, but after beating up the English Channel for a short distance it was evident that the vessel was unseaworthy and likely to founder. So the vessel returned ignominiously to Dover (Gray, *History of the Gambia*, pp. 27–28).

p. 13—The Fort on St. Andrew's Island was originally built in 1651 by certain subjects of the Duke of Courland. In 1661 Robert Holmes on behalf of the African Company forcibly evicted the occupants and gave the island the name of James Island (Gray, *op. cit.* Chapters IV, V and VI).

p. 16—Footnote (1). Particulars of John Vermuyden's exploration of the Upper Gambia are to be found in Gray, *op. cit.*, pp. 71–74. He was the son of Sir Cornelius Vermuyden, the drainer of the Fens, who was one of the patentees of the Royal Adventurers in 1661.

p. 16—Footnote (2). Between 1669 and 1678 the Royal Adventurers underlet their trading monopoly in the Gambia to a body known as the Gambia Adventurers, who, however, went more or less bankrupt (Gray, *op. cit.*, pp. 69, 84–90, 93).

p. 17—There had been at least one attempt to explore the upper reaches of the Gambia between the date of the explorations of Jobson and Stibbs. In 1690 Cornelius Hodges sent a report of his explorations to the Royal African Company. This has been reproduced by Thora B. Stone, "The Journal of Cornelius Hodges in Senegambia", *English Historical Review*, CLIII, pp. 89–95.

p. 24—Other evidence shows that the account which Charles Johnson gives of Howel Davis' exploit is unreliable. See Gray, *op. cit.*, pp. 158–9. A full account of George Lowther and Captain John Massey's mutiny in the Gambia shows that here again Johnson is not reliable. See Gray, *op. cit.*, pp. 162–177. Massey was guilty of the grave military offence of mutiny, but as the judge at his trial wrote, he was "an unfortunate man and an unhappy object of great compassion" and in later times would most certainly never have gone to the gallows.

Reference should also be made to the following publications which have been issued since 1940.

Davies, K. G., *The Royal African Company* (London, 1957).

Gailey, H. A., *History of the Gambia* (London, 1964).

Gamble, D. P., *The Wolof of the Senegambia* (London, 1957).

Hailey, Lord, *Native Administrations in British African Territories*, Vol. III (London, 1951).

Mattiesen, O. H., *Die Kolonial und Übersee Politik der Kurländischen* Herzöge im 17 and 18 Jahrhundert (Stuttgart, 1940).

For early notes on the Mandingo *see* Adanson *Voyage to the Senegal the Isle of Goree and the Gambia* (London, 1939), Jobson, *The Golden Trade*, pp. 51–83, and Moore, *Travels in the Inland Parts of Africa*, p. 29 and Labouret, *Les Mandings et leur langue* (Paris, 1934).

April 1967 J. M. GRAY

INTRODUCTION TO THE FIRST EDITION

The purpose and scope of this volume can be so readily understood from a glance at the Table of Contents that an explanatory introduction of any great length is considered unnecessary. I am glad, however, to be able here to take the opportunity of acknowledging much invaluable assistance that has been given to enable me to prepare the work, notably by His Excellency the Governor, who, by encouragement and by affording every facility, has greatly lightened my task. Most of the illustrations are from photographs taken by him on his official tours; for others I am indebted to Capt. L. F. Scott, Mr. G. H. Sangster, Lieut. W. B. Stanley, Lieut. H. C. W. Hoskyns, Monsieur F. Orcel (Consular Agent for France), and Dr. F. A. Baldwin, and to the courtesy of Messrs. Cassell & Co., Limited, whose admirable "Story of Africa and its Explorers," edited by the late Dr. Robert Brown, M.A., I have used freely.

In compiling the section of the book in which an attempt has been made to fit the earliest knowledge of the Gambia into its place in relation to West African exploration generally I have been confronted with the half-mythological character of ancient records and the disagreement of later authorities. It has been no part of my purpose to reconcile conflicting authorities; I have, rather, steered clear of them, with the intention of compressing into limited space a broad view of the history of the Gambia, from our remotest knowledge of it through the period when, as in all the early settlements on the Guinea Coast, it saw the slave-trading posts established in the face of the opposition of the Portuguese, French and Dutch —a period that carries us to the treaty of 1783, which first recognised the Gambia as a British river, though with the reservation of Albreda; through the time of prosperity for the "factories" which ended with the prohibition of the slave trade in 1807; and thence through the decade of practical desertion of the district until, in 1817, British merchants from Senegal formed a settlement on St. Mary Island, and substituted for the iniquitous bartering of human lives a legitimate trade in ivory, ground-nuts, beeswax and other tropical products. Four years later the Gambia and the Gold Coast were joined with Sierra Leone to form the "Colony of West African Settlements;" but in 1843—the growing trade in ground-nuts having revived its prosperity, and its area having been increased by various additions of territory along the banks of the river—the Gambia was rendered independent of Sierra Leone, and it remained a separate colony until 1866, when all the settlements were again combined under one Governor-in-Chief, though each continued to have its own Legislative Council. When, in 1874, the Gold Coast and Lagos were united as the Gold Coast Colony, the Gambia still remained attached to Sierra Leone, and the name "West African Settlements" was in official documents somewhat inconveniently and inaccurately confined to it and the last-named dependency, the Governor residing at Sierra Leone, and the Administrator of the Gambia being subordinate to him. Its existence as British territory has often been seriously menaced—as in 1870, when it was proposed to hand it over to France, or in 1874-75, when the French offered for it Bassam, Assinie and Gaboon—but it has, so far, proved the truth of the proverb as to threatened lives. After its many changes, it finally became, in 1888, an independent Crown Colony, and such it is to-day.

I am led to believe that THE GAMBIA COLONY AND PROTECTORATE will provide a useful medium of reference for many directly concerned with this region; but I am not without hope that it will also interest the wider circle of the public who are now, as never before, watching with keen and sympathetic appreciation the building up of their England beyond the seas. They may, I hope, gather from it that enlightened rule, administered, in the spirit of modern knowledge, with probity and tolerance, has done something not only to uphold the interests of Great Britain in Western Africa, but to advance the welfare of the native races there. The horrors of the over-sea slavery traffic are a shadow of the past; barbaric sacrifice of life has been stayed by the advance of civilisation; paths of free commerce have been opened; peace has been substituted for internecine slaughter. Even death from disease, in a country once accurately defined as "The Land of Death," has been fought with a success which is ever growing; and there is now justification for modifying the belief that to administer a West African colony it takes three Governors—one dead, one acting, and one on his way out. While I do not suggest that the time has yet come to hold up the Gambia as an ideal health resort for Europeans, I can fairly claim that with each succeeding year the well-directed efforts of the medical and sanitary scientist are producing results which afford ample encouragement to a continuance of their labours. Already they have effectively altered the conditions which were suggested—and in early days not altogether without reason—in the mariners' caution against the Bight of Benin, "where for one that came out there were forty stayed in." That the Gambia has in the past taken its full toll of precious lives these pages will show. "If blood be the price of Admiralty, Lord God we have paid it fair." But my book on the Gambia will not wholly justify its making if it do not tend to prove that the price, in this instance, is neither an exorbitant outlay nor a sterile investment. At least to us who are endeavouring in this far-off outpost to uphold, to the utmost of our powers, the best traditions of our national history, this firm belief, the outcome of accumulated experience, is an incentive without which the mere calls of duty would be but as a voyage without a hope of port. It is the beacon light of the mission which, each in his degree, we are striving to fulfil :—

Clear the land of evil, drive the road and bridge the ford,
Make ye sure to each his own
That he reap where he hath sown.
By the peace among our peoples let men know we serve the Lord!

And thus, in our little way, we seek to serve the King, and our countrymen at home.

F. BISSET ARCHER.

BATHURST,
GAMBIA.

CONTENTS.

PART I.

THE HISTORY AND DEVELOPMENT OF THE GAMBIA.

CHAPTER I.

FROM THE EARLIEST RECORDS TO THE FOUNDING OF BATHURST.

CHAPTER II.

FROM 1820 TO 1852.

CHAPTER III.

From 1852 to 1865.

CHAPTER IV.

From 1865 to 1904.

PART II.

PARTICULARS OF THE DISTRICTS UNDER THE TRAVELLING COMMISSIONERS.

CHAPTER V.

The Districts under the Travelling Commissioners.

PART III

THE COLONY DURING THE PAST DECADE.

CHAPTER VI.

The Colony during the Past Decade.

PART IV.

RETURNS AS TO THE VARIOUS DISTRICTS IN THE GAMBIA PROTECTORATE.

CHAPTER VII.

PART V.

THE CHIEF ENACTMENTS IN FORCE FOR THE GOVERNMENT AND ADMINISTRATION OF THE COLONY AND PROTECTORATE.

CHAPTER VIII.

The Chief Gambian Enactments.

PART VI.

PARTICULARS OF THE DIRECT MARCHES THROUGHOUT THE GAMBIA PROTECTORATE, AND A RETURN OF CHIEFS RECEIVING STIPENDS.

CHAPTER IX.

PART VII.

AN ENGLISH-MANDINGO DICTIONARY OF SOME EIGHT HUNDRED WORDS AND PHRASES IN COMMON USE.

CHAPTER X.

PART VIII.

PERSONNEL OF IMPERIAL AND COLONIAL DEPARTMENTS CONCERNED IN THE GOVERNMENT AND ADMINISTRATION OF THE GAMBIA: SERVICE REGULATIONS: GENERAL INFORMATION AS TO COLONIAL APPOINTMENTS: FINANCIAL AND OTHER DETAILS AS TO THE COLONY AND ITS INSTITUTIONS: FISCAL ARRANGEMENTS: LOCAL DIRECTORY.

CHAPTER XI.

CHAPTER XII.

Miscellaneous Information.

CHAPTER XIII.

Miscellaneous Information.

PART IX.

A RECORD OF OFFICERS' SERVICES.

CHAPTER XIV.

A List of Officers, with Records of their Services: Adminstrators of the Gambia.

INDEX.

MAPS AND ILLUSTRATIONS.

MAPS AND PLANS.

ILLUSTRATIONS.

CORRIGENDA.

Page 78 (line 19). For "the latter" read Mr. Kortright and Sir Samuel Rowe.

Page 90 (second line from bottom of page). For "ten" read five.

Page 92 (line 25). Mansah Koto's death was prior to the attack on Dumbutu. He was wounded when Mr. Sitwell and Mr. Silva were killed (*vide* page 91), and died the following day.

Page 236. The hours of attendance of the Customs Out-Door Branch are as given on page 298.

PART I.

THE HISTORY AND DEVELOPMENT OF THE GAMBIA.

CHAPTER I.

From the Earliest Records to the Founding of Bathurst.

Position and Extent of the Colony—The River Gambia—Mungo Park's Tree—McCarthy Island—Trade Centres and Agents—The Staple Export of the Country—Earliest Discoveries—Cadamosto's Voyages—Diogo Gomez—French Claims—Diogo Cam—Slavery—The Status of Women—Superstition—Portuguese Privileges—The Earliest English Trading Companies—Troubles with the Dutch—James Island—The Royal African Company—Voyages of Stibbs and Jobson—The Story of Job—Native Potentates—British Traders—The African Association—Mungo Park's Explorations—Later Explorers—Mollien discovers the Source of the Gambia—Riddle of the Niger solved—Pirates—The Treaty of 1783—Formation of the Gambia Settlement and its Annexation to Sierra Leone—Bathurst.

The Colony and Protectorate of the Gambia, the most northerly of the British West African dependencies, is situated as nearly as possible in the north latitude 13° 24′ and 16° 36′ west longitude, and comprises both banks of the River Gambia from the north inland due east to a small village on the north bank some 3 miles above Konia, where the French sphere of influence is reached. It contains roughly, including both Kommbos, some 5,000 square miles.

The seat of the Government is at Bathurst,* on the Island of St. Mary, which was ceded to the British Government by the Treaty of June 14, 1827, made with the king of Kommbo on the formation of the Gambia into a British settlement, although some twenty years earlier the country was under the influence of the Government at Sierra Leone. It includes, also, a tract of land in Kommbo which was acquired by the treaty of 1840, the whole of Upper Kommbo being declared British in 1853; Albreda, an original French settlement on the north bank (or Senegal side) of the river; and the Ceded Mile, commencing at Yadoo Creek on the west and extending to Jakado Creek on the east, so called on account of its

* Named in honour of the Right Hon. the Earl of Bathurst, His Majesty's Principal Secretary for War and the Colonies in Lord Liverpool's Ministry (1812 to 1827), from whom the Australian city also takes its name. Up to the year 1801 the business of the colonies was carried on at the Home Office. The Colonial Office, in its present form, was not constituted until 1854, the business of the colonies being under the control of the Secretary of State for War from 1801 to that date.

having been handed over by Brunnay, the then king of Barra, by the treaties entered into by Governor Macauley in the year 1826 and by the treaty of 1832. The king of Barra received by way of exchange an annual stipend.* The above-mentioned places, with the Island of McCarthy (purchased by the Government in 1823), form the Colony. The Protectorate includes all those territories on both banks of the river not already alluded to.

Before proceeding with the detailed history of the country it will be as well to give a few particulars of the river itself. It is one of the greatest waterways of the world, measuring at its mouth no less than 27 miles across, but narrowing opposite the town of Bathurst, 18 miles distant, to some 2½ miles. Next to the Congo, it is probably the safest river to enter on all the West African coast, and among all African rivers it is remarkable for a bar which can be crossed at any time of the tide. At this bar there is never a less depth than 26 ft. of water, and, as there is a wide channel, ships of war on the station and ocean-going steamers have no difficulty in crossing the bar and entering the port at any time, and gunboats can proceed without trouble right up to McCarthy Island, the charts available being fairly accurate. At first, and probably more accurately, this waterway was known as the "Gambra." For hundreds of years it baffled the heroism of the explorers who sought to discover the secret of its source; and even at the date when England was almost making the world her own the birthplace of the mysterious waterway was hidden from the ken of civilised man. The then sum of European knowledge of it is shown by the statement in the "Annual Register" of 1758 that: "The River Niger, according to the best maps, rises in the East of Africa, and, after a course of 300 miles nearly due west, divides into three branches, the most northerly of which is the Senegal, the middle is the Gambia or Gambra, and the most southern the Rio Grande." Three centuries had passed since Europeans first came to West Africa; and, as will be seen hereafter, sixty years more were to pass before this cloud of obscurity was lifted from the Gambia.

The river is tidal as far as the so-called "Falls"—really shallows—of Barraconda, distant some 350 miles, and is navigable up to this point by steamers drawing 6 ft. of water. At Barraconda navigation is impeded during the dry season by a ledge of rocks, which stretches practically across the river. The average flow of water is about 1 mile an hour up to

* Ships of all nations, on entering the Gambia, were wont to salute the King of Barra, who owned the mouth of the river, and to pay a toll of one bar of iron.

the frontier, but at Bathurst the current, owing to the tides, is as much as 4 to 5 miles an hour. The water is salt to Devil's Point, 60 miles up-river. The width as far as McCarthy Island probably averages 800 yards, and at a distance even of 300 miles is greater than the Thames at Kingston. Numerous creeks branch off, the most important being that of Vintang, on the south bank, which eventually, after a course of some 40 miles, forms itself into a huge system of waterways only navigable by small craft.

As one proceeds up-river the scenery is interesting, and large numbers of birds of beautiful plumage are to be observed, the banks not being wholly composed of mangrove bushes, as is the case along most of the other waterways on the West African coast. In fact, after passing McCarthy the banks are lined with beautiful palms and other trees and with masses of ferns and varied vegetation. Beyond this are vast plains of swamp lands, covered with grass, and interspersed with clumps of timber leading up to the farms and villages. The river contains an abundance of fish, and hippopotami are to be found in numbers at Sea Horse Island, some 16 miles this side of McCarthy, and they abound thence to the upper reaches of the river. On both banks good shooting is to be obtained.

The source of the river is situated in a group of mountains a short distance to the north-east of Timbo, in Futa Jallon, a few days' journey from the Niger, which no doubt gave rise to the original theory that the Gambia owed its origin to the River Niger. It was not until 1818 that Gaspard Mollien, a Frenchman who had ascended the Senegal to Bondu, crossed the Gambia and halted at the village of Cocagné, on the borders of Futa Jallon. Thence he visited the Tangué mountains, and discovered the sources of the Gambia, as well as those of the Rio Grande (Comba), near Bandeïa.

One of the most intrepid travellers in these parts was the renowned Mungo Park, who made the Gambia the starting-point for both of his interior expeditions.* A tree exists some 2½ miles from Bathurst, along the Cape road, known as "Mungo Park's tree," under which, it is stated, he used to rest on his way to the Cape St. Mary. It stands in a sylvan glade, and was near an old village called Juku, since forsaken. This record is mentioned, as most of the people in the colony know the place as "Mungo Park."

The River Gambia is of a serpentine nature, and is some 1,000 miles in length. There are several islands situated in it,

* Mungo Park started for his first expedition in 1795; his second in 1805. His travels are referred to later in this chapter.

among the principal being St. Mary's, Elephant, Deer, McCarthy, Pappa, Sea Horse, Baboon and Kai Hai Islands.

In addition to the settlement on St. Mary's, there is one also on McCarthy Island, on which stands a Government House. The settlement of McCarthy was founded when the island was purchased, in 1823, by the Government, and is situated 158 miles up-river, deriving its name from Governor McCarthy.* At the time of the formation of the settlement a detachment of the West India Regiment was stationed there, and land was granted to retired men of the regiment. Several factories are on the island, the principal being those of the Bathurst Trading Company and the Compagnie Française. The Wesleyans have established a school, which is well attended. As a centre for scientific research no better place than McCarthy could be found, and it would be most suitable for the formation of a rich collection of fauna and flora. The island is reached without much difficulty, transport by the river always being available. Beyond it the banks of the Gambia become steep and thickly wooded, and the valley of the river up to Barraconda is enclosed by ironstone hills, of volcanic character, surrounded by park-like scenery. On the north bank, some twenty miles beyond McCarthy, there is a hill with a plateau top known as "Monkey Court." Here, every Friday, an assemblage of monkeys can always be seen sitting in solemn conclave, possibly adjudicating upon domestic disputes. The place appears to be the supreme court of their kingdom, and the name by which it is known to the people dates from ancient history. It is extraordinary, but it is a fact, that Friday is the only day in the week on which monkeys meet here in any great number.†

The majority of the mercantile firms have factories situated at various places up the river, with jetties at which the trading steamers call and are loaded for direct export. Beyond McCarthy Island, however, the decrease in the depth of water makes it necessary to employ cutters, of which there are a number, and these bring down the produce to the island, where it is transhipped to ocean-going steamers.

The main towns at which factories and trading centres exist having responsible agents are as follows:—

* Brigadier-General Sir Charles McCarthy, one of the most famous of West African administrators, who was killed at Ensikuma, in an action with the Ashantis, on January 21, 1824. In 1811 he was promoted to the Lieutenant-Colonelcy of the Royal African Corps, and the following year he was created Governor of Sierra Leone. When Cape Coast Castle was taken out of the hands of the African Company he assumed the government there also. He was knighted in November, 1820.

† The Rev. T. Eyre Poole, who was Colonial Chaplain of Sierra Leone, records that the inhabitants of Tendaba were twice driven from their homes by force, the disturbers of their peace being "dog-monkeys," so called from the barking noise they make.

NORTH BANK DISTRICT.

The Compagnie Française, Albreda.
Do. Jamey Kunda.
Do. Ballanghar.
The Bathurst Trading Co., Kuntu-Ur.
Ballanghar.
Do. Kau-Ur.
Maurel & H. Prom, Kau-Ur.
Do. McCarthy.
Maurel Frères, Ballanghar.

UPPER RIVER DISTRICT.

The Compagnie Francaise, Kanube.
Do. Basse.
Do. Fattatenda.
Do. Walia.
Do. Peri.
Do. Yarbutenda

KOMMBO DISTRICT.

The Compagnie Francaise, Gunjour.
T. Waelter & Co., Vintang.

MCCARTHY ISLAND DISTRICT.

The Compagnie Française.
McCarthy Island.
Do. Nianimaroo.
The Bathurst Trading Co.,
McCarthy Island.
Do. Nianimaroo.
Maurel & H. Prom, Nianimaroo.
Do. McCarthy Island.
Do. Kuntu-Ur.
Maurel Frères, Nianimaroo.
Do. Kuntu-Ur.
Do. McCarthy Island.
T. Waelter & Co., Kuntu-Ur.

SOUTH BANK DISTRICT.

The Bathurst Trading Co., Kudang.
Maurel Frères, Kudang.

At these stations produce—principally ground-nuts *(Arachis hypogœa)*, the staple export of the country—is collected. The nuts are bought from the natives, who bring them to the factories, and at the end of the season—say about April, or as soon as proper arrangements can be made and the European markets permit—they are shipped by special steamers chartered for the purpose and known as "Ground-Nut Boats."

To return to the history of the Gambia. With one exception* it is the oldest colony possessed by Great Britain on the West African coast; but no such colony has so ancient a history, as the Gambia was practically the original starting-point of that West African trade which has of late years made such marvellous strides

According to Herodotus the earliest circumnavigation of Africa (Libya) was that of the Phœnicians sent by Pharaoh Necho, of Egypt, about B.C. 600. Another African, Hanno of Carthage (B.C. 450), is said to have sent his explorers to the mouth of the Gambia, or even to the Sherbro Island, but the exact extent of the voyage is conjectural. Eudoxus of Cyzicus (B.C. 117) apparently reached Senegambia, but mutiny broke out on his two small ships and he had to return to Barbary. Egypt under the later Ptolemies made no further progress with African exploration, little was made by the Romans, the Carthaginians made none which has been recorded. From the Arabs we get our first information concerning the interior of Northern Africa. By means of the camel they travelled along the coasts as far as the

* The Gold Coast also grew out of the operations of the trading company (referred to later) chartered in 1618. Sierra Leone was acquired as a settlement for liberated African slaves in 1787. Lagos dates only from 1861, when the native ruler ceded it to the British Government.

Senegal and the Gambia on the west, and to Sofala on the East. It was left to the fifteenth century to open up a new era in maritime discovery, and to the voyages of the Portuguese to give us anything like an accurate outline of the two coasts.

For opening up the way to this achievement the world is indebted to one of the noblest figures in later history—Prince Henry of Portugal, who, beyond all others, has been honoured as "the father of modern discovery." He was born in 1394, almost exactly a century before his countrymen found their way round the Cape of Good Hope. His father was King John I; his mother a Plantagenet princess, Philippa, daughter of "old John of Gaunt, time-honoured Lancaster." Great were the difficulties with which he had to contend. Cape Non ("Not," or No Further), near the southern boundary of Morocco, then marked the horizon; and beyond it for 1,100 miles, to the mouth of the Senegal, stretches an inhospitable coast, without harbours and without rivers, with the Gambia river some 240 miles farther southward. In 1418 two members of his household reached the little island of Porto Santo, and in the following year the neighbouring land of Madeira was discovered. In 1434 a great step forward was taken. Cape Bojador, the "bulging" cape, was doubled, as referred to later;* and the Portuguese sailors now began to work their way along the barren coast of the Great Desert. An expedition, sent out in 1441, brought back some Moorish captives; in the following year two of the Moors were exchanged for ten negro slaves and some gold dust—first instalments of the two baleful products whose existence subsequently brought such untold misery on West Africa.

But as yet the land of the negroes had not been reached, and such slaves as were brought to Europe had been procured through the Moors of the Desert. In 1445, however, Dinis Diaz passed the mouth of the Senegal, discovered the westernmost point of Africa (Cape Verde), and came back to Portugal with four negroes whom he had taken in their own country. The navigators had at last passed the dry bare waste of northern desert, and had reached the towns and cornfields of the negroes, a settled and watered land full of promise of great wealth. The first Portuguese to reach the Gambia were the members of an ill-fated expedition which started in 1446, and nearly all of whom, including their leader Nuño Tristam, perished at the hands of the natives. It was left to the young Venetian now to be mentioned to explore the river some ten years later.

As far back as the year 1455 Alvise Cadamosto undertook a voyage to this country at the request of Prince Henry, one at-

* (Page 8).

traction being the gold which was said to exist in the neighbourhood of the upper reaches of the River Gambia, where auriferous deposits, it is believed even to the present time, can be found in territory now under the French sphere of influence. Alvise Cadamosto was a Venetian, whose detailed account of his voyages, written by himself, was published at Vicenza in 1507, under the title of "La Prima Navigazione per L'Oceano alle terre de'Negri della Bassa Ethiopia di Luigi [Alvise is the Venetian form of Luigi or Louis] Cadamosto." On his first voyage, owing to the opposition of the natives, he was unable to explore the Gambia. On his second he sailed his three caravels about ten miles up stream, and buried one of his sailors on an island named, after the dead mariner, S. André. Cadamosto was told by natives that their country was called Gambra, and their prince Forosangoli, who lived about ten days' journey from the river, between the south and south-west; that he was a vassal of the Emperor of Melli; and that they would take Cadamosto to Batti (Mandingo for "king") Mansa. The offer was accepted, and Cadamosto met Batti Mansa at a point sixty miles from the river's mouth, made a treaty with him, and exchanged European goods for slaves and gold—the latter in disappointing quantity. According to the narrator, the natives offered for sale, among other merchandise, cotton cloths, white and striped nets, and gold rings. They also brought baboons and marmots, civet, and skins of the civet cat. They were generally idolators, and superstitious with regard to charms and enchantments; but they believed in a God, and among them were Mohammedans who travelled about trading with other countries. There was but little difference between their food and that of the natives of Senegal, except that they eat dogs' flesh.* They dressed in cotton pagns (native coverings), which they had in abundance. The women dressed like the men, but for ornament tattooed their skins with hot needles when they were young. There was a great number of elephants, which the people hunted on foot with bows and poisoned darts or javelins. Cadamosto also mentions the serpents called "calcatrici," and the horse-fish (hippopotamus). He returned to the sea at the end of eleven days, as fever began to make itself felt, not having discovered either gold or the kingdom of Prester John, and thus the principal export from these shores for hundreds of years after this venture of Cadamosto was "slaves." †

* "Upon the Kroo coast a dog is esteemed a singular delicacy, and in the kingdoms of Dahomy and Whidaw the flesh of dogs is exposed in the public market for sale."—Dr. Winterbottom's "Account of the Native Africans in the Neighbourhood of Sierra Leone" [1803].

† It is not suggested that the Portuguese were the first to deport natives as slaves. Without searching more ancient history, it is certain the Moors, from a very early date, conveyed them across the desert for sale in the Gulf of Tunis. It has been asserted—and contradicted—that Jean de Bethencourt, a Frenchman, anticipated the Portuguese by thirty years in exporting slaves by ship from the West Coast of Africa.

Mr. R. H. Major gives—in "The Life of Prince Henry of Portugal"—a translation, from a manuscript, of the narrative of Diogo Gomez, another Portuguese, who in 1460 visited the Gambia. He saw many canoes full of men who at first fled at the sight of his party, in fear, as they were the natives who had slain Nuño Tristram and his men on the Rio Grande in 1446. Afterwards they told him their chief was called Frangazick, and was the nephew of Farisangul (Cadamosto's "Forosangoli"). He went up the Gambia "as far as Cantor [Kantora], which is a large town near that river's side," and brought back wondrous stories of a land of gold. "They told me that the king's name was Bormelli, and that the whole land of the negroes on the right side of the river was under his dominion, and that he lived in the city Quioquia [Kukia]. They said further that he was lord of all the mines, and that he had before the door of his palace a mass of gold just as it was taken from the earth, so large that twenty men could scarcely move it, and that the king always fastened his horse to it, and kept it as a curiosity on account of its being found just as it was, and of so great a size and purity. The nobles of his court wore in their nostrils and ears ornaments of gold."

It is but fair to interpolate that the French claim to have traded with West Africa prior to the discoveries made there under Prince Henry the Navigator. According to the Portuguese, Gil Eannes was the first emissary of the Prince to succeed (in 1434) in passing Cape Bojador. Next year Prince Henry's cupbearer, Affonso Gonsalves Baladaya, set out, accompanied by Gil Eannes, in a caravel, and got south of Bojador; and in the following year they went again to what is now Pedra de Galla, their great achievement being the discovery of the Rio d'Oura. By its name it commemorates the first West African district from which the Portuguese got gold-dust.

The French story is that there was a deed of association of the merchants of Dieppe and Rouen. This deed was dated 1364, and it provided for the development of the then existing French trade with West Africa. The original is said to have been burnt in a conflagration in Dieppe in 1694. The French authorities say that under the association's auspices factories were established at Sierra Leone, and that as early as 1382 a fort was built at what is now Elmina, the first European settlement on the West Coast.

Round this fort controversy rages. The Portuguese claim to have discovered in 1470 the coast called by them La Mina, by us the Gold Coast, through an expedition commanded by João de Santarim and Pedro de Escobara—the last expedition made in the reign of Affonso V. But his son João II. energetically pushed on the exploitation of the Guinea Coast, sending out explorers under the command of the celebrated Diego de Azambuja, who selected Elmina as a suitable site for a fort as a base from which to keep up constant trade in gold-dust with the natives. Having obtained a concession from the King Casamanca, Azambuja built his stronghold, and a church as well. He gives plenty of details of these buildings, but none as to any French fort already there. Yet Sieur Villault, Escuyer, Sieur de Bellfond,* speaks of it with detail and certainty. Moreover, M. Robbe says that one of the ships sent out by the Association of Merchants in 1382 went to the place where the fort stood, next year built there a strong house in which they garrisoned ten or twelve men, and thence carried on trade until 1413, when, owing to the wars in France, the stores of these adventurers being exhausted, they were obliged to quit not only Elmina, but Sierra Leone and their other settlements.

Judiciously leaving this perplexing conflict of testimony where it is, it may be briefly noted that in 1484 Diogo Cam made a remarkable voyage on which he was accompanied by Martin Behaim, the inventor of the application of the astrolobe to navigation. Behaim's famous globe records that they "came to the kingdom of Gambia, where the malaguette [pepper] grows."

In 1460 the Portuguese had established a "factory" for the nefarious traffic which to-day is responsible for a disastrous condition of things, not only in the Gambia but throughout West Africa, inasmuch as the population existing is not sufficient by tens of thousands to cope with the cultivation of the vast tracts of fine lands available.† To this is, in a measure, due the unhealthiness of the continent, as, owing to the absence of cultivation and clearing, thousands of malarious swamps exist—an evil which only the steady advance of civilisation will remedy.

The export of the people into bondage, and the consequent depopulating of the country, is what is specially called attention to, as it must not be inferred that slavery, as a system, was introduced into Africa by European nations. Domestic

* "A Relation of the Coasts of Africa called Guinea, collected by Sieur Villault, Escuyer, Sieur de Bellfond, in the years 1666—1667." London: John Starkey, 1670.

† "I find it impossible to avoid the conclusion that the average number of slaves introduced into America and the West Indies annually exceeds *one hundred thousand*, and this estimate affords but a very imperfect indication of the real extent of the calamities which this trade inflicts upon its victims. No record exists of the multitudes who perish in the overland journey to the African Coast, or in the passage across the Atlantic, or of the still greater number who fall a sacrifice to the warfare, pillage, and cruelties by which the Slave-trade is fed" (Lord John Russell, in his letter to the Lords of the Treasury, proposing the Niger Expedition. in 1839). This was thirty-two years after the Abolition Act was passed. It has been calculated that from 1680 to 1786 fully 2,130,000 negroes were imported into English Colonies alone. Sir Fowell Buxton estimated that as late as 1830, 150,000 human beings were annually carried across the Atlantic and sold into bondage, in spite of the fact that all nations, except Spain, Portugal, and Brazil, had made the trade penal. Captain Maclean, when Governor of the Gold Coast in 1834, put the number deported in that year from the Bights of Benin and Biafra at 140,000. It must be remembered, too, that these figures refer to the best working manhood of the country, as none but able-bodied men were taken.

slavery has always been known throughout the western coast of the African continent,* and, odd to relate, these domestic slaves, in the greater number of cases, would not accept their freedom if it were forthcoming. Having been born in slavery they know no other condition; and, seeing that they are well cared for by their masters and treated practically as outside members of the family, they consider themselves well off.

West Africa differs vastly, however, from every other portion of the known globe. Here the females, especially the lower classes, do all the hard labour, and the men do little or nothing; but the treatment of women-folk is greatly improving. A man's wealth is frequently estimated by the number of wives he possesses. They do all the work, from petty trading to toiling on the farms. An odd thing about the Gambia up-country "rich man" or "chief," as the case may be, is that all his wealth is invested in cattle, and the idea of turning over his money by judiciously investing it in any other way has apparently never entered his head. In fact, so highly do they prize their cattle that it is a difficult matter to get them to sell. The consequence is that a bad year among beasts may ruin a man who was comparatively rich. Another factor in the degradation of Africa is the influence of its superstitions; but this point is of too great a magnitude to be touched upon here, beyond allusion to the fact that there is hardly a native of the Gambia who, either around his neck or body or attached to a portion of his clothing, does not wear some extracts from the Koran, or other supposed beneficial charm,† enclosed in a neatly-made leather pouch varying in size and shape. Superstition is known to exist in most parts of the world in some form or other, but nowhere to such an extent as in West Africa.

To continue the early history of the country. The Portuguese, as the original discoverers of this portion of Africa, for a period had trading affairs all in their own hands, their position on the west coast being strengthened by a "Bull," granted in 1454 by Pope Nicholas V., under which they

* As elsewhere. The Pentateuch makes frequent mention of slaves among the Hebrew people. Joseph was sold by his brothers to the Ishmaelitish merchants, and by them again sold into Egypt. The Greeks and Romans practised it to an almost incredible extent. At a council in London, in 1102, it was determined that no one should sell men like brute beasts, as had been done formerly in England, says Fleury.

† In an interesting note, Dr. Winterbottom points out that the wearing of amulets, or "gree grees," as they are called in West Africa, is a practice of great antiquity and general prevalence. It seems probable that the teraphim which Rachel stole from her father were such gree grees. Homer makes Ulysses wear a ribbon to preserve him from drowning. It is not many years since, in Europe, anodyne necklaces ceased to be worn as a preventative against convulsions in teething, or a cure for worms; and it is not impossible that the modern necklace of fashion is a survival of such superstitious practices. The author has himself known people in England who carry a dried potato to ward off rheumatism, a twentieth-century custom of civilisation which would seem to invite invidious comparison with the Gambians' faith in gree grees.

claimed the right of prohibiting other European powers not only landing but even participating in any existing commerce of the country. King John II. of Portugal in 1493 obtained from Pope Alexander VI. a confirmation of this Bull, with an additional clause assigning the spiritual jurisdiction of all lands and islands which had been, or might be, discovered, from Cape Bojador *usque ad Indos*, to the Portuguese Order of Christ.

In 1481, however, a movement, initiated in England, was made to obtain a share in the African trade, and a fleet was equipped upon the inspiration of the Duke of Medina Sidonia, by John Tintam and William Fabian, at Bristol. This expedition, unfortunately, never sailed, as the then King of Portugal, John II., on hearing of the enterprise, at once despatched an envoy to his cousin, King Edward IV., at the Court of St. James, requesting that the fleet be dispersed and the Portuguese rights observed. The appeal was upheld, and Portugal appears to have remained in undisputed possession of the trading rights of the West African coast up to the middle of the fifteenth century, when we find that English merchants were again making a bid for a portion of the trade. Probably John Tintam and William Fabian would have been the first Englishmen to disregard the Papal interdict if they had not been restrained as mentioned above. As it is, the honour of being the first Englishman recorded as actually visiting West Africa (1530-32) was "old Mr. William Hawkins of Plymouth," as Hakluyt calls him, the father of the famous Sir John Hawkins, whose Armada fame is tarnished by remembrance of the further fact that he was also the first Englishman to convey (in 1562) the first cargo of negro slaves carried to America under the British flag. Next to him in date comes what Hakluyt terms "The first English Voyage to Guinea and Benin," * that made in 1553 by Thomas Windham, who had with him Antonio Pinteada, a Portuguese. Neither of these explorers returned alive. They were followed by John Lok, who brought home with him 400 lb. of gold, in 1554, and William Towerson in 1555 and 1556. Besides these we have record of a Mr. Stephen, who went out in 1573 in a Portuguese vessel, and of several others; all these were private adventurers and not under government approval.

In 1588 Queen Elizabeth granted a patent to certain rich merchants of Exeter and of London to carry on trade in Senegal and the Gambia. The supremacy of the Portuguese in the country at this time appears to have been at an end, as little or no opposition was met with on the arrival of the English

* William Hawkins's voyages were to the Coast of Brazil, but in the course of them "he touched at the river of Sestos, upon the Coast of Guinea.

travellers, although, as was expected, they were not received favourably by the existing Portuguese settlers. This company does not appear to have prospered. That its voyages were not slave-trading ventures, but were made for legitimate commerce, is shown by Hakluyt's account of one of them made in 1591 by Richard Rainolds and Thomas Dassel.

In 1592 Queen Elizabeth issued another patent for the West African trade to Thomas Gregory and others, of Taunton, for traffic between the River Nunez and Sierra Leone.

In 1618 King James I. of England granted a charter to Sir Robert Rich and other London merchants for purposes of trading up the River Gambia. Their enterprise was entitled "The Company of Adventurers of London trading into Africa," and they made two settlements—Fort James in the Gambia, and the other at Kromanti, on the Gold Coast. To them belongs the honour of being the first Englishmen to establish settlements ashore, earlier private adventurers having traded only from their ships. George Thompson, a Barbary merchant, was entrusted with the first of their ventures. He ascended the river as far as Tenda, a distance of about 370 miles from Bathurst—further than any previous European had ventured. Here he was murdered by one of his own men, but unaware of his fate the Company sent the "Lyon," of 200 tons, and the "St. John" pinnace of 50 tons, under Richard Jobson, one of the most notable pioneers in the field of exploration of the Gambia and the development of its trade.* He reached what became known as the mouth of the Nerico River,† and returned safely to England. Factories, with stockades for the safety of traders, were erected; but the Company, like its immediate predecessors, does not appear to have been successful. It is noteworthy that, as yet, with the exception of Hawkins, Englishmen had kept clear of slave-trading. Jobson mentions a negro trader on the Gambia who came to him, bringing women to be sold for slaves. The answer was that Englishmen did not buy or sell one another, "or any that had our own shapes."

About the year 1631 another British chartered company was formed, King Charles I. having granted a charter to Sir

* His amazing story may be found in the following: "The Golden Trade; or the Discovery of the River Gambra, and the Golden Trade of the Ethiopians. Also the Commerce with a Great Black Merchant called Buckar Sano, and his Report of the Houses Covered with Gold, and other Strange Observations, for the Good of our own Country. Set down as they were Collected in travelling part of the years 1620 and 1621, by Richard Jobson, Gent" [1623]: "A True Relation of Mr. Richard Jobson's Voyage, employed by Sir William St. John, Knight, and others, for the Discovery of the Gambra," "Purchas his Pilgrimes," vol. ii., p. 1567.

† It is so called on the map which accompanied the Blue Book (1881) relating to Administrator Gouldsbury's expedition (referred to later), where it is noted that the river flows into the Gambia from the north, is at its mouth 25 yards wide and 6 feet deep, and has high banks, well wooded, especially with palm trees. The author thinks that the place indicated is the Jorunko Creek. The native pronunciation of the name might have led to its being written "Nerico."

B. Young, Sir R. Digby, and others. It is recorded that the merchants under this charter supplied the British settlements in the West Indies with slaves for working estates. At this time many stations in West Africa were formed with similar objects, and not only the English, but the French, Dutch, Spaniards, and Portuguese, were shipping consignments of slaves to their various possessions in the West Indian Islands. In fact, the whole West African trade at this period was in slaves.

In the year 1662 a charter was granted by Charles II. to a third company known as the "Royal Adventurers of England trading to Africa," the king's brother, the Duke of York—afterwards King James II.—being connected with the enterprise, which was undertaken with a view to the protection of trade generally against the oppression of the Dutch, who had at this time usurped the original position held by the Portuguese. The company contracted to supply 3,000 slaves annually to the British colonies in the West Indies, evidence that the slave trade was now sanctioned by the Government in the most formal and direct manner.

The British Government, having failed to obtain any redress from the Dutch for their interference with British interests, proclaimed war against Holland in the year 1664. This war was carried on with varying success, but the capital of the company having been exhausted, they surrendered their charter to the Crown, and in the year 1672 a fourth company was incorporated under the name of the "Royal African Company." Not only was the Duke of York interested in it, but the King himself. It started with a capital of £110,000, out of which it had to pay the "Royal Adventurers" £34,000 for James Fort on the Gambia, Cape Coast Castle, and Bence's Island at Sierra Leone. This company took possession of the Island of St. James, in the Gambia River, and considerably strengthened the fort which had been erected on it previously. A brief reference to this island may not be out of place here.

In defiance of the French, the first fort on James Island was built, as mentioned above, by the great chartered company of 1618. It must, apparently, have been rebuilt, for in 1663 an expedition was sent out to West Africa to protect British trade. Its commander, Capt. (afterwards Admiral Sir Robert) Holmes, took all the Dutch forts upon the Gold Coast with the exception of the two strongest, the fort at Axim and the Castle of Elmina. At the Gambia, according to Barbot, he founded Fort James "for the principal seat of the English commerce and to secure their new conquests over the Hollanders on this coast." The same writer says it was "the next best fortification to Cape Coast

Castle," and, with this one exception, it was the head settlement of the Royal African Company. Several smaller factories on various branches of the river were subordinate to it, and its importance was shown by the fact that it was garrisoned by sixty or seventy white men in addition to "gromettoes." *

War with the Dutch on the Gold Coast was followed by war with the French in Senegambia. In 1692 an English expedition from the Gambia took Goree and St. Louis from the French, but St. Louis was retaken at once, and Goree in the following year. In 1695 came the turn of the French, who levelled Fort James to the ground. It appears to have been soon rebuilt, for it is stated to have been again twice taken (in 1702 and 1709) by the French between the peace of Ryswick in 1697 and the treaty of Utrecht in 1713. In the eleventh article of the latter treaty mention is made of some outstanding French claim in connection with the capitulation of the "castle of Gambia."

The schedule of the Act of 1752, which completed the dissolution of the African Company, enumerated the forts of the company according to a survey which had been held in 1749. They were nine in all, eight on or near the Gold Coast, and James Island. There were, no doubt, subsidiary factories, but none others that were garrisoned or fortified. A clause in the treaty of Versailles (1783) guaranteed to the English their possession of "Fort James and of the River Gambia," which was immediately afterwards by Act of Parliament again transferred from the Crown to the company of merchants. Fort James was abandoned after the abolition of the slave trade, but it must always remain a prominent landmark in the history of the English in West Africa.

James Island is a small rocky piece of land situated about 35 miles from the mouth of the river and some 17 miles from Bathurst. When the headquarters of the Royal African Company were situated here, on the island was the stronghold above-mentioned—named after the Duke of York, afterwards James II.—a most substantial and well-fortified structure, and it was occupied by the company's governor or chief agent in the Gambia. A description of it is given by Francis Moore, a writer in the service of the company in 1730. As well as the merchant who acted as governor there was a second who was warehouse-keeper, and a third who was accountant. In addition there were eight factors, thirteen writers or clerks, a wax-refiner, a tanner, a surgeon, three surgeon's mates, a surveyor, two gardeners, two masons, an interpreter or "linguister," a steward, an armourer,

* Grumĕte in Portuguese means a ship boy. The word constantly occurs in early notices of West Africa.

a "bombay" [bombardier], two coopers, a joiner, a carpenter, a purveyor, and a gunner. The garrison consisted of a company of soldiers, with several European officers, and, seeing that the island lies in the centre of the stream, it should have been almost impregnable. That it was not so previously was proved by Monsieur de Gennes, who destroyed it in 1695. Captain de la Roque captured it in 1702; and a squadron of privateers, under Monsieur Parent, attacked it for the last time in 1709.

The stores of the company were lodged at the fort, which became the medium of the main supply for the company's factories up-river, and also preserved to the company the right of trading and other privileges in accordance with its charter. For its commerce the company had sloops, shallops,

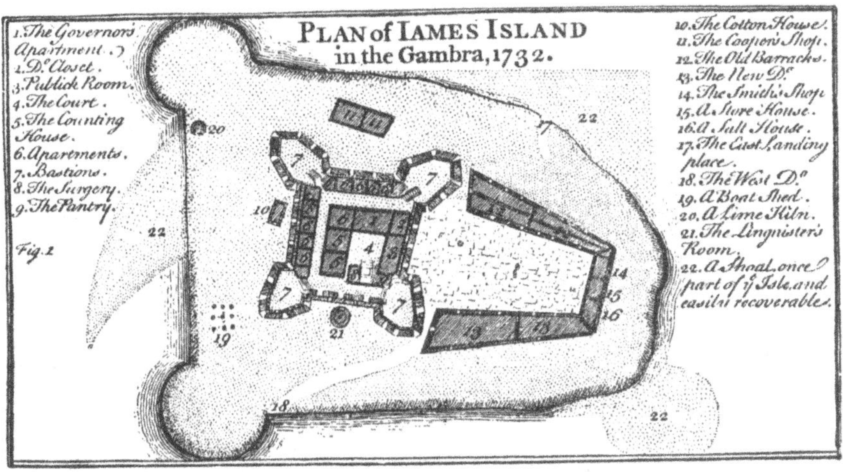

JAMES ISLAND IN 1732.
(After an old Print.)

canoes, and boats, with their crews, and eight out-factories with black servants belonging to them, besides the white factors, writers, and "linguisters." These included Joar and Jilifri, where a large business was done in beads, beeswax, ivory, slaves, and gold. The gold was brought—by Mandingo merchants known as Joncoes, who were extremely reticent as to the country from which they came—in the form of bars turned round into rings, worth from ten to forty shillings each.

The principal trade of the company was the export of slaves (for which they had for a time an exclusive right) for the encouragement of the plantation industry in America. Parliament, however, in 1697 curtailed the company's monopoly, allowing it, in exchange, 10 per cent. upon all freights to Africa other than its own shipments.* Eventually, in 1730, this percentage was commuted for an annual payment of £10,000 towards the cost of maintaining the company's forts and other properties.

This policy was a good one for the Government, as it was beneficial for British rights in the Gambia that the forts on the river should be properly maintained, and had the agreement not been entered into it would have been incumbent upon the Government, at a much greater expenditure, to maintain these safeguards against foreign intrusion.

By the new agreement free trade was permitted and traders were assisted to dispose, at good prices, of cargoes for exportation to America, the Crown benefiting by the extra duties obtained through the increase in trade. Slaves at this period were worth £10 per head.

For the Royal African Company, however, the arrangement did not prove satisfactory. Probably the private adventurers seldom paid up the 10 per cent. the Company were authorised to charge, and the upkeep of forts and settlements cost considerably more than the amount of the Government subsidy. Under the enlightened presidency of the Duke of Chandos the Company made one notable effort to open up new markets in the interior, and in 1723 Captain Bartholomew Stibbs was despatched on a voyage up the Gambia.† At James Fort he found that the governor to whom he was accredited had succumbed to the climate. At Barraconda he found a mass of blackened ruins; it had been burnt by a slave-hunting king and its inhabitants carried down the river for sale to the English factories. His expedition was a failure, and he returned without even having reached the limit of Jobson's voyage of more than a century before. By 1744 the Company had only one fortified settlement left—that on James Island. They petitioned Parliament in 1749, with the result that two Acts were passed —one making the slave trade free and open to all King George II.'s subjects who were willing to pay a fee of forty shillings

* It has been noted by the late Miss Mary H. Kingsley that the worst horrors of the slave trade commenced from this date. There were sad cases before, but the men and women exported to America and the West Indies by the Company were mainly criminals, sold by the natives instead of being killed for their crimes; and the slaves were carefully transported. When the private adventurers were let in there commenced the carrying in small ill-found vessels, and the era of kidnapping. The old Company dared not kidnap. It had given hostages to fortune in its settlements and goods ashore; it had to keep on good terms with the natives. But not so the man with a ship that could make a coup and sail away from the consequences. Moreover, the intense competition for slaves between the interlopers and the Company and their foreign rivals led, undoubtedly, to the fostering of wars which were raiding wars to capture slaves.

† Stibbs appears to have read the journal of "Vermuyden," a merchant of Charles the Second's day, who, after accumulating much wealth on the Gambia, had visited some of the interior gold mines, with remarkably splendid results. If he spent these three months in travelling after passing Barraconda he must have gone far beyond the then bounds of European knowledge of the Gambia, but his names and descriptions of places look as if they had been taken from Jobson, and as no one except Stibbs has seen his journal its authority will always be questionable.

for membership of the new Company of Merchants trading to Africa, created by the Act, though the corporation was not itself, as a body, allowed to trade. The second Act fixed the amount of compensation to be paid to the outgoing Royal African Company. That compensation was duly paid, and in April, 1752, the Royal African Company disappeared, after having in its early days reached the highest point of commercial prosperity that had been touched by England in Africa. The new corporation, it may be noted here, lived long enough to be shattered by the Act which abolished the slave trade in 1807, though it lingered on, with an annual subsidy which was then increased to £23,000, until its possessions were taken over by the Crown in 1821.

Though Stibbs was the first voyager up the Gambia of whom any record has been kept since Jobson made his attempt to reach Timbuctoo by that route, there had been minor essays in the same direction during the interval, but they were probably even more pronounced failures than Stibbs's. Nor was Stibbs the only explorer of English name until the era of the journeys under the African Association set in; for in 1732 Harrison, apparently an employee of the Trading Company, reached as far as Fattatenda, where, finding that his sloop could not proceed, he sent Captain Leach, with boats, for over sixty miles farther, when he was stopped by what he describes as an insurmountable ledge of rocks in the river.

But what did more for West African exploration than these unsuccessful expeditions was the episode of Job, Son of Solomon, "a king in his own country." Job—or Ayûb ibn Suleyman ibn Ibrahim, to give him his full Arabic name—was the son of a chief of the Foulahs who was at once prince and Moslem pontiff of the Bondu country. Job was enjoined by his father not to cross the Gambia River, lest he should fall into the hands of the Mandingoes, who were bitter enemies of his race. He disobeyed, was captured, and was brought to Joar, where he was sold to Captain Pyke, then engaged in "completing an invoice of servants" for the "American plantations." There Job was sent as a slave, but his servitude was not destined to be lasting. He wrote in Arabic to his father. Owing to the vessel by which it was to reach the Upper Gambia having left England before the letter arrived, Job's message lay several months in London, where, by chance, it was seen by the famous Mr. (afterwards General) Oglethorpe—the founder of Georgia and the friend of Wesley, Pope, Johnson, and Boswell—who occupied a high place in the African Company. Touched by the pathetic tale of the royal captive, Oglethorpe had him ransomed, and in April,

1733, Job arrived in London. By that time Oglethorpe had left on the voyage that resulted in the founding of the now flourishing city of Savannah; but Job found many friends, among them Sir Hans Sloane, founder of the British Museum, by whom Job, after he had learned to speak English, was employed to translate some Arabic manuscripts. After more than a year's stay he set out for Africa, and arrived at James Fort in August, 1734. His father had died almost immediately upon hearing of his son's return, but Job set out for Bondu—and vanished from history. The interest his romantic story and remarkable mental gifts aroused during his stay in London had far-reaching influence on African exploration and subsequent agitation against the slave trade.*

By this time the Gambia and Senegal were becoming familiar rivers and a voyage to Barraconda or to Galam was no longer regarded as remarkable. The natives, if the King of Barsalli be accepted as an average type of the kind of potentate who had grown up under the slave trade, had not improved. The journals of Francis Moore, already referred to,† record how he seized upon the traders' stores at Joar, was drunk for days upon stolen cognac, and only left after rifling the factory. Like himself, his chiefs drank and robbed, kidnapped and enslaved, and when mad with rum joined in his favourite pastime of shooting at the canoes passing up the river, shrieking with drunken merriment when a bullet made the paddle drop from a dead man's hands. At Fattatenda, where the limit of the African Company's traffic was reached, the agent seems to have had similar experiences with another bibulous sovereign who ruled over the country of Kantora.

The factors at this time seem to have been little better. Their business was largely receiving stolen property. They were in every way intemperate. Mr. Robert Forbes, writer, died at Joar of hard drinking and McHoughton at James Fort of too heavy a dose of laudanum. Captain Major was killed by the natives ot Kasson in revenge for an injury, and several men of Captain Williams's Company were killed by a mutiny of his slaves. Mr. Lowther, supercargo of the *Bumper* sloop, was shot by his negroes; Mr. Railton, factor at Brako, died from "a fall, correcting his black boy, perhaps too passionately"; Mr. James Ellis ended his career as a martyr to rum. The traders even quarrelled bitterly among themselves, and were not above instigating the natives to insult and rob the white man against whom they had a grudge.

* The story of Job is contained in Bluet's "Some Memoirs of the Life of Job, the Son of Solomon, the High Priest of Boonda, in Africa" (1734), and in Moore's "Travels into the Interior Parts of Africa" (1738).

† Page 14.

It was not until 1788 that it began to be believed in England that the Niger was not to be found and followed by expeditions up either the Gambia or the Senegal, a belief which led to the foundation, by Sir Joseph Banks, President of the Royal Society, and others, of the African Association, which was finally incorporated in the Royal Geographical Society of London. John Ledyard, who died on African soil, was the first of their emissaries; the next, equally unsuccessful, Mr. Lucas, who had been directed to try to reach Fezzan, on the route to Timbuctoo, by way of Tripoli, returning *viâ* the Gambia, or the West Coast generally, as found most convenient. The Association then made the West

MUNGO PARK.

Coast their basis, and from Sierra Leone, where the settlement for freed negroes had then been formed, Messrs. Watt and Winterbottom, in 1794, explored Futa Jallon by sailing up the Rio Nunez to Kakundi, and thence, for sixteen days, through a country in many places barren, but in others extremely fruitful, and abounding in vast herds of cattle. They returned to Sierra Leone by another route. The Association next engaged Major Houghton to try to reach the Niger and Timbuctoo by way of the Gambia. He left England in 1790, and, shunning the river route, went overland to Medina,* the capital of Wuli. All tidings of him ceased after July, 1791. Frederick Hornemann, a learned

* Medina is the equivalent to the Arabic word for "a city."

German, another agent of the Association, reached Fezzan by way of Egypt, and from this point he set out on a journey to Bornu. In 1800, like Houghton, he disappeared from view, and was heard of no more.

Of the next explorer sent out by the Association it is impossible here to speak at adequate length. He was destined to win a great name in the history of African exploration, and to redeem with his life the failures of his predecessors. This was the young Scottish surgeon, Mungo Park, the son of a Selkirkshire farmer. On May 22, 1795, in his twenty-fourth year, he started on board a trader for Pisania (since destroyed), on a part of the Gambia River above McCarthy Island. There he was nursed through a fever by Dr. Laidley, and spent some months in studying the Mandingo language and collecting information as to the interior and the Gambia trade—then, as formerly, almost solely in slaves. Gold-dust and gum, kola-nuts and dye-woods were mere incidents of commerce. Even his host, Dr. Laidley, was actively engaged in the terrible traffic of the barracoons and caravans. When the rains stopped Park set out for the interior with Johnson, a free negro who spoke English (and who afterwards deserted him) and Demba, one of Dr. Laidley's negro boys. Their arms were two fowling-pieces and two pairs of pistols—all flint-locks. On December 3rd the Pisania friends who had escorted him bade him good-bye, and left him to plunge into what seemed a boundless forest, the commencement of the vast unknown. By the time he arrived at Kaarta, on the Upper Senegal, he had been victimised for the payment of "custom" to such an extent that he had little left of which he could be plundered further. In the kingdom of Wuli he was hospitably entertained at Medina, and thence he marched for two days across a waterless desert to Bondu, where the old fertility of the land returned. At Silla, little more than two hundred miles from Timbuctoo, the hostility of the Moors compelled him to set his face homewards. With varying fortunes, and penniless, he passed as far up the Niger as Barnaku, and thence to Manding, the land of origin of the great Mandingo race. His route thenceforward was marked by intense sufferings, but at Kamalia his worst misfortunes came to an end. There he met one Karfa Taura bound with a "coffle," or gang, of slaves to the Gambia.

On April 19, 1797, he set out with the party, having recovered from a four weeks' attack of fever, and eventually he again reached Pisania, where he was welcomed as one risen from the dead. He sailed for England from Goree, voyaging first in a slave-ship to Antigua, and finally landing at Falmouth on December 22, 1797, after a journey which, from its circumstances and the results to which it led, is perhaps the most extraordinary in all the story of Africa and its explorers.

It had now been ascertained that the Niger was not identical with either the Gambia or the Senegal, but Park's theory was that it terminated in the Congo. The ostensible object of his second journey (which was organised by Government) was, however, not exploration, but to ascertain whether commercial intercourse of a profitable nature could be opened up with Central Africa. A captain's commission was given to him, and to his second in command, Dr. Alexander Anderson (Mrs. Park's brother) was given the rank of lieutenant, in order to enable them to exact obedience from the soldiers of the African Corps who were to be taken from the garrison of Goree, at that time in

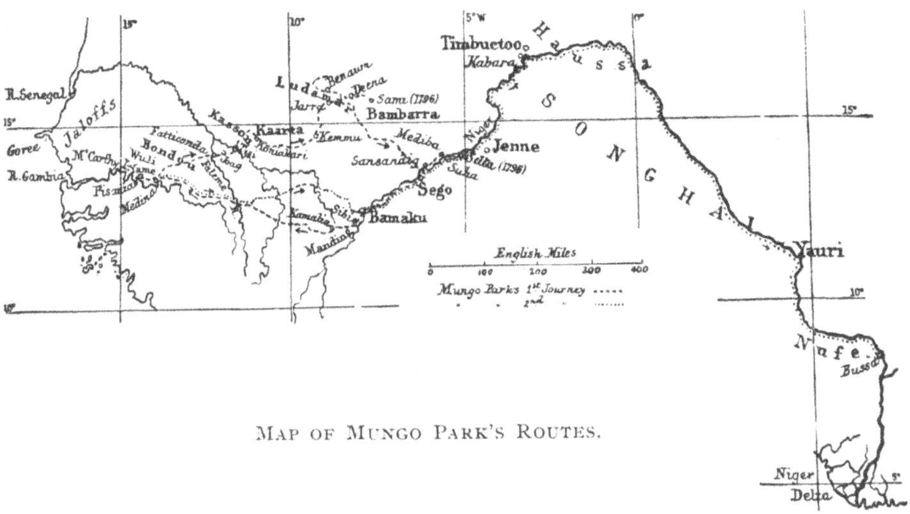

MAP OF MUNGO PARK'S ROUTES.

the possession of England. The expedition met with so many delays that the rainy season was at hand before it could reach the Gambia, on April 27, 1805. Thenceforward it met with a series of disasters. Of the thirty-eight men who had left Goree only seven remained by the time they were five hundred miles in the interior. Continuing past Sego, Park came to Sansanding where, out of some half-rotten native boats, he patched up the schooner *Joliba*, in which he hoped to descend the Niger. By the time it was launched the party had been reduced to three Europeans, besides the Commander, and Lieutenant Martyn (who had joined with the troops brought from Goree). On November 12, 1805, the little force set out on their voyage, taking with them three slaves, and a native named Amadi Fatuma, who agreed to go as far as Houssa. Isaaco, Park's interpreter, had left him at Sansanding, and carried his letters and journals in safety to the Gambia. For a long time nothing was heard of the explorer, and it was not until 1806 that Isaaco was despatched in search of news. The story he brought back remains substantially all that is known of the fate of Park. It is probable that the end came soon after Houssa was left, and that off the village of Boussa—a point now familiar as the limit of steam navigation from the sea—the party were attacked by a force sent by the Yauri King. Seeing there was no escape Park took hold of one of the white men, and, jumping into the river, was drowned. Martyn followed his example, and the only slave remaining in the boat was captured. For many years Park's widow held to the belief that her husband was a prisoner somewhere in the centre of Africa; and this idea she transmitted to her three sons, the second of whom landed in 1827 on the Gold Coast, with the intention of ascertaining the fate of his father. But he, also, disappeared in the Dark Continent.

The death of Park, instead of damping the ardour for African exploration, rather stimulated it. Nicholls, Roentgen and Captain Tuckey were among those who went to their deaths. Major Peddie, who started from the mouth of the Rio Nunez, perished of fever before he had gone far on his road; and Captain Campbell, who succeeded to the command, met with no better luck, though he managed to reach Futa Jallon. He did not long survive his arrival at Kakundi, and Lieutenant Stokoe, a naval officer who then assumed the leadership of the expedition, perished as he was on the eve of making another attempt to retrieve its fortunes. Major Gray, with Dr. Dochard, in 1818 travelled, by way of the Gambia, through Wuli, Bondu, and the neighbouring countries. Gray covered, to a large extent, the ground which Park had traversed, but he found that the thirteen years which had elapsed since that traveller's death had not lessened the hostile feeling of the natives. Dr. Dochard journeyed as far as Sego in order to obtain the king's permission to visit that region, but after endless delays he was compelled to return to die on the Senegal. All these parties included too large a proportion of Europeans; were too considerable to escape attention, and too small to defy it; and none of them was conducted with adequate ability. To all intents and purposes they were fruitless as well as fatal.

The activity of the English in African exploration had not been without its influence in stimulating French endeavour, and among those who, after the cessation of the long Napoleonic wars, turned their attention to discovery was a cousin of one of Napoleon's ministers, Gaspard Mollien, whose name has been referred to earlier as the finder of the source of the Gambia.* His name deserves a larger place than it has received in the history of African development; it certainly merits more than a passing mention in any record, however slight, of Gambian history. When in 1818—the year of the Gray and Dochard expedition—he started from St. Louis to discover the sources of the Gambia and the Senegal he left with no more sumptuous equipment than a donkey-load of stores and trading goods, and the escort of a single marabout, who spoke the language of the countries through which it was intended to pass. Marching through the great forests of Ferlo, he reached Saldé, ascended the Senegal to Bondu, and, as already stated, crossed the Gambia, eventually discovered its sources, and arrived at Timbo, where he met with some opposition, the natives regarding the country in which the Senegal arose as so sacred that they threatened with death the impious person who should attempt to penetrate the secret of the river's birthplace, though he obtained sufficient information to fix the quarter whence it sprang. Worn out with fatigue and weakened by fever, he was forced to lie for a month at Bandeïa, surrounded by an unfriendly population, and in the hands of a treacherous host who endeavoured to kill him for the purpose of obtaining what little property remained unpillaged. He lived to escape, however, and to reach the coast by way of the Portuguese settlements of Geba and Bissao, after an absence of a year. Afterwards he became Consul-General in Havana, and died at Nice as recently as 1872.

Among the new men who now appeared was Major Alexander Gordon Laing—the first Briton to reach the long-sought-for City of Timbuctoo—who in 1823, while on the West Coast of Africa, was sent on a mission which enabled him to dispel the fast-vanishing notion that the Niger was in any way connected with the Nile. In 1825 he began at Tripoli the journey which landed him in Timbuctoo on August 18, 1826. His after fate is unknown, but it is believed he was murdered on his return journey by the Gambia. It would be impossible within limited space to follow the later explorers, even those whose travels had direct bearing upon the opening up of the Gambia. The last to be mentioned here must be the Landers, who in 1831 returned to England with news of the discovery of the mouth of the Niger in the broad delta along the shore of the Bights of Biafra and Benin. Then was revealed the riddle left unsolved by so many explorers who, like Thompson and Jobson, had ascended the Gambia under the belief that it was the Niger.

* Page 3.

Piracy was one of the main causes that retarded the development of the African trade in the seventeenth and eighteenth centuries, and there is on record at least one instance of a notable sea-thief who was the officer in command of a Guinea fort.

Among the most notorious of the pirates who infested the West African Coast was Howel Davis, of Milford, who had the boldness to anchor under the guns of Fort James, and to partake of the governor's hospitality, on the plea that he was seeking refuge from the pursuit of two French men-of-war. He managed, when the garrison were off their guard, to take possession of the place and to ransack the castle. Having secured, by way of plunder, £2,000 in bar gold, as well as other articles of value, he dismounted the guns and demolished the fortifications. After a few more successful depredations he was eventually shot, according to one account, by the Portuguese Governor at Principe (then Princes Island).

George Lowther was another of the rascally corsairs of this period. He sailed from the Thames as second mate of the *Gambra Castle*, an armed vessel belonging to the Royal African Company. On board were Major Massey and a troop of soldiers intended to regarrison Fort James, recently sacked and dismantled by Captain Davis. Massey joined with Lowther in seizing the ship, and they started on a course of piracy. Massey afterwards separated from the pirates, and found his way back to England; but his plausible explanations were met by the African Company with the answer that he should be "fairly hanged." Accordingly he was hanged, upon the evidence of his own letters and of the witnesses to his proceedings on the Gambia River. Lowther transferred his operations to the West Indies, where, having been worsted by a ship that proved too strong for him, he shot himself.

Prior to 1783 the trade of this portion of Africa, on both sides of the Gambia River as far as the Senegal on the north and the Cassamance Rivers on the south was absolutely free, neither Great Britain nor France actually extending either claims or protection to these countries. But about this time the French Government took over considerable territory on both sides of the River Gambia, and the policy of Great Britain at the time not being one of acquiring a large sphere of influence in West Africa, the British Government decided to retain only the Gambia River and those countries immediately bordering it which had been practically in its occupation for a considerable period. Accordingly, by the treaty*

* The Treaty of Versailles.

entered into in 1783, Great Britain retained the exclusive right of trade on the river and its vicinity, but agreed to permit France to occupy Albreda, on the north bank, some few miles from Bathurst, as an outlet for French trade. The dimensions of the territory granted were 300 yards by 400 yards.* This concession, and the troubles it eventually led to, are specially alluded to later. The treaty, in addition, gave France the Senegal River, with the exception of the exclusive right of trading for gum with the Moors or Arabs at Portendic, a trade that eventually fell away to nothing, owing to friction between the French and the Moors.

ALBION SQUARE, BATHURST.

In 1807 Great Britain formed the settlement of the Gambia, which was subject to and controlled by the Government of Sierra Leone, and ultimately annexed to that colony by Act of Parliament in 1821.

On the Island of Goree being ceded back to the French it was the intention to repair James Fort, but at this period —1814—the fort was found to be in so shattered a condition that it was deemed advisable to remove the seat of government and to form a new settlement, which was ultimately established at the Island of Banjole (Bathurst). The position, from a health point, was at the time not considered good, owing mainly to swamps surrounding the island, but the commercial advantages of the place were sufficient to counterbalance the detriments of malaria and other ills, which had been the cause of the natives leaving it. The decision at this

* Poole's "Sierra Leone and Gambia."

date—1905—has been proved to be a judicious one, as not only is Bathurst the only really possible place for shipping, but, now that the Government have carefully drained a large portion of the island, made roads, built suitable houses, and improved the sanitary conditions, Bathurst may be considered to be, at any rate during the dry season, fairly healthy. In the rains,* however, when the prevailing north and north-westerly winds (which are generally in evidence from the end of November to the end of May) practically cease, the island is deprived of their purifying influence, and it is then that the humidity of the air and the oppressiveness of the climate is felt.

CLIFTON ROAD, BATHURST.
(From the Secretariat.)

There is also a great evil to contend with, and that is the considerable range in the thermometer, varying, as it at times does, some 30 degrees at Bathurst and up-country as much as 59 degrees. As an instance, during the month of January, 1904, the Governor, on one of his tours in the Protectorate, found the temperature recorded at 6 a.m. as low as 40 degrees, and at 1 o'clock it was 99 degrees. This great variation is, of course rare, but a difference of 40 degrees is of common occurrence. How really dry the atmosphere is on Bathurst Island in January is shown by a difference of 22 degrees recorded between the wet and dry bulbs. This excessive dryness

* The tornados begin in the River Gambia at about the commencement of June, and the rainy season at about the commencement of August.

is undoubtedly due to the severe "harmattan"* experienced in the locality.

The Island of St. Mary, which is occupied by Bathurst, is nothing more nor less than a sandbank, $3\frac{3}{4}$ miles long by $1\frac{1}{2}$ miles broad, something like Lagos, in the Gulf of Guinea. When the restitution of Goree and Senegal was in contemplation it was deemed necessary that a post on the River Gambia should be occupied, as a deterrent to the slave trade and a centre from which participation in the gum trade by British merchants might be encouraged. James Island was first fixed

VIEW IN BATHURST.
(From the Roof of the Bank of British West Africa.)

upon, but the option of selection was left to Colonel Brereton, who decided upon the Island of St. Mary, which was accordingly occupied in May, 1816.

The Marina—on which are situated Government House, Government buildings, business premises and shops—faces nearly north. The end of the island, known as Half Die, is as nearly as possible east. At the western end there is Oyster Creek, so called from the quantity of oysters that used to be collected in the vicinity. This creek is some 200 yards wide at its mouth, and narrows gradually until the southern side of the

* The dry East wind which blows, generally for periods of about two weeks at a stretch, in December, January, and February.

island is approached. There a system of small waterways branches off right round to Lamin, on the south-east side, the waterways being bordered by dense mangrove swamps. At Oyster Creek there is a fine iron bridge, and by this one proceeds into British Kommbo and to the Cape St. Mary, crossing to the right a further iron structure known as the Cape Bridge. At the junction of the road, if the left turning be taken, one crosses another iron bridge, the "Kammallo," and proceeds into South Kommbo.

A substantial Government House stands on the lofty rocks of the point at the Cape, some 50ft. above high water, and most of the mercantile firms and well-to-do members of the community here have houses, used as sanatoria and for week-end residence. The climate is very pleasant, as the district derives the full benefit of the pure breezes from the Atlantic.

A Gambian Chief and Followers.

CHAPTER II.

FROM 1820 TO 1852.

The Jolloffs—The Mandingoes—The Foulahs—The Jolahs—Hairdressing—Hospitality—"Griots"—Judicial Management of Native Affairs—First Missionaries appointed—Military Protection—Captain Owens's Survey—Barra Point occupied—Mr. George Rendall appointed first Lieutenant-Governor—The Protection of McCarthy—Outbreak at Barra—France's Occupation of Albreda—Drainage of Bathurst in 1841—Importation of Freed Slaves—The Acquisition of British Kommbo—Cost of Civil Establishment in 1832 and 1833—Colonial Accounts first Audited in London—Exploration of Vintang Creek—Outbreak of Wuli and Nianibantang Natives—Petition for Separation of Gambia from Sierra Leone—The Defences of McCarthy Strengthened—Exports of Rice and Cotton in 1833—Vessels entering Bathurst in 1834—British Squadron first placed on the West African Station—Mr. Rankin appointed first Government Chaplain—Improvements in McCarthy in 1837—Appointment of first Queen's Advocate—The Competition of Albreda—The Origin of "Half Die"—Deaths of Lieutenant-Governors Rendall and Mackie—Exports in 1837-38—Lieutenant-Governor Huntley Appointed Administrator—Appointment of first Chief Justice—McCarthy Invaded by "Refugees"—Gambia Separated from Sierra Leone—Governor Huntley's Improvement Works—Survival of Slavery Difficulties—Improvements at Government House—Pacification of the Kataba and Upper Niani Districts—The Military Force in 1841—Emigration to St. Vincent—Increase in Imports and Exports—Currency Revision—Treaty with Nianibantang Chiefs—The Cape St. Mary Convalescent Home—Mr. H. P. Seagram Assumes the Administration, and is Succeeded by Governor E. Norcott—Ratification of the Independence of the Colony—First Provision of a Government Steam Vessel—Emigration to the West Indies still Unpopular—Commander Fitzgerald Assumes the Administration—Enhanced Value of Ground-Nuts; their Importance to the Colony—Legislation as to Palm Wine Duties—First Ferry Provided—An Abortive Improvement Scheme for Bathurst—First Local Auditor Appointed—Mr. Macdonnell Assumes the Administration—Imperial Grant of £20,000—Shipping and Trade in 1848—The "Dover" Replaces the "Albert"—The Keeming and Bambako Punitive Expedition—Commercial Depression in 1848-49—An Improvement in 1850—Establishment of Roman Catholic Mission—First Colonial Engineer Appointed—House Assessment—The River Buoyed—Establishment of a Supreme Court—Erection of Court House, Treasury, and Customs Buildings—First Census—Sierra Leone Ordinances Adopted—Col. O'Connor Assumes the Government—Provision of Public Hospital—Construction of Road to St. Mary.

BEFORE recording the later history of the settlement it will be as well to give some idea of the peoples inhabiting the countries bordering the river who had to be governed. They can be classified into four great tribes—the Jolloffs, the Mandingoes, the Foulahs, and the Jolahs.

The Jolloffs are a well-built people of medium height. Their skin is very black and their hair woolly, but their noses are not as flat as those of the other negroes of West Africa. They are intelligent and peaceably inclined, though if driven to it they are warlike and brave. As a race they are generous, and are very attached to each other. Their country is situated on the north bank (or Senegal side) of the river, and in religion they are Mohammedans. They are proud, and claim for themselves a very ancient descent. The women are fond of gay apparel and personal adornment of every description., The moral character of the race is not high.

The Mandingoes are the most numerous people on this portion of the West African coast. They derive their name from having originally migrated from a place called Manding,* an elevated region some 700 miles in an easterly direction from the coast, and are now spread right along the territories of the Gambia. The people as a rule are true Mohammedans, though many are Sonninkees. They are a very superstitious race. The term "Sonninkee" is applied by Mohammedans to all people, irrespective of race, who drink spirits. Physically the Mandingoes are a spare, though athletic, race of medium height, with better features than the average typical negro. In colour they are not so dark as the Jolloffs. The Mandingo language is that principally used in the Gambia colony and protectorate.

The Foulahs can be divided into at least three sections—known as Teucolors, Loubis, and Foulahs proper. The first section are physically like the Mandingoes, and are very strict Mohammedans. The Loubis possess no definite settlements, and can be classed as the "gypsies" of the Gambia. They are a handsome race, bearing a stronger resemblance to the Foulahs proper than to any other people. In religion most of them are Pagans. They have no definite laws of their own, but are guided by those of the people among whom they may be residing.

The Foulahs proper are easily distinguished from the pure negro of Africa, inasmuch as their features are more of the European type and their skins fairer than those of the average native of the country.† They are not only good farmers, but

* See the earlier reference to Mungo Park's first expedition (page 21).

† The root "Ful" means red, to distinguish their colour from the prevailing black of their neighbours. They are in all probability an Asiatic race, who entered Africa by the narrow Isthmus of Suez. Their nomadic life is well exemplified by the many names they bear throughout the region occupied by them. According to Gray and Dochard ("Travels in Western Africa") they have had possession of Futa Jallon for about 140 years, having subjugated the aboriginal pagan Jallonkeas and enforced Mohammedanism upon them. Dr. Winterbottom, who was surgeon to the Sierra Leone Company, says he saw one Foulah youth "whose features were exactly of the Grecian mould, and whose person might have afforded to the statuary a model of the Apollo Belvedere."

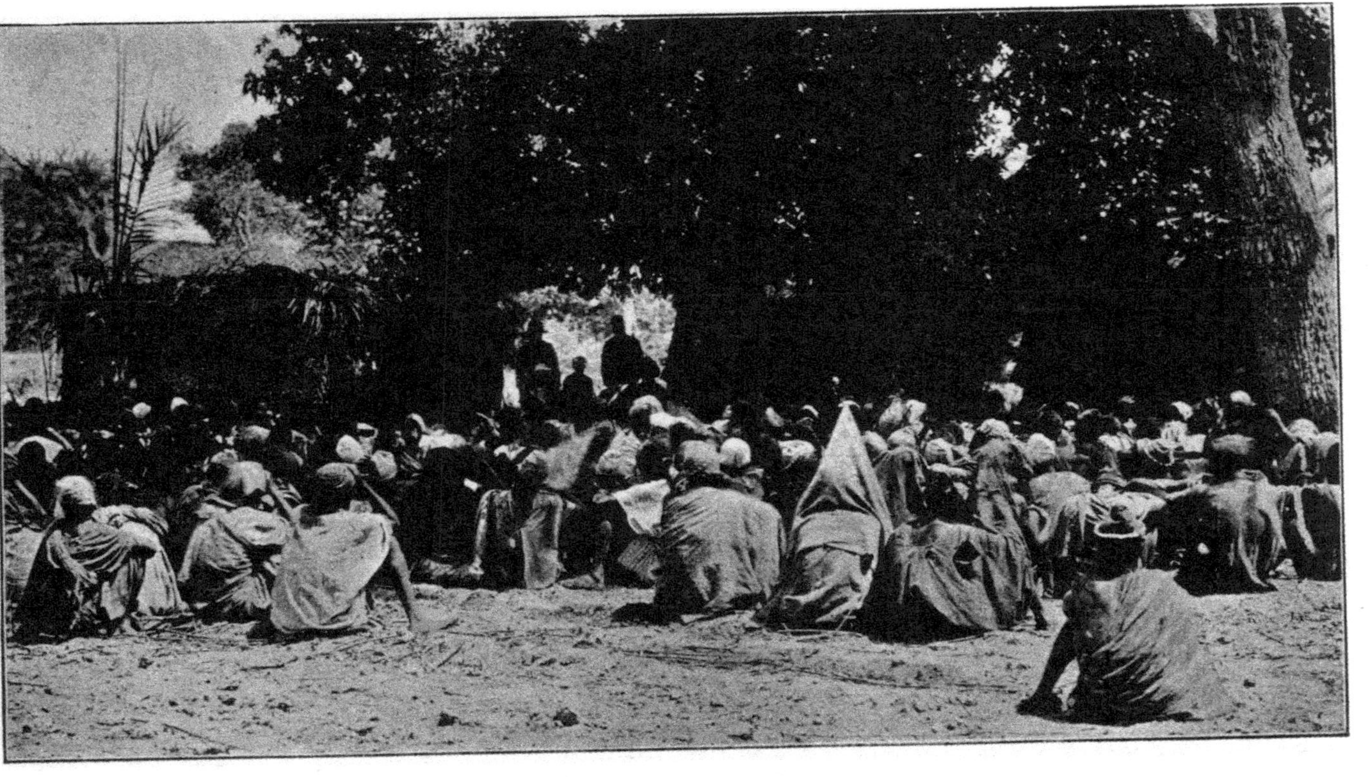

A Palaver in the Jolah Country.

excellent herdsmen, and as they do not usually possess extensive lands of their own, they leave their own country, which is small, and settle in other places where they can rent land from the chief to whom it belongs. The capital of the Foulah country is Timbo in Futa Jallon, the town being situated in north latitude 10° 38′ and west longitude 11° 10 .

The Jolahs are usually of short stature, but strong. Their colour is very black, and they have regular features, though physically they are not an attractive race. Both sexes wear little or no clothing. They are the most backward of all the tribes of the Gambia, and are a wild, unsociable people, dirty in the extreme, and very vindictive. The history of this primitive people is involved in much obscurity. No idea seems tc exist among themselves in explanation of their origin, and even tradition is silent as to it.

The territory known as the Jolah country, or Fogni, com prises those lands situated between the southern limit of foreign Kommbo and the north bank of the Cassamance River, and runs in a north-easterly direction towards the south bank of the Gambia River as far as the mouth of the Vintang Creek.

It would appear that the Jolahs, whether from persecution or some other cause, have always been an isolated race, and have shunned contact with the other peoples to be found in the Gambia. They are Pagans and worshippers of the Devil.

The custom that strikes one most about the people of the Gambia is the method of doing their hair, which is very noticeable among the races of this portion of Africa. Lower down the Gulf of Guinea the hair of the negro is woolly, and grows in tight curls. Here it grows some 6 in. to 8 in. long, and is arranged in numerous plaits all round the head and neck, and in the case of the women large amber beads are often attached to it, somewhat in the manner of the coiffure adopted by the early Egyptians.*

Much can be said for the hospitality of the people generally, and they are most willing and obliging. On entering a town or village everything possible is done for one's comfort, from providing well-made huts of cane bamboo to procuring and bringing water from the wells. This trait in the character of the people cannot altogether be attributed to the influence of the Government, as old travellers' records mention the kindness and attention received. Before the author are the travels of Gaspard Mollien, who writes: "We should have been a long time without finding a lodging had not one been pro-

* In the valuable Blue Book report for 1885 (Parl. Paper C—5071, 1887) Mr. (now Sir) Gilbert Carter deals at some length with the ethnology and distribution of the native races in the valley of the Gambia.

vided for us by a Teucolor, who also shared his supper with us. What civilised country would have exhibited such an example of hospitality?"*

In most of the towns the head chiefs have a band of musicians and dancing women known as "Griots"; they are a distinct section in themselves, and their music and dancing are weird in the extreme. Their principal instruments are the "cohra"—played like a harp, tom toms, guitars, and so-called "violins," introduced, it is stated, by the Moors, and an instrument called the "ballandjin," made on the lines of a xylophone. These people are expert musicians, and it is a pity that they are not provided with musical instruments of more modern make.

The headman, or chief, of each town is called among the people "Tobanbo Mansu," which, being interpreted, is "White Man's King." Bu· the general term applied to him, and universally recognised, is that of "Alcaide." The priest of the town is known as the "Almamy."† The alcaide has great power among his immediate people, and he is responsible for the law and order of the town and for the settlement of all disputes. By the passing of a most excellent and far-reaching enactment—the Protectorate Ordinance 7, of 1902—the Government have appointed tribunals or councils for the management of native affairs. The head chief of each district, who is specially nominated by the people and whose appointment is confirmed by the Government, acts as head of the tribunal, and the members are chosen by the Governor from the alcaides from the chief towns in the district. Any disagreement with the findings of the tribunal is referred to the Commissioner, and the Governor during his tours through the various districts is prepared to deal with any special questions that may arise from time to time, acting as an Executive Appeal Court. In this way the management of interior questions is thoroughly dealt with and the people have just treatment meted out to them. Important cases dealt with in the Commissioners' Court are of course not interfered with, all committals for trial being sent to Bathurst for hearing at the Quarterly Assizes before the chief magistrate. On the occasions of the Governor's visits representative meetings of the chiefs and people are held in the towns occupied by head chiefs, and the headmen or sub-chiefs, members of the tribunal, and people, are called together, and then have an opportunity of bringing their grievances direct to the notice of the Governor. By this means the people come directly in touch with the Government; and this tends to create a spirit

* "Travels in Africa to the Sources of the Senegal and Gambia in 1818."

† Or "Almami," a corruption of Al-Iman, the Arabic word for Sovereign Pontiff.

of confidence and acts as a check on any malpractices that might be committed. At these meetings the Commissioner is present, and all appeals as to unjust treatment by the native tribunal or other bodies are dealt with at once.

During 1820 the Gambia was recommended by Sir Charles McCarthy to the General Wesleyan Missionary Committee as an eligible spot for missionary enterprise; and at the general conference of that year the Rev. J. Baker and Mr. Morgan were appointed and sent to the settlement as the first missionaries. The establishment of a Colonial Church was collateral with the occupation of St. Mary's by the Government. The number of worshippers was small. The Wesleyan communion numbered 150, of whom 100 usually attended. The only provision for the instruction of the youths was that afforded by the Wesleyan missionaries, and the children numbered, in 1826, forty; several of them were French lads from Goree and Senegal, but the majority were Joloffs, Mandingoes and other native residents.

In 1823, Sir Charles McCarthy visited Bathurst for the purpose of strengthening the hands of British merchants engaged in the gum trade at the neutral port of Portendic, and for negotiating with the Moorish chiefs a treaty intended permanently to encourage the trade. In 1824 a petition was addressed to Earl Bathurst, the then Secretary of State for the Colonies, by Mr. William Stockdale and five other British merchants of Bathurst, asking for military protection of the island, no definite arrangements to this end having hitherto been made, although there was a small garrison there of fifty to sixty effective black soldiers. The petition set forth that from July, 1823 to August, 1824, upwards of 200 tons of beeswax had been exported from the Gambia, and the duty paid in the Colony on that particular commodity was £10,000, apart from revenue collected on gold, ivory, gum, and about 40,000 hides. In response to the petition, Major-General Turner was instructed to reinforce the garrison, and to appoint a competent commandant. Consequently, of the five hundred men granted to Major-General Turner for service in the West Africa Settlements, two hundred were selected and sent to the Gambia to relieve the detachment of the 2nd West India Regiment stationed there.

In 1825-26 the river was surveyed by Captain Owens, from the mouth to Pisania.

Barra Point was first occupied in 1826, when a tract of land on the northern bank of the river—about thirty-six miles long and one broad, and extending from Buniadu Creek to Junkada Creek—was ceded to the British Government by the King of Barra. By a treaty of the same date, the duties formerly paid annually by the British Government for vessels harbouring and watering at the Point were abolished by General Turner, and in lieu an annual stipend was allowed to the King.

In April, 1830, H.M.S. "Ariadne" arrived at Bathurst, conveying dispatches appointing Mr. George Rendall the first Lieutenant-Governor of the settlement, with powers which prior to this had been vested in a board of merchants.

At this time, owing to tribal wars in the Upper Niani country, the Government post at McCarthy was threatened by the people engaged in the Carbo differences, which, it is stated, had been in progress for no less than twelve years. The surrounding countries were devastated and the inhabitants much disturbed owing to repeated raids, during which numbers were carried off into slavery by one Kementeng, the king of Upper Niani, who committed numerous outrages. Some protection at McCarthy against invasion was considered necessary, and a proclamation was issued instructing the people to arm themselves and enroll as a volunteer force. In addition, the majority of the sailors employed on the river craft were also enrolled. Further, the Royal African Corps, a militia force, was embodied, all these being colonial troops paid from local revenue.

The active measures taken to guard against the invasion of McCarthy had a salutary effect generally and tended to settle existing troubles. Unfortunately, however, as soon as they were disposed of in one place they arose elsewhere.

During 1831 there was grave trouble at Barra with the king of that place and his people. They threatened to cross the river and attack Bathurst. Prompt action was necessary to quell this outbreak, and Fort Bullen, situated on the Point —a square structure, with bastions on which four-pounder guns were mounted as a defence to the river entrance—was reinforced, and the king and his people attacked. They received a severe lesson, but, unfortunately, several men of the Royal African Corps were killed and many wounded.

The trade of the colony in 1831 was in a fairly satisfactory condition, but the merchants considered that if the upper reaches of the river could be dealt with a great increase would be the result. Accordingly they formed themselves into an association, with a capital of £5,000, to prospect and to open up communication for trade purposes with the countries above McCarthy and as far as Tenda. The venture was in a measure successful, but it was found that unless some settlement of the existing feuds among the people could be arrived at progress to trade would be impeded.

The chief Kementeng was the stumbling-block, and until his power was broken trade in the upper river was bound to suffer, as his marauding proclivities were not only a bad example to the countries in the upper reaches of the river, but caused the other chiefs to be always on the defensive, and compelled them to neglect the cultivation of their lands and farms.

An additional source of trouble to the settlement and trade generally was the exclusive occupation of Albreda, on the north bank of the river, by France, many malpractices being carried on by the people there, who openly ignored the local government. By the Treaty of 1814 the British Government maintained the exclusive rights to the navigation of the river, and allowed the rights of France to Albreda in view of that country having had possession of it in 1792. Numerous complaints and petitions were addressed to the Home Government, but at the time it was not found possible to arrange to take Albreda over, by any exchange, from the French Government. It is worthy, however, of note that, although at this period there was free trade to the Gambia, British vessels were debarred from passing up the River Senegal as far as St. Louis, and, moreover, trade by British merchants that had been in force for centuries was being curtailed up the Cassamance River.

The slave trade was carried on in an intermittent manner, but strenuous efforts were being made to suppress it, care being taken to point out to the various chiefs the destructive tendency to any people of such a traffic.

In the year 1831, after the assumption of the Government by Mr. Rendall, special endeavours were made to lay out the town of Bathurst and to effect proper drainage on the island. The sluice-gates on the western side were erected, and also the dyke embankment on the south-east side of Half Die, to protect the low-lying portion of the town from floods during the rainy season, when vast volumes of water accumulate in the system of creeks at the back of the island. At this period Bathurst practically consisted of two hamlets—Mocamtown and Melvilletown. Mocamtown was that portion at the Half Die, or the eastern end and side of the island, occupied by the poorer inhabitants, who made a living by burning the oyster shells for lime and collecting palm wine, Melvilletown being inhabited by the better class of people. The present division of the town of Bathurst is specially alluded to later.

An important factor in the Gambia during 1831 was the importation of liberated Africans, some thousands being brought into the colony.

A Liberated African Department was formed, specially to look after these poor people rescued from slavery, and everything that a Government could do was done to make life acceptable to them. The headquarters of the Department were at McCarthy Island, where numbers of liberated Africans were not only housed but provided for and taught farming and trades. The Wesleyan Mission, under a Mr. Dove, did excellent work, and assisted the Government in every way to deal properly with this section of poor humanity. The annual outlay up to the year 1843 on these people was considerable. It was also thought that if Deer Island, near McCarthy Island, were obtained, it could be given over to the liberated Africans. It was ceded to the Government in 1834 by the chiefs of Niamina, but it was eventually found impossible to utilise the island, which nearly the whole year round is nothing but a swamp.

In addition to the liberated Africans at McCarthy Island, a small settlement was started at Lamin for purposes of brick-making and other industries, but it was eventually given up in 1839, land being acquired from the chiefs of Kommbo, and the village of Newcastle started. There these people finally settled.

Under the Treaty of July 18, 1840, Soulong Jarta, the King of Kommbo, ceded to the Government that portion of land from Oyster Creek to the Cape St. Mary, and thence following the beach in a south-westerly direction for 5 miles and in an east-by-south (true course) for a further 5 miles—all the country in the above-mentioned limits being included and eventually known as British Kommbo.

As an item of interest the cost of the Civil Establishment of the Government for the year 1832 is mentioned—it was £3,173. In 1833 this amount had increased to £4,552, but these figures do not include the emolument of the Governor, or several special charges which were defrayed from Imperial funds.

The cost of the upkeep of the Gambia Militia for the year was £718. The revenue at this time amounted to £2,500.

The auditing of the colonial accounts was first undertaken by the Audit Department in London during 1830.

In 1833 the Vintang Creek was partially explored, and commerce opened up with the people residing in the neighbouring country. Hitherto they had been unknown. The curse of the trade generally here, as elsewhere, was the exorbitant system of "custom" levied by all chiefs before they permitted any intercourse with their people; in fact, so serious did this question of "custom" become that the merchants, to protect themselves, entered into a bond to the effect that they would not take produce for goods unless at prices specially agreed upon by themselves.

On March 3, 1834, serious trouble was experienced with the people of Wuli, and those from Nianibantang, who in great numbers proceeded to McCarthy Island and wrecked the place, burning Government buildings and the houses of the liberated Africans. Lieutenant-Governor Rendall at once proceeded to McCarthy, but, owing to contrary winds, H.M.S. "Britomart" took six days to accomplish the journey. In the meantime the marauders had retired, carrying off numbers of the people for slavery and a large quantity of cattle. It will be seen that in these days, without a considerable armed force and endless expenditure, the question of pacifying the people and opening up trade must have been a most difficult one; moreover, merchants sending goods up-river for trading purposes stood in a most precarious position, as there was practically no certainty that their cutters or stations might not be raided and glutted. This condition of things was, it must be admitted, most trying, and eventually led to the Home Government being petitioned for the separation of the Gambia from the Government of Sierra Leone, so that proper measures might be enacted to enable matters to be placed on a firmer basis.

The buildings at McCarthy were eventually rebuilt and a substantial mud fort and barracks erected, two companies of the Royal African Corps, together with a battery of three small field guns, being stationed on the island, in addition to the Volunteers. It is recorded at this period that the settlement of McCarthy had somewhat recovered its normal condition, which had been affected by the raid made by the Wuli and Nianibantang people, and it became practically the centre of the upper river trade.

Among the exports of the settlement during the year 1833 we find 72 tons of Gambia-grown rice and 2 tons of cotton. By way of encouragement a quantity of Sea Island cotton seed was distributed among the liberated Africans for their plantations or farms.

The number of vessels entered inwards at Bathurst for the half-year ending June 30, 1834, were:—

British	113	..	Tonnage	5,607
Foreign	71	..	,,	4,298
	184			9,905

In May, 1834, a squadron of warships was first placed on the

West African Station, under the command of the Admiral at the Cape of Good Hope, for the purpose of controlling generally the West Coast trade, particularly that of the Gambia, and to aid in the question of the gum trade from Portendic in Senegambia, which at the time was considerable. Although the British were on good terms with the Moors (Trazzars), who controlled the gum trade, difficulties arose between the Trazzars and the French Government which so militated against the development of the trade that in a few years it had practically ceased.

By the year 1836 the liberated Africans in the Gambia under charge of the Government were no less than 2,386, and a manager was specially appointed to look after them.

BATHURST: THE SIX-GUN BATTERY NEAR GOVERNMENT HOUSE.

The first Government chaplain to the settlement, Mr. Rankin, was appointed during this year, and the old mess-room at the public works yard was used as a church, and utilised during the week by the garrison as a school-room. This building was demolished in 1900, the Government giving the new site for the present church of St. Mary.

In 1837 special sanction was received for the renovation of the barracks and buildings at McCarthy Island, and in a great measure the presence of a strong force at this place was responsible for keeping the people of the surrounding countries in check. The population of McCarthy was 1,500. Good farms were made and the ground on the island cleared. The Wesleyan body, who started in 1822, were doing really excellent work in their schools and on the farms, teaching the people the art of cultivation; and in view of this, by way of encouragement, the Government granted them an annual subsidy of £100.

The system of justices of the peace was in force and worked well, but great delay was experienced from time to time in dealing with the number of cases before the courts. It was therefore strongly urged, seeing the importance of the settlement was increasing, that the pressure of business demanded the appointment of a law Officer of the Crown, who might also act as police magistrate; consequently the first Queen's Advocate was appointed, the Chief Justice from Sierra Leone coming up for the Quarterly Sessions.

The interference with British merchants through the occupation by the French of Albreda had now become most acute, and a memorial was addressed to the Home Government suggesting the giving up of the right of trade at Portendic, under the Treaty of 1783, in exchange for Albreda. The traders of the colony were much hampered by the trade carried on by the French at this place, as the merchants there, owing to the non-payment of duty, were enabled to undersell their Bathurst competitors. Moreover, they had the advantage of using the French ports of Goree and Senegal as depôts for their goods, obtaining "drawbacks" on exports for Albreda.

During the year 1837 the battlements facing the military barracks, and near the market-place, were erected. The former had two 24-pounders, four 18-pounders and two mortars; the latter twenty 4-pounders. There was also a one-gun battery at Half Die.

The origin of the name of this special portion of St. Mary's known as "Half Die," originally "Wildman Town," is amusing. The appellation arose from a conversation between Governor Rendall and the then Colonial Surgeon. The Governor took some interest in a patient of the doctor's in this locality and one day asked how the patients were. The doctor replied that "down there" they were all nearly "half dead." Hence the district became known as "Half Die." It was greatly improved, eventually, by Governor Rendall.

In July, 1837, a terrific tornado swept the island, doing immense damage. Moreover, an epidemic of yellow fever caused an almost total cessation of business, and among those who succumbed to it was Lieutenant-Governor Rendall, who had administered the government for some six years. He was succeeded by Lieutenant-Governor Mackie who, unfortunately, also died, after a short residence.

The most important exports from the colony between October, 1837, and September, 1838, were:—Cotton, 26 tons; ivory, 13 tons; hides 99,209; wax, 258 tons; ground-nuts, 671 tons. The revenue for the year ending March, 1839, was £6,780, and the expenditure £6,633.

In April, 1840, Lieutenant-Governor H. V. Huntley assumed the administration.

The pressure of work in the court of the colony had so increased by 1840 that it was found necessary to apply for the special appointment of a police magistrate in addition to the Queen's Advocate, an office created in 1839. However, the first judge, Mr. Macdonnell, who was granted the rank of chief justice, was not appointed until 1842.

BATHURST: ANOTHER VIEW OF THE SIX-GUN BATTERY.

Owing to the various tribal disputes around the McCarthy Island district, great numbers of armed people, calling themselves refugees, were beginning to assemble at the settlement, and, as serious trouble arose between them and the garrison on the island, an order was accordingly issued to check this invasion. The various chiefs were informed that it was not the intention of the Government to harbour refugees, or to interfere in any way in tribal troubles, which they must settle among themselves. The Government would only mediate between contending parties who desired an amicable and definite ruling on any standing dispute.

In 1840 the application of 1834 to grant the Gambia a separate charter from that of Sierra Leone was repeated; but it was not until 1843 that the request was complied with by Her Majesty's Government, and the Colony granted a Governor and Commander-in-Chief who was also Vice-Admiral of the Port.

Soon after the arrival of Governor Huntley steps were taken to follow the good work, started by Lieutenant-Governor Rendall, of laying out in definite form the town of Bathurst by constructing a system of proper drains, forming new streets, and raising the old streets to a suitable level. These improvements were pushed on with and a great amount of good was derived therefrom.

Although the traffic in slaves had for many years been abolished by local law, numerous cases were continually coming before the courts, and great difficulty was experienced in dealing with them. Slaves were now deserting their masters and flying to various portions of the colony.

Government House—which in 1840 comprised merely three ground-floor rooms with three bed-rooms above and a verandah to the upper storey, erected about 1831-32—was in a dreadful state of repair, and it was taken in hand and thoroughly renovated. This building in one way and another cost the Colony some £17,000. About this time a wall was built round the grounds to keep the people from depositing refuse there. A portion of the land in the neighbourhood of the building was utilised as paddy fields, and as it was of a swampy nature a good deal of filling in must have been undertaken, as at the present day the land on which Government House stands is as dry as any portion of the island. Many further improvements have of recent years been carried out, two new wings having been added and kitchens built, but at best the building is neither architecturally imposing nor convenient in accommodation.

Since the trouble in 1834 the condition of the Niamina countries had been fairly satisfactory, but during the early portion of the year 1840 news arrived at headquarters that the chief of Kataba in Lower Niani, and Kementeng of Upper Niani, had been causing further trouble. Lieutenant-Governor Huntley therefore proceeded to the upper river, and with a detachment of troops entered the Kataba country, where he was, however, cordially received. The chief declared that the trouble was not of his making, but was due to the raiding of Kementeng. The Kataba people wanted peace, he said, and he was only too ready and willing to enter into any treaty under which he would be protected by the British Government. Accordingly the Treaty

No. 9 of April 23, 1841, was entered into, the Government agreeing to protect these people against the chief of Upper Niani, who had again been raiding slaves and ruining the trade of these countries. As a safeguard a fort was built in Kataba territory, a detachment of troops stationed there, and an order issued stopping all communication with Kementeng. By these means it was hoped that this troublesome person would be brought to his senses as it would be awkward for him not to be able to obtain his various supplies, such as cotton goods, salt, and the like. It must be understood that all our dealings with the people were merely on defensive and conciliatory lines and

MAKING "CRINTING" (INTERWOVEN BAMBOO) WALL FOR GOVERNMENT COMPOUND.

great forbearance and tact was at the time necessary—and indeed, will always be necessary—to avoid bloodshed and a consequent rupture to the trade generally of the country. It was not long after the troops were stationed in Kataba that information was received of the death of Kementeng, and by May, 1842, the towns of Niamina quieted down, and the troops were withdrawn.

The total number of soldiers in the colony during 1841 was 447, of whom 173 were stationed at McCarthy and the remainder at headquarters and Barra. In addition, the garrison of McCarthy comprised pensioners of the 2nd West Indian Regiment and discharged men from the Royal African Corps, together with liberated Africans.

In that year a visit was paid to the colony by the agent of the West Indian Emigration Society, and many of the liberated Africans, with the sanction of the Government, took the opportunity of proceeding to the Island of St. Vincent. But the system of emigration did not appeal favourably to the people, the majority preferring to remain in the Gambia.

In 1829 the imports and exports amounted only to £30,000 and £40,000 respectively; in 1839 they had risen to £153,000 and £162,000.

A troublesome matter in 1842 was the influx of the five-franc piece and the Spanish dollar, each valued in the country at 4s. 4d. whereas the true valuation in London was about 3s. 9d. These dollars were, for trade purposes, frequently halved and quartered, and were therefore useless outside the Gambia, entailing a loss not only to the Treasury but to the mercantile community. In addition, Portuguese copper was current, and the Home Government were petitioned to adopt English currency throughout the colony. In December, 1844, this came into force, and the currency was placed on a satisfactory basis. The cutting of coins was abolished and the value of the five-franc pieces was fixed at 4s. These coins are still largely in circulation at this valuation for trade purposes.

An important treaty was entered into with all the chiefs in the Nianibantang country in 1824—a good measure, in view of the fact already mentioned that in this neighbourhood troubles had frequently arisen with the garrison at McCarthy. By this treaty the traffic in slaves was finally abolished and free trade opened up. The only troublesome tribe left to be dealt with was the Baddibus; and there was also the final settlement of differences in the Barra and Kommbo countries to be achieved.

The house at Cape St. Mary, built in the year 1835, was now utilised as a convalescent home, the troops having been withdrawn thence in November, 1841.

In 1843 Mr. H. P. Seagram assumed the administration of the colony, but shortly afterwards was succeeded by Governor E. Norcott, who only remained to the end of the year. At the same date, as previously mentioned,* the approval of Her Majesty was received to the granting of a charter to the Gambia as an independent colony, with Executive and Legislative Councils for the proper administration of its affairs.

A long-felt want in the Gambia was also met this year in the introduction of a government steamer, the "Wilberforce." Numerous delays had in the past occurred owing to the inefficient transport available. One of the first services executed

* Page 42.

by this vessel was the voyage nearly to Tenda, in 1844, when a chart of the river from McCarthy Island was made by Major Cobb and Mr. Wildman, Ordnance Clerk of Works. This was a great boon, as the Admiralty charts at the time terminated at Pisania, an old settlement of the Portuguese and, as previously mentioned, the original starting-point of the renowned Mungo Park.

In 1844 the emigration from the colony to the West Indian Islands was still being encouraged, with the sanction of the Government, special transports visiting the Gambia and the West Coast of Africa from time to time for this purpose. The records show, however, that emigration was not received by the people of the Gambia with more favour at that time than it had found in 1841.

During 1844 Commander G. Fitzgerald, R.N., assumed the administration of the Government.

As far as can be ascertained from local records nothing of importance took place from a political point of view during the years 1844 to 1848. The country, as will be seen from the statements of exports from the colony, must have been, during these years, in a fairly peaceful and flourishing condition, as the staple industry, the ground-nut crop, more than doubled itself. The nuts must also have been very good as exceptional prices were received for them. In 1835 the value of nuts was only £4 4s. per ton; in 1848 it had risen to £12 per ton.

To show the progress of the colony's trade from 1840, the following return of imports and exports is given, as also a return of the ground-nuts exported from the year 1835:—

TOTAL IMPORTS AND EXPORTS FOR THE YEARS MENTIONED.

	Imports.		Exports.		Imports.		Exports.
1840	£105,441	...	£124,588	1845	£119,187	...	£154,801
1841	96,708	...	144,611	1846	95,403	...	164,806
1842	111,154	...	146,939	1847	90,706	...	178,090
1843	85,828	...	108,404	1848	68,960	...	152,082
1844	96,153	...	156,753				

EXPORT OF GROUND-NUTS FROM THE GAMBIA DURING THE YEARS MENTIONED.

	Quantity.			Value.				Quantity.			Value.		
	Tons.	Cwt.		£	s.	d.		Tons.	Cwt.		£	s.	d.
1835	47	5½	...	199	13	0	1842	2,169	1	...	27,659	4	0
1836	129	16	...	1,557	12	0	1843	2,608	5	...	31,900	14	0
1837	671	—	...	8,052	6	0	1844	3,425	17	...	43,581	14	0
1838	661	16	...	8,038	19	0	1845	4,027	1	...	52,270	2	0
1839	882	2	...	11,202	7	0	1846	5,596	16	...	74,635	18	0
1840	1,211	—	...	15,209	4	0	1847	8,237	—	...	99,937	16	0
1841	2,540	5	...	29,766	4	0	1848	8,637	—	...	103,778	0	0

Ground-nuts for the past seventy years have been the chief

production of the country,* and consequently the mainstay of the colony. In fact it is hard to see how the necessary requirements of the Gambia could be met without this industry. From the above table of exports it will be seen that for the year 1848 £152,082 was received, and of this amount no less than £103,778 was for ground-nuts.

In 1845 an enactment was passed for the better regulation, extension, and collection of duties on palm wine, and the first government ferry across the Oyster Creek was started during this year. These appear to be the only enactments promulgated affecting the general community.

To obviate as far as possible the flooding of the back portion of Bathurst, and if practicable to complete the draining of the mangrove swamps to the west of the town, it was proposed during 1846 to build a lock with sluice gates at the Malfa Creek, and to form a road to Oyster Creek. This, indeed, if carried into effect, would have been beneficial to Bathurst; but unfortunately from various causes, principally military expenditure, the funds of the colony were not sufficient to enable the scheme to be carried into effect, and to this day granite blocks specially imported from England are to be seen on the banks of the Malfa Creek, the work having been underestimated and abandoned in 1848.

Early in 1848, owing to many discrepancies that had been brought to light during previous years, the question of local audit was raised, but it was not until 1850 that an auditor was appointed to see that the revenue of the colony was properly dealt with.

During the year 1848 Mr. R. G. Macdonnell assumed the administration of the Gambia.

At this time the Home Government provided an annual Parliamentary grant of £20,000 to the colony, the revenue not being sufficient to meet all the local expenses and the heavy cost of keeping up the military establishments necessary to protect trade rights throughout our territories in the Gambia.

The tonnage of British vessels entered at the Port of Bathurst during 1848 was only 3,549, as against 21,838 foreign, the value of exports being £47,797 to Great Britain and the colonies, as against £130,441 to foreign countries. These figures might be compared with those given for 1834.

In 1849 the Admiralty placed at the colony's disposal the steam vessel "Dover" to replace the "Albert," which in turn had succeeded the original boat, the "Wilberforce." It can

* Mr. (afterwards Sir) Alfred Moloney, when Administrator, called *Arachis hypogæa*, "the commercial idol of the Gambia." (Parl. Report C—4842, 1886.)

hardly be alleged that the superannuation of the "Albert" was premature. She was one of the three steamers which took part in the terribly fatal Government expedition, under Captain Trotter, which in 1841 ascended the Niger to Egga, and made a sheaf of treaties. It may be remarked parenthetically that the value of them can be inferred from the fact that thirty-nine "kings" of the Gambia region had, not long before, agreed to abolish their slave trade for a yearly subsidy of £300, or £7 13s. 10d. apiece—that is, less than half the then price of a single captive. After her palmy days the "Albert" was bought by the Government for colonial and mercantile purposes, and an annual allowance of £2,000 was allocated for her repairs. The Rev. T. Eyre Poole, who journeyed up the Gambia in her some five or six years later, vigorously anathematizes her as then a specimen of abominable dirt, neglect and disrepair. Her boilers were constantly bursting, on occasions more than once within twenty-four hours. On her return journey she ran ashore, "bearing down boughs and limbs of trees which overhung the river's side and knocked one side of the vessel pretty well to pieces." When Sir Richard Burton visited Bathurst some thirteen years after the ill-starred "Albert" had been replaced he saw her lying in a ruinous state on the left bank of the river. He suggests that "she died probably of grief from the abuse heaped upon her by the Rev. Mr. Poole."

In February of this year Governor Macdonnell made a lengthy trip into the interior, many miles beyond Barraconda, but nothing special was the outcome of the journey. On his way back to headquarters he called at Tendaba to inquire into a gross outrage and robbery that had been committed at this trading station, at the instigation of the king of the town of Keeming, in the neighbourhood of Kwinella. Keeming, which was in Kiang, was strongly fortified with high palisades. Mr. Macdonnell and his party proceeded to the town of Keeming to interview the king and his people. They were roughly handled, and an attempt on their lives was only frustrated by the intervention of a certain section of the people, aided by a party from Kwinella, who considered themselves bound to protect the "strangers" in their country in accordance with Mandingo law. The Governor and his suite eventually escaped to Kwinella.

It was necessary that this further outrage should be speedily punished, and a force of the colony's troops was sent against Keeming and Bambako, the people of the latter town having joined those of the former.

The result of the expedition, but only after hard fighting, was satisfactory, a severe lesson being administered, as the towns of

Keeming and Bambako were destroyed. This success did an immense amount of good for trade generally, and the thanks of the whole mercantile community were tendered to the Government for the prompt action that had been taken. The lawless king and his people soon after tendered their submission to the Government.

The years 1848 and 1849 were far from satisfactory with regard to trade in the colony, both imports and exports falling off considerably, although the quantity of nuts exported was the highest recorded. The unsettled state of France at the period had something to do with the condition of affairs. It may be asked how the troubles of a foreign state affected the finances of a small British colony. The explanation is that the main quantity of our ground-nuts was shipped to France, and our largest mercantile houses were French. Owing to the markets on the continent being affected, no doubt they found prices bad, and accordingly did not import to the colony on the usual scale. Anyhow, the revenue of the Gambia fell off during this period no less than 10 per cent.

It is satisfactory to record that 1850 saw a decided improvement in the colony's finances, the revenue being £7,057, due to increased imports and the steady commercial progress made generally. The exports during the year amounted to £142,366, which—although showing that the trade was recovering itself somewhat, this total being £34,564 over that of 1849—was still much below the figures for 1847. There is no doubt that the just rule of the British Government was now beginning to have a beneficial effect in the country as the people were never willingly interfered with except to enforce some obviously just principle of international law and convenience, or to promote general peace by punishing aggressive outrages. To this policy is due the high appreciation at the present day of His Majesty's Government in West Africa.

In 1849-50 the Roman Catholic Mission that has done such good work here and elsewhere in the West African colonies was first started in Bathurst; and in addition to the fathers who came from Paris, three sisters arrived from the convent of St. Joseph of Cluny in France. These good people have done much for the community, including invaluable educational work.

During 1850 the first colonial engineer was appointed. It is recorded that the drains, streets and general sanitary arrangements of the town received considerable attention.

This year also saw the introduction of the Rating System Ordinance No. 2 of 1850, now embodied in No. 11 of 1891, 4 per cent. (since reduced to 3 per cent.) being levied on the annual value of buildings. Huts under the value of £5 were originally assessed at a fixed rate of 3s. per hut. All moneys received were utilised for the proper upkeep of the town, as is the practice now under the control of the Board of Health.

At the close of the year 1850 the first arrangements were made for the "buoying" of the river from the entrance to Bathurst.

The next year saw the establishment of a Supreme Court and Court of Requests, under Ordinance No. 46 of the 11th June, finally embodied with other Ordinances in the Supreme Court Ordinance No. 5 of 1888.

The building of the present court house, treasury, and customs buildings was commenced in 1849 under contract, but through the subsiding of the foundations the court house collapsed, and it was not until some years later that the

THE ROMAN CATHOLIC CHURCH, BATHURST.

works were properly completed and the offices occupied, the premises now occupied by Messrs. Maurel Frères being meanwhile utilised by the customs.

The first census was taken in 1851, and the following is the return, only the Island of St. Mary, McCarthy Island, Barra Point, and the Cape St. Mary, in British Kommbo, being included:—

Males	.. ..	3,173
Females	.. ..	2,520
Total	..	5,693

During this year Ordinance No. 6 was passed bringing into operation those Ordinances of Sierra Leone applying to the Gambia, prior to the granting to it of the Charter in 1843.

In 1852 Colonel L. S. O'Connor arrived and assumed the Government. The question of building a public hospital was brought forward, but it was not until June, 1853, that the work was commenced and the foundations of the existing hospital laid. Of late years the building has been much improved. The year 1852 also saw the commencement of a proper road to Cape St. Mary.

A GROUP OF GAMBIAN YOUTHS.

CHAPTER III.

FROM 1852 TO 1865.

Inter-Tribal War in Kommbo Quelled, and British Kommbo Acquired—Settlement of the Barra-Baddibu Feud—The Paving of Wellington Street—Governor O'Connor's 1854 Expedition—Provision of Market, Bridge, and new Ferry Boat—Foulah Raids—Military Force Augmented—The Gold Coast Government Assisted—River Police Provided—Brikama Attacked by Marabouts—Opening of Colonial Hospital—Financial Position in 1854—Anglo-French Expedition against Sabijee—Power of the Futah Foulahs Broken—Commercial Relations with Bucari Chillas Opened up—Salum Jartar Shot—Sale of Munitions of War Regulated—Peace Convention between Sonninkees and Marabouts—Barracks Rebuilt in Bathurst—The African Steamship Company—Settlement of the Barra Trouble—Port of Albreda Regained for the Colony—Enlargement of Barracks—High Postal Rate—Fall in Exports—Abolition of Ferry Toll—Attorney-General given a Seat in the Executive Council—Militia Ordinance Revised—Financial Position in 1857-58—Satisfactory Features of 1859—An Appreciation of Governor O'Connor—Colonel D'Arcy succeeds to the Governorship—Epidemic of Yellow Fever—Pacification of the Baddibu Country—Construction of Sea Wall—First Manager of Kommbo Appointed—Provision of Pilots—Tax on Importation of Kola Nuts—Cotton Industry in 1860—Flood Prevention Measures—Death of the Prince Consort—Trading Restrictions Abolished—Militia Force raised for Service in Kommbo—Troops Lent to Lagos—Wellington Street Paved and Bridges Rebuilt—The Lawlessness of Mahaba—Founding of Hamilton—Fall in Value of Ground-Nut Oil—Taxation of British Kommbo—Further Pacification of Sonninkees and Marabouts—Swamp Reclaimed and Sea Wall Erected—First Fairway Buoy Provided—Police Force in 1864.

FOR some time previous to 1852 trouble had been brewing in Kommbo, owing to the religious differences between the Marabouts and the Sonninkees. It must be understood that the latter were the original owners of the soil and the king's people. The Marabouts had, however, greatly increased in numbers, and party feeling was so strained that not only property, but life was insecure at the time, owing to the various marauding parties of both sections.

Kommbo being so near Bathurst, these feuds among the people had a most prejudicial effect, as the principal part of the supplies for the community of St. Mary's came from there. Moreover, they were dependent on it for grazing grounds for their cattle. The Government, as related earlier, formed a settlement in Kommbo for a portion of the liberated Africans, and these poor people, who were struggling for an existence in a strange country, together with many of the leading inhabitants of Bathurst, who had houses in Baccow and farms in the neighbourhood, looked on the differences in Kommbo with grave anxiety, dreading the influence they might have on the prosperity of the colony itself. It was not the desire of the Government to proceed against the malcontents by force, if such a measure could be avoided; and to overawe the people a garrison of 100 men was placed at the Cape barracks, as it was thought that the presence of the troops would have a sufficiently salutary effect. The king and his opponents speedily settled their religious, civil and political differences, recognising that their trifling but constant struggles would weary and exhaust both parties. The people, harassed and disgusted by frequent raids, the destruction of their property, the stagnation of trade, the cessation of cultivation of the lands and consequent difficulty of procuring foodstuffs, would, it was thought, insist on peace, and cause the principals of both sections to seek gladly the mediation of the local Government, as, although strenuous enmity existed, and will continue to exist, between the Marabouts and Sonninkees, both parties had every faith and confidence in British protection as an honourable and powerful arbitrator in their differences. However, the desired settlement of the troubles was not effected, the people of Sabijee openly defying the king of Kommbo and strongly fortifying their town.

There is no doubt that the problems the Government in these countries had to contend with at the time, as complications in dealing with the native chiefs frequently arose, required most careful handling, and questions in which the usages of trade entered largely also made matters most difficult to settle.

However, by May, 1853, all reasoning had failed to settle the disputes in Kommbo, which were making the whole of the colony and protectorate disaffected—for news soon travels in West Africa. An armed force, comprising 463 rank and file from the 1st, 2nd, and 3rd West India Regiments, Gambia Pensioners and the colony's Militia—603 all told—with seven guns, a mortar and a rocket tube, was therefore organised and proceeded against the Sabijee people, who to the last doubted the ability of the Government to subdue them. On May 30th the troops left Bathurst viâ Jeshwang, some six miles from headquarters, and on June 1st advanced on Sabijee, completely destroyed it and removed the stockade. Casualties were small. The alcaide and leading Marabouts were taken prisoners and confined in the gaol at Bathurst. It was a pity that more severe chastisement was not administered, for two years later, as recorded further on, trouble again occurred.

On the termination of proceedings, in accordance with a previous arrangement with the king of Kommbo, that portion of his territory now known as British Kommbo was formally taken over by Governor O'Connor by Treaty No. 14 of May, 1853, and it was not long before the people began to settle down. The lesson taught was a wholesome one, as messages were received from the king of Barra, the alcaide of Jilifri, the kings of Keeming and Kwinella, and from many other chiefs, expressing their great satisfaction at the termination of hostilities and assuring the Government that they were now anxious to end their several wars and to reduce their rebellious subjects to obedience, so that trade might again be opened up and their territories cultivated.

The foregoing particulars of the Kommbo troubles are recorded at some length, as a permanent settlement was of vital importance to the colony, and was an object that it had for years been the desire of the Government to attain. There is no doubt punitive expeditions are not generally desirable, but the teaching of interior chiefs that they can be speedily reached by the strong arm of the Government has done much towards the steadily advancing pacification of the countries of West Africa, which those who best know the people understand would never otherwise have been accomplished.

In August, 1853, a feud of long standing between Demba Sonko, king of Barra, and Jawlior of Baddibu, who was supported by the king of that place, was by the tact of Governor O'Connor amicably settled, Jawlior at last acknowledging Demba Sonko as his paramount chief. Thus was terminated an internecine war which for nearly thirteen years had blighted the agricultural pursuits and commercial prosperity of the fertile and widely extended kingdom of Barra. Jawlior was no doubt afraid that the Government would adopt similar measures to those which were so successful against Sabijee in Kommbo.

As an item of interest the author here mentions that the estimates of 1854 contained an item of £200 for the paving of Wellington Street.

In February, 1854, Governor O'Connor proceeded to the upper reaches of the river and was received on both sides with great cordiality and marked respect. At this time the following were among the leading men in power in the countries bordering the river: Demba Sonko, of Barra; Mamady Sonko, king of Jarra; Sandigee Bar, king of Nianimaroo—a most important chief who had great influence over all the adjacent tribes—and

Musa Narmar, king of Kataba. It was from this last-mentioned chief that the British purchased Lemain (McCarthy Island) in 1823. The Governor recorded that the so-called "Falls" of Barraconda were misnamed, and suggested that a good channel might without much difficulty be made, on the left side of the river, by blowing up some of the rocks on the shoals.

When Governor O'Connor proceeded up-river he took with him the sons of the kings of Barra and Kommbo, so that these young men might see something of the protectorate and understand the extent of the sphere of influence of the British, and this diplomatic course had a very good effect. The king of Wuli, who exercised paramount control of the territories up to the country of the king of Bondu, and down to that of the Kataba kingdom, was visited. He was a shrewd man, and on seeing the lads with the governor at once suggested that his own son should return to Bathurst "so that his head might be made large" by learning the white man's ways, as if he lived always in a hut what could he learn about a city?

In 1854 the market of Bathurst was erected, and the first bridge constructed by the Government was built over Mandingo Creek, some distance from the Cape. It is now replaced by the iron structure known as the Cape Bridge. During this year, also, the old Government ferry-boat at Oyster Creek was replaced by a well adapted boat or scow propelled by paddle-wheels; the tolls imposed were 2d. for each person, 6d. for each head of cattle and 1s. for each horse.

It was not long after the troubles in Kommbo were settled when information reached the Government that the Foulahs of Futa Jallon — a country high up the Gambia River — were coming down and harassing the riparian tribes. This kind of excursion, by the way, seems to have provided an annual "outing" for these people, who threatened to go as far as McCarthy Island. But prompt action in reinforcing the garrison there put a stop to any aspirations they may have had of raiding a Government settlement.

As the Foulahs had good horses their mobility was great, and it was always difficult to forecast the direction of their operations. Their raiding proclivities were distressing to the country, but nothing could be done by the troops available to deal with them, and the feelings of enmity, want of confidence, and jealousy existing between the chiefs foolishly prevented them from joining forces and thoroughly routing these marauders. However, as stated later, the power of the Foulahs was eventually crushed, and to-day those in our protectorate are a quiet people, and the best herdsmen and farmers in the Gambia.

During 1854 the Militia force was increased to 450, fifty of these being trained specially as artillerymen, and it is recorded that these auxiliary troops did good work. The colony at this time had to augment its military establishment for the better protection of trade and the object of pacifying the country generally.

In the same year application was received from the Government of the Gold Coast for the assistance of 300 troops from the Gambia. It was impossible fully to comply with this request, but some aid was given, a detachment of the West India Regiment being sent down, the Militia meanwhile doing garrison duty in Bathurst.

During 1854 Brikama, the chief town in Lower, or Foreign,

IN THE MARKET AT BATHURST.

Kommbo—a clean and flourishing place—was attacked by the Gunjour Marabouts and completely destroyed.

The new colonial hospital was opened in July of this year.

The revenue during 1854, notwithstanding the native troubles in the Gambia, had amounted to £9,738. In 1853 the returns had been £10,515, the decrease being no doubt due to the troubles in Kommbo. The expenditure in 1854 was £15,273. The exports during the year had reached £215,803 and the imports £126,454.

The inauguration took place during 1855 of a river police—a vessel and ten men—under a specially engaged European in the colony, being provided for the prevention of smuggling. This movement was strongly supported by the mercantile community, who assisted with funds in support of the service.

In July, 1855, a further rising occurred among the Sabijee people, and another expedition had to be sent against them, in which a detachment of French troops, numbering some eighty, at the invitation of Governor O'Connor to the French Governor at Goree, joined and assisted in the most disinterested and friendly manner. By August of that year Sabijee was again taken at the point of the bayonet, the French troops ably assisting those of the colony. The casualties in this engagement were very heavy on both sides. It was afterwards ascertained that the Marabouts of Sabijee were led by one Omar, a Moor, who had formerly been an officer in the army of Abdel Kader, which no doubt accounted for the skilful tactics displayed in resisting our attack. It must be recorded that in this engagement the leading men of Kommbo on the king's side, and the mercantile community of the colony, did all they could to aid the Government. In the assault on Sabijee Governor O'Connor was twice wounded, once in the arm and again in the shoulder. There is no doubt that at this period the Marabouts in the Gambia were responsible for much of the existing strife and were instigated by so-called missionaries of the "Prophet." The Omar mentioned was, for example, entirely responsible for this further rising in Sabijee and for the troubles in the neighbourhood of Gunjour. He was, however, eventually taken by the French and conveyed to Goree.

In November, 1855, news reached Bathurst that the Futah Foulahs, several thousands strong, had shut themselves up in the strongly-stockaded town of Suraja and were surrounded by the Mandingoes of the upper river. Among the Foulahs was their leading chief, Bakary Koi, as well as Omera Katu, another influential and troublesome chief who had been worrying the garrison at McCarthy Island. Suraja was eventually taken, with great loss to the Foulahs, and Omera Katu was made a prisoner by the king of Kataba, and beheaded. This sweeping victory destroyed the prestige of the Futah Foulahs, who had hitherto been considered invincible, and few events could at that period have occurred so opportunely for the interests of the Gambia.

In January, 1856, Governor O'Connor proceeded to the town of Joal, on the sea-coast to the north, for the purpose of opening up trade between that place, Boor Sin (now French territory), and the Gambia. He was received with every courtesy by the king, Bucari Chillas, and his people. A convention on a satisfactory basis was entered into, but the king was keenly jealous of any foreign settlement being made in his territory.

In May, 1855, Salum Jartar, the king of Kommbo, was shot during an attack made by the people of Busumballa. He was succeeded by the Sallatte of Yundum, who received the "Cap" in January, 1856.

Owing to the enormous trade at this period in arms and ammunition, it was necessary to pass an Ordinance (No. 4 of 1856) to regulate the sale of munitions of war. It was afterwards repealed by No. 13 of 1899, for which Nos. 4 and 7 of 1892 have since been substituted.*

The year 1856 saw the signing of an important convention

THE WEST AFRICAN FRONTIER FORCE: OFFICERS' QUARTERS IN MCCARTHY SQUARE, BATHURST. (The Building to the right is the Men's Barracks.)

between the Sonninkees and Marabouts of both Upper and Lower Kommbo, by which they agreed to abstain in future from hostilities, and to promote, maintain, and preserve peace throughout the kingdoms of Kommbo. But on no account were the original malcontents of Sabijee permitted to return into British Kommbo.

During this year the men's portion of the old barracks in McCarthy Square was practically rebuilt, the structure as now existing being erected; but it was not until 1858 that the

* See Chapter XIII.

officers' quarters were thoroughly overhauled and put into proper condition.

The main line of steamers running to the Gambia and the West Coast of Africa at this period were those of the African Steamship Company, the head of the concern being Mr. Macgregor Laird.

In May, 1857, there were serious troubles between the king of Barra and his son-in-law, Ansumana Jaggi, a powerful Serrahooli chief. As an outcome the kingdom of Barra was again devastated, entailing at the time of the year (the harvest) very serious losses to the commercial branches of the community.

There was much to be said on the side of Ansumana, who was only endeavouring to obtain the rights he had fairly earned from Demba Sonko, who was a grasping old man. But the Government could not permit this strife to continue.

A meeting was arranged at Fort Bullen, Barra Point, between the disaffected parties. The Governor was present with a strong escort, and Ansumana stated that he was willing to stand by the Governor's decision in the matter. Terms were finally agreed upon, and at the request of the Serrahooli chief and his party, some 300 strong, they finally left Barra in the Government yacht "Dover" for Fatatenda, *en route* for Tilliboo in the Serrahooli country. The residue of Ansumana's followers at Fort Bullen dispersed, the Bambarra people taking service with the king of Barra, and others being permitted to come over in small parties to Bathurst, where they were willingly employed by the merchants and traders. These people eventually settled on land given them in British Kommbo. From the many troubles in these countries already mentioned it will be obvious that a perfect pandemonium would have existed at this time throughout the Gambia had it not been for the steady and guiding influence of the Government. It is true that bloodshed has been in a small measure the outcome of punitive expeditions, but it can readily be understood how much more blood would have been spilt by the people themselves had the restraining power of our military forces been absent.

The year 1857 marks a special epoch in the history of the Gambia, for it was in this year the convention entered into between Great Britain .and France regained for the colony the Port of Albreda, about which so much has already been written on the baneful effect on our trade caused by the presence of a foreign free port in our territories. In 1678, by the peace of Nimeguen, Goree was ceded to France, and henceforward French influence was consolidated on the Senegal. But, in addition, they had Albreda on the Gambia. As previously recorded, in

1783 the intermittent struggle with France was concluded by the French recognition, under the Treaty of Versailles, of exclusive British trading rights on the Gambia, with the exception of the French factory at Albreda, in return for a similar concession to themselves of the commercial monopoly of the River Senegal; but as a set-off against the French factory on the Gambia the British retained the exclusive right to trade for gum with the Arabs or Moors of Portendik, on the Senegal coast near Cape Blanco, about 120 miles north of St. Louis. It cannot be said that the intention of the treaty was very strictly observed by our competitors, for in 1786 they contended that, though the agreement guaranteed the Gambia to Great Britain, the river only began at James Island; and that therefore they were free to build a fort at or slightly below that point.* When all the French possessions in Senegal which had been held by the British from time to time during the Napoleonic wars were given back to France by the Treaty of Paris in 1814, and the British hold over the Gambia was more clearly defined, the French only retained their one post on the river—Albreda. Finally, as mentioned above, by the convention of 1857 a most unsatisfactory condition of things was adjusted by the withdrawal of the French from Albreda in return for the relinquishing, by the British, of their trade monopoly with Portendik.

During this year the barracks at Cape St. Mary were enlarged and thoroughly repaired, as were also the barracks at Fort Bullen and McCarthy Island.

The postage at this time from England to the colony was 6d.

The exports of gold, gum, ivory and teak wood, which in 1836 had amounted to £45,229, fell during 1857 to £632, and had it not been for the increase in the ground-nut industry the outlook for the colony would have been black indeed.

The toll at the Government Ferry at Oyster Creek, created in 1854, was abolished this year, and the ferry made free, thus bringing about increased trade between Kommbo and Bathurst.

In 1858 the Queen's Advocate of the colony, now Attorney-General, was first given a seat in the Executive Council.

During the year the Ordinance "To embody and constitute a Militia in the Colony" was amended. The enactment as it originally stood provided for 300 men in Bathurst, 100 at McCarthy Island and fifty at Fort Bullen. It was found, however, as the majority of the men were petty traders and small agents up the river, mechanics and other workmen, that the number enrolled was too great, as it interfered with the men's occupation. Accordingly the amendment provided only for 100 men at

* Lucas: "Historical Geography of the British Colonies," Vol. III., p. 110.

Bathurst, to be trained as artillery. The men were clothed by the Government, the condition of enlistment being twelve days training during the year, and a liability to be employed on special duties for which they might be required during times of trouble.

The revenue of the colony during 1857 was £12,329; that for 1858 showed a slight falling off, £12,245 being received, but it clearly indicates that the Gambia trade was fairly satisfactory, when the commercial crisis which existed at this time between Europe and the United States of America is taken into consideration. In 1857 the ground-nuts exported amounted to 13,554 tons, of the value of £162,649; in 1858 this was increased to 15,728 tons, having a value of £188,736.

As an evidence of the good work that had been done in both British and Foreign Kommbo, the author may mention the satisfactory conditions existing in 1859.

Governor O'Connor was about to proceed on leave and to vacate the Government of the colony, and to show the respect in which he was held a numerous deputation from the people of both Kommbos, who had been at enmity and the most inveterate foes only a few years back, now met together in friendly palaver to wish the Governor "*bon voyage.*" Among those present were Toumanni Mousa, the king of Yundum, who succeeded to the "Cap" on the death of the king of Kommbo in 1856; and the almamies and alcaides from Brikama, Baccow, Brufut, Busumballa, Faraba Bunta, Tamboor, Gunjour, Mandwari and Old Sabijee, attended by their followers. Governor O'Connor's *régime* in the colony can be characterised as certainly one of its foundation stones.

In September, 1859, Colonel G. A. K. D'Arcy succeeded Colonel O'Connor as Governor of the colony.

After a lapse of nearly twenty-two years an epidemic of yellow fever again visited Bathurst, in the latter part of 1859. All trade was, for the time, paralysed by the absence of the European merchants who, on the breaking out of the sickness, promptly left for the islands and England. The year consequently saw a falling off in the revenue and in the export of the ground-nut During this epidemic the troops lost many officers, non-commissioned officers and men who were serving in the Gambia; and a monument, which stands on the western side of McCarthy Square, near the barracks entrance, was erected to their memory by the remaining officers of the garrison.

Early in 1860 trouble was reported in the Baddibu country, owing to the lawless manner in which the king and his people interfered with trade, robbed the agents of firms and generally pillaged all those strangers who happened to come within Baddibu territory. Matters became so acute that the merchants petitioned the Government to take decisive remedial measures, and at last it was decided to blockade the ports of the river and creeks by which communication with the Baddibu country was maintained. This was the only course feasible at the time, as the Baddibus on land were too strong for military measures to be undertaken successfully by the existing troops in the colony.

As the blockade failed in its object it became of serious moment that special measures should be taken to obtain the troops necessary for land operations. Governor D'Arcy accordingly proceeded to Sierra Leone and there discussed matters with Governor Hill. They both agreed upon the urgency for the expedition, as the numerous tribes around the settlement and along the banks of the river were eagerly awaiting Government action against the powerful king of Baddibu.

The Governor of Sierra Leone at once placed his garrison at the disposal of the colony, and they proceeded to the scene of operations on February 15th. The forces available were three companies of the 1st West India Regiment, four companies of the 2nd West India Regiment, the Gambia Militia Artillery, and 600 allies. H.M.SS. "Arrogant" (Commodore Edmonstone), "Torch" (Commander Smith), and "Falcon" (Commander Heneage), and the colony's steamer "Dover," with cutters, conveyed the troops and impedimenta, and ably assisted in shelling the huge earthworks the enemy had thrown up off the landing-place at Suarra Kunda Creek. The place to be attacked was a strong and well-made stockade twenty miles up the river, three up the creek, and one of marching. The little "Dover" carried the Europeans to the attack and brought them back to sleep on board their ship. After desperate resistance our troops succeeded in effecting a landing and driving the Baddibus from their defences, which were demolished and the towns of Saba and Suarra Kunda destroyed. Our loss was four Europeans (Lieutenant Hamilton of the "Arrogant" and three seamen) killed, and twenty-one wounded. The West Indians lost but one. Four of the king's sons were slain. After this victory the king of Baddibu and his chiefs begged for peace, and for reasons of humanity this was acceded to, a heavy fine being levied, and the Treaty of August 18, 1861, signed.

The sea-wall at Half Die, running from the corner of Hill Street to Cotton Street (originally Wildman Street), was commenced in 1860 by penal labour and finally completed in 1861.

This was an immense boon to the north-east portion of the island.

The year 1861 saw the first manager of Kommbo appointed, the duties originally being carried out by the officer in charge of the detachment of troops at the Cape, an arrangement which was not found to work satisfactorily.

In August of this year the colony was provided with a special pilot boat, the "Grace Darling," for the convenience of ships entering the port that required pilots. The year 1862 saw the introduction of Ordinance No. 7, which specially defined the duties of Gambia pilots. Pilots have since, however, been abolished, and an improved system of "buoying" the harbour adopted.*

The taxation on the import of kola-nuts (*Sterculia acuminata*) was introduced on March 25, 1861, by Ordinance No. 1 of that year, since repealed and embodied in the present Customs Ordinance.* At this period the duty on ground-nuts exported was 1d. per bushel (equivalent to 6s. 8d. per ton), the same as at the present day.

As an item of interest, the author mentions the following fact with respect to cotton grown in the Gambia in 1860, compiled from returns given by the traders during this year to the Government. The number of native "pagns" (or cloths) actually purchased amounted to 104,904, the quantity of cotton utilised in the weaving of each cloth being estimated at 3 lb. This gives 314,712 lb. of cotton, to which must be added 147,840 lb. of raw cotton that was purchased, making in all a total of 462,552 lb., or roughly 206 tons, of cotton actually obtained by the traders. Beside this amount another 14 tons was locally consumed in the various districts, making a grand total of 220 tons of cotton grown in the colony and protectorate during the year. From this it will be seen that if the cultivation of cotton is now taken up seriously by the people, with the opportunities the Government are offering, the export return for this product should shortly become a substantial one.

As long ago as 1760 the London Society of Arts judged, from specimens of Senegambia cotton they had seen, that an adequate supply could be obtained from Africa, and they offered a gold medal for the greatest quantity, "not less than two tons," the growth of any of His Majesty's settlements on the coast of Africa, and imported by private adventurers into any of the ports of Great Britain in 1761. That cotton of the best quality can be got outside America the author has no doubt. What is now known

* **Particulars as to buoyage dues and details as to Customs arrangements will be found in Chapter XIII.**

as Sea Island cotton, from the seeds of which the finest qualities have been obtained, is a native of Honduras. It spread thence to the West Indies, and was carried to the United States shortly after the Revolution. No finer cotton has ever been grown than that raised in the island of Tobago between the years 1789 and 1792; and Egypt has furnished a staple which for quality and length holds a high rank, and comes next to Sea Island. In South America the cotton plant thrives in all the varied climates, from Para to Rio Grande. In India the quantity for export, though not of the highest quality, can be increased. In East Africa the outlook is very promising. As for West Africa, a part of the greatest potential market for raw material in the world, it is capable of producing more cotton than the present world's supply; and one authority—Mr. Alfred Hulton, President of the Manchester Chamber of Commerce—expects that within the next five years West Africa will send home a million bales.

Those most directly interested in lessening our dependence upon America have, perhaps, been rather slow to move effectively, but an important beginning was made in May, 1902, when —largely through the instrumentality of Sir Alfred Jones, who has always been in the forefront of every good work for the development of West Africa—there was formed the British Cotton Growing Association, which had for its object the widening of the area of cotton cultivation under the British flag, and more especially in West Africa. This meeting was followed by another in June, 1902, when it was decided to raise a guarantee fund of £50,000. Experimental plantations were inaugurated, large quantities of seeds were distributed, ginning and baling machinery were sent out, advances were made to planters, and grants were given to various colonies. In October, 1903, the guarantee fund was doubled; but it was soon seen that this was still inadequate, and it was decided to increase it to £500,000, and to petition the King to grant a Royal Charter of Incorporation to the Association, a privilege which was duly accorded in August, 1904. For seven years from this date the Association may not distribute any profits, which in the meantime must be applied to the furtherance of the objects of the Association. It has to deal with the four essentials to profitable cultivation—(1) a suitable soil, (2) a regularly-recurring rainfall and adequate irrigation, (3) sufficient labour, and (4) transport facilities; and its success will be watched with the deepest sympathetic interest by all who have the welfare of West Africa at heart.*

* It may be put on record here that the first shipment of cotton, grown and ginned locally, left Bathurst on September 19th, 1904, per ss. "Teneriffe," consigned to the British Cotton Growing Association. The shipment consisted of 160 bales of ginned cotton, weighing nearly 70 tons, and 293 bags of cotton seed, weighing over 20 tons.

An authoritative estimate of the loss that would be incurred if all the English cotton mills were running three-quarters time instead of full time puts it at £15,000,000 per annum. If this be so, and when it is borne in mind that no fewer than 10,000,000 of the population of the United Kingdom are directly or indirectly interested in the cotton industry, it will be seen how important are the considerations involved, and their extent must be the author's excuse for this digression here on a subject which directly concerns the Gambia.

In 1862, as it was even then found impossible to complete the work of building the lock (commenced in 1846) at Malfa Creek, Governor D'Arcy caused to be erected the small sluice

BATHURST: MCCARTHY SQUARE (GOVERNMENT PLACE).
Showing site of Recreation Ground laid out as a Memorial to her late Majesty Queen Victoria, the cost being met by Local Donations and Government Grant.

gates, now known as "Box Bar," to prevent in a measure the flooding of the centre of the island during high tides or heavy rains. The Box Bar acts as a lock on a small branch stream that bends to the north from Malfa Creek and circles through the mangrove swamp to the west of the town. In addition, an embankment was thrown up from the top of Clifton Road to the left, opposite the cemetery, and thence to the swamp bordering the Malfa Creek, as a further impediment to the flooding of that portion of the island.

On the death during this year of His Royal Highness Prince Albert, Her Most Gracious Majesty's Consort, a memorial was addressed to our late Queen Victoria tendering the profound and respectful sympathy of her loyal subjects in the colony.

To enable the trade of the Gambia to be placed on a firmer

basis and to obviate as far as possible the perpetual differences arising between the headmen of towns and the traders, agreements were during this year entered into by the Government with the various kings and chiefs of the country, by which it was decided that the existing system of "custom," as between the merchants and themselves, should cease, thereby freeing the mercantile community from the obnoxious quibblings that always arose before dealings between them and the people could be carried into effect. To avoid any trouble or misunderstanding the Government at the time issued "passes" to the traders, and to meet the expenditure arising from the above-mentioned arrangement certain duties were increased. These "customs'

BATHURST: NORTH END OF WELLINGTON STREET.

were superseded by "stipends," such as still continue in operation, which lapsed on the death of the recipient but might be continued at the discretion of the Government. Trade licences came into force under Ordinance No. 6 of 1893, since repealed by No. 13 of 1895,* so that all difficulty as to trade between the merchants and the people at the present day is at an end.

An infantry militia force was raised in 1862 for special service in Kommbo, and to this end Ordinance No. 1 of that year was passed. It was subsequently repealed by No. 13 of 1899, the idea being to enroll, in substitution, the West Indian pensioners in British Kommbo. These men were settled at a new village near the ruins of the town of Sabijee. During 1862, also, the colony assisted Lagos with troops during the trouble at

* See Chapter XIII.

Abeokuta, and the Militia in St. Mary's were once again called out for garrison duties, which shows that these auxiliary troops were useful in time of need.

The paving and draining of Wellington Street, the main business thoroughfare in Bathurst, was completed, and the "Kammalo" and Cape bridges were practically rebuilt at this time, having been first erected in 1852.

The years 1862 and 1863 saw great trouble on the north bank of the river, in the countries of Barra, Salum, and Baddibu, caused by further religious differences between the Sonninkees and Marabouts. The latter section had the aid of the

BATHURST: MIDDLE SECTION OF WELLINGTON STREET.

Mohammedan priest, specially alluded to later, who had a following of some 3,000 well armed men, and who was the cause of endless strife throughout the north bank. He was formerly a trader, named Hamah Bah, but was commonly called Maba, or Mahaba. The kingdom of Baddibu was his "happy hunting ground."

This civil war lasted some two years, although many promises had been made that it would be discontinued—in fact, an agreement for peace had, at the intervention of the Government, been signed by both parties, the Sonninkees promising to refrain from their lawless proceedings and the Marabouts undertaking to live peaceably and not to seek the aid of

Maba or any other foreigner. No doubt this was the wish of the people themselves, but as Maba had everything to gain, and practically nothing to lose, he instigated and abetted fresh outrages, causing practically at this period the desolation of the country from Essau to Sabagh, with immense loss of life. He even went so far as to attack the French at Kowlack. This unnecessary bloodshed and destruction of property—numerous towns being burnt—affected the trade and prosperity of the country to no little extent, but unless there had been maintained a huge military force, which the Government could not afford, it was in the sixties impossible to stamp out these disputes, and it is only after the lapse of time and through

BATHURST: THE SOUTH END OF WELLINGTON STREET.

the advancement of civilisation that the country has at last, it is hoped, become finally tranquil.

It should be specially emphasised that the continual intervention on the part of the Government in the settlement of tribal disputes was a sore drain on the finances of the colony, and this is one of the main reasons why many important works at the time were left unattended to.

Owing to this civil war no less than 2,000 of the people from Salum and Baddibu, known as Sereres,* and practically destitute, fled to Barra for Government protection, and the only way they could be provided for was by giving them permission to cross the river and settle in Kommbo. A few settled in Bathurst, at

* A distinct race, with a language having no affinity either to the Mandingo or Jolloff.

Half Die. A number of these people were utilised on the formation of the road to Oyster Creek, which was completed by their labour.

Towards the end of 1863, Maba, having practically got all he could from the people of the north bank, crossed the rive. at Tendaba and proceeded against Keeming and Kwinella and other places, where, owing to illness among his troops and other causes, it is pleasing to be able to record that he received just chastisement, and was completely routed, losing some 800 killed. But it was in French territory that Maba died eventually, from elephantiasis.*

To provide for the limited service men discharged from the West India Regiments who had fixed upon the Gambia as their final home, it was after some difficulty arranged with them, in 1863, that they should band themselves together and establish a town in Kommbo, on land granted to them by the Government. This town eventually received the name of Hamilton, and formed one of a series of armed military posts raised for the pacific settlement of the Kommbo country. It must be understood that for the most part these men were in the prime of life, but with no pensions, professions, or formed habits of industry; consequently on their discharge from the army they became an incubus to the Government. The idea, therefore, of settling them in Kommbo was excellent.

For purposes of comparison between the then and the now the author gives here some of the impressions of the famous Sir Richard Francis Burton, as recorded by him in his "Wanderings in West Africa. By a F.R.G.S.," published in 1863. "As we approached the land," he writes, "the sun burst through the thick yellow swamp-reek and the dew-clouds with a sickly African heat. Far to the right, in the Port St. Mary, stood a whitewashed building upon a dwarf red cliff. On our left, the river's proper right bank, was Fort Bullen, an outpost on a tongue of land dead-green as paint, and scattered with tall Bentangs (*Pullum cerba*), or bombax trees. This silk-cotton differs greatly in shape from its congener in Eastern Africa . . . It is everywhere, however, a noble tree, useful for shade, and supplying the people with canoe materials and a poor cotton. At Fort Bullen, which is about one hour's row from Bathurst, there is a detachment of one officer—*alias* Commandant and Governor of the Queen's Possessions in the Barra country—and seventeen men. The place is by no means wholesome, and there is no high ground within reach."

* According to Sir Gilbert T. Carter (Parliamentary Papers C-5071 of 1887, p. 98) he was killed in the war he waged in 1867 against the Serere king of Seine.

"Another half hour placed before us Bathurst in full view. It suggested the idea of a small European watering-place, and contains barely 5,000 souls. The site has none of those undulations which render a place picturesque; everything is horizontal, straight-lined, and barely above sea level. Beginning from the westward are a few detached houses, a colonial hospital, a military ditto, the Governor's quarters, large barracks . . . the market, the slaveyard, and the esplanade, behind whose line of trees lay the mass of the settlement. The houses might be those of Byculla, Bombay—in fact they date from the same epoch—large uncompact tenements, washed glistening white or yellow, with slates, tiles, or shingles, which last curl up in the sun like feathers. Further on are heaps of native huts, like beehives, or a crowded rickyard, rising from swamp and sand, and terminating abruptly up the river. There is an Octagon, not a concert room or chapel, but a coal depot, and there are two one-gun martello towers at the angles of the fort looking towards the town, which may relieve the view, but which look anything but dangerous. A nearer glance shows the house walls stained and gangrened with mildew; a fearful vegetation of Guinea grass, palms, plantains, cotton trees, and caoutchouc figs, which at a distance resemble whitethorns, occupies every inch of soil, and the inundations of the river sometimes find their way into the ground floor. In fact, the island and settlement of St. Mary (of old a cemetery) seem to be selected for unhealthiness, for proximity to mud, mangrove, miasma, and malaria."

"The island . . . is an island within an island; the latter, also called St. Mary, is the northernmost of that mass of continental islands which, formed by the Gambia and the Cacheo River, extend south to the Rio Grande. . . . St. Mary-the-Less is a mere strip, a sandpatch, which potent heats and tropical rains clothe with a vivid and profuse vegetation. Water may everywhere be found 3 feet beneath the surface, but it is brackish and bad. There is hardly any versant—in places the town is below the level of the river; excellent brick sewers have been built, but the rains prefer to sop the soil. And lest the island be gradually carried away, there is a penalty for removing even a pailful of sand from the beach . . ."

"Under charge of Dr. Martin [the then 'superintending surgeon,' Dr. Sherwood being the 'colonial surgeon'] I visited the military hospital on the west of the town, close to the swamp. The place is murderous. There is a sick ward upon the ground floor!—one night on the ground floor is certain fever in most parts of tropical Africa—and that ground floor is, like the latrinæ and other offices, frequently under water. In the first story the beds are crowded together, each patient having 800, whereas 2,000 feet of air should be the minimum. Moreover, in these regions no first story is thoroughly wholesome, unless a free current of air flows beneath it. Jalousies or shutters take the place of glass windows. On the second floor are the quarters of the medical officers, within pleasant distance of an atmosphere fraught with small-pox and dysentery, typhus, and yellow Jack. This caution of a hospital is built to 'accommodate' 23, at times it has had 32, and the average may be set down at 12; when I visited it there were 18 fever and dysentery cases. . . . I was not astonished after going the rounds to hear of 92 deaths out of 96 admissions, and that at times *el vomito* 'improves off' everybody. . . ."

The troops were then under the command of Captain Ivey. Referring to the barracks, Sir Richard Burton mentions, as one of their features, "a clock so artificially disposed that the soldiers for whom it is intended cannot see it without going outside. This and the loopholes have been standing jests at Bathurst. . . The loopholes look from the road into the barrack-yard, kitchen, and cellar; the enemy will find convenient shelter while firing down upon the former, and the friend concealment during his pilfering the latter. . . ."

"The garrison at Bathurst now consists of three companies (304 men) of the 2nd West: they are thus distributed. Bathurst has 212, Macarthy's Island 41, Cape St. Mary's 34 invalids and convalescents, and Fort Bullen 17. . . ."

Of the missionaries he records that while the French had two or three, and the same number of Sisters of Charity, and the Wesleyans had two chapels, two European missionaries, and a large school which received a Government annuity of £100, the Established Church of England had, neither at Bathurst (where there was a colonial chaplain) nor at McCarthy Island, any house of worship, except a building which was once an officers' mess.

In connection with his visit to the old convalescent-house at Cape St. Mary, the writer refers to the burial ground. "A few tombstones, mostly without inscriptions, are scattered on the sand and in the bank, and they are so near the shore that corpses and coffins have been washed into the sea. . . . Three governors are buried in the sand-bank."

In 1864 there was a decided fall in the value of ground-nut oil in the European markets, the price dropping from some £15 to £10 per ton, due to its being in a measure superseded by Canadian petroleum and American "belmontine."

On the taking over of British Kommbo, it was for several

years exempted from the payment of any taxation, for the purpose of encouraging settlers to cultivate the land; but in 1864 it was considered desirable to impose a trifling tax as an addition to the revenue, as a return for the many benefits derived since the Government occupation, and for all that had been done in quelling disturbances, making roads, and effecting other improvements. An Ordinance No. 1 of this year was passed, since repealed by No. 2 of 1897, by which the following taxes became payable: 4s. per annum for all lots of land containing one or more dwelling-houses or huts, and 8s. for groundnut and other farms of one acre. British Kommbo, however, ceased in 1903 to be treated as colony, being merged into the protectorate, and becoming amenable to the provisions of Ordinance No. 7 of 1902 and to the scale of taxation as provided by Ordinance No. 7 of 1895.

Although a large tract of land on the north bank of the river was practically uncultivated, owing to the depredations of Maba, the revenue for 1863 was £17,263. This increase was no doubt due to the contented state of Kommbo and to the rapid strides made in that country, as well as to a decided increase in the imports. At this time the civil wars in the countries adjacent to the lower river had practically ceased; but in May, 1864, troubles between the Sonninkees and Marabouts were again commencing around McCarthy. However, prompt measures being taken by the Government, matters were settled without bloodshed, and a treaty of peace between the contending parties signed. Had it not been for the intervention by the troops, under Major Harley, of the West India Regiment, the Marabouts would have been severely handled. Naturally our action caused distrust in the minds of the Sonninkees as to the Government's neutrality in party feuds; but this intervention could not be avoided, as quite enough bloodshed had already taken place, leaving in its wake terrible distress among the people.

During 1864 a good deal of swamp land was reclaimed at Half Die by filling in, and a sea-wall was erected there. To reimburse the Government to some extent for its outlay this land was sold by public auction, £500 being realised.

The first fair-way buoy was placed in position at the mouth of the river during this year.

The police force available in the colony at this period numbered thirty-seven only of all ranks.

Before concluding this chapter it may be noticed as a matter which might have had an exceedingly important bearing on the Gambia that in the next year (1865) a select Parliamentary

Committee reported "that all further extension of territory or assumption of government, or new treaties offering any protection to native tribes would be inexpedient; and that the object of our policy should be to encourage in the natives the exercise of those qualities which may render it possible for us more and more to transfer to them the administration of all the Governments, with a view to an ultimate withdrawal from all, except, probably, Sierra Leone." It was recommended that McCarthy Island should be no longer occupied, and that the British settlement on the Gambia should be confined as much as possible to the mouth of the river. As the expression of a pious opinion the report is interesting, but it does not appear to have had any practical bearing on the future course of events.

A PRIVATE OF THE GAMBIA COMPANY OF THE WEST AFRICAN FRONTIER FORCE.

CHAPTER IV

FROM 1865 TO 1904.

Mahaba (Maba) and the Marabouts—Postal Facilities extended—Colonel Blackall appointed Governor-in-Chief—Removal of Troops from McCarthy Island—Amar Fall's Outbreak—Further Punitive Expedition against the Marabouts—Another Epidemic of Yellow Fever—Sale of the "Dover"—Rear-Admiral Patey assumes the Government—Financial Position in 1866-67—Further Postal Reform—First Epidemic of Cholera—Withdrawal of Imperial Troops—Rumoured Cession to France—Mr. Callahgan assumes the Government—Revenue and Expenditure from 1870 to 1880—Mr. Kortright and Sir Samuel Rowe successively assume the Government—Gambia progresses towards Independence—New Government Steamer supplied—Dr. Gouldsbury becomes Administrator—His Expedition to Timbo—Further Postage Stamps introduced—Oyster Creek Bridge commenced—Sir Alfred Moloney assumes the Government—Uneventful Period from 1870 to 1887—Fogni and Jarra added to the Protectorate—Treaties of Peace in 1887—Anglo-French Boundary Agreement—Mr. Gilbert Carter, as Administrator, visits Kwinella and Batelling—Expedition against Fodi Kabba—Mr. R. B. Llewelyn becomes Administrator—Proceedings of the Anglo-French Boundary Commission—Fodi Kabba's Power finally broken—Troops again stationed in the Colony—Travelling Commissioners appointed—Acquisition of New Police Barracks—Construction of New Wharf—Troubles in Foreign Kommbo and Fulladu—Expedition against Fodi Sillah—Further Delimitation of the Anglo-French Boundary—Domestic Conditions in 1893-95—Police Provision in 1895—Prosperity of 1897—Female Hospital Erected—Oyster Creek Bridge Freed—Construction of Up-river Wharves—Sir G. C. Denton appointed Administrator—Expedition against Dumbutu—Anglo-French Force deals with Fodi Kabba—His Associates Deported—Subsequent Permanent Pacification of the Protectorate—British Fulladu added to the Protectorate—Visitation of Drought and Locusts in 1901—St. Mary's Church built—The Death of Queen Victoria—Detection of Crime in 1901—Satisfactory Revenue in 1902—Accession of King Edward VII.—Cost of Living in the Gambia.

As the Mohammedan priest Mahaba, or Maba, has been specially alluded to in these details of the Gambia, it would perhaps be as well to give a short sketch of his career and of the origin of the Marabout section of inhabitants in the Gambia. About the year 1774 there was not a Mohammedan or Marabout in the country. The inhabitants were composed of Mandingoes, Jolloffs, Jolahs and Foulahs, who were all pagans, but gradually a small body of Mohammedan Arabs found their way along the coast from Fez and Morocco, preaching to the people and teaching them their religion, and obtaining leave from the kings and chiefs to establish schools in the villages. It then became a custom to allow the young men on arriving at years of discretion to select their religion—*i.e.*, either to remain Sonninkees or to adopt the new faith. But with regard to the Mohammedans, that renowned traveller Mungo Park says: "Although frequently consulted in affairs of importance, yet they are never permitted to take extensive share in the country's Government, which rests solely in the hands of the king and his chiefs." This system has, however, changed; and at the present time most of the principal chiefs are Marabouts, showing the hold the faith of Mohamet has taken on the people of this country. Shortly after Mungo Park's time the number of Mohammedans vastly increased, the religion being favoured by a great number of the people, who eventually rose in rebellion against the Sonninkees, but were defeated at the Sonninkee stronghold at Kwinella, where Maba was routed in May, 1864.

The system of Sonninkee government has been handed down in this country from time immemorial and it presents some interesting features. Life, for instance, was held so sacred that even if the king shed blood, without just cause, he was liable to be deposed, or heavily fined, by the chiefs. The Sonninkees were marauders of the deepest dye, but murder was seldom or never added to their crimes. On the other hand, under the Mohammedan rule in Baddibu human life was taken on the slightest pretext. Maba was born in Salum and was a Jolloff by birth. Owing to some crime he committed when a boy he was expelled from his country and for a time lived in Bathurst, working as a labourer. He eventually seems to have acquired a considerable sum of money—how, history does not record—finally settling in Baddibu by leave of the Sonninkee king, building a town there, and, by the aid of slaves, making big farms. Later on he embraced the Mohammedan religion, becoming a Marabout of great sanctity.

When the Government had to send the expedition against the king of Baddibu, at Sawarra Kunda and Saba, Maba played an important part. The power of the king of Baddibu being practically broken, and having lost nearly all his warriors, Maba, after the departure of our troops, hoisted his standard of rebellion, calling upon all good Mohammedans to assist him to exterminate the Sonninkees or pagans, with the result recorded earlier. He conquered Baddibu, burning all the Sonninkee towns, and driving a great number of these people across the river into the Sonninkee kingdom in Kiang. But even in this district the Marabouts have greatly increased, and as an interesting fact the author records that Fodi* Brima Saniang, the present

* "Fodi" means Mahdi, or Defender of the Faith.

chief of Kwinella, has given up the faith of his forbears and become a Marabout.

Fortunately for Maba, at this period (1862) the old king of Barra (Demba Sonko) died, and as by the Mandingo law the title remains in abeyance for three months, this was an opportunity for Maba; for having subdued Baddibu he proceeded against Barra, during this unsettled time, ignoring his promises made at Saba to the Government. Under the cloak of religion he was joined by the Marabouts, and his conquest of the greater portion of the Barra kingdom was easy. Although outside our influence, the Government had to interfere, as it was not safe or just for us to stand by and witness the numerous acts of inexcusable oppression against unoffending people which were being committed in the immediate vicinity of the colony, and were causing the devastation of a fine country. Maba, on the intervention of the Government, returned to Baddibu, whither, during his absence, the king of Salum had proceeded and burnt his town. A long fight, with varied fortunes, followed, between Maba and the Salum people, with the deplorable result that a rich and flourishing country became practically a desert. These successes of Maba's Marabouts were soon heard of in Kommbo, and it was with the greatest difficulty that Governor D'Arcy prevented a further religious rising in that country. It has been recorded earlier how Maba eventually crossed the river into the Kiang, Jarra, and Fogni countries, where fortunately he was thoroughly routed and had to fly for his life.

The influence of this man Maba was a dreadful calamity for the country, as the strife between the Marabouts and Sonninkees afterwards broke out on the slightest provocation. It was in this year (1865) that there became prominent a chief, Fodi Kabba, who is specially mentioned later.

In February, 1866, alteration in the scale of postage was made in the Gambia, the half ounce weight for letters being introduced. The money-order system that came into force during 1863 had proved a great boon to the community of small traders, as hitherto they had had to take their goods from the resident European firms at a valuation that left their profits unremunerative. The money orders enabled the petty traders and others to remit to, and buy direct from, the manufacturer, and consequently to save the profit that hitherto went into the pockets of the large mercantile firms.

This year Colonel Blackall was appointed Governor-in-Chief of the West African colonies of Sierra Leone and the Gambia, the title of the chief executive officer of the Gambia becoming once again "Administrator," or "Officer Administering the

Government," instead of Governor. It may be recalled that in 1843 the Government of the West Africa Settlements had been broken up, and the Gambia constituted a separate colony; but in this year (1866) all the settlements were again combined under one Governor-in-Chief, though each continued to have its own Legislative Council.

On May 18, 1866, the imperial troops were removed from McCarthy Island, their place being taken by a limited armed constabulary, with forty trained militia artillery, to be called out as occasion arose. These men resided at George Town, McCarthy Island.

In July of this year the Marabouts on the Ceded Mile, under one Amar Fall, broke the peace by endeavouring suddenly to burn the Sonninkee town of Siterunnko, and by lifting cattle from Masamba Kokey's town of Bantang Killing. Severe fighting ensued, but fortunately for the Government H.M.S. "Mullet" came into port, and the Governor proceeded to the scene of the trouble and raised the siege. Masamba requested permission to go to British Kommbo with his people, unless proper protection could be assured to him, as he feared the Marabouts in the towns of Sicca, Jilifri, Tubabcolong, and other places. His request, however, was not complied with, as it was thought that it would lead to the destruction of Albreda, Fitzgerald Town, and also Essau and Berwick.

As the Marabouts had been a cause of serious trouble in the neighbourhood of the Ceded Mile for some considerable time it was decided to send a force against them. On June 27th H.M.S. "Mullet" and the "Dover" proceeded to Albreda with 262 rank and file and nine officers. These troops disembarked on the 28th, and the Marabouts of Albreda were disarmed without bloodshed. On the 29th our forces were joined by 500 allies under the Soma of Essau, who made common cause with Masamba, and on the 30th the town of Tubabcolong was attacked. The place was strongly fortified, but was eventually taken, with considerable loss to the Marabouts.

This taking of life is to be regretted, but the presumption or the Marabouts in recent hostilities had to be checked; as had it not been for the timely arrival of H.M.S. "Mullet" great slaughter would have occurred in British territory among the natives of the countries involved in these broils.

The civil wars that have been incidentally alluded to in this chronicle caused endless loss of life, and greatly retarded the advancement of the Gambia; but it is impossible to see what more could have been done by the Government to prevent or quell these disturbances. History demonstrates that, where civilised races are in immediate contact with barbarians and warlike tribes, no matter how careful the former may be, there must be occasional collisions, and herein is the explanation of the Government's numerous expeditions, which indeed in every instance appear to have been necessary.

In August, 1866, a further epidemic of yellow fever visited the colony, and fourteen of the thirty Europeans resident at the time in Bathurst died.

The colonial steamer "Dover," which had done yeoman service for the colony from the time she arrived in 1849, was now condemned. Her hull was nearly worn through, and as her engines and boiler were quite unfit for further work her sale was ordered by the Admiralty.

On December 18, 1866, the Government of the Gambia was assumed by Rear-Admiral Patey, Colonel D'Arcy retiring after a tenure of office of nearly seven years.

Much good work was done during Colonel D'Arcy's administration, but owing to the constant feuds between the Marabouts and Sonninkee raids by Maba, Amar Fall, Omar and others, these years, 1859-1866, are among the most sanguinary in the annals of the colony.

The imports to the Gambia during 1866 amounted to £108,190 and the exports to £158,370. The revenue for the same period was (exclusive of the Parliamentary grant) £15,782, and the expenditure £13,971. In 1867 the revenue had increased to £22,415, the expenditure being £18,665.

The year 1868 saw the first introduction into the colony of postage stamps of 4d. and 6d.

During 1869 the Gambia was visited for the first time with a most serious epidemic of cholera, imported, it is believed, from the adjoining French territory of Senegal. The deaths in the colony were numerous. The Government provided temporary hospitals and did all they could for the people, but it was not until the end of the year, when the dry season and the strong harmattan winds set in, that the disease abated. It is recorded by the then Administrator, Rear-Admiral Patey, that the visitation of this terrible epidemic cost Bathurst a fourth of its population, 1,162 deaths occurring up to July, 1869.

The tribesmen have more than once threatened Bathurst, and it may be noted that this same year (1869) was the last occasion on which it was seriously menaced. The opportune arrival of two French men-of-war possibly saved the colony, which had then no adequate garrison to safeguard it.

In 1870 all imperial troops were removed from the Gambia, the existing armed police force being increased to 100 men, and these, with the militia force, were still the only protection available.

At this time it was rumoured that the colony was about to be ceded to France, owing no doubt to the cholera scare. Little or nothing, however, of interest happened in the Gambia, pending the arrival of Mr. T. F. Callahgan, C.M.G., in 1871. In fact up to 1880 the colony was in a most tranquil state, as the following return of revenue and expenditure shows, few disturbances occurring and none worthy of record:—

REVENUE AND EXPENDITURE OF THE GAMBIA FROM 1870 to 1880.

Year.	Revenue.	Expenditure.	Year.	Revenue.	Expenditure.
1870	£18,969	£21,937	1876	£19,786	£21,489
1871	17,490	16,662	1877	19,254	18,728
1872	17,249	17,873	1878	26,546	18,376
1873	19,335	24,068	1879	28,505	20,674
1874	20,380	23,425	1880	23,341	18,361
1875	22,700	22,468			

Mr. C. H. Kortright succeeded Mr. Callahgan in 1873, and was in turn relieved by Sir Samuel Rowe, K.C.M.G., in 1875, both the latter becoming in succession Governors-in-Chief at Sierra Leone.

In 1874 the settlements on the Gold Coast and at Lagos were constituted one colony, under the name of the Gold Coast Colony; while Sierra Leone and the Gambia, still under one Government, retained to themselves the family title of the West Africa Settlements, a retention somewhat illogical and frequently inconvenient. Lagos, it may be mentioned here, was separated from the Gold Coast in 1886; and the Gambia was finally cut off from Sierra Leone in 1888.

In 1875 a new Government steamer, the "St. Mary," was sent to the colony to replace the "Dover," condemned, as already mentioned, in 1866. From the latter year to the arrival of the "St. Mary" the colony had been without any special means of communication with the upper river, except by an occasional ground-nut boat and by slow-moving cutters.

In 1877 Dr. V. S. Gouldsbury, C.M.G., arrived in the colony and assumed the administration.

In 1880 new denominations of Gambia stamps were introduced, ½d., 1½d., 2d., 3d., 1s. being added to the 4d. and 6d. introduced in 1866.

On November 27, 1880, Sir Samuel Rowe, K.C.M.G., the Governor of the West Africa Settlements, reminded the Colonial Office that there was, in the previous June, a current balance the credit of the settlement on the Gambia of over £19,000; and he suggested that a portion of this should be devoted to defraying the cost of an expedition in the neighbourhood of the Upper

Gambia, to obtain accurate information of the value of the stream as a commercial highway, and to promote friendly relations with the chiefs in the district. He proposed that Timbo should be reached, and the return journey made thence to Freetown. As a guide to the time that might be occupied he prepared the following interesting table:—

Journey.		Name of Traveller.	Dates of Travel.		No. of days' travelling.	No. of days' rest.	Days' actually travelling.
From	To		From	To			
Pisania	Medina	Major Gray	April 29, 1818	May 3, 1818	5	—	5
Medina	Kussaye	Major Gray	May 6, 1818	May 7, 1818	2	—	2
Kussaye	Badou	Mungo Park	May 14, 1805	May 28, 1805	15	4	11*
Badou	Cacagne	Mollien	March 19, 1818	March 28, 1818	10	1	9
Cacagne	Timbo	Mollien	March 29, 1818	April 20, 1818	23	4	19
Timbo	Freetown, Kambia only	Blyden	1873	1873	21	8	13†
					76	17	59

* Easy distances. † Only 67 hours actually travelling.

Lord Kimberley, the Secretary of State for the Colonies, approved of the expedition, and of its command by Dr. Gouldsbury; and he arranged that Lieutenant Dumbleton, R.E., and Surgeon Browning, R.N., should accompany it. Various gifts were provided by the Home authorities, including a handsome ram's head "in a tin case" for the Alimamy of Timbo; and a supply of threepenny pieces to the value of £300 was furnished to facilitate the keeping of "an accurate account of the cash expenditure on the march, as well as of the disposal of the merchandise." For the three officers Fortnum and Mason prepared cases containing supplies for ninety days of the following rations: Cocoa and milk ¼ lb., biscuit ¾ lb., and preserved meat or soup ½ lb., per day. There was also a case of Navy rum each, to allow of one ration per day. Each officer was provided with a horse at the cost of the expedition, but the national exchequer was not further deplenished for saddlery, the cost of which was debited to the officers.

On January 22, 1881, Dr. Gouldsbury embarked at Bathurst on the colonial steamer "St. Mary," with his two officers, a sergeant and nineteen native constables of the Gambia Police, one native clerk, two interpreters, and twenty-eight other natives, with one horse and three donkeys. The day before he had despatched sixty carriers and three horses on the cutter "Collingwood." It was the 26th before, owing to a breakdown in the machinery of the "St. Mary," they reached McCarthy Island, where additional carriers were engaged. Towing the cutter, on the 29th they reached Yarbutenda, the highest point to which the "St. Mary" could go. This wharf village, where they disembarked, had been destroyed by the king of Bondu two years before, and on Dr. Gouldsbury's arrival it consisted of a few huts occupied by a trader representing Mr. A. C. Verminck, of Bathurst. Here the expedition divided (to re-unite later) into a land party and a boat party, the former going through Kantora to Jallacotta. The Kantora country had been invaded in 1879 by the combined forces of Bakary Sardho, king of Bondu, Molloh, king of Firdou, and Sorie or Alpha Ibrahema, chief of Laby, and its villages and farms were laid waste, many of its people being carried into slavery and the remainder dispersed. Some had, at the date of the expedition, returned to Kantora and rebuilt a few villages; but as the king had died, and no proper successor had been appointed, the nation—like the Wuli country on the opposite side of the river—was broken up.

The boat party, with whom went the Administrator, passed the rocks of Barraconda without difficulty on February 1st; on the 3rd they reached the mouth of the tributary Grey River; and on the 7th the mouth of what Dr. Gouldsbury calls the Nerico, the limit of Jobson's historical journey in 1620-21. Proceeding up that tributary they reached Jallacotta "wharf" (like other so-called wharves merely the point on the bank where the pathway for the town strikes the river) eight miles from the town of Jallacotta, where they made a treaty with the chief Farrumba Walli. Jallacotta then consisted of about 250 huts, was stockaded, and stood in an open plain interspersed here and there with trees. A twelve hours' march brought them to Bady, and thence they reached the wharf of Bady, some twelve miles from the town, and 180 miles from Yarbutenda by river. Not a single canoe or other vessel was seen throughout this length of river, "and from the date of Governor McDonnell's expedition in 1849 until we appeared—a lapse of thirty-two years—" writes the Administrator, "its surface bore no other burden than the floating leaf, the broken branch, and the fallen tree."

It is impossible, within reasonable compass, to follow the course of the expedition in detail,* but it may be noted that Toobah was the most extensive place seen, and Dr. Gouldsbury was informed that it was the largest town in Futa Jallon. Exclusive of outlying villages, it was estimated to contain about 800 houses, and its mosque was believed to be the biggest in the kingdom. "Toobah," wrote the Administrator, "is the seat of the Mohammedan hierarchy of the nation and is, as it were, the Canterbury of the country. When the Foulahs are about to

* Particulars are given in a Blue Book (C—3065) presented to Parliament in August, 1881.

make war they send to Toobah to invoke the prayers of its priests for success in their enterprise." And he adds, "I never saw keener persons at a bargain than its inhabitants."

Many were the speculations and anticipations respecting the magnitude, importance, and barbaric splendour of Timbo, the "key of the Western Soudan," which was permitted to fall to France by the delimitation of 1889. About this capital of the Futa Jallon country there had been almost as many mythical stories as about Timbuctoo. "But," writes Dr. Gouldsbury, "before we passed within its environs the dream of my followers as to the vast dimensions of the town and its great population were rudely dispelled." There was the reality, a town at an elevation of 2,000 feet above sea-level, situated on a flat tract of ground surrounded by hills, numbering 100 houses, or, with the outlying villages, 814 houses, including the smallest and broken-down huts. Allowing the fair average of three persons to each hut, this would give the population of the far-famed metropolis as 2,442. The country around it, for two days' route, was found to be very rocky, and the roads hilly and rugged.

On April 21st the expedition arrived at Freetown, having, from the day of embarkation at Bathurst, extended over exactly three months. Some of its tribulations were due to the difficulties of overcoming "the laziness, lies, and bad faith of the natives," and satisfying their avarice. The carriers, with few exceptions, proved to be "a lazy, lagging, womanish, weak-hearted lot." Small-pox and fever claimed their victims. At Bady the expedition was literally cut off from its supplies, and routed, by multitudinous and aggressive bees.* The Foulahs generally were addicted to thieving, and on a scale which approximated to meanness. Even the horses' tails were not exempted, but were "converted from long-flowing appendages into the short crop of a hunter." And subsequently the robbers stole the tail stumps, with the horses attached.

The result of the expedition cannot be said to have been encouraging, and the report closes on a note of pessimism. The Administrator concluded that the Gambia, above Barraconda, was hopeless for transport purposes; and that even the lapse of centuries would not bring about the concourse of circumstances essential to any very great expansion of trade with the countries bordering the upper river. The chief of these necessities was population, and he believed that in West Africa this was stationary, if not decreasing, owing to polygamy, wars, or the enormous infant mortality. Probably all three combined in

* The enormous number of bees inhabiting the mangrove swamps and coast lands of Guinea excited the amazement of André de Bruë, who really founded the French empire in West Africa, and who—it may be noted incidentally—visited the Gambia in 1700.

the causation of a standstill or diminishing population, but of the three factors he deemed the last-named to be the most active.

To return to the main chronicle, it may be recorded that in 1885 the bridge over the Oyster Creek was opened, with due ceremony, by Captain (now Sir) C. Alfred Moloney, C.M.G., who had been appointed Administrator the year before. The bridge had been commenced in 1879 under the auspices of Mr. Bauer, the then Colonial Engineer, but for long the only visible result of a considerable expenditure of money was a straggling array of screw piles all standing at different angles and reaching only a third of the way across the creek. At length the construction was placed in the hands of English contractors—Messrs. Wakefield & Co.—who sent Mr. R. Challis out to supervise the work. Under his experienced guidance the screw piles gradually assumed an upright position, and by May 1, 1885, the complete structure was ready, as mentioned above, for public inauguration amidst much enthusiasm. The bridge is 300 yards long and 16 feet wide, and has a substantial platform of tarred pitch pine. Its total cost was £5,495.

In the same year (1885) Captain Moloney was promoted to be the Administrator of Lagos, which was erected into an independent colony; and Mr. (now Sir) Gilbert T. Carter, then treasurer, assumed the administration of the Gambia.

Early in 1887 overtures were made to the Government by the people in the countries of Fogni and Jarra to be placed under British protection, and after mature consideration treaties were entered into with the chiefs of these countries, and the Union Jack was hoisted in the principal towns. The reason why the native tribes named appealed to the Government was that they were unable any longer to resist the repeated attacks made upon them by their foreign foes, the marauding chief Fodi Kabba (first mentioned in 1865), and Fodi Sillah, and therefore were most desirous that the British Government should extend protection to them.

The troubles that led up to this request were the outcome of the lawlessness of the Mohammedan Maba, whose career has been specially alluded to. On the death of Maba, Fodi Kabba, who had been his right-hand man, was engaged by Mahmoud N'Dare Bah,* then king of Baddibu, for the purpose of slave-raiding on the south bank of the river. After a time, Fodi Kabba appears to have considered himself strong enough to act on his own behalf; this was about 1877, and, instead of returning to Baddibu, where he went to from Gunjour, his original home,

* Maba's nephew, who, according to one story, merely acted as regent for Maba's young son, Saide Mattee.

he remained in the Jarra country, carrying out his nefarious designs and depredation at will. At this time the north bank of the river was also once more in an unsatisfactory state, Beram Ceesay, one of Maba's generals, having commenced to carry out marauding expeditions in the country of Baddibu, and having attacked and plundered Sanjally and many Mandingo towns.

To show what a troubled state the country was again in, due no doubt to the inactivity in the colony from 1870 to 1887, the customs revenue dropped between the years 1884-1887 some 30 per cent. (from £20,000 to £13,000). The internal disputes and native wars desolated the countries adjacent to the river, and the cultivation of the fine lands in Baddibu and the surrounding country was entirely neglected. The revolt of Beram Ceesay against Mahmoud N'Dare Bah, referred to above, resulted in the partition of Baddibu, but the latter was recognised both by the Government and by Beram Ceesay as chief of the kingdom, and continued to receive the stipend granted to him for protecting traders on the river. Peace, unhappily, was of short duration. In 1884 Saide Mattee, who had then arrived at manhood, got together a number of followers and claimed the throne by right of inheritance from his father. Beram Ceesay took the side of his chief. Civil war raged, and it was not until 1887 that treaties of peace, as on the south bank, were entered into, and an improvement generally was anticipated. Unfortunately, however, Saide Mattee soon after got into trouble with the French Government, and the consequence was that progress was again put back.

On August 10, 1889, was signed the agreement which laid down a line of demarcation between the English and French protectorates, in accordance with which the frontier was delimited in 1891, as referred to later.

Returning to Fodi Kabba and the south bank, in February, 1890, the Administrator—Mr. (now Sir) Gilbert Carter—visited Kwinella and Battelling, and the people, though anxious for the removal of Fodi Kabba from their territories, had to admit that he had not for the time being worried them since they had entered into the treaties and adopted the British flag.

Proceeding northward from Kwinella the Governor met Musa Molloh, the recognised king of the whole of the Fulladu country, at Boraba Kunda, and there discussed with him the question of his assisting the British Government to put an end to Fodi Kabba's malpractices. Musa Molloh stated that he would be only too willing to assist in any way; and soon after this it was decided by Her Majesty's Government to send an expedition against Fodi Kabba. Unfortunately this expedition was delayed pending the delimitation of the boundary between the British and French spheres of influence.

In 1891 Mr. (now Sir) R. B. Llewelyn succeeded Mr. Carter as Administrator of the colony, and the French contingent of the Boundary Commission arrived in the Gambia. The Commission proceeded at once with its work, but received repeated checks from both Fodi Sillah and Fodi Kabba, in consequence of which British gunboats had to patrol the river near to where the Commission was engaged.

In the same year the Commission arrived at Kansala, and in the neighbourhood of this place one Frangwoi, Fodi Kabba's headman, was stated to be bringing up large reinforcements of men. Off Kansala we had three ships of war, the "Swallow," "Widgeon" and "Alecto," but open hostilities were deprecated, an amicable settlement if possible being considered advisable for the sake of the people and the trade of the country. Many palavers took place between Frangwoi, the Administrator, and the officers of the ships of war; and after men and guns had been landed, as a hint of what the resisters had to expect in the event of any continued resistance, the commissioners were permitted to proceed with their work.

It having been reported that Fodi Kabba had entered into a treaty with the French at the Cassamance, all went well until the town of Kankuran was reached. Here information was received by the commission, through Jolahs, that Fodi Kabba was preparing to attack them with a large force. Preparations were accordingly made by the gunboats at Kansalla to resist any interference; but, as a matter of fact, if it had not been thought inadvisable at the time, little difficulty would have been experienced in dealing with Fodi Kabba and his followers, as the hatred against him and his people was most pronounced. A message was sent to Frangwoi explaining the reasons of an armed force being present, and requesting him to come to discuss the situation with the Acting Administrator. He assented at once, and solemnly declared that Fodi Kabba had no intention of molesting the expedition and that the rumours to the contrary were untrue.

This apparently satisfactory settlement of hostilities enabled the boundary delimitation to be completed through the troublesome country occupied by Fodi Kabba, and there now remained only the higher reaches of the river as far as Yarbutenda to be dealt with.

On May 5, 1891, the Administrator, Mr. Llewelyn,, proceeded up-river in the yacht "Countess of Derby," borrowed from the

Government of Sierra Leone, with the Commissioners, who were introduced to the important chiefs of Kantora, Wuli, Sandu, Karantaba, Kunting, and the king of all Fulladu, Musa Molloh. Every assistance was given to the expedition, which by the end of May completed the work of fixing the boundary of the Kantora and Wuli districts. In addition an excellent survey was made of the river from McCarthy Island to the frontier.

The apparent submission by Frangwoi at Kansalla, when the ships of war were present with the Boundary Commission, was unfortunately of short duration, as no sooner had the expedition returned to Bathurst than Fodi Kabba again commenced molesting the people, and returned in force to Sangajor. A communication was addressed to him stating that Her Majesty's Government refused to recognise his authority in any way throughout the Jolah country on the British side of the line of demarcation, and that he was to remove to the French side of the boundary. The protests by the Government were ignored, and it was finally decided to proceed against this robber chief, and, if possible, to force him to leave British territory, or, better still, to capture him. Musa Molloh was again asked to co-operate and to prevent Fodi Kabba from passing into the Fulladu country. On December 29th a detachment of troops left Sierra Leone for the Gambia, and, with the assistance of the naval brigade present in the colony, attacked Fodi Kabba at Marigo, some 30 miles up the Vintang Creek on January 2, 1892. Marigo, Bondali and the adjacent villages were totally destroyed, but unfortunately Fodi Kabba escaped into French territory, after heavy loss. Subsequent fighting took place at Toniataba, in Western Jarra, and elsewhere, between our troops and the followers of Fodi Kabba, who were completely crushed, but it was not until the end of May that these disturbances were brought to a satisfactory termination, and this troublesome chief finally driven to Mandina in French territory.

After the troubles above recorded, a detachment of the 1st Battalion West India Regiment, comprising some 100 men, three officers and a European non-commissioned officer, was again permanently stationed in the colony; and it was now considered time that proper legislation should be introduced for the control of the territories as deliminated by the Boundary Commission. To this end two travelling commissioners were appointed, Mr. Ozanne for the countries bordering the north bank of the river, and Mr. Sitwell for the south bank.

At the 1891 census the population of the 69 square miles which comprised the settlements was returned at 14,266. The numbers must of course be taken as approximate only, but they afford a comparison with the parallel returns of 1881, which amounted to 14,150, and seem to show that the population of the settlements remained stationary during the ten years, any increase being counterbalanced by considerable emigration from the district of the Upper Kommbo.

In 1892 the value of the ground-nuts exported was £150,000, as against an average of £154,000 in the five years 1880-84, £188,000 in 1858, and only £199 in 1845. The export of india-rubber had quadrupled in the three years ending with 1891. Revenue in 1892 reached £31,000, the highest yet realised in any year except the preceding one. The imports were valued at £170,000, and the exports at £172,000; as compared with

THE RIVERSIDE AT BATHURST, SHOWING THE GOVERNMENT WHARF AND CUSTOMS WAREHOUSES.

£69,000 and £79,000 respectively in 1886, and £174,000 and £255,000 respectively in 1882.

In 1893 the police force was stationed at premises known as Lloyds Estate in Wellington Street, but the accommodation offered having been found unsuitable the commodious buildings and stores of a Mr. Barriere, at No. 10 Wellington Street, were purchased by the Government and handed over to the police force as barracks.

At this time considerable difficulty was experienced by the customs because there was no Government wharf. Looking to the increase of trade it was necessary that this should be provided, as hitherto cargo had to be delivered by cutters, from which it was discharged at the various wharves belonging to

DEMBO DENSA, HEAD CHIEF OF WESTERN BRITISH FULLADU

MOUSA MOLLAH, KING OF FULLADU (or FIRDOU.)

MARANSARA, ONE OF DEMBO DENSA'S PRINCIPAL MEN.

Both Dembo and Maransara were under Mousa, but since 1901, when Dembo's part of Fulladu became British Protectorate, that chief has been responsible to the Colonial Government only. By far the larger part of Mousa's kingdom is in French territory, but he has lost control of it since 1903, when he took refuge under British Government.

merchants. Accordingly, in 1893, an adequate T-shaped wharf was designed, and the work of constructing it commenced in October of that year. Its ultimate cost to the Government was some £9,600. It is a fine structure, measuring 165 feet from the customs enclosure, with a width of 31 feet, and has a T end 215 feet long. The available depth at high water is approximately 18 feet, with 14 feet at low tide.

The chief Fodi Sillah, of Foreign Kommbo, who had been quiet for some time and had been observing the conditions of his treaty with the British Government with regard to his territories, and who was in receipt of an allowance of £50 per annum, again commenced to give trouble in 1893, stopping traders and robbing them of money and goods; and in addition to these disturbing elements, trouble was occurring in Fulladu between Musa Molloh and one Decore Cumba, who was aided by many of Fodi Kabba's followers. But in December, 1893, it was reported that Decore had been killed, and these disturbances put a stop to. Musa Molloh himself had been always open in his dealings with the British Government, and had as far as possible been ready and willing to assist in the settlement of tribal differences when called upon.

Early in 1894 the behaviour of Fodi Sillah had become so aggressive that active measures had to be taken, and an ultimatum addressed to him. No definite result was obtained by these communications, neither would he meet the Administrator to discuss matters. It was accordingly decided to send an expedition against him.

Brikama, Gunjour, Sukuta and Busumballa—troublesome districts during the Kommbo troubles—were the four places in the occupation of Fodi Sillah and his people, and it was against these towns that a special demonstration was considered desirable. On February 22nd a force under Captain Gamble, composed of 200 men from the ships of war present, proceeded to Bakote, a short distance from Sukuta, which town was demolished. The force then proceeded against Brikama, but owing to opposition was unable to reach there, receiving a severe check and losing several officers and nine men from H.M.S. "Raleigh," besides having many other serious casualties. This was a most disastrous commencement of hostilities. However, a large force was soon assembled, comprised of men from the West India Regiment, blue-jackets and marines; and on March 6th it proceeded into Kommbo. Fodi Sillah was routed and his remaining strongholds destroyed. The chief and certain of his followers fled to the boundary to the east, but found that they were prevented by the Jolahs from escaping that way. This forced them to surrender to the French, who deported

Fodi Sillah to Saint Louis, where he eventually died, Foreign Kommbo being annexed by the British Government.

It was, at this time, considered necessary further to delimit the Anglo-French boundary in the Gambia, and Mr. Henry Reeve, with Mr. Ozanne, were appointed to act on behalf of the Government, in conjunction with M. Fargue and Lieutenant de Jussuin, who were the French commissioners.

The Commission left Bathurst on December 17, 1895, and proceeded with its work, not returning to headquarters until April, 1896, when matters affecting the upper reaches of the north bank of the river were concluded. The intelligence Map No. 848, prepared after the Commission of 1891, was used as the basis of operations. It was not until 1898-1899, however, that the boundary on the south bank was completed and the delimitation as now defined decided upon. The boundary marks placed by the Commissioners were stone cairns, and these are visited at intervals by the colony's travelling commissioners, who see that they are maintained in good order. Prior to the demarcation the total area of the Gambia settlements was taken to be not more than 69 square miles—rather less than half the size of the Isle of Wight. Outside the settlements the sphere of British influence was wholly undefined. After the delimitation the territory owned by, or under the protection or influence of, Great Britain was found to amount to 3,550 square miles, or a little less than twice the size of Lancashire. Now, as already mentioned (page 1), it is put at some 5,000 square miles.

Returning to the conditions of the colony and its people, it must be recorded that—what with tribal wars, and raids by the before-mentioned chiefs and the consequent punitive expeditions—the people had a good deal to disturb them, but in 1892 their troubles were increased by disease which caused heavy loss amongst their cattle. In 1893, great havoc was caused by locusts and a phenomenal rainfall. The Government, however, did all in their power to alleviate the troubles of the people by encouraging a proper system of commetee, and by establishing peace in the country. In 1894 the troubles already recorded no doubt militated in a great measure against trade, and the year was a bad one, as also was 1895, although the protectorate was becoming gradually settled. The opening up of Kommbo, and the freedom of the people from the oppression of Fodi Sillah, gave a great impetus to the rubber industry ; but, unfortunately, the trees were not tapped judiciously. In 1894 the passing of an important Ordinance (No. 11) to provide for the exercise in the protected territories of certain powers and jurisdiction by native tribunals, as well as by the commissioners, aided in the pacific settlement of the country and no difficulty was experienced in its introduction.

The detachment of the West India Regiment, which had been in the colony since 1891, was withdrawn in February, 1895, and was replaced by an armed frontier police force. However, this force, after being embodied only some nine months, was disbanded, owing to local troubles between the men and the townspeople. Moreover, the men of the force, who were principally recruited from the hinterland of Sierra Leone, were found, at the time, not amenable to discipline The removal of the imperial troops and the disbanding of the short-lived frontier police, left only the armed local police force of 100 men available in the colony, but the troublesome era had, so far, subsided, and it was thought that the local constabulary would be sufficient to enforce the observance of law and order in Bathurst, and to deal with any immediate trouble that might arise.

The year 1897 saw great strides in the prosperity of the country, and the revenue nearly doubled that of 1895. Her late Majesty's "Diamond Jubilee" was celebrated by the erection of a permanent female hospital and by the removal of the existing tolls at the Oyster Creek Bridge.

The year 1898 again saw continued good trade, and this, undoubtedly, was due to the improvement in the administration and to the pacific state of the protectorate. Trading centres increased, and up-river several wharves were constructed, from which ocean-going steamers could load for direct export of produce.

In November, 1900, Sir George Chardin Denton, K.C.M.G.—the present Governor—was appointed to succeed Sir Robert Llewelyn as Administrator of the colony; and, from the great experience gained by him during many years service as Colonial Secretary and as Lieutenant-Governor of Lagos, his appointment was a happy one for the Gambia. Sir George arrived in the colony on January 10, 1901, with the expedition of that year, particulars of which are given below, and assumed the administration, which, however, was raised in March, as in the early days of the colony, to a Governorship.

The most recent punitive expedition was that against the rebellious people of Dumbutu, a town on the south bank of the river, who had assisted the people of Sankandi when they deliberately murdered Messrs. Sitwell and Silva, Sergeant Cox and ten constables of the police force. A most beneficial effect in the protectorate was the result, as the people were shown convincingly that His Majesty's Government, while ready and willing to assist in the pacific administration of the country, would not tolerate gross acts of injustice and insurbordination. This expedition is of the greatest importance in the annals of the Gambia, for it led to the proper administration of the protectorate, and the author therefore gives the following details concerning it.

For some time previous to the trouble there was a long-standing dispute between the people of Sankandi and those of Battelling, a town close by, with regard to the ownership of

A Village Bantaba Tree.
(This one is at Manna, Suntu Koma's town).

some rice-fields situated between the two towns. In 1900 this dispute assumed serious dimensions, and a visit was paid to Sankandi by one of the commissioners, to endeavour to settle the trouble. Unfortunately, no result was obtained, and the dispute became more acute, the fact of the Battelling people being staunch Sonninkees, and those of Sankandi strict Mohammedans, probably adding to the trouble.

The Government could not, of course, permit this state of affairs to continue and decided to bring matters to a settlement. Accordingly, on June 14, 1900, Mr. Sitwell and Mr. Silva, with an escort of a sergeant and ten constables, proceeded to Sankandi. On the way Mansah Koto, the chief of Battelling, a very influential Sonninkee with a large following, joined the party.

On the arrival of the commissioners at the outskirts of Sankandi the chief and people were asked to discuss the subject of the dispute, but declined to do so unless the palaver was held under the village bantaba tree, as usual. Mr. Sitwell accordingly complied with the request and entered the town, where no one was to be seen. Suddenly the headman Dari Bana Dabu appeared. This chief was known to be opposed to the Government, and when Mr. Sitwell, the senior of the two commissioners, called upon him to come to his compound and discuss matters he refused to do so. Mr. Sitwell then left the compound and tried to arrest him. Dari Bana Dabu resisted, and called upon his people, who were lying close by in ambush, armed with guns. They at once fired on the party, with the lamentable and unexpected results already recorded. The expedition, which comprised five companies of the 3rd West India Regiment and a wing of the Central African Regiment under command of Lieutenant-Colonel Brake, D.S.O., proceeded in January, 1901, to punish the people of Dumbutu, who participated in the above-mentioned crime. After a short resistance, resulting in a few casualties to our force, the participators in the revolt were thoroughly routed and subdued, and the town of Dumbutu was destroyed. In the attack Mansah Koto was unfortunately wounded, and very shortly after it he died from the wounds he received.

The ringleaders of the trouble, refugees from Sankandi, had after the murders already joined Fodi Kabba at Mandina, in French territory, and requests for the surrender of the culprits were made to the Government of Senegal. Nothing, however, was done; and at the latter end of January Sir George Denton suggested to M. Ballay, the then Governor-General of French West Africa, that concerted action should be taken against Fodi Kabba. This, after some delay, was agreed to, and on March 23, 1901, hostilities were commenced, our troops, under Lieutenant-Colonel Brake, guarding the frontier, whilst the French attacked the town of Mandina, Fodi Kabba's stronghold. The fort and compound were demolished; and the powerful old marauder who had in his time caused so much trouble, was shot. Lansaniang Dabu and Bakary Job are supposed to have lost their lives at the taking of Mandina. Bakary Bajo was arrested in British territory and together with N'Farli Dabu and Dari Bana Dabu, who had been handed over by the French, was tried by the Supreme Court at Bathurst. All these men were convicted, and were

ANGLICAN CHURCH, BATHURST, COMPLETED IN 1902.
(The Buildings in the Distance are the Barracks.)

eventually hanged at Dumbutu. The other chiefs known to be implicated were deported to Sierra Leone and to other places in the protectorate.

The names of those sent out of the colony were Jummo Sanyang of Kwinella; Mai Dabu and Bakary Dabu of Dumbutu; and Fodi Bakary Ceesi, Fodi Malek Ceesi and Fodi Dabu Ceesi of Sallikenni, turbulent firebrands of that town who had been responsible for sending an armed party to the commissioner of the north bank, threatening to use force if he did not at once quit their country.

As a warning to the people of the protectorate as to what to expect on any recurrence of hostilities of a similar nature, columns, in some instances accompanied by the Governor, proceeded through the principal towns. The desired effect was produced, and the country was not only pacified but was opened up for trade, with the result that, at the present time, it is perfectly safe for anyone to travel throughout the length and breadth of the protectorate, the various chiefs who possibly might eventually have become troublesome having thoroughly learned that it would be against their own interests and those of their people to resist law and order. Several of the unreliable and incompetent chiefs were superseded and stronger men appointed in their stead, the consequence being that the Protectorate Ordinance No. 7 of 1902—a far-reaching enactment*—was accepted without any difficulty arising.

Following on the expedition, one of the most important measures effected during 1901 was an agreement entered into with Musa Molloh under which, in consideration of an annual stipend of £500, he handed over the administration of British Fulladu to the government of the Gambia, and agreed to its forming part of the protectorate.

There was a slight falling off in the revenue during this year. This was due to the ground-nut crop, on which there is an export duty, suffering from an insufficient rain, and from a visitation of locusts, which destroyed other food-stuffs and left the people on the verge of famine. However, the Government came to the rescue and issued a large quantity of rice, which enabled the trying period to be tided over. It must be recorded that from the following year's crops the whole of the issues were repaid in full by the people, not only without the slightest trouble, but with expressions of their gratitude for the timely assistance which undoubtedly tended to strengthen the bond of union between the protectorate and the Government.

In 1900 the Anglican Church of St. Mary was commenced.

* See Chapter VIII.

It was finished in 1901, and was consecrated by Bishop Taylor Smith in December of that year. The building is a fine structure, capable of accommodating a congregation of 400.

The death of Her Most Gracious Majesty Queen Victoria on January 22nd, cast a gloom over the whole country, the grief of the people being most genuine, as the name of Queen Victoria was as well known and as much reverenced in the Gambia as in any part of the British dominions.

Several important ordinances were passed during 1901, but these will be found in a tabulated return given separately for easy reference.* There was an increase in the criminal statistics but this is accounted for by greater activity throughout the country in the administration of the laws. Crimes that would probably otherwise have escaped detection were brought to light by the commissioners, who, travelling continually up and down the protectorate, came directly in touch with the chiefs and people. Moreover, the Governor's frequent tours throughout the country made it difficult, as well as impolitic, for the chiefs to hide misdemeanours.

In 1902 the revenue for the first time exceeded £51,000, which must be considered most satisfactory. Many important works that had long been neglected received attention, and the Gambia of to-day is a very different place to what it was even a few years back. Everything is progressing apace, and general tranquillity exists.

The accession of His Most Gracious Majesty King Edward VII. to the throne of the empire, on the death of our late lamented Queen, must be recorded. His coronation in 1902, after His Majesty's most unfortunate illness, gave rise to general rejoicing throughout the country.

There is just one point that should be mentioned before closing the foregoing particulars of the Gambia, and that is the cost of living, which is much greater than in the other British possessions in the West Coast of Africa. From personal experience the author estimates that it is at least 20 per cent. dearer in Bathurst than either at the Gold Coast or Lagos. Wages in the last-mentioned colonies rarely exceed 30s. or 35s. per month for a good steward, and £2 for a cook, but in the Gambia £3 is not considered excessive for either cooks or stewards. Good servants are at premium and difficult to obtain. The reason for this is to be found in the fact that market prices are high and few things can be purchased locally at the stores at anything but comparatively costly rates. It is hoped, however, that the progress the colony is making will at no distant date put matters on a better footing in this respect.

* See Chapter VIII.

PART II.

PARTICULARS OF THE DISTRICTS UNDER THE TRAVELLING COMMISSIONERS.

CHAPTER V.

THE DISTRICTS UNDER THE TRAVELLING COMMISSIONERS.

Detailed Particulars as to the following Districts under the Five Travelling Commissioners: The North Bank, McCarthy Island, Upper River, South Bank, and Kommbo and Fogni.

THE particulars of the districts under the five travelling commissioners are given in the following short reports. It will be gathered from them that a most satisfactory condition of affairs exists in the colony of the Gambia.

THE NORTH BANK DISTRICT.

Lower Niumi is a very large district, extending from the coast line to the Memene Creek. General improvement has been noticeable in the country and its people during recent years. The head chief is Maranta Sonko, one of the few remaining hereditary chiefs of the lower river. All the Government compounds are in excellent order, and the roads throughout the districts are good.

At the tidal creek between the towns of Bakkendick and Buniadu a good bridge has been erected.

The crops are steadily improving, but the old trouble of the people persisting in pulling their ground-nuts before maturity has been detrimental to the crop. However, in 1903 the Government and merchants distributed among all the districts of the protectorate some 200 tons of Rufisque nuts, and the results have been most satisfactory, as the 1904 crop was very heavy.

In Niumi there are but few cattle and the tsetse fly is said to be very prevalent. The condition of the people, however, is reported as being satisfactory and prosperous. The largest town is Bakkendick, with a population of some 600. This district is peopled by Mandingoes near the river and Jolloffs on the boundary side. In Upper Niumi, Sicca—a Mandingo town 3½ miles east of Albreda—has been selected as the chief town of this district. Ibraima Sonko is the chief, and is an intelligent man who carries out his duties in a very satisfactory manner.

The native court is composed of the head chief, with two

Mandingo and two Jolloff members who are respectively the headmen of the Mandingo towns of Tubabcolong and Jurunku, and of the Jolloff towns of Pakkau and Bantan Killing.

The roads in the district are fairly good, and have been much improved during the past few years; where necessary bridges have been erected by the people.

It has been suggested that the reason why cattle do not thrive in either Upper or Lower Niumi is the presence of the tsetse fly, which has been specially noticed as existing in these districts.

The largest towns in Upper Niumi are Sika, Aljamadu, and Tubal-Kolong, all Mandingo towns, with Bantankilling, a Jolloff town. The country is very fertile and it is hoped that cotton will do well there.

The territory of Jokadu, which runs from the Memene Creek on the west to the Suarra Kunda Creek on the east, is not large and is somewhat sparsely populated; the people are Mandingoes along the land immediately bordering the river, but Jolloffs near the boundary.

Dasallami, on the creek of that name, is the chief town, with a population of some 300. The largest town, however, is that of Sajuka, a Jolloff town having a population of 650. It is pleasing to record that this is quite a new town, erected during the past few years by people from Senegal who have come over to British territory to settle.

The main road, running due east, is in very good order and receives continual attention. The Memene Creek is crossed by a bridge some 600 feet long, entirely erected by the people of Jokadu, and of great use.

Crime in the district is very rare, and the native tribunals have little to do beyond keeping general order and settling petty disputes. The health of the country is good and the people careful and hard-working. They are prosperous, and the crops have been excellent of recent years.

Lower Baddibu extends from the Suarra Kunda Creek to half-way between the towns of Kunti Kunda and Illiassa. It is the largest and most important district throughout the north bank. The majority of the people are Mohammedan Mandingoes, but there are a considerable number of Jolloffs and Foulahs in the upper towns. The town of the head chief is Sallikenni; and Arafang Buli Dabu is an energetic and able man who gives entire satisfaction to the Government. He, moreover, is held in great respect by his people.

The work done in this district has been good, every support being given to the commissioner by the chiefs and people. It was at Sallikenni that the Gambia company of the West African

Frontier Force had their camp in 1903, during the period the barracks at headquarters were under extensive repairs. The town of Sallikenni is probably the largest in the protectorate, having no less than 4,000 inhabitants, and the fact that the troops made it the headquarters for their annual course of field training had an excellent moral effect.

Other large towns in this neighbourhood are Karawan on the Suarra Kunda, Saba, Kunguru, Bunni, Jabba Kunda, No Kunda, and Kunti Kunda, all inhabited by Mohammedan Mandingoes.

The health of the people has been good, the protectorate medical officer having quite recently been through the district on a tour of inspection.

IMPROVISED RIFLE BUTTS OF THE WEST AFRICAN FIELD FORCE AT SALLIKENNI.

Good progress had been made at Marong Kunda, where improvements in the town and streets have been carried out. The inhabitants here are very well off, being possessed of large herds of cattle, sheep and goats, together with many horses.

The roads in the district are, however, none too good, owing to the sandy soil, which makes the going heavy.

Upper Baddibu includes Sabagh and Sanjal. The head chief is Jato Silang Jani, one of the few remaining hereditary chiefs of the country. He is much respected by his people, but unfortunately he is a very old and infirm man who cannot get about, which is bad for the district.

The population of Upper Baddibu is not numerous, but there are one or two towns with over 1,000 people—namely, Katchang and Farafenni. The inhabitants are chiefly Mandingoes, with a slight sprinkling of Jolloffs and Foulahs. In Sabagh and Sanjal the Jolloffs predominate, but there are a good many Foulahs, who are always found to be excellent farmers.

Throughout Baddibu the main roads are good and as the Government distribute valuable annual prizes for the best protectorate roads of the year, awarded on the recommendations of the commissioners, it is thought that they will continue gradually to improve.

Lower Salum was originally known as No. 4 District. The head chief's town is at Kau-ur, and Arafang Jani is a first-rate and energetic man and, moreover, one who can be relied upon to carry out instructions and who is held in high esteem by his people. The district is not a large one and the inhabitants, with the exception of those of the Mandingo town of Kau-ur, all Jolloffs. In this district is the important wharf town of Ballanghar, a big centre of trade.

McCARTHY ISLAND DISTRICT.

The people of this district are of a quiet disposition and the head chiefs and alcaides do their work well, although, as elsewhere in the protectorate, prior to 1901, disaffection on the part of one or two of the important chiefs showed itself. But, as a whole, they are an intelligent lot of men who take great trouble to carry out the wishes of the administration, and to do what they can for the general welfare of their people.

At the Island of McCarthy a good deal of trade is carried on, due to its being the "half-way house" between the upper reaches of the river and Bathurst.

The roads throughout the district are receiving special attention, and the majority of the main thoroughfares, if so they may be called, are in fair condition; but work on them can only be performed in the wet season, as great difficulty is experienced in treating the hard ground and removing the old roots and stumps of trees. Moreover, the labour required can only be obtained for short periods between the planting season and the "harvest," the population of the country, as it is, being hardly sufficient to cultivate the lands available. This applies to the whole protectorate, but each year sees progress with the good work in hand, and time will witness the desired and necessary improvements.

Throughout this district large quantities of cattle exist, and if a trade could be established on a sound, commercial basis it would not only be remunerative but beneficial generally. As mentioned elsewhere, however, the people are disinclined to sell their beasts—they invest all their capital in them—and the fact that their cattle are frequently reduced by disease does not deter them from continuing this short-sighted practice. The reason for it is no doubt due to a man's social position frequently being estimated from the size of his herds.

The ground-nut industry has progressed, and cotton is receiving due attention; but the people do not show the interest in the latter product that they should. All their energy is apparently thrown into the ground-nut cultivation, and it is only from the reduction in price, as will eventually be found to be the case, that

NATIVE CATTLE AND SHEEP AT BALLANGHAR.

the people will realise that they must look to a second staple product to provide for necessary and increasing wants.

In referring to this district mention must be made of the head chief of the Upper Niani country, Sunta Koma, as he is a most important factor in the adminstration of the McCarthy area. He is a powerful chief in whom reliance may be placed, and when called upon he assists the Government in every way possible. His town is Manna, and though but a small place his power throughout Upper Niani is omnipotent. The Government, in view of the assistance received from Sunta Koma, has recently increased his stipend.

In Sandu there is a scarcity of good farm lands and this has been the cause of a number of the permanent inhabitants migrating into the Fulladu country. But each year, from various causes, there is an influx of strange farmers from the adjoining French territory; and this counterbalances the emigration, and is beneficial to the country, as these temporary settlers are a peaceful and hard-working people comprised principally of Foulahs. They experience some difficulty, however, in leaving French territory, as can readily be supposed, the French Government not desiring to lose any of their people from a country so sparsely populated.

The roads in this portion of the country are fair, and, considering the comparatively short time during which the upper river territories have had the services of a commissioner, the district is very free from disturbances of any kind, the people being most amenable to British rule, under which they have learnt that if they do their best to comply with existing regulations they will always receive justice and protection.

In Wuli it is found that the population is gradually increasing, and the crops have of recent years been excellent. But, as elsewhere, the people are a little grasping, being very ready to put "tong"—a native term equivalent to the English "prohibition"—on the sale below a certain price of their ground-nuts. In some instances this has recoiled on themselves, as the market has of recent years been a falling one; but, on the other hand, on occasions it has proved most useful in forcing the hand of the merchant. As a rule, however, a fair price per bushel is agreed upon at the commencement of the season, and adhered to.

Kantora is one of the most fertile districts in the upper river and still has plenty of good lands available for cultivation. The population here also is increasing and the health of the people is good.

In Fulladu great progress has been made, the revenue in 1902 more than doubling itself, showing plainly the prosperity of the people. The population has greatly increased, owing to the immigration of Musa Molloh and his people from French territory. The roads throughout Fulladu are receiving attention and the people are keeping their bridges in good repair.

At Gambasara and Numuyelle an unsettled feeling at present exists, and, although Gambasara is one of the largest towns in British territory, some questions of abandoning it arose. The reason apparently was that as the town is so near French territory the domestic slaves desert their masters. The Gambasara people are Serrahoulis, and like most of this section probably are too hard on the people working for them. Consequently, their so-called slaves run away. There is, however, one good point in favour of the Gambasara people—they teach their children to read and write, having a school of their own in the town; but,

WINNOWING GROUND-NUTS.

as explained elsewhere, the extent of the learning imparted amounts only to the writing of Arabic and the reading of passages of the Koran. This was one of the special towns from which His Excellency the present Governor suggested one or two lads should be sent to the Mohammedan school in Bathurst, but the proposal was not received with favour.

There has been good progress in the cultivation of the farm lands, due again to an influx of people from French territory.

In Western Fulladu the roads have been well looked after, the head chief Dembo Densa being a first-rate man. In all the districts proper tribunals exist and do good work without party favour. As an instance, a member of the tribunal under Dembo Danso was himself tried for unlawfully hearing cases. This tends to show that Section XXI. of Ordinance 7 of 1902 is being complied with by the native tribunals. The revenue in this district has increased some 75 per cent. Cotton in the upper river towns is receiving careful consideration, the soil apparently being most suitable; but, again, ground-nuts pay the people best and do not require such absolutely close attention, although it is a mistake to think that the ground-nut when planted can be left until ready to be pulled. To quote information received from Mr. W. B. Stanley, the commissioner of the upper river, "the ground-nut, being a low creeping plant, is easily smothered by weeds and grass, which both flourish prolifically, and therefore it requires continual hoeing. As the plant arrives at maturity the ground beneath it has to be dug up very carefully in order that the tendril-like stems on which the nuts are produced may more readily strike down into the earth. If this operation be neglected the nuts ripen on the surface and are empty and valueless." An acre of ground-nuts, however, is found to yield some 60 per cent. more than cotton, as cultivated at present, but the tuition that the people will receive from the cotton expert now employed in the colony, and at the model farm at Willinghara, will undoubtedly tend to increase the cotton crop, which hitherto has received but little attention. Moreover, it is hoped that the encouragement the people are receiving from the Government, in the shape of presents of seed and prizes for the best cotton produced, will have a beneficial effect. The old system of "barter" payment in goods is fast disappearing, and, as less credit is given by the merchants than was the case years ago, the people are getting more independent and now prefer cash for their produce. The consequence is that the merchant has to supply his up-country traders with coin and the circulation of British silver is on the increase. Great quantities of five-franc pieces, however, still remain in circulation.

Although the lands throughout the upper river districts are excellent, they are unfortunately somewhat cramped, owing to the vast ridges of iron stone running parallel to the river at a distance of three to four miles. On both banks exist great swamps, running inland about a mile. In the dry season these lands become a kind of bog, but in the rains, when the river rises rapidly and overflows, they are inundated,

Camp of H.E. the Governor at Madina, Native Servants in Foreground

and are useless for cultivation except on the borders, where rice is grown.

In the dry season the swamp lands are most picturesque, being covered with long golden grass, and the shooting to be obtained in them is excellent—antelope, bush-fowl (partridge), duck and teal abounding.

From Gambasara to Basse is about ten miles, the district up to the village of Damfa Kunda being comprised of fine farm lands and the country open.

Just before reaching Damfa Kunda the town of Madina is found, and a creek between the two places is crossed by means of a native bridge formed of woven bamboo-cane known as "crinting." On the other side of this creek a vast plain stretches right away for miles, being bordered on the river side by trees of a fair size. When—as in February, 1904—this immense level is covered with the golden grass already mentioned, the picture is a beautiful one.

Tambasansan, the town of the head chief Farli Cora, is nine miles from Basse. There, a commissioner reports, they "were well received, everything possible to the native mind having been prepared for our comfort. The camp was excellent, and on the approach of His Excellency [Sir George Denton] he was met by some forty or fifty horsemen, preceded by musicians and dancing Griots, who escorted him through the town. This is only recorded to show the hospitable welcome extended throughout the protectorate at the present day; and, at the same time, I should say this is not an isolated case but a general procedure met with in nearly all the districts of this country. On the day following our arrival all the chiefs and a number of the people in the Eastern Fulladu district attended at the Government compound, and the Governor explained to them several questions affecting their welfare, such as vaccination, education, and the extended cultivation of cotton."

The system of placing "tong" on the sale of produce was gone into and the people advised not to proceed to it unless it was absolutely necessary to protect themselves against exceptionally low prices; they were told that they should only adopt such a measure as a last resource, as sometimes the first prices offered by the merchants were as high as it was possible to pay, and if the markets in Europe became glutted by large imports of ground-nuts from other countries, such as India and elsewhere, prices would be sure to drop and they would be the losers. It was also pointed out that the market prices of produce did not depend entirely on the merchants, and as long as fair prices were obtainable they should be accepted, as profit had to be made on both sides, and the increasing production of the ground-nut throughout the world would probably in the future reduce the high prices of previous years.

THE SOUTH BANK DISTRICT.

In the East Central Kiang district all the towns are well looked after and the roads have been widened, the people themselves seeing the advantages to be derived from good roads instead of the old "bush paths."

As in the other districts contentment and prosperity reign supreme, all the crops for several years having been excellent. Here, as elsewhere, the foolish mistake of pulling the nuts too soon has been made and in consequence the crop has been reduced, but no doubt the lesson that has been learned of late will be a useful one.

There were but few cases before the native courts in 1903. Those most prevalent throughout the country were assault and seduction, and these were dealt with by the native tribunals.

A certain amount of ill-feeling exists at Kwinella against the present head chief Fodi Sanniang, but he has done good work and will be supported by the Government while he continues to do so. The dissentient section are Sonninkees and the followers of a man named Jumo N'Ding, who for the part he took in the Sankandi trouble was deported to Sierra Leone and subsequently allowed to return to Borroba only. Application for his return to Kwinella has been frequently made, but so far it has not been thought advisable to permit him to do so.

It was at this town that, in 1902, the Gambia Company of the West African Frontier Force went into camp for their first training. Every assistance was given to the officers of the force by the chief Fodi Sanniang, and no complaints were received by the Government from either the detachment or from the people of Kwinella.

In Eastern Kiang the people are now of a quiet disposition and give little or no trouble. The only serious crime that can be recorded of late is the attempted murder of the head-man of the town of Jiniri by a stranger from French territory. The man was arrested and received ten years' penal servitude.

The people of this portion of the protectorate have accepted the principles of vaccination as against the old native remedy of inoculation; and thus, in this part of the protectorate, the smallpox which is so common amongst the people of West Africa has been checked. Throughout the greater portion of the protectorate vaccination is readily being adopted, but in the upper-river district, the people, through ignorance, still prefer their own remedy, to which, unfortunately, it is estimated that at least 50 per cent. of the infant mortality is due.* The Government have, however, appointed a protectorate medical officer to travel throughout the country, and it is confidently hoped that good results will be the outcome of his mission, as he is well received by the people and is an expert in vaccination. The towns in Eastern Kiang are clean and the roads in good order.

Progress in Western Jarra has of late been most marked, the head chief being Arafang Lang Jaju, a strong and energetic man, who was appointed quite recently in succession to Fodi Dabu, an old and infirm chief who had little or no hold on his people. As can be readily imagined, a strong head chief in a district is of vital importance to the progress and welfare of the people, who require leading rather than driving. The Government compounds and the towns are frequently visited by the commissioners, and this keeps them in touch with the people and tends to their being maintained in good order. The roads throughout Jarra are receiving attention, and consequently are losing the appearance of a bush path; but, owing to the scarcity of labour really good roads must of necessity be a question of gradual development throughout the protectorate.

Central Jarra is not only the smallest but the poorest country in the south bank between Vintang Creek and the McCarthy Island district; but even here improvements in roads and in other directions have taken place and the general prosperity and health of the people continues to be satisfactory. It will perhaps appear odd to those who do not know the country to read that in nearly every portion of the protectorate satisfactory progress is being made. But such is nevertheless the case, and the people during recent years have become law-abiding and peaceful, the commissioners experiencing but little difficulty in the administration of their various districts.

Eastern Jarra, during 1902 and up to the commencement of the following year, was very unsettled, owing to the head chief Arafang Lang Sedi Sali making mis-statements to the people with regard to their sheep and goats. He represented that the Government desired them to be slaughtered and would not permit any to be retained. No such order had, of course, ever been given or thought of; but the opportunity was taken during the

* The Medical Officer (Dr. Hopkinson) in charge of the West African Frontier Force vaccinated some 400 people in 1902 in Quinella and the neighbourhood. In 1903 smallpox broke out in Kwinella itself. Amongst those who had been vaccinated there was not a fatal case, and the few who contracted the disease had it very lightly, and all recovered. In contradistinction to this, in a certain town some 40 or more children were inoculated according to the native custom, and it was stated by the chief of the town, at a public meeting, that every one of these had died. At the town of Jassong His Excellency the Governor was speaking at a public meeting on the subject of vaccination and he invited the people to bring their children to be vaccinated. The chief of the town stated that he was very sorry he could not do as he was asked, because there were no children to bring—they had all died the previous year.

rainy season and in the absence of the commissioner to circulate this malicious rumour. In addition, a rumour was spread that a specially large Government ground-nut measure was going to be issued. That the people are willing to believe such canards shows their simplicity and the power the head chiefs have among them.

This man Sedi Sali was superseded as soon as the Governor visited Eastern Jarra; and the headman of Buraing, Afarmara Dabu—a nephew of an old district chief—was appointed. Buraing thus reverted, after many years, to its former position as the principal town in this part of the country.

The natives here are very prosperous and most industrious, being good farmers and herdsmen.

Early in 1903 there was an influx of people from French territory, and at their special request they were granted land, and the new town of Sukuta N'Ding was built.

Western Niamina is most populous and would be as well a prosperous district, but the people, who are Sonninkees, are extravagant and lazy, spending most of their money in drink.

On the other hand, the only four Marabout towns which form the sub-district are most prosperous and flourishing, having good farms and large herds of cattle. These four towns are Dunkunku, Barro-Kunda, Sami, and Jakoto.

Eastern Niamina is one of the largest and best cultivated of the districts on the south bank. Although not permanent settlers, the "strange farmers" (principally Foulahs from French territory) do excellent work here, clearing the land and making large farms. The head town is Kudang, with a population of 1,000—which is large for up-country towns in the Gambia. The head chief is Fodi Sani Ceesay, who is a strong man; but, unfortunately, he does not give the detailed attention to his district that he might, the result being that many of the district towns are not kept clean and the people are dirty in their habits. However, the present commissioner (Mr. Withers) is giving special attention throughout his district to the question of cleaning towns, widening the lanes or streets, and improving the roads every year; the future therefore will, with careful administration, undoubtedly see great improvements throughout the country. A fair revenue is received each year in the protectorate from depasturage fees for cattle grazing, the land in French territory not being as good as that on our side of the frontier. The herdsmen drive their beasts to suitable pasture lands with the permission of the chiefs of the districts concerned, and pay a fee for the accommodation granted. All amounts received in this way are in the first instance dealt with in the commissioner's accounts and brought to the revenue of the colony, one-fifth of the fees thus collected being handed to each chief concerned at the end of the year.

In Eastern Niamina little or no crime is committed, the majority of cases that come before the native tribunal or commissioner's court being very trivial.

THE KOMMBO AND FOGNI DISTRICT.

Available information proves that the people of Kommbo and Fogni are perfectly satisfied and are proud of being under British protection.

Comparing the people of Fogni of to-day with those of even as recent a period as ten years ago, their improvement is remarkable; then they would barely listen to reason and were ignorant in the extreme. The past few years, with a guiding hand, fair treatment and kindness, have, however, done wonders, and although not yet quite all that they should be, the people are steadily improving and are ready and willing to carry out the instructions given to them. The general health, also, has improved; and this, no doubt, is due to the people being made to keep their compounds and towns clean and in good order. The tour of the travelling commissioners in the Gambia covers the eight months, from November to the end of June, of the dry season, and during this period the commissioners go up and down their districts, advising and guiding the people and seeing that law and order is observed. Serious crimes are rarely committed and when they do occur as a rule strangers from over the boundary are responsible for them.

The crops have been fairly good throughout Kommbo, but the drought caused by the small rainfall in September and October of 1903 did much harm.

Along the frontier of Kommbo and Fogni the French Government have recently established customs stations. It is hoped that responsible persons may be placed in charge of them, so that the people who come into British territory to trade may not be robbed. This is merely mentioned owing to complaints that have been received from the town of Siliti.

The cotton in this district does not appear to have done very well. Probably this may, in the past, have been due to planting at the wrong season of the year; but the question is now receiving serious attention, and all instructions possible as to cultivation, planting and other points, are being given to the people.

Cattle are not very plentiful in the Kommbo and Fogni

Party travelling with H.E. The Governor through Kommbo.

countries, and, as elsewhere, their owners cannot as a rule be induced to sell. Heavy losses are therefore at times experienced owing to disease.

Rubber has, of recent years, been scarce, and in fact it is at present almost a negligible export from the Gambia. This may be due to the small quantities still collected being passed through French territory, where it is understood better prices can be obtained than from the merchants of Bathurst.

The district of Kommbo is divided into five parts—Kommbo St. Mary (hitherto British Kommbo), North, South, Central and East Kommbos. Bakau is the head town of St. Mary and the chief is Bakary Jammeh. The population in 1903 was 1,438. Originally this portion of Kommbo was colony, but during 1902 it was brought under the protectorate ordinance.

The head town of North Kommbo is Sukuta, and its chief is Kabba Cham. The population is 2,279. Originally Busumballa was the head chief's town, but when he was deposed in 1898 Kabba Cham was appointed. Kabba Cham is very intelligent and understands English fairly well.

Gunjour, years ago a hotbed of insurrection, is the principal town in South Kommbo, and has a population of 1,117. Tumani Ture is the chief, and he and his people are strong Mohammedans.

Brikama is the head town of Central Kommbo, and has a population of 596. It was, with Gunjour, one of Fodi Sillah's strongholds, destroyed by the expedition of 1894. The present chief is Fodi Musa Bojan.

The landing-place for Brikama is at Kembugie, up the Mandina Creek, and it was here that the naval brigade, soon after disembarking, suffered a severe repulse in February, 1894.

Faraba Bunta is the head town of Eastern Kommbo and Mamady Sannian is the chief. The population of this district is 1,260.

The only timber fit to cut for export in the whole of the Gambia is obtained in Eastern Kommbo, but in no great quantities. There is fair rosewood, but so far trial shipments have resulted in loss to the exporter; such timber as is at present cut is utilised merely for shipbuilding and for repairing purposes at headquarters.

The estimated number of people throughout Kommbo, in 1903, was 7,022, the total area being roughly 400 square miles.

The country of Kiang is divided into West, West Central, East Central and Eastern Kiang, the west and west central portions being under the commissioner of Kommbo. The principal town of Western Kiang is Jali, the chief being Janko

Sammati. This is a large district, but numbers only some 2,540 inhabitants.

The head town of West Central Kiang is Batteling, the chief being Lansaniang, an excellent man and a strong supporter of the Government, as was his predecessor—Mansah Koto—before him. The population is 944. In this portion of Kiang, Sankandi, the town where Messrs. Sitwell and Silva and the constables were murdered, was situated, as was also Dumbutu, against which the expedition of 1901 was sent.

The whole of Kiang is in a satisfactory condition, and no trouble has been given there recently. The present chiefs

H.E. The Governor. Chief Kabba Cham.

A PALAVER AT SUKUTA.

throughout it are a fairly intelligent and amenable class of men, and this means everything to the towns for which they are responsible.

After Sankandi and Dumbutu were destroyed the Government refused permission for them to be rebuilt, leaving them in their dilapidated condition as a warning to the people in the surrounding country. In 1903, the land in the neighbourhood of the above-mentioned places having lain fallow for two years, the Government granted permission to build an entirely new town there on quite a different site, so that the available farms might be again cultivated. A position a short distance away was decided upon, and the new town of Sannian Kunda has arisen. The lesson taught these people in 1901 will never be forgotten.

The total area of Kiang is 317 square miles.

The Fogni country is divided as follows;—West Fogni, Vintang, Brefet, Karrenai, East Fogni, Kansalla and Bondali. There are wharves for shipping at Vintang, Karrenai and Brefet, which are inhabited mostly by Mandingoes. The head Jolah town is Bullelai, in Vintang, West Fogni; and the chief of this district is Kekota Daramai.

The Jolahs are a wild people, but are gradually settling down and becoming amenable to the protectorate laws.

In addition to the wharves at the above-mentioned towns there are jetties at Kansalla, Bondali and Jarrol. The chief of this portion of Fogni is Nianki Baji, and his town is Kangaramba. At the eastern end of this section of Fogni the Binoonka country commences. It was in this neighbourhood that Fodi Kabba was routed by British troops in 1892, and driven to Mandina, in French territory.

The population of Fogni in 1903 was approximately 5,753, and the area 355 square miles.

The Jollahs who inhabit this portion of the protectorate are an unsociable race, but are receiving careful attention, and during this year (1904) they have performed a good deal of work on their roads, which is a step in the right direction. At one time, not so long ago, it was dangerous for traders to go through Fogni, but now they are perfectly safe.

The only navigable waterway in this district is the Vintang Creek, which is navigable up to the Sandeng Creek, 1 mile from the frontier, for vessels drawing 8 feet.

The Jollahs are an extremely hard-working and thrifty race and will in time improve materially; at present, however, although they give no special cause for worry, they are erratic and require careful handling.

All the roads throughout the whole of the Kommbo and Fogni districts have been well looked after and are being widened, but what is specially required throughout the country is to get the people to understand the usefulness of carts and other vehicles. They will then see that good roads are essential and a saving of time and labour

PART III.

THE COLONY DURING THE PAST DECADE.

CHAPTER VI.

THE COLONY DURING THE PAST DECADE.

Revenue and Expenditure from 1890 to 1903—Remarks on Financial Conditions—Expenditure accounted for—Additional Taxes during the Past Decade—Currency—Boards of Health and Education—Friendly Societies—The Slave Trade—Chief Exports—Paucity of Timber—Importance of the Ground-nut—The Prospect for Cotton—Excellence of Native Cloth—The Problem of Irrigation—A Future for Indigo—The Philosophy of Farli Cora—Area of Colony and Protectorate—The Principal Imports—Comparative Table of Imports and Exports for 1895-1904—Principal Trading Companies—Lack of Mineral Wealth—Native Conservatism—Gambasara and the Cart—The Steady Advance of Civilisation—The "Mansah Kilah" and "Thistle"—The Botanical Station at Kotu—Model Cotton Farms—The Rhun Palm—Steamship Service—Ground-nut Boats—Government Yacht Service—Telegraphic and Postal Service—Educational Facilities—The Colonial Hospital and its Work—The Contagious Diseases Hospital—Hospital Expenditure—"Gree Gree"—Native "Doctors" and Diseases—Care of the Destitute and the Insane—The Prison—Table of Convictions for Crime—Climate—The Harmattan—Rainfall—Improved Sanitary Conditions—New Slaughter-House—Military and Police Forces—An Optimistic Conclusion.

As it is considered unnecessary to give in detail returns of revenue and expenditure from the time the British Government took over the Gambia in 1821, the following synopsis of the progress of the colony is limited to the past decade, and it is hoped it may be found an interesting feature of the handbook.

FINANCIAL.

The actual general Revenue and Expenditure from 1890 to 1903 was as follows;—

Year.	Revenue.	Expenditure.	Customs' Revenue.	Year.	Revenue.	Expenditure.	Customs' Revenue.
	£	£	£		£	£	£
1890	30,573	22,759	25,687	1897	39,415	27,059	31,463
1891	31,038	27,697	25,934	1898	43,717	29,035	34,762
1892	30,978	28,740	26,691	1899	46,840	30,405	37,786
1893	31,899	38,143	27,446	1900	49,080	29,818	40,255
1894	23,797	31,640	19,370	1901	43,726	48,518	34,168
1895	20,561	28,867	15,302	1902	51,016	51,536	40,555
1896	26,172	25,300	20,029	1903	55,564	67,504	42,752

The invested funds at the end of 1899 amounted to £43,490. At the end of 1903 they amounted to £53,153.

Up to the end of the latter year the financial condition of the colony was prosperous, although there was not much difference in the actual receipts.

In 1894 a bad year was experienced, owing to an abnormal rainfall, which affected not only the whole trade and prosperity of the people, but contributed to a general depression of business. The consequence was, that a very poor revenue was collected, and this was the case up to 1896. The ground-nut crop during the seasons 1894-1896 was very poor indeed; to remedy this unfortunate state of affairs the Government considered it advisable to procure a change of nut from the French colony of Senegal, and this seed was issued to the planters throughout the protectorate. In 1896 the export of ground-nuts was 12,000 tons. In 1897 it had increased to 20,000, and the average weight of the nuts was better. It is presumed, therefore, that the experiment of importing the fresh seed from Senegal was most successful.

This year of 1897, as will be seen, was a most prosperous one, the largest revenue to date being recorded; and it is pleasing to note that since the bad years ending with 1896 the colony has thrived, the revenue at the present time having doubled itself as compared with that year.

As the expenditure during the past few years shows an increase greater in proportion than the increase in the colony's revenue, it should in fairness be stated that more substantial works have been carried out since 1900 than, probably, in the whole previous history of the country. The condition of public buildings was deplorable; but these have now been put in proper repair. Among the most noticeable works completed are the military barracks, which have practically been rebuilt. A new wing to the hospital has also been erected, the central building renovated, and all the wards put thoroughly in order. The secretariat was rebuilt in 1902; two double bungalows, a special bungalow for European nurses, and a new female hospital were erected in 1903. The existing customs warehouses and other buildings have been improved and extended; a new post office, well ventilated and suitable to the increased postal service of the colony, has also been provided; and the police barracks, as well as the collector-of-customs' quarters have been thoroughly repaired. These are a few of the works carried out since the arrival of Sir George Denton in the colony. Small necessary requirements have also received due consideration as they arose, and have been dealt with without unnecessary delay. Special attention must also be called to an expenditure, which is dealt with later, of some £17,000 on the punitive expedition in 1901. From

Bungalow Quarters built in Bathurst in 1903.

this it will be seen that, although the colony's expenditure has apparently been large, value in full has been received.

The actual balance standing to the colony's credit at December 31, 1903, amounted to £47,676.

The following additions have been made in the taxation during the past decade:—

An additional duty of one farthing on kola-nuts became permanent by Ordinance No. 5 of 1890.

A dog licence of 5s. was imposed for the first time in 1890, by Ordinance No. 4 of that year. During the year 1893 trade licences were first issued; this ordinance was, however, repealed by the Gambia Protectorate Trade Ordinance of 1895,* the charges substituted being £10 for an "A" licence, to enable trade to be carried on at a factory where produce is collected for direct export; £3 for a "B" licence to trade at a station and to employ sub-traders not exceeding four; and £2 for trading and employing two sub-traders. In addition to the rate payable for the licence, a charge of 10s. is made for each sub-trader employed. To be a petty trader in kola-nuts, corn, salt and fish only, 4s. per annum is charged. Petty canoe traders in corn, fish and salt pay 8s. for each canoe. This trade-licence ordinance was a most beneficial enactment for all classes of traders, as it abolished finally the old system of "custom" charges, levied formerly by the chiefs and alcaides of towns, over which many disputes arose. The Government first attempted its abolition as long ago as 1862. Naturally, the headman did not like the change, as they originally purloined the custom, or "dash," paid by the merchant, and made a good thing out of their pilfering. But the new system is far more satisfactory, as it enables free trade to be carried on without "buying" the influence of the alcaides.

In 1895 the "hut and yard tax" was instituted, and it has been collected without opposition. The rate is 4s. annually for a yard containing not more than four huts, and 1s. for each additional hut if occupied by a member of the family; should the additional hut be occupied by a stranger, this amount is increased to 2s.

The above taxation in the colony is specially mentioned as affecting the people.

Ordinance No. 16 of 1903 was introduced to amend the Customs Tariff Ordinance, of 1899, and by it the import duties on spirits were increased to 4s. per imperial gallon.

An excellent Bill (No. 13) was passed in 1903, to regulate the sale of intoxicating liquors, and special spirit licences became payable in the protectorate, £10 being charged for an annual, and £6 for a half-yearly licence.

* See page 65.

CURRENCY.

The currency in the colony is sterling, but the five-franc piece is largely circulated throughout the protectorate, and is accepted at the treasury as legal tender at an exchange value of 3s. 10½d.

BOARDS OF HEALTH AND EDUCATION AND FRIENDLY SOCIETIES.

A board of health was organised in the year 1891, by Administrator Sir Robert Llewelyn, and it has done excellent work in keeping the town of Bathurst clean. All questions respecting the sanitary condition of buildings, streets, and the town generally, the filling of disused drains, the covering of old wells, the causing of all compounds and yards to be kept clean, and other matters of detail affecting the general health of the town, come within the scope of the board, which consists of the senior medical officer, the colonial engineer, assistant colonial surgeon and superintendent of police as official members, with three other members specially appointed by the Governor. A meeting of the board is held once each week, when all matters brought before it receive close attention. The revenue of the board is derived from an annual Government grant, from a rate of 3 per cent. on the annual value of house properties, and from the fees collected at the Government slaughter-house and market.

There is in the colony a Board of Education, whose functions are defined by Ordinance No. 14 of 1903 and the rules thereunder, for the promotion and assistance of primary and secondary education. The president is the Governor, who is supported by the members of the Legislative Council and by the principals of the Anglican, Wesleyan and Roman Catholic missions. The average annual Government grant-in-aid for division among the various schools has been, for the past ten years, £350. It is earned by results based on the examination held by the Government Inspector of Schools, and there is also a capitation given on the average attendance of pupils.

Bathurst is well supplied with friendly societies, there being no less than thirty-one. To deal separately with them would be out of the question; the author therefore merely makes passing mention of them to show that the various interests of the "Banjolian"* receive due attention.

TRADE, AGRICULTURE AND INDUSTRIES.

As is recorded particularly elsewhere, the main trade of the Gambia up to the time the country came directly under the

* From "Banjole," the early name of Bathurst.

Crown, in 1807, was the exportation of slaves, which continued even to a much later date in the sister colonies on the West African coast. In Lagos, for instance, the traffic survived right up to the late fifties.

The chief exports of the country are ground-nuts, wax, and small quantities of palm kernels. Up to the end of 1901 rubber was exported in some quantity, but latterly none has come in from the protectorate, no doubt because of the avaricious methods adopted by the collectors in the past, under which the trees, not being judiciously tapped, withered and died.

The timber of the country has already been referred to. It is small, and with very few exceptions not worth exporting. Small quantities only are now being cut annually, for repairs to cutters, schooners, and similar purposes.

The salvation of the Gambia is its staple article of cultivation, the ground-nut, the people devoting their whole attention to this product, and growing but small quantities of rice and corn for private consumption. The Government is doing all in its power, however, to push the cultivation of cotton as a second string; and it is hoped, now that an expert has arrived in the colony, that the people will soon learn the art of properly planting and treating it. But the wants of the country are small, and sufficient profit is made during the ground-nut season to tide over the rains; if it is seen that cotton pays to cultivate, it will, the author thinks, be taken up readily, as the population are hard-working and thrifty. The main drawback, however, is the lack of labour, the country being so very sparsely populated.

It must not be inferred that cotton has been entirely neglected in the past, as small quantities have been grown for local consumption, and utilised in the making of the native cloths known as "pagns." The weaving is primitive, native looms of an ingenious kind being used, and the cloth woven in long strips of some 27 yards in length by about 9 inches wide. It seems incredible but the native cloth spun by hand on these native looms bears favourable comparison with Manchester cotton goods, and the author even goes further and asserts that the cloth itself is certainly of a more durable nature.

An expert in irrigation visited the colony a short time ago, and he reported that the people thoroughly understood the art of cultivating rice and other cereals. In fact, he considered that they were quite as proficient in this respect as the natives of the East. Irrigation in some shape or form, however, is much needed, but the cost is so very heavy that it is impossible for the Government to take up the question at present.

Indigo is cultivated on a small scale. In nearly every village or town the author has visited an indigo "patch" was to be seen. This product, again, is utilised only for local purposes, such as the dyeing of "pagns" and other materials; but from the healthy look of the plants there is no doubt that the industry might well be extended. The small quantities that have been exported have been reported upon as being most excellent.

But in all these questions of extension of exports, the answer must at present be—insufficient population to deal with side issues on a large scale, outside ground-nuts. Farli Cora, the

BAITING CAMELS (AT NIANIBANTANG) THAT HAVE BROUGHT GROUND-NUTS FROM FRENCH TERRITORY TO THE GAMBIA RIVER.

chief of Tambasansan, an extremely intelligent man, thus put the case to the Governor during a recent visit: "I am ready and willing to take up these things you tell me about, but which of them pays best? As my people are so few they could not deal with them all."

The principal imports to the Gambia are rice, salt, spirits, wines, kola-nuts from Sierra Leone, provisions, hardware, sugar and tobacco. A statement of imports and exports for the ten years to 1903 is given for comparison with the colony's trade:—

TOTAL VALUE OF IMPORTS AND EXPORTS FOR THE TEN YEARS 1895-1904.

IMPORTS.

Years.	United Kingdom. £	s.	d.	British Colonies. £	s.	d.	Foreign Countries. £	s.	d.	Total. £	s.	d.
1895	51,067	15	4	17,399	6	2	28,932	7	3	27,399	8	9
1896	57,568	0	0	19,986	18	2	32,769	7	10	110,324	6	0
1897	97,180	18	11	25,146	13	5	53,999	3	1	176,326	15	5
1898	127,464	18	8	24,167	5	8	96,459	6	6	246,091	10	10
1899	115,306	4	8	36,309	7	1	89,291	4	9	240,906	16	6
1900	124,126	8	4	44,068	9	6	109,463	18	0	277,658	15	10
1901	116,919	19	7	25,532	11	5	110,194	6	6	252,646	17	6
1902	136,326	9	4	40,385	12	10	126,902	14	9	303,614	16	11
1903	142,560	8	11	48,007	15	2	150,494	12	1	341,062	16	2
1904	109,887	14	6	71,864	17	3	124,396	11	3	306,149	3	0

EXPORTS.

Years.	United Kingdom. £	s.	d.	British Colonies. £	s.	d.	Foreign Countries. £	s.	d.	Total. £	s.	d.
1895	33,999	8	3	993	11	11	58,543	10	10	93,536	11	0
1896	41,022	0	2	1,756	16	3	74,201	14	3	116,980	10	8
1897	35,235	7	1	1,469	8	8	129,189	8	3	165,894	4	0
1898	45,500	14	9	1,955	4	4	200,375	15	10	247,831	14	11
1899	26,545	16	10	2,751	7	3	212,638	17	11	241,936	2	0
1900	42,177	15	11	2,283	7	8	237,514	11	11	281,975	15	6
1901	26,058	3	8	2,236	18	11	205,371	8	6	233,666	11	1
1902	18,758	11	3	1,468	13	1	227,912	8	5	248,139	12	9
1903	22,080	1	3	11,077	1	6	300,860	6	5	334,017	9	2
1904	13,781	4	7	15,011	4	7	282,490	9	3	311,282	18	5

The most important factories in the colony are those of the following companies: The Bathurst Trading Company, The French Company (Cie. Française), Messrs. Maurel Frères, Messrs. Maurel & H. Prom, and Messrs. T. Waelter & Co., and these are sufficient for the trade of the country. They are of old standing, and the formation of any further commercial houses cannot be recommended. Among the natives there are several big traders and innumerable petty traders.

The main trade of these enterprises is the purchase of produce and the sale of cotton goods, haberdashery, spirits, and a few other articles. Provisions are dealt in, but in small quantities only, most of the substantial inhabitants of the colony themselves obtaining their stores direct from Europe.

There are neither mines in the country nor apparent mineral wealth, but vast ridges of ironstone are to be met with throughout the upper-river territories. Many miles north of the Gambia, in French territory, gold is said to have been found, and one or two companies have been formed to obtain it.

The people of the Gambia—and, for that matter, the people throughout the West African coast—are most conservative and strongly opposed to the introduction of any new methods, their industries, abodes, and habits being much the same at the present date as travellers found them centuries ago. Any suggestion put forward for their advancement that involves alteration in their existing customs is met with "passive resistance." Practically, they are without ambition. Their aversion to new measures they express in their ineradical belief that, as their fathers lived and worked as they do, what was good enough for their progenitors ought to be good enough for them.

As an instance the following fact is recorded. The Governor, in an endeavour to reduce labour and to induce the people to improve their roads, introduced a few two-wheeled carts into the protectorate. The chief of Gambasara, a large town on the south

MESSRS. MAUREL & H. PROM'S PREMISES AT BATHURST.

bank of the upper river, stated at a public meeting that he did not require carts; he had no use for them. It was pointed out that by using them for taking produce to the wharves a great deal of manual labour would be saved. His reply was that he preferred the system they had always been used to—namely, carrying loads, of 60 lb. and upwards, on their heads. As it was useless to argue with a man of this stamp, the Governor had to cause one of the carts to be left at Gambasara, and the commissioner received instructions to see that it was used.

The above is given as an example of the difficulty of convincing the people by verbal reasoning only. It is true that the advancement of our African colonies is steadily and surely being brought about, but it will be long before the possibilities that exist are fully made use of. The example set by the Europeans, and their continual contact with the native inhabitants of the interior, will no doubt gradually educate these ignorant people, but their advancement will of necessity be a question of time. The educated Africans at the various Government stations —alert, intelligent and, as a rule, good business men—prove convincingly how much the gradual and inevitable advancement of civilisation will do.

As a means of transport, to enable the Government and others to keep in easy touch with the protectorate and its people, the steam yacht, "Mansah Kilah" (King's Messenger), was purchased

A MONO-WHEEL-CART TRIAL IN THE PROTECTORATE.

in 1894, when a regular weekly mail and passenger service was introduced. This boat has done excellent service, and has more than repaid the Government. Her original cost, delivered at Bathurst, was £3,500. The service, however, has so enormously increased during the past ten years that a larger steamer with better accommodation would appear to be necessary, and no doubt arrangements for acquiring a suitable vessel will be made as soon as practicable. In addition to the "Mansah Kilah," a new launch—the "Thistle"—was purchased in 1901 for special use in the upper-river country; and the commissioner, whose district extends over a tract of country of some 120 miles, has found the "Thistle" of great assistance for administrative purposes, as it enables touch to be kept with practically the whole of his territory, without long and tedious marches that would otherwise take days to accomplish.

In 1894 a Government botanical station was started at Kotu, in British Kommbo, 11 miles from Bathurst, but it has not been found altogether successful, although small quantities of cotton and ground-nuts have been obtained from the land. It is now proposed to form, at various places up-country, model farms at which the people may receive proper instruction in the art of

THE MANSAH KILAH (SANTAMBA WHARF AT BACK).

planting and treating cotton and other produce—in fact, a special farm has already been started at Willinghara, under the management of the cotton expert.

In the Gambia there is no such export of palm oil as tends to swell the returns of other colonies in the Gulf of Guinea; but the Rhun palm flourishes, and its timber, which is of a fibrous nature, is very useful in bridge-work and for piling and the like

MEANS OF COMMUNICATION.

The following return shows the total shipping through the Port of Bathurst "inward" and "outward" during the past fifteen years:—

ACCOUNT OF SHIPPING IN THE COLONY OF THE GAMBIA, 1890-1904.

Years.	INWARDS. Vessels entered.	Tonnage of Vessels entered.	OUTWARDS. Vessels cleared.	Tonnage of Vessels cleared.
1890	170	111,777	168	109,909
1891	173	114,682	175	115,276
1892	159	108,590	159	108,834
1893	169	114,126	169	114,580
1894	174	115,110	175	114,592
1895	143	94,096	142	94,100
1896	151	116,236	150	115,389
1897	176	129,532	174	128,866
1898	194	163,962	195	164,183
1899	177	142,938	172	141,697
1900	150	132,839	146	128,430
1901	167	140,419	166	144,652
1902	188	143,407	188	143,471
1903	231	193,873	232	193,844
1904	215	183,879	219	183,681

Transport between the colony and Europe is effected by the steamers of the African Steamship Company, which run fortnightly between Liverpool and Bathurst, and those of the Woermann Line, from Hamburg, which communicate with the colony once each month, but these latter steamers do not call at Bathurst on the homeward passage, but proceed direct to Europe from Sierra Leone. There is a French line, the Messageries Maritime, that sails to Bordeaux from Dakar fortnightly, and passengers often join at Dakar, as these vessels are first-rate and get to Europe in eight days. The cost of the passage, though, is between £22 and £25, according to cabin, while that by the English line is £18 10s. only.

In addition to the above-mentioned vessels, ground-nut boats run frequently during the export season, and are prepared, as a rule, to take passengers at a lower figure than the usual mail boat charge; but the accommodation and service are, of course, not of the best.

The service up-river by the Government yacht, which leaves headquarters at Bathurst each Tuesday morning for McCarthy Island, returning on Friday, is 2d. per mile for first-class passengers and 1d. per mile for deckers. Freight and towage is afforded at a fixed rate.

Bathurst is in communication with Europe by telegraph cable, the African Direct Telegraph Company having a station on the island. The company receives a subsidy from the Government of £500 per annum, and charges the general public 3s. 6d. per word cabled.

The postage of letters to the United Kingdom, India and certain colonies is 1d. per ½ ounce, letters for interior costing 1d. per ounce. The return given below shows the average of postal matter dealt with during the past five years:—

LETTERS.

1900	1901	1902	1903	1904
66,612	77,937	77,918	94,365	94,358

PARCELS.

1900	1901	1902	1903	1904
782	1,151	1,340	1,532	1,677

MONEY ORDERS ISSUED.

1900	1901	1902	1903	1904
£9,653 2 6	£9,865 4 1	£3,254 0 9	£2,410	£1,490 4 2

MONEY ORDERS PAID.

1900	1901	1902	1903	1904
£175 19 5	£365 8 4	£815 19 9	£159	£292 14 2

POSTAL REVENUE RETURN.

Year.	Amount.	Year.	Amount.
	£		£
1895	686	1900	459
1896	1,506*	1901	769
1897	1,845*	1902	1,452*
1898	2,140*	1903	553
1899	589	1904	597

* Including extra issues due to the sales to stamp dealers and collectors.

As far as the postal revenue is concerned it will be observed that at the present time there is a considerable decrease as compared with previous years. The increase during 1902 was due to the purchase of stamp denominations, since obsolete, bearing the head of Her late Most Gracious Majesty Queen Victoria. The falling off in the money order system is accounted for by the establishment at Bathurst of a branch of the bank of British West Africa, Limited, which issues bills of exchange, for any amount from £1 upwards, at charges that compare more than favourably with those imposed by the Government, the consequence being the majority of traders and private persons prefer bills of exchange to money orders. Outside the money order system the postal revenue is decidedly on the increase. A postal order system between the United Kingdom and British colonies has been introduced, and is a decided boon to the community. In addition six new denominations of postage stamps have been brought into use, and the colony's issues are now—½d., 1d., 2½d., 3d., 4d., 5d., 6d., 7½d., 10d., 1s., 1s. 5d., 2s., 2s. 6d. and 3s.

EDUCATION.

There is no Government school in the colony, education being denominational, but the various governing bodies have the following six schools in Bathurst:—

ROMAN CATHOLIC.—St. Joseph's Convent and Hagan Street School.

WESLEYAN.—Dobson Street School and Stanley Street School.

ANGLICAN.—St. Mary's School.

MOHAMMEDAN.—Buckle Street School.

At McCarthy Island there is another school, under the management of the Wesleyan missions.

All the expenses of these schools are defrayed by the respective religious denominations, who have special grants-in-aid made to them by the Government in proportion to the educational results reported by the Government Inspector of Schools.

The total number of children on the registers at the present time is roughly 1,000, and the grants distributed by the Government have averaged during the past ten years £350 per annum. The Board of Education is responsible for the disbursement of the amount and for ensuring that the expenditure of the schools, and their general management, is satisfactory. To enable proper supervision to be given in the various schools the Government have generously provided another annual amount of £450 for division equally between the three European denominations, to enable inspectors to be appointed for each section. To further secure the effective administration of these schools special educational rules have just been passed and will come into operation at no distant date. These rules invest the Government inspector with considerable powers; and by this means it is hoped that, with constant and careful supervision, great progress generally will be the outcome.

Prior to the year 1901 the Gambia shared with Sierra Leone the services of a Government inspector of schools, but as the arrangement was not found to work satisfactorily the appointment of the inspector, as far as the Gambia was concerned, was terminated; and the examination of the various schools is now conducted by the attorney-general, who has been appointed the Government inspector.

The only secondary school in the colony is that established in Dobson Street by the Wesleyan Missionary Society. It has an average attendance of some twenty scholars.

In 1903 the Government provided another annual grant of £300 for the formation of a technical school, where lads may receive instruction in suitable trades. The number of students now in attendance is twenty, and it is satisfactory to record that good progress is being made in this establishment, which has a competent master-tradesman as an instructor. The technical school is under the immediate management of the Wesleyan body, but is strictly undenominational, and on this condition only is the Government grant made.

In addition to the above, the Mohammedan school was opened in 1903, and has an excellent attendance. The Government grant to this institution is £110 per annum. The pupils, with very few exceptions, are Bathurst children; but the Governor impressed on the protectorate chiefs the necessity of educating their children, has received promises from several influential head chiefs that they would send down one or two children, and to date six boys and girls have been sent. This school is conducted on sound lines, under a committee of management comprised of six leading Mohammedans of Bathurst.

HOSPITALS: NATIVE DISEASES AND TREATMENT.

Of recent years great improvement has been effected at the hospital, which has been enlarged and thoroughly repaired until to-day it is one of the best on the west coast of Africa. It contains three excellent wards—first, second and third class—and a new bungalow has been erected for the treatment of female patients. In 1903, as already mentioned, three sisters from the Convent of St. Cluny, in France, were engaged as European nurses, and they have done excellent work.

In a report of the senior medical officer he writes: "I cannot speak too highly of the present nursing arrangements at the hospital. The nurses are well trained and well up in their work; their devotion to it is unceasing, and all patients speak highly of the kindness of the nurses. I do not think that they, on their part, ever let religious bias enter into, or interfere with, their duties. Their establishment here in the Gambia has done much to increase the popularity of the hospital with the natives."

The nurses are always available for duty, living as they do in a special bungalow in the hospital compound. The medical staff of the colony comprises the senior medical officer and three assistant medical officers, two of whom are permanently resident at headquarters, and one detailed for duty in the protectorate, throughout which he travels, thereby coming in close touch with the people. To show at a glance the number of cases treated during the last ten years the following statement is given:—

PATIENTS TREATED AT THE COLONIAL HOSPITAL.

Period.	Patients admitted into Hospital.	Patients treated out and in Hospital.	Deaths in Hospital.
1895	258	—	19
1896	204	—	13
1897	224	—	21
1898	264	2,882	14
1899	220	2,462	27
1900	221	1,961	28
1901	598	4,608	26
1902	441	4,420	20
1903	591	9,068	37
1904	666	1,014	34

NOTE.—The figures as to out-patients prior to 1898 cannot be obtained.

In addition to the general hospital there is a contagious diseases hospital on an outlying portion of the island.

The expenditure on the hospital during the past ten years has been as follows :—

Years.	Amount.	Years.	Amount.
1895	1,504	1900	1,672
1896	1,519	1901	2,023
1897	1,574	1902	2,797
1898	1,601	1903	3,110
1899	1,525	1904	3,615

The work at the hospital is doing much to dispel the superstition which is most prevalent among the people of the country, that all their diseases are attributable to one of two causes—either they have been "witched" or some enemy has made "gree gree" against them. There are two forms of "gree gree," one that is administered internally and most usually consists of an infusion made from roots, leaves, and the bark of trees supposed to possess the desired properties; and the other that acts through external influences, which are brought to bear with considerable ceremony and to the accompaniment of incantations and dancing.

The treatment relied upon for cure in many cases, and much practised in the country, is to call in a "native doctor," who, after examining the patient, writes in Arabic characters on a wooden slate a long "prescription," generally extracts from the Koran. The slate is then washed and the dirty infusion drunk by the patient. But the people have many herbs that they boil for internal as well as external application. Shea butter is also used for rheumatism, sprains, bruises, and the like; but the increasing number of cases treated by the medical officers shows clearly that the old superstitions of the people are rapidly dying out. The diseases most commonly fatal among West Africans are pneumonia and phthisis. Intermittent fever among them is very common but seldom fatal. Many of the up-country people suffer from aggressive types of elephantiasis and small-pox, but vaccination, in preference to the country system of inoculation, is progressing apace, and will do much to abate the latter scourge.

There is no poor-house or reformatory in Bathurst, but destitute persons properly recommended and brought to the notice of the Government are maintained and cared for from public funds. Nor has the colony a lunatic asylum, all cases requiring detention being sent to the Kissy Asylum at Sierra Leone.

THE PRISON.

The prison of the colony is not as good a building as could be wished, but it answers the present requirements of the country. There are nineteen cells and four association wards for male prisoners, with one cell and two association wards for female prisoners. In 1903 the prison was repaired and the cells enlarged, but the "separate system" is not in force, owing to want of accommodation. The prisoners are employed by day in gangs and at night are located in separate cells as far as possible, but in some cases three or four have to be located in one ward. The labour in force, during the first three months, for prisoners pronounced medically fit, is shot-drill for three hours per diem, and subsequently stone-breaking, washing, carting stones, and such similar assistance on public works as may be necessary. There is no tread-wheel in use, although years ago this system of hard labour was in force. The diet of the prisoners is substantial, and sick prisoners receive such special diets as are prescribed by the medical officer. The average cost to the Government of this institution is about £700 per annum, or about £6 per head.

The following statement shows the comparative table of convictions for crime during the past decade :—

Years.	Male.	Female.	Juvenile.	Total.	Executions.
1895	58	5	—	63	1
1896	63	6	1	70	1
1897	34	3	—	37	—
1898	48	4	1	53	—
1899	38	6	—	44	—
1900	25	1	1	27	—
1901	56	1	—	57	3
1902	94	6	—	100	4
1903	86	1	—	87	1
1904	88	—	—	88	1

CLIMATE AND PUBLIC HEALTH.

The climate of the Gambia during the dry season is very pleasant and healthy, which is more than can be said for any other of our possessions on the West Coast of Africa. But during the wet season (July to October) the conditions are much the same as elsewhere, though the change from excessive dryness to the damp atmosphere of a miasmatical nature, so prevalent in the Gulf of Guinea, is probably more trying to the inhabitants.

The lowest reading of the thermometer during the last dry season was at Bathurst 56 degrees, the highest recorded temperature being 100; but up-country—at Boraba Kunda, on the south bank of the upper river district—the lowest temperature experienced by the Governor in a trip in February, 1904, was 40 degrees, the highest on the same day being 99 degrees. In the wet season of 1903 the lowest temperature recorded at headquarters was 67 degrees and the highest 91 degrees.

The harmattan wind, as previously mentioned, usually sets in early in December, and is welcomed after the oppressive weather of October and November. It is an exceedingly dry wind, and though cool and bracing in the morning becomes hot under the influence of the sun. The highest temperature of the day is usually between two and three o'clock. The harmattan is an intermittent wind, blowing for a few days and then being succeeded by a refreshing sea breeze, which in turn gives way again to the harmattan. This state of things continues well into April, the month of February being the time when the harmattan is most prevalent.

The months of July to October are considered the most unpleasant and unhealthy in Bathurst. In July the sea breeze has abated and the atmosphere becomes very hot and oppressive, the days previous to the rains being most stifling, and generally closing with tornadoes and heavy rain. The first rains generally appear about the middle of June, but the wet season does not finally establish itself until well into July, that month, August, and September, seeing the principal rainfall of the season. The following are the records of rain for the past decade:—

RECORD OF RAINFALL, 1895 TO 1904.

Years.	Highest occurring in one month.		Total for the year.	Years.	Highest occurring in one month.		Total for the year.
		in.	in.			in.	in.
1895	August	36·63	66·86	1900	July	20·53	43·38
1896	August	17·30	51·18	1901	August	19·90	45·31
1897	September	11·84	33·61	1902	August	14·36	29·42
1898	August	19·20	48·65	1903	August	35·87	57·87
1899	August	14·26	56·17	1904	August	17·27	38·2

As a rule a heavy rainy season is considered healthy, especially if tornadoes are frequent, as the air becomes unusually pure and clear. The population of the colony to-day is—if strange farmers and herdsmen, and the number of persons continually in transit, be taken into account—approximately 140,000, as will be seen from the following return taken at the last census in 1901.

CENSUS RETURN, 1901.

	Males.	Females.	Total.
THE COLONY.			
Bathurst	4,911	3,896	8,807
British Kommbo	823	818	1,648
The Ceded Mile	1,184	1,027	2,211
McCarthy (Island)	465	332	797
	7,383	6,073	13,456
THE PROTECTORATE.			
North Bank...	12,534	15,007	27,541
McCarthy (District)	5,390	5,810	11,200
Upper River	6,303	6,929	13,232
South Bank	5,556	6,191	11,747
Kommbo and Fogni ...	6,769	6,459	13,228
	36,552	40,396	76,948
Total	43,935	46,469	90,404

To this total must be added at least 40 per cent. for the Protectorate, as the people are very shy and object strongly to their numbers being taken; moreover, at best the return can only be approximate, owing to the movements of the inhabitants.

The public health of the colony has of recent years been good, and the cleanliness of the town exceptional, due in a measure to the energies of the Board of Health. There has of late been no epidemic in the Gambia. The sanitary conditions of Bathurst have been considerably improved generally; new latrines have been erected in several quarters of the town, and the drains are kept in good order. The streets, also, have received considerable attention, and are being levelled where necessary. A commodious new slaughter-house has been erected, conveniently situated near the market. The fees derived from it go to the Board of Health, and are devoted to the general upkeep of the town.

MILITARY FORCES.

The present defences of the colony are in the hands of a company of the West African Frontier Force, comprising one captain (commanding), two lieutenants, two European serjeants, and 120 rank and file, with an armed Police Force of eighty rank and file, commanded by a superintendent, with an assistant superintendent. The Police Force have an excellent brass band, under a European bandmaster, who has charge also of the band of the West African Frontier Force.

Both forces are armed with the Martini-Enfield carbine, have field guns, and are very efficient. It is needless again to record the various garrisons that have from time to time been provided in the colony, as they have been mentioned previously; but it may be mentioned that the old militia does not at present exist, and that the forces particularised are at this period considered all that are necessary for the due ensuring of law and order in the colony and protectorate. It has, however, been suggested that a Volunteer Artillery, as at the Gold Coast, should be raised, but nothing definite has as yet been decided upon.

In closing the foregoing particulars of the colony of the Gambia, the author takes pleasure in recording, by way of summary, that during the past few years a great deal of work has been accomplished and the protectorate is now in a most tranquil state, no doubt mainly due to the close touch that is kept with native affairs by means of the many tours made throughout its length and breadth by the Governor and the commissioners. The colony is united, prosperous, and free from endemic disease, and Bathurst, the seat of the Government, can now be compared favourably with any other town on the West Coast of Africa. Both colony and protectorate would seem to have emerged from the darkness of a troubled past into the dawn of a future which, it may reasonably be hoped, shall never be seriously overclouded.

PART IV.

RETURNS AS TO THE VARIOUS DISTRICTS IN THE GAMBIA PROTECTORATE.

CHAPTER VII

RETURNS SHOWING THE VARIOUS DISTRICTS IN THE GAMBIA PROTECTORATE, TOGETHER WITH THEIR BOUNDARIES, AND THE CHIEF TOWNS, APPROXIMATE POPULATIONS, HEAD CHIEFS AND NATIVE TRIBUNALS.

In this chapter is given a list of the various districts in the Protectorate, with the names of the head chiefs and other details.

NORTH BANK DISTRICT.

LOWER NIUMI.

Chief Town, Essau; population 320. Head Chief, Maranta Sonko.

Native Court: President, Maranta Sonko; Members, Siluman Sonko, Maling Kambai, Koli Mani, Sainya Ba.

Number of Towns in District: Twenty-six.

Boundaries of District: West, sea coast; East, all that country lying within a line drawn north from the river to the boundary line half-way between the towns of Aljamadu and Bakkendick.

UPPER NIUMI.

Chief Town, Sicca (Mandingo Town); population 12c. Head Chief, Ibraima Sonko.

Native Court: President, Ibraima Sonko; Members, Ihamia Job, Jonko Sonati, Ibraima Ba, Braima Manjang.

Number of Towns in District: Twenty-four.

Boundaries of District: West, all that country lying within a line drawn north from the river to the boundary line half-way between the towns of Aljamadu and Bakkendick; East, Memene Creek.

LOWER SALUM.

Chiet Town, Ka-uur; population 898. Head Chief, Arafang Jani.

Native Court: President, Arafang Jani; Members, Macumbo So, N'Juka Turay.

Number of Towns in District: Forty.

Boundaries of District: West, all that country lying within a line drawn north from the river to the boundary line half-way between the towns of N'Geyen and Ballanghar; East, Bantanto Creek.

Jokadu.

Chief Town, Dasallami; population 330. Head Chief, Bulli Forfana.

Native Court: President, Bulli Forfana; Members, Karramu Sila, Lamin Jagu, Munka Janmi.

Number of Towns in District: Twenty-four.

Boundaries of District: West, Mememe Creek; East, Suarra Kunda Creek.

Lower Baddibu.

Chief Town, Sallikenni; population 3,990. Head Chief, Arafang Buli Dabu.

Native Court: President, Arafang Buli Dabu; Members, Ansumana Singate, Ansumana Jaiti, Kouli Damfa.

Number of Towns in District: Sixty-six.

Boundaries of District: West, Suarra Kunda Creek; East, a line drawn due north from a point on the river half-way between the towns of Kunti Kunda and Illiassa to the boundary.

Upper Baddibu.

Chief Town, Illiassa; population 620. Head Chief, Jato Silang Jani.

Native Court: President, Jato Silang Jani; Members, Bomba Sansu, Sitafa Debachako, Maliffi Kamara, Modi Gay.

Number of Towns in District: Thirty-five.

Boundaries of District: West, a line drawn due north from a point on the river to the boundary half-way between the towns of Kunti Kunda and Illiassa; East, a line drawn due north from a point on the river to the boundary half-way between the towns of N'Geyen and Ballanghar.

Sub-District, Sabagh..

Number of Towns in District: Twenty-two.

Sub-District, Sanjal.

Number of Towns in District: Twenty-four.

McCARTHY ISLAND DISTRICT.

Lower Niani.

Chief Town, Nianibantang; population 174. Head Chief, N'Garry Sabali.

Native Court: President, N'Garry Sabali; Members, Fodi Suaneh, Tague N'Dau, Beram Joof.

Number of Towns in District: Thirty-four.

Boundaries of District: East, Paleng Creek; West, the town of N'Jai Kunda No. 2; North, the town of M'Baien; South, the River Gambia.

UPPER NIANI (PRINCIPAL DISTRICT).*

Chief Town, Manna No. 1; population 67. Head Chief, Sunta Koma.

Native Court: President, Sunta Koma; Members, Burrema Kassema, Arafa Madi Cisi, Saneh Jang, Bobodun, Saliman Jang, Lamin Touri, Samba N'Jie, Amadu Jano.

Number of Towns in District: Seventeen.

Boundaries of District: East, the town of Bani; West, Paleng Creek; North, the town of Kibiri; South, the River Gambia.

SUB-DISTRICT NO. 1 (UNDER PRINCIPAL DISTRICT).

Native Court: President, Ha Fodi Jowla (Sub-Chief); Members, Fodi Kamera, Kutubo Kanhi, Burrema Konti.

Number of Towns in District: Nine.

Boundaries of District: East, the town of Toniataba; West, the town of Kujow; North, the River Gambia; South, the River Gambia.

SUB-DISTRICT NO. 2 (UNDER PRINCIPAL DISTRICT).

Native Court: President, Omar Backi (Sub-Chief); Members, Madu Jara Cisi, Samba Jallow, Amadi Aruna.

Number of Towns in District: Eight.

Boundaries of District: East, Kunchow Creek; West, the town of Sinchi Baia; North, the boundary pillar quarter of a mile from Sami; South, the River Gambia.

EASTERN SALUM (N'JAU).

Chief Town, N'Jau; population 134. Head Chief, Sa Wallo Cisi.

Native Court: President, Sa Wallo Cisi; Members, Nauhauteh Seck, Sarochi Seck, Batchi Seck.

Number of Towns in District: Thirty-five.

Boundaries of District: East, the town of M'Baien; West, the town of Madina; North, boundary pillar half a mile from N'Jau; South, by Nianija Creek.

NIANIJA.

Chief Town, Nianija; population 190. Head Chief, Jero Cham.

Native Court: President, Jero Cham; Members, Marmadu Allieu, Sidi Cham, Dembo Cham.

Number of Towns in District: Twelve.

* Originally Upper Niani was divided into a principal district and four sub-districts. These have now been altered, the original sub-districts 2 and 4 being merged into the principal district, under the powerful chief Sunta Koma, with increased members to the native tribunal and to the governing council.

Boundaries of District: East, the town of Boodook; West, Nianija Creek; North, Nianija Creek; South, the River Gambia.

UPPER RIVER DISTRICT.

SANDU.

Chief Town, Misera; population 870. Head Chief, Jimbermang Jowla.

Native Court: President, Jimbermang Jowla; Members, Arafang Yarmadu, Bakary Kassima, Fodi Sambu, Kakora Silla.

Number of Towns in District: Forty-six.

Boundaries of District: West, the Kunchow Creek; North, the Anglo-French boundary; East, the Chamois Creek; South, the Gambia River.

WULI.

Chief Town, Bantonding; population 711. Head Chief, N'Yakadu Walli.

Native Court: President, N'Yakadu Walli; Members; Fodi Lamin, Maserang Kamati, Sekunda Baja, Kulum Bio.

Number of Towns of District: Forty-two.

Boundaries of District: West, Chamois Creek; North, Anglo-French boundary; East, Anglo-French boundary; South, River Gambia.

The following ten Foulah and Mandingo towns are situated west of Chamois Creek: Illo Kunda, Sambagubudayah, Yoromganyah, Farato Kunbali, Yorobywall Chamois, Kea Kunda, Kollingkhan, Harmadisereyah, Limbambulu, and Barro Kunda.

KANTORA.

Head Town, Sunkunda; population 417. Head Chief: Manjang Sanyan.

Native Court: President, Manjang Sanyan; Members, Ansumana Sanyan, Suliman Sani, Duadending Sesse, Sourahatta Goumani.

Number of Towns in District: Sixteen.

Boundaries of District: East, the Anglo-French boundary; West, the Simoto Creek; South, the Anglo-French boundary; North, the River Gambia.

EAST FULLADU.

Chief Town, Tambasansan; population 432. Head Chief, Farli Cora.

Native Court: President, Farli Cora; Members, Bundunkera Silla, Demba Numa, Mansa Jang, Fodi Bah.

Number of Towns in District: Fifty.

Boundaries of District: East, Simoto Creek; North, the Gambia River; West, Mansafa Creek; South, Anglo-French boundary.

Gambasara.

Chief Town, Gambasara; population 2,343. Head Chief, Bakandi Tunkura.

Native Court: President, Bakandi Tunkura; Members, Baba Asseh Kamara, Madi Wandeh Dukereh, Mahamadi Fesereh.

Number of Towns in District: Two.

Boundaries of District: The town of Gambasara and Numuyelle and adjacent farms.

Fulladu West.

Chief Town, Borroba; population 324. Head Chief, Dembo Danso.

Native Court: President, Dembo Danso. Members, Sanna Bio, Mousah Bojo, Wullum.

Number of Towns in District: Sixty-two.

Boundaries of District: East, Mansafa Creek; North, river Gambia; West, a small marsh about 7½ miles west of the village of Banding; South, Anglo-French boundary.

SOUTH BANK DISTRICT.

Eastern Niamina.

Chief Town, Kudang; population 1,000. Head Chief, Fodi Sani Ceesay.

Native Court: President, Fodi Sani Ceesay; Members, Fodi Alaji Kassama, Alakali N'Ding Fati, Ansumana Samara.

Number of Towns in District: Ten.

Boundaries of District: All that district lying within a line drawn from the river to the boundary line between the towns of Banding in Fulladu and Tenning Farra in Niamina on the east, and a line drawn from the river to the Sofyaniama Creek, passing half-way between the towns of Jarrang and Kumbani on the west.

Western Niamina.

Chief Town, Katamina; population 290. Head Chief, Tambaring Jadama.

Native Court: President, Tambaring Jadama; Members, N'Famara Damfa, Isiaka Samara, Jumbo Jada.

Number of Towns in District: Eleven.

Boundaries of District: All that district lying within a line drawn from the river to the Sofyaniama Creek, passing half-way between the towns of Kumbani and Jarrang on the east, and bounded south by the Sofyaniama Creek and on the west by the river.

Sub-Chief Town, Dunkunku; population 700. Sub-Chief, Fodi Ali M'Boge.

Towns in Sub-District: Sami, population 40; Barro Kunda, population 250; Jakoto, population 100.

Eastern Jarra.

Chief Town, Buraing; population 550. Head Chief, Afamara Dabu.

Native Court: President, Afamara Dabu; Members, Arafang Lang Sedi Sali, Madi Barro, Mousa Kani.

Number of Towns in District: Nine.

Boundaries of District: All that district lying between the Sofyaniama Creek on the east, and a line drawn south from the river to the boundary line, half-way between the towns of Jassong and Badumi, on the west.

Central Jarra.

Chief Town, Jappinni; population 310. Head Chief, Jalali Damfa.

Native Court: President, Jalali Damfa; Members, Buli Lyne, Mansa N'Ding Sunko, Lang Kode Damfa.

Number of Towns in District: Eight.

Boundaries of District: All that district lying within a line drawn due south from the river to the boundary line half-way between the towns of Badumi and Jassong on the east, and a line drawn south from the river to the boundary line, passing half-way between the towns of Buiba and Karantaba on the west.

Western Jarra.

Chief Town, Soma; population 430. Head Chief, Arafang Lang Jajusi.

Native Court: President, Arafang Lang Jajusi; Members, Seri Sidi Ba, Alkali Jobe, Lamin Jadama.

Number of Towns in District: Eleven.

Boundaries of District: All that district lying within a line drawn south from the river to the boundary line half-way between the town of Karantaba and Buiba on the east, and a line drawn south from the river to the boundary line half-way between the town of Giffin and Kaiaff on the west.

Eastern Kiang.

Chief Town, Kaiaff; population 820. Head Chief, Lamin Dabu Sani.

Native Court: President, Lamin Dabu Sani; Members, Alkali Jaja, Mansali Sani, Jumbo Sani.

Number of Towns in District: Seven.

Boundaries of District: All that district lying within a line drawn south from the river to the boundary line half-way between the town of Kaiaff and Giffin on the east, and a line drawn south from the river to the boundary line half-way between the towns of Kolior and Mandina on the west.

East Central Kiang.

Chief Town, Kwinella; population 810. Head Chief, Fodi Brima Saniang.

Native Court: President, Fodi Brima Saniang; Members, Dibong Sani, Suma Jambang, Imfali Kamara.

Number of Towns in District: Ten.

Boundaries of District: All that district lying within a line drawn south from the river to the boundary line half-way between the town of Mandina and Kolior on the East, and a line drawn from the west of Tendaba south to the boundary line half-way between the town of Saniang Kunda and Urokang on the west.

Western Kiang.

Chief Town, Janni Kunda; population 173. Head Chief, Fodi Karum Janni.

Native Court: President, Fodi Karum Janni; Members, Arrafang Soan, Lansonkor Jammeh, Dowda Kambi, Bakary Jadama.

Number of Towns in District: Fourteen.

West Central Kiang.

Chief Town, Battelling; population 476. Head Chief, Lansaniang.

Native Court: President, Lansaniang; Members, Tumani Sani, Fodi Kinti, Arrafang Ture.

Number of Towns in District: Nine.

Boundaries of District: North, Gambia River; South, Vintang Creek.

KOMMBO AND FOGNI DISTRICT.

Fogni West.

Whart Town, Vintang; population 298. Head Man, Masserai Sisi.

Chief Town, Mansa Kinda; population 47. Jolah Chief, Kekota Darrami.

Jolah Court: President, Kekota Daramai; Members, Araji

Jaju (Kussamai), Juria Baji (Kanuma), Aio Sannian (Kianga), Cajagor Sonkor (Upert).

Number of Towns in District: Forty.

Boundaries of District: From main river along Brefet Creek, thence along Baijana Creek, thence to French frontier, crossing Baijana Road at that point where Demba Creek crosses close to the town of Kangabina; in the north, the main river and Vintang Creek to Urambang Creek, thence along the latter creek and crossing the Anglo-French boundary, between the town of Luluchor and Anglabatta; South, Anglo-French frontier.

BREFET.*

Chief Town, Brefet; population 153. Head Chief, Lansaniang.

Native Court: Nil.

Number of Towns in District: Four.

KARRENAI.

Chief Town, Karrenai; population 139. Head Man, Malan Dabu.

Native Court: None, there being a Commissioner's Court only.

Number of Towns in District: Twenty.

FOGNI EAST.

Wharf Town, Kansalla; population 149. Head Man, Janko Dahaba.

Commissioner's Court.

Number of Towns in District: Twenty-eight.

Boundaries of District: North, Vintang Creek, from Urambang Creek to Anglo-French frontier on east; South, Anglo-French frontier; East, Anglo-French frontier; West, Urambang Creek to Anglo-French frontier between Anglabatta and Luluchor.

BONDALI.

Chief Town, Kangaramba; population 66. Chief, N'Yanki Baji.

Native Court: President, N'Yanki Baji; Members, Jaringo Baji, Sori Samba, Abino Baji, Blapp Kolli.

Number of Towns in District: Sixteen.

WESTERN KIANG.

Chief Town, Jali; population 323. Head Chief, Janko Sammati.

* There is no Jolah chief, the head man of Brefet (a Mandingo) acting in that capacity. The commissioner holds a court at Brefet when necessary.

Native Court: President, Janko Sammati; Members, Junkun Sannian, Mamudu N'Jie, Arafang Sisi.

Number of Towns in District: Eight.

Boundaries of District: North, Gambia River; South, Vintang Creek.

KOMMBO DISTRICT.

EAST KOMMBO.

Chief Town, Faraba Bunta; population 303. Head Chief, Mamady Sannian.

Native Court: President, Mamady Sannian; Members, Nali Bojan, Arafang Forfanna, Maserai Souho.

Number of Towns in District: Thirteen.

Boundaries of District: Commencing on south boundary of the protectorate on east boundary of Central Kommbo and following such boundary north to Kembugi Creek, thence by the left bank of that creek and Mandina Creek to the left bank of the Gambia River, thence upwards along the left bank to the mouth of Brefet Creek, thence by the left bank of that creek and the left bank of Baijana Creek upwards to a point on the south boundary of the protectorate between the towns of Baijana and Kangabina, thence west along such boundary to the point of commencement.

SOUTH KOMMBO.

Chief Town, Gunjour; population 1,117. Head Chief, Tumani Ture.

Native Court: President, Tumani Ture; Members, Brima Sannian, Lan Bojan.

Number of Towns in District: Five.

Boundaries of District: Commencing on the sea coast on the south boundary of Kommbo North, thence by such boundary east 4½ miles, thence south 2½ miles, thence east 4½ miles, thence south to the boundary post on the left bank of Allahai River the boundary of the protectorate, thence by the left bank of such river to its mouth, thence by sea coast northwards to the point of commencement.

CENTRAL KOMMBO.

Chief Town, Brikama; population 275. Head Chief, Fodi Musa Bojan.

Native Court: President, Fodi Musa Bojan; Members, Madi Bojan, Lan Bojan.

Number of Towns in District: Eight.

Boundaries of District: Commencing at boundary post on the left bank of Allahai River, thence along the boundary of South

Kommbo as follows—*viz.*, north 5½ miles, west 4½ miles, north 2¼ miles to south boundary of North Kommbo, thence along the said boundary east 5 miles, north 1¾ miles, east 4 miles, to left bank of Mandina Creek, thence by the creek and Kembugi Branch upwards till it cuts the meridian of 16° 35′ west longitude, then by said meridian of longitude south, to south boundary of the protectorate, and thence by said boundary west to the point of commencement.

North Kommbo.

Chief Town, Sukuta; population 703. Head Chief, Kabba Cham.

Native Court: President, Kabba Cham; Members, Karranta Cham, Karrafa Bojan, Seku Sisi, Bakary Bojan.

Number of Towns in District: Thirteen.

Boundaries of District: Commencing on the sea coast on the south-west boundary of British Kommbo, thence following said boundary south-east and north-east to Abuku branch of Lamin Creek, thence by the right bank of the creek to the mouth of the Gambia River, thence by left bank of the river, including all creeks, &c., to the mouth of the Mandina Creek, thence by left bank of the creek to a point half a mile north of Kubune, thence west 4½ miles, thence south 1¾ miles to a point 1 mile north of Brikama, thence west to the sea coast midway between Tujure and Sannian, and thence by the sea coast north and north-east to the point of commencement.

St. Mary.

Chief Town, Bakau; population 392. Head Chief, Bakary Jammeh.

Native Court: President, Bakari Jammeh; Members, Fodi Konti, Alasan Cham, Sanba Silibi, Ali Jobe.

Number of Towns in District: Nineteen.

Boundaries of District: East, Oyster Creek to main river from sea to opening of Lamin Creek; West, sea coast a point midway between Kotu and Bijilo; South, a point ¼ mile south-west of Bakote, on Sukuta Road; at the stream on the Sukuta and Sabijee Road, 1 mile south of Sabijee, on the Busumballa Road along the bank of the Abuku Creek to Lamin Creek, thence to the Gambia River.

PART V.

THE CHIEF ENACTMENTS IN FORCE FOR THE GOVERNMENT AND ADMINISTRATION OF THE COLONY AND PROTECTORATE.

CHAPTER VIII.

THE CHIEF GAMBIAN ENACTMENTS.

Text of the Letters Patent constituting the Office of Governor—Synopsis of Most Important Enactments in Force—Regulations as to writing Letters for Illiterate Persons—Text of the Gambia Protectorate Ordinance of 1902.

IN the following chapter the full text of both the Letters Patent constituting the office of Governor and Commander-in-Chief of the colony and of the Protectorate Ordinance of 1902 are given; and a synopsis of the most important enactments in force in the colony is added. In view of the fact that irregularities in connection with the writing of letters for illiterate persons are of such frequent occurrence as to become a growing nuisance in the colony, the author has also included here the main provisions of the Ordinance which regulates this practice.

The full text of the Letters Patent of 1888, passed under the Great Seal of the United Kingdom, constituting the office of Governor and Commander-in-Chief of the Colony of the Gambia, and providing for the Government thereof:—

Letters Patent dated 28th November, 1888.

Victoria by the Grace of God of the United Kingdom of Great Britain and Ireland Queen, Defender of the Faith, Empress of India: To all to whom these presents shall come, Greeting.

Preamble.

Whereas by Our Letters Patent under the Great Seal of Our United Kingdom of Great Britain and Ireland, bearing date at Westminster the Seventeenth day of June 1885, We did constitute the office of Governor and Commander-in-Chief of Our West Africa Settlements, then comprising Our Settlement of Sierra Leone and Our Settlement on the Gambia, as therein defined, and did provide for the Government of Our said West Africa Settlement:

Recites Letters Patent dated the 17th June, 1885.

And 11th October, 1887.

And whereas by certain other Letters Patent under Our said Great Seal, bearing date at Westminster the Eleventh day of October 1887, We did make provision for the appointment of a Deputy or Deputies to Our Governor and Commander-in-Chief of Our West Africa Settlements in Our Settlement on the Gambia:

And whereas We are minded to make separate provision for the Government of Our Settlement on the Gambia hitherto comprised within Our West Africa Settlements:

Recites Revocation of Letters Patent of 17th June, 1885, and 11th October, 1887.

Now know ye that We have, by Letters Patent of even date herewith, revoked and determined Our above-recited Letters Patent, but without prejudice to anything lawfully done thereunder:

Erection of separate Colony of the Gambia.

And further know ye that We do hereby erect Our said Settlement on the Gambia into a separate Colony, to be called the Colony of the Gambia, and We do by these presents order and declare that there shall be in and over Our said Colony of the Gambia and charged with the Government thereof, a Governor and Commander-in-Chief, or a Lieutenant-Governor or an Administrator as We shall from time to time direct, and that appointments to such offices shall be made by Commission under Our Sign Manual and Signet.

Boundaries.

2. Our Colony of the Gambia (hereinafter called the Colony) shall, until We shall otherwise provide, comprise all places, Settlements, and territories which may at any time belong to us in Western Africa, between the twelfth and fifteenth degrees of north latitude, and lying to the westward of the tenth degree of west longitude.

Governor's powers and authorities.

3. We do hereby authorize, empower and command Our said Governor and Commander-in-Chief or Lieutenant-Governor or Administrator (each of whom is hereinafter called the Governor), to do and execute all things that belong to his said office, according to the tenor of these Our Letters Patent and to such Commission as may be issued to him under Our Sign Manual and Signet, and according to such instructions as may from time to time be given to him under Our Sign Manual and Signet, or by Our Order in Our Privy Council, or by Us through one of Our Principal Secretaries of State, and to such laws as are now or shall hereafter be in force in the Colony.

4. And we do by these Our Letters Patent declare Our will and pleasure as follows:

Publication of Governor's Commission.

5. In the first instance the Government of the Colony shall be vested in an Administrator, and every such Administrator, and every Lieutenant-Governor, if We shall think fit to vest the Government in such an Officer, and every person appointed to fill the office of Governor, shall with all due solemnity, before entering on any of the duties of his office, cause the Commission appointing him to be read and published, at the seat of Government, in the presence of the Chief Magistrate, and of such members of the Executive Council, of the Colony as can conveniently attend, which being done he shall then and there take before them the Oath of Allegiance, in the form provided by an Act passed in the Session holden in the Thirty-first and Thirty-second years of Our reign, intituled, "An Act to amend the Law relating to Promissory Oaths"; and likewise the usual Oath for the due execution of the office of Governor, and for the due and impartial administration of justice, which Oath the said Chief Magistrate, or, if he be unavoidably absent, the Senior Member of the Executive Council then present, is hereby required to administer.

Oaths to be taken by Governor.

Imperial Act, 31 and 32 Vict., c. 72.

Public Seal.

6. The Governor shall keep and use the Public Seal of the

Colony, for sealing all things whatsoever that shall pass the said Seal; and until We shall otherwise direct the Public Seal hitherto used for Our Settlement on the Gambia shall be used as the Public Seal of the Colony.

Executive Council.

7. There shall be an Executive Council in and for the Colony, and the said Council shall consist of such persons as We shall direct by Instructions under Our Sign Manual and Signet, and all such persons shall hold their places in the said Council during Our pleasure.

Legislative Council.

8. There shall be a Legislative Council in and for the Colony, and the said Council shall consist of the Governor and such persons, not being less than two at any time, as We shall direct by any instructions under Our Sign Manual and Signet, and all such persons shall hold their places in the said Council during Our pleasure.

Powers of Legislative Council.

Recites Imperial Act, 50 and 51 Vict., c. 54.

9. In pursuance of the powers vested in Us by an Act of the Imperial Parliament, passed in the Session holden in the Fiftieth and Fifty-first years of Our reign, intituled "An Act to enable Her Majesty to provide for the Government of Her Possessions acquired by settlement," We do hereby delegate to the persons who shall from time to time compose the said Legislative Council full power and authority, subject always to any conditions, provisoes, and limitations prescribed by any instructions under Our Sign Manual and Signet, to establish such Ordinances, not being repugnant to the Law of England, and to constitute such Courts and Officers, and to make such provisions and regulations for the proceedings in such courts and for the administration of justice as may be necessary for the peace, order, and good government of the Colony.

Governor's Veto.

The Governor shall have a negative voice in the making and passing of all such ordinances.

Disallowance of Ordinances.

10. We do hereby reserve to Ourselves, Our heirs and successors, full power and authority, and Our and their undoubted right, to disallow any such Ordinances and to signify such disallowance through one of Our Principal Secretaries of State. Every such disallowance shall take effect from the time when the same shall be promulgated by the Governor in the Colony.

Powers of Legislations, &c., reserved to the Crown.

We do also reserve to Ourselves, Our heirs and successors, Our and their undoubted right, with the advice of Our or their Privy Council, from time to time to make all such Laws or Ordinances as may appear to Us or them necessary for the peace, order and good government of the Colony.

Governor and Legislative Council to observe Instructions.

11. In the making of any Ordinances the Governor and the Legislative Council shall conform to and observe all rules, regulations and directions in that behalf contained in any Instructions under Our Sign Manual and Signet.

Governor empowered to make grants of lands;

12. The Governor, in Our name and on Our behalf, may make and execute, under the Public Seal, grants and dispositions of any lands within the Colony which may be lawfully granted or disposed of by Us; Provided that every such grant or disposition be made in conformity, either with some Law in

force in the Colony, or with some Instructions addressed to the Governor under Our Sign Manual and Signet, or through one of Our Principal Secretaries of State, or with some regulation in force in the Colony.

And to appoint Judges and other officers.

13. The Governor may constitute and appoint all such Judges, Commissioners, Justices of the Peace, and other necessary Officers and Ministers, as may be lawfully constituted or appointed by Us, all of whom, unless otherwise provided by law, shall hold their offices during Our pleasure.

Suspension of Officers.

14. The Governor may, upon sufficient cause to him appearing, suspend from the exercise of his office any person holding any office within the Colony, whether appointed by virtue of any Commission or Warrant from Us or in Our name, or by any other mode of appointment. Every such suspension shall continue and have effect only until Our pleasure therein shall be signified to the Governor. In proceeding to any such suspension, the Governor is strictly to observe the directions in that behalf given to him by any Instruction as aforesaid.

Grant of Pardon.

Remission of fines.

Proviso. Banishment prohibited.

Exception. Political offences.

15. When any crime has been committed within the Colony, or for which the offender may be tried therein the Governor may, as he shall see occasion, in Our name and on Our behalf, grant a pardon to any accomplice in such crime who shall give such information as shall lead to the conviction of the principal offender, or of any one of such offenders, if more than one; and further, may grant to any offender convicted in any Court, or before any Judge or other Magistrate within the Colony, a pardon either free or subject to lawful conditions, or any remission of the sentence passed on such offender, or any respite of the execution of such sentence, for such period as the Governor thinks fit, and may remit any fines, penalties or forfeitures due or accrued to Us. Provided always, that the Governor shall in no case, except where the offence has been of a political nature unaccompanied by any other grave crime, make it a condition of any pardon or remission of sentence that the offender shall be banished from or shall absent himself or be removed from the Colony.

Succession to Government.

Administration.

Senior Member of Executive Council.

Proviso. Lieutenant Governor, &c., to take Oaths of Office before administering Government.

Powers and authorities of Administrator.

16. Whenever the office of the Governor is vacant, or if the Governor become incapable or be absent from the Colony, then such person or persons as We may appoint under Our Sign Manual and Signet, and in default of any such appointment the Senior Member of the Executive Council, shall, during Our pleasure, administer the Government of the Colony, first taking the Oaths hereinbefore directed to be taken by the Governor and in the manner herein prescribed, which being done, We do hereby authorise, empower and command any such Administrator as aforesaid to do and execute, during Our pleasure, all things that belong to the office of Governor and Commander-in-Chief, according to the tenor of these Our Letters Patent, and according to Our Instructions as aforesaid, and the Laws of the Colony.

Appointment of Deputy to Governor.

17. In the event of the Governor having occasion at any time to visit any territories adjacent to the Colony, in pursuance

of any Instructions from Us, or through one of our Principal Secretaries of State, he may by an Instrument under the Public Seal of the Colony appoint any person or persons to be his Deputy or Deputies within the Colony, and in that capacity to exercise, during his pleasure, such of the powers hereby vested in the Governor, except the powers of suspension and pardon, as the Governor shall think fit to assign to him or them. The appointment of such Deputy or Deputies shall not affect the exercise by the Governor himself of any of his powers or authorities. Every such Deputy shall, in the discharge of his office, conform to and observe all such Instructions as the Governor shall address to him for his guidance.

18. And we do hereby require and command all Our Officers and Ministers, Civil and Military, and all other the inhabitants of the Colony, to be obedient, aiding and assisting unto the Governor and to such person or persons as may from time to time, under the provisions of these Our Letters Patent, administer the Government of the Colony.

Officers and others to obey Governor.

19. In the construction of these Our Letters Patent the term "the Governor," unless inconsistent with the context, shall include every person for the time being administering the Government of the Colony.

Term "the Governor" explained.

20. And We do hereby reserve to Ourselves, Our heirs and successors, full power and authority from time to time to revoke, alter, or amend these Our Letters Patent as to Us or them shall seem fit.

Power reserved to Her Majesty to revoke, alter, or amend present Letters Patent.

21. And We do direct and enjoin that these Our Letters Patent shall be read and proclaimed at such place or places within the Colony as the Governor shall think fit.

Proclamation of Letters Patent.

In witness whereof We have caused these Our Letters to be made Patent. Witness Ourself at Westminster, the Twenty-eighth day of November, in the Fifty-second year of Our Reign.

By Warrant under the Queen's Sign Manual,

MUIR MAKENZIE.

The most important enactments in force in the Colony, with a *précis* of the main provisions.

No. 1 of 1859. *Artisans, Labourers, Servants.*—Artisans, labourers, servants may be punished for neglect of work, insolence, or engaging with more than one employer. Persons enticing them may be fined.

No. 9 of 1862. *Marriage.*—By publication of banns or license of Governor. Void unless solemnized by person in holy orders or minister of Christian religion.

No. 3 of 1865. *Friendly Societies.*—Must submit Rules to Legislative Council. Must be registered and supply annual statement of funds.

No. 8 of 1873. *Fraudulent Debtors.*—Abolishes imprisonment for debt and the punishment of fraudulent debtors.

No. 10 of 1873. *Cruelty to Animals.*—Persons ill-treating may be fined. Maintenance of animals impounded.

No. 2 of 1880. *Currency.*—Spanish Mexican and South American silver dollars not legal tender (see Orders of Queen in Council of 10th June, 1843, 30th June, 1852, 14th January, 1871, 28th November, 1874, on pp. 106–

108, Vol. II. of Ordinances Revised Edition, 1900, fixing rates at which certain foreign and colonial coins shall be received in payment, also Ordinance No. 12 of 1903).

No. 5 of 1880. *Registration of Deeds.*—All instruments, wills, powers of attorney, contracts affecting land may be registered. Gives priority according to date of registration (see Ord. No. 4 of 1904).

No. 8 of 1882. *Customs.* Amended No. 17 of 1901, No. 6 of 1902, No. 2 of 1903.—Importation, Exportation, Warehousing of goods. Smuggling Regulations, 25th March, 1902 (see Ord. of 1904 as to Tariffs, also Ord. No. 10 of 1887, and Rules thereunder 14th July, 1903).

No. 11 of 1884. *Savings Bank.*—Interest at the rate of 2½ per cent. per annum paid on deposits over £1.

No. 9 of 1885. *Married Woman's Property.*—Married woman may hold property acquired after date of Ordinance and contract and dispose of same by will as if *femme sole.*

No. 11 of 1886. *Births, Deaths, Marriages.* — Makes provision for registration of.

No. 4 of 1887. *Public Health.*—Local rates at disposal of Board (see Ordinance No. 11 of 1891). Board exercises powers in Island of St. Mary generally over sanitation, also slaughter-house, market, nuisances, burial-ground. Regulation of streets, buildings and open spaces. Regulations 7th July, 1902, and 20th February, 1903.

No. 4 of 1889. *Supreme Court.* Amended by Ordinances Nos. 9 of 1901 and 11 of 1903.—Court exercises powers of Chancellor over infants and persons of unsound mind, powers of High Court of Justice in England (except Admiralty not conferred by Act of Parliament). Statutes of general application in England on 1st November, 1888, in force in the Colony.

No. 11 of 1891. *Rates.* Amended No. 8 of 1903.—Local Rate of 3 per cent. of annual value on lots exceeding £5 in annual value.

No. 4 of 1892. *Firearms and Ammunition.* Amended by No. 5 of 1903 and No. 7 of 1892.—Regulates the importation and carrying of Firearms and Ammunition.

No. 4 of 1893. *Alien African Children.*—Alien African Children coming into the Colony must be registered. They are allotted to guardians and educated.

No. 7 of 1894. *Naturalisation.* — Aliens residing for one year may obtain certificate of naturalisation on taking the oath of allegiance.

No. 12 of 1894. *Slave Trade Abolition.* — Persons unlawfully compelling or attempting to compel by any coercion or restraint the service of any person, or slave dealing, liable to imprisonment for seven years with hard labour.

No. 8 of 1899. *Shipping Casualties.*—Makes provision for due inquiry into the causes of wreck and other casualties to shipping occurring on the coasts of the colony. Appointment of receiver of wrecks. Appointment of salvage. Conveyance of shipwrecked passengers to their destination.

No. 9 of 1899. *Police.* Amended Ordinance 16 of 1901.—Consolidates Law relating to Gambia Police.

No. 15 of 1899. *Court of Requests.* Amended No. 12 of 1902.—Civil Jurisdiction up to £50. Rules 29th January, 1891.

No. 9 of 1901. *Acquisition of Lands for the Public Service.* — Lands required for the Public Service may be bought or taken and compensation given.

No. 11 of 1901. *Auctions.*—Regulates sale by auction. Auctioneers must be licensed.

No. 13 of 1901. *Hospital and Dispensary.* Amended No. 15 of 1901.—Regulates management. Rules passed 2nd July, 1902.

No. 14 of 1901. *Contagious Diseases.* Amended No. 4 of 1902.—Rules passed regulating quarantine of ships.

No. 3 of 1902. *West African Frontier Force.* Amended No. 9 of 1902, No. 20 of 1902 and No. 2 of 1905.—Establishes Gambia Company.

No. 5 of 1902. *Grants of Public Lands* —May be granted by the Crown Regulations passed 5th July, 1902.

No. 7 of 1902. *Protectorate.* Incorporates as "Protectorate System," Nos. 7 of 1895, 13 of 1895, 6 of 1896. Amended No. 3 of 1903.—Makes provision for management of Protectorate. Regulations 19th June, 1902 (Native tribunals under Headmen). Regulations 28th April, 1905 (roads, bridges, &c., and the procedure to be followed by Native Tribunals).

No. 10 of 1902. *Weights, Weighing Machines and Measures.* Amended No. 19 of 1902.—Regulates use of. Regulations 20th February, 1903.

No. 9 of 1903. *Vacant Lands.*—Provides for disposal of.

No. 13 of 1903. *Sale of Liquor.*—Specifies conditions.

No. 14 of 1903. *Education.*—Board may make grants to primary and secondary schools for attendances and proficiency of pupils, also to an industrial school. Rules passed 18th July, 1904.

No. 1 of 1904. *Navigation.*—Regulates navigation of River. Hiring and right of sailors.

No. 3 of 1904. *Market.*—Meat and Fish not to be sold outside Market.

No. 4 of 1904. *Land Transfer.*—Titles to land may be registered.

No. 9 of 1904. *Public Holidays.*—Specifies days.

Particulars from Ordinance No. 17 of 1902 of Regulations as to the Writing of Letters for Illiterate Persons.

Any person who shall write any letter or other document for, on behalf, or in the name, of any illiterate person, or shall write or set the name or mark of such illiterate person thereto, shall also write on such letter or other document his own name as the writer thereof or has having written or set the name or mark of such illiterate person thereto, and his full and true address; and his so doing shall be taken to be equivalent to a statement—

(*a*) That he was instructed to write such letter or document by the person for whom it purports to have been written, and that the same fully and correctly represents his instruction; and

(*b*) That prior to execution it was read over and explained to such illiterate person, and that he understood and desired to execute the same:

Or in the case of a person merely writing or setting the name or mark of such illiterate person thereto, then the latter part (*b*) of such statement shall be implied.

If the writer of any such letter or document, or person writing or setting the name or mark of the illiterate person thereto, shall fail to write thereon his full and true address, or if having done so any statement which under the Ordinance is in consequence implied shall be found to be untrue, then and in every such case the writer or such other person as aforesaid shall be guilty of a misdemeanour, and shall be liable on summary conviction before the Chief Magistrate, a Travelling Commissioner, or any two

Justices of the Peace, to a penalty not exceeding twenty pounds or in default of payment to imprisonment with or without hard labour for a term not exceeding six months.

The above conditions do not apply to any officer in the public service of the Colony properly acting in the discharge of his duty, and must be observed in the Protectorate as well as in the Colony of the Gambia.

In the preceding chapter particulars were given of the various districts in the Gambia protectorate, with details of the native tribunals and other matters. In amplification of this information the Ordinance No. 7 of 1902 is introduced here, as, *inter alia*, it explains the general scheme of executive government of the protectorate and the constitution and powers of the native tribunals, and sets forth the offences that can be dealt with summarily by these courts. In view of the importance of the Ordinance the author has thought it desirable to give, as follows, its full text—

THE GAMBIA PROTECTORATE ORDINANCE.

No. 7, 1902.

Title. An ORDINANCE passed to make better provision for the management of the Protectorate, and for the administration of justice therein.

Preamble. WHEREAS by an Order of Her Late Majesty in Council made at the Court at Windsor the Twenty-third day of November One thousand eight hundred and ninety-three it was ordered that it should be lawful for the Legislative Council for the time being of the Colony of the Gambia, by Ordinance or Ordinances, to exercise and provide for giving effect to all such jurisdiction as Her Majesty might at any time before or after the passing of the said Order-in-Council have acquired within divers territories on the West Coast of Africa, near or adjacent to the Colony of the Gambia: AND WHEREAS in pursuance of the said Order-in-Council and to give effect to such jurisdiction as aforesaid to Her Majesty belonging sundry Ordinances have from time to time been made and passed by the Legislative Council of this Colony, and among others (1) the Protectorate Ordinance, 1894; (2) the Protectorate (Yard Tax) Ordinance, 1895; (3) the Protectorate (Trade Licence) Ordinance 1895; and (4) the Protectorate (Public Lands) Ordinance 1896; which Ordinances are in general made applicable to those portions of such territories as aforesaid, and those portions only, to which the same might from time to time be notified by Proclamation to be specially applied: AND WHEREAS FURTHER by certain other Ordinances, to wit, (5) the Brefet and Bajana (Administration) Ordinance 1895; (6) the M'Carthy's Island (Administration) Ordinance 1896; and (7) the Ceded Mile (Administration) Ordinance 1897, certain portions of the Colony have now been brought and are under the system of laws and administration by the Protectorate Ordinance 1894 and other above-mentioned Ordinances established, but without prejudice always to His Majesty's rights of sovereignty and other the like rights, powers, jurisdiction and privileges in such portions possessed, held, exercised and enjoyed: AND WHEREAS all and every part of that whole extent of territory near or adjacent to the Colony of the Gambia recognised and defined as British territory by the terms of an arrangement entered into by Her Late Majesty and the President of the French Republic dated the tenth day of August 1889, has now been formally, fully and effectively brought under His Majesty's protection, and all or most of the Ordinances above particularly mentioned, and certain other Ordinances and laws thereto made applicable, whether by Proclamation or otherwise: And Whereas in particular by an agreement recently made and entered into between His Excellency SIR GEORGE CHARDIN DENTON, Knight Commander of the most Distinguished Order of St. Michael and St. George, Governor and Commander-in-Chief of this Colony, on the one part, and MOOSAH MOLLAH, paramount Chief of the territory commonly known as Fulladugu, on the other part, upon the 7th day of June 1901, and since by the consent of both parties revised and modified in various particulars, that portion of Fulladugu which lies within British territory as recognised and defined by the arrangement aforesaid has been brought and is now under His Majesty's protection, and the Protectorate system of laws and administration made applicable thereto; And Whereas experience of the working of the said system as applied to Brefet and Bajana and other portions of the Colony above referred to, as shown the same to be well suited to the habits and usages of the people, and it is deemed expedient that it should be further extended to that portion of the Colony commonly known as British Kommbo: And Whereas Finally it is desirable to amend the said Protectorate system in certain particulars, and to make clear the application thereof in and to the whole territories above mentioned;

Be it, therefore, enacted by the Governor of the Colony of the Gambia with the advice and consent of the Legislative Council thereof, as follows viz.:— Enacting Clause.

PART I.—PRELIMINARY.

I. This Ordinance may be cited as "The Protectorate Ordinance, 1902," and shall be read and construed along with the Protectorate (Yard Tax) Ordinance, 1895, the Protectorate (Trade Licence) Ordinance, 1895, and the Protectorate (Public Lands) Ordinance, 1896; and the three last-mentioned Ordinances together with the present Ordinance may be cited collectively as "The Protectorate Ordinances, 1895 to 1902." Short Title and construction, etc.

II. The Protectorate Ordinance 1894, the Brefet and Bajana (Administration) Ordinance 1895, the M'Carthy's Island (Administration) Ordinance 1896, and the Ceded Mile (Administration) Ordinance 1897, are hereby repealed: provided that this repeal shall not affect— Repeals.

(1) Anything duly done or suffered before the commencement of this Ordinance under any Ordinance hereby repealed;

(2) Any writ, warrant or instrument made or issued before the commencement of this act;

(3) Any imprisonment, fine, forfeiture or other punishment incurred or to be incurred in respect of any offence committed before the commencement of this Ordinance under any Ordinance hereby repealed;

(4) The institution or prosecution to its termination of any investigation or legal proceeding, or any other remedy for prosecuting any such offence, or enforcing or recovering any such imprisonment, fine, forfeiture or punishment as aforesaid:

And any such investigation, legal proceeding, remedy, writ, warrant and instrument, may be carried on and executed as if this repeal had not been enacted.

Interpretation of terms.

III. In this Ordinance, unless the context otherwise require—

"Protectorate" means all territories whatsoever (whether lying beyond or forming part of the Colony) made subject to the Protectorate system;

"Protectorate System" means the Protectorate Ordinances 1895 to 1902, together with any Ordinances for the time being in force amending the same, and any Rules made thereunder, being read and construed together as one system; and shall be taken as applying to all British territories on the River Gambia lying beyond the Colony and such portions of the Colony as are hereinafter in section four made subject to the said system;

"Head Chief" means a Head Chief duly appointed under the provisions of this Ordinance to exercise authority over a District;

"Headman" means a Headman duly appointed under the provisions of this Ordinance to exercise authority over a Sub-District.

"District" means a District duly appointed by the Governor under section seven, or any existing district continued under section eight hereof;

"Sub-District" means any Sub-District duly appointed by the Governor under section seven or any existing sub-division of any district continued under section eight hereof;

"Territory of a Commissioner" means any District or Districts placed under the charge or supervision of such Commissioner;

"Commissioner" means a Travelling Commissioner or any Officer appointed by the Governor to exercise jurisdiction under this Ordinance, whether permanently or temporarily, or in certain cases, as the Governor may direct;

"Supreme Court" means the Supreme Court of the Colony of the Gambia;

"Prescribed" means prescribed by any regulations to be made under section forty-four hereof.

IV. The following portions of the Colony are hereby made and declared to be subject to the Protectorate System, that is to say, the territories commonly known as Brefet, Bajana, M'Carthy's Island, the Ceded Mile and British Kommbo: but without derogation always to all rights, privileges, powers, jurisdiction or sovereignty which His Majesty now possesses, holds, exercises or enjoys therein; and without prejudice to any enactment or law of the Colony at present in force in such territories, unless such enactment or law be inconsistent with the Protectorate System.

Portions of the Colony subject to Protectorate system.

PART II.—GENERAL SCHEME OF EXECUTIVE GOVERNMENT IN THE PROTECTORATE.

V. The Governor may do and execute within the Protectorate all things that belong to his Office, and shall have full power and authority for the maintenance of law and order, the suppression of disorders, riots or insurrections, and all other the like purposes.

Governor to have authority over Protectorate.

VI. (1) The Governor may banish any person from the Protectorate, or from any part thereof; and may also order him to reside within any limits in the Colony or Protectorate when he shall deem it expedient to do so for the promotion of security, peace or order.

Governor may banish troublesome persons.

(2) If any person so banished returns within the limits from which he has been so banished, or departs from the limits within which he has been ordered to reside, he shall be guilty of a felony, and on conviction thereof shall be liable to imprisonment with or without hard labour for a period not exceeding two years.

VII. The Governor may from time to time by proclamation—

Divisions of Protectorate.

(*a*) (*i.*) divide the Protectorate into Districts as he may deem most convenient for judicial and executive purposes;

(*a*) Districts to be under Head Chiefs.

(*ii.*) may alter or vary the boundaries of any District, merge two or more Districts into one, redivide the whole Protectorate, or re-arrange the Districts in any portion thereof in such manner as he may deem most expedient;

(*iii.*) appoint Head Chiefs to exercise authority over Districts;

(*iv.*) dismiss any Head Chief and appoint a successor;

(*b*) (*i.*) Sub-divide any District into Sub-Districts;

(*b*) Sub-Districts to be under Headmen.

(*ii.*) alter or vary such sub-division;

(*iii.*) appoint a Headman subordinate to the Head Chief of the District to have supervision of any sub-district;

(*iv.*) dismiss any Headman and appoint a successor;

VIII. Except in so far as they may hereafter be expressly altered by proclamation as above provided, all Districts and sub-divisions of Districts presently existing and approved by the Governor shall continue.

Existing Districts, etc., to continue.

Responsibility of Head Chiefs.

IX. A Head Chief is responsible to the Governor for the good order of his District, and may in case of misconduct be punished by fine, suspension or removal as the Governor shall deem fit; but without prejudice always in case such misconduct shall include any offence punishable by law, to the institution of criminal proceedings against him, if the Governor shall so direct.

Responsibility of Headmen.

X. The Headman of any Sub-district shall be responsible to the Head Chief of the District for the good order of such Sub-district; and may on the report of the Head Chief or Commissioner be punished by fine, suspension or removal as the Governor may direct, but without prejudice always to the institution of criminal proceedings as in the immediately preceding section provided.

Powers of Head Chiefs and Headmen—

XI. Every Head Chief and Headman shall possess and exercise all powers requisite—

(*a*) For maintenance of the peace;

(*a*) for preventing or suppressing riots and affrays, and for the maintenance of the peace, whether by the employment of necessary force, binding over unruly persons to be of good behaviour, or any other means reasonable and fitting under such circumstances as may arise;

(*b*) The prevention of crime;

(*b*) for the prevention and detection of crime, the arrest and detection of offenders, and all other such duties as are usually performed by a civil police force; and

(*c*) Carrying out Sentences, etc.

(*c*) for carrying into execution and enforcing, or assisting in the carrying into execution and enforcing within their Districts and Sub-districts of all sentences, judgments and orders of any native tribunal, or of any court of law in the Colony, in such manner and subject to such provisions as may be contained in any regulations to be made under Section forty-four hereof.

Protection of Head Chiefs and those employed by them.

XII. In the exercise of the powers in the last preceding section contained, and for the performance of any duty assigned to them by law, every Head Chief and Headman, and all messengers, servants and other persons duly authorised and employed by them, shall have and enjoy all such authorities, rights, privileges, immunities and protection as are by the law of England, or any law or Ordinance of the Colony enjoyed by any justices, sheriffs, bailiffs, constables or other officers or public servants, or the like persons whatsoever, in the like cases.

Commissioner's powers, general nature of.

XIII. (1) The commissioner shall have the superintendence of all Districts within his territory; and it shall be the duty of the Head Chief and Headman to be guided by any advice, and to obey all orders given by the Commissioner for the order and general management of the District, or for carrying into effect any law or Ordinance made applicable to the Protectorate.

(2) A Commissioner may at any time at his discretion exercise all or any of the powers belonging to his office within or in respect of the territory of any other Commissioner, or any portion of the Protectorate whatsoever, subject to any regulations to be made as hereinafter provided in Section forty-four.

Commissioner's powers exercisable outside the territory.

XIV. Where in any district, sub-district or locality no Head Chief or Headman shall have been appointed, or where the Head Chief or Headman shall have died, or shall be absent from the district, or under suspension or in any way incapacitated from the discharge of his duties, it shall be lawful for the Commissioner to exercise all and sundry the powers and authorities hereinabove conferred on Head Chiefs and Headmen; and in the exercise of such powers and authorities the Commissioner, and all constables, interpreters, messengers and persons whatsoever authorised and employed by him, shall have the like protection as is above conferred on Head Chiefs and Headmen and those employed by them.

Powers of Commissioner in districts where no Head Chief or Headman appointed.

PART III.—COURTS AND TRIBUNALS IN AND FOR THE PROTECTORATE.

A.—Jurisdiction of Colonial Courts in respect of matters occurring in the Protectorate.

XV. The Supreme Court, the Police Court and the Court of Requests at Bathurst, and any other Courts of law of the Colony, are hereby declared to have in respect of matters occurring within the Protectorate the same jurisdiction, civil and criminal, original and appellate, as they may respectively possess from time to time in respect of matters occurring within the Colony.

Colonial Courts declared to have jurisdictions.

XVI. (1) Judgments, decrees, orders and sentences of any Court of law of the Colony made or given in the exercise of the jurisdiction in the immediately preceding section hereof declared may be enforced and executed, both within the Colony and the Protectorate, as follows:

Execution of judgments, etc., in Protectorate.

> in the case of process of the Supreme Court, by the Sheriff or his bailiff;
>
> in the case of process of the Court of Requests, by the Beadle thereof;
>
> in the case of process of the Police Court, by members of the Gambia Police Force and any other peace-officers of the Colony;
>
> and generally by the like officers and persons, and in like manner in all respects, whether as to the form of writs or warrants used or any other matter, as if such judgment, decree, order or sentence had been made or given under the ordinary jurisdiction of the Court;

but without prejudice always to the enforcement and execution thereof in any other manner, or by any other officer or person, duly authorised by any court or tribunal having competent jurisdiction for such purpose.

Head Chief, etc. to assist, Sheriff, etc.

(2) In the case of the enforcement or execution of any such judgment, decree, order or sentence within the Protectorate, the Head Chief of the District, and the Headman of the Sub-District where such enforcement or execution may be intended, and the Commissioner, shall render all necessary assistance to the Sheriff, bailiff, beadle, constables, peace-officers or persons aforesaid in the performance of their duty.

Appeals in Protectorate cases.

XVII. Appeals may be had and prosecuted from the Court of Requests and the Police Court at Bathurst to the Supreme Court of this Colony, and from the Supreme Court of this Colony to the Supreme Court of the Colony of Sierra Leone, in respect of all judgments, decrees, orders and sentences made and given in the exercise of the jurisdiction above declared in section fifteen hereof, in the same way as if such judgment, decree, order or sentence had been made or given under the ordinary jurisdiction of the Court.

Special sittings of Supreme Court for trial of Protectorate cases.

XVIII. (1) It shall be lawful for the Governor, at any time when he shall see fit, by public notification to appoint a special sitting of the Supreme Court to be held in any place in the Colony or Protectorate for the trial of Protectorate cases; and such sitting shall be deemed, if the said Court be then in session, to be a part of such session, or, if the Court be in vacation, to be a part of the session then last held.

Attendance of Officers may be dispensed with.

(2) The attendance of the Attorney-General, and of the Sheriff, Clerk of Courts and other officers attached to the Supreme Court, or any of them, may be dispensed with at any such special sitting, when the Governor shall so direct; or it shall be lawful for the Governor to appoint a Commissioner, or such other person or persons as he shall select, to perform at such special sitting the duties of public prosecutor, or of the Clerk of Courts or any other regular officer of the Court.

Relaxation of rules of Court at discretion of Chief Magistrate.

XIX. It shall be lawful for the Chief Magistrate on application made to him in Court or in Chambers by the Attorney-General or public prosecutor, or person acting as such, to relax any rule of Court with reference to the supplying of copies of informations to persons committed for trial, or the time appointed for supplying the same, or any other the like matter: provided always that no such relaxation shall be made save where the Chief Magistrate shall be of opinion that the same is necessary or expedient for facilitating or expediting the administration of justice, and will not prejudice the accused in making his defence.

Colonial Courts may remit cases to Native Tribunals.

XX. If it shall appear to any Court of law of the Colony that any cause or matter brought before it is properly cognizable by a Native Tribunal, and of a nature to be more conveniently or expeditiously disposed of by such tribunal, the Court may stop the further progress of such case before it, and remit the case to the Native Tribunal accordingly, and may award such costs as shall seem fit.

B.—Native Tribunals, their constitution and powers.

XXI. (1) There shall be in every District a Court or Tribunal to be styled the Native Tribunal of that District; which tribunal shall have jurisdiction both civil and criminal, in respect of matters occurring wholly or in part within the district as follows, *viz.*:— **Native Tribunal in every District.**

(*a*) In respect of crimes and offences so occurring, a Native Tribunal shall have and exercise all and sundry the powers below mentioned in Sections thirty-one and thirty-two hereof, together with such further or other powers as may for the time being be exercisable by the Police Court at Bathurst in the like cases, including the power of committing offenders for trial before the Supreme Court: **Criminal proceedings.**

(*b*) In respect of personal actions, actions of ejectment or other the like matters or proceedings, a Native Tribunal shall have and exercise the like powers and jurisdiction as shall be for the time being exerciseable by the Court of Requests at Bathurst, subject always to the following provisions:— **Civil proceedings.**

(i.) The Tribunal shall have jurisdiction only where the defendant, or one at least of the defendants, is resident within the district; or

(ii.) Where the lands, or other hereditaments which are the subject of any action, are situate within the district; or

(iii.) In suits and matters relating to the succession to the estate of any deceased person, where such deceased person was at the time of his death permanently resident within the district.

(2) For summoning and compelling the attendance of witnesses and accused persons, examining witnesses on oath or affirmation, calling for documents and all other the like purposes, a Native Tribunal shall have and may exercise all such powers as are exercisable by the two Courts last above mentioned. **Summoning witnesses, etc.**

XXII. A Native Tribunal shall be constituted as follows: **Constitution of Tribunal.**

(*a*) By three or more native members duly appointed by the Governor as hereinafter provided; or

(*b*) By the Commissioner, sitting alone or along with one or more native members.

XXIII. (1) The Governor shall in all districts where he shall deem it expedient appoint fit persons, not being more than seven in number, to be members of the Native Tribunal of such district. **Appointment of members.**

(2) Not less than three members shall be a *quorum* of the Tribunal, and the judgment of the majority shall be the judgment of the Tribunal; in the event of an equality of votes as to the verdict, sentence, or decision of any matter whatsoever, the President shall have a casting vote in addition to his original vote. **Quorum.**

Removal of members.

(3) Members may be suspended or removed by the Governor at any time in case of misconduct.

Commissioner may hold tribunals when expedient.

XXIV. (1) Subject to any regulations to be made under section forty-four hereof, it shall be lawful for the Commisioner to hold Native Tribunals at such times and in such places as he shall deem expedient.

Head Chief ditto.

(2) The Head Chief of any District may in like manner, and subject to any such regulations as aforesaid, convene Native Tribunals consisting of duly appointed native members, and shall, in the absence of the Commissioner, preside thereat and maintain order during the proceedings.

Judgment of Commissioner to be decisive.

(3) Where the Commissioner is present, he shall preside, and the judgment of the Commissioner shall be the judgment of the tribunal.

Other native jurisdictions excluded.

XXV. (1) The jurisdiction of the Native Tribunal of any District shall be exclusive of all other native jurisdictions, and shall not be exercised by any Head Chief or Headman sitting alone, nor by any other native authority whatsoever on any pretext.

Unauthorised persons sitting with Tribunal punishable.

(2) Any unauthorised person who shall pretend to hold a Court, or to adjudicate upon and determine any cause or matter, or who shall sit with any Native Tribunal or take part in its proceedings, consultations, or judgments, may be tried before the Supreme Court, and shall on conviction be liable to be punished by imprisonment with or without hard labour for a period not exceeding six months or by fine which may extend to twenty-five pounds, or by both.

Arbitrations, etc., saved.

(3) Nothing in this section contained shall interfere with the amicable settlement of disputes by arbitration or otherwise.

President to sign summonses, etc.

XXVI. (1) Subject always to the prohibition contained in sub-section one and sub-section two of the immediately preceding section, it shall be lawful for the Commissioner, or for the Head Chief of any District, to do and execute on behalf of the tribunal of such district all matters of a ministerial nature, including the hearing of informations and of complaints, issuing summonses, warrants and other process, giving orders for the apprehension of offenders, authorising searchers and all other the like acts, orders and instructions preliminary to the trial of any cause or matter, or in execution of any judgment duly given by the tribunal.

Process to be served by authorised messengers.

(2) All summonses, warrants and other process issued by the Head Chief of any District may be served and executed by an authorised messenger of such Head Chief duly appointed with the approval of the Commissioners. Every authorised messenger shall, when serving or executing any manner of process, wear a badge of office of such nature as may be prescribed.

C.—Committal of persons charged with Indictable Offences for trial before the Supreme Court.

Commissioners, Head Chiefs, etc., to investigate Crimes, etc.

XXVII. It shall be the duty of all Commissioners, Head Chiefs and Headmen to inquire into and investigate all crimes and serious offences committed in any place subject to their authority; and to make and cause to be made due search for all persons charged with, or believed to be concerned in, any such crime or offence wheresoever committed, who may reside or be, or be suspected to reside or be within any such place; and to take all due measures for bringing the same to trial as hereinbelow provided.

XXVIII. (1) Persons charged with murder, manslaughter or any other crime or serious offence, not being of a nature punishable summarily by a Native Tribunal, or being attended with such circumstances of aggravation as to render the same incapable of being adequately punished by the maximum punishment awardable under section thirty-two hereof, shall be committed for trial before the Supreme Court: such committal may lawfully be made by— **Persons charged with murder, etc., to be committed.**

(*a*) Any Native Tribunal, or

(*b*) Any Commissioner, Head Chief or Headman—

before whom the accused shall be brought.

(2) The procedure to be followed in connection with committals shall be such as may be prescribed; and in the absence of any regulation prescribing the same, shall be, so far as practicable, in conformity with the Indictable Offences Act, 1848, and any other Acts of the Imperial Parliament for the time being regulating the performance of the duties of Justices of the Peace with respect to persons charged with indictable offences. **Procedure.**

PART IV.—DECLARATION OF LAWS.

A.—General.

XXIX. So far as consistent with the Protectorate system, and without prejudice to any such reasonable native laws and customs as are hereinafter mentioned, all laws, statutes, Ordinances and rules for the time being in force in the Colony, being of general application throughout the same, shall extend and apply to the Protectorate, and to all matters, civil and criminal, arising therein, and shall be so extended and applied in all Courts of law whether within the Colony or the Protectorate: Provided that such laws and others may and shall be construed with such verbal alterations in the name or functions of any officer, Court, office or place therein mentioned or referred to as to render the same applicable to any person performing a like duty, and to any tribunal, office or place of a like nature in or in respect of the District concerned; also with such changes or omissions in any legal forms or documents or any technical matters whatsoever as may render the same suitable to the circumstances of such district; Provided notwithstanding that such alterations and omissions shall in no case affect the substance of the said laws, statutes, ordinances and rules. **Colonial laws to be in force in the Protectorate.**

XXX. All native laws and customs existing in the Protectorate, whether relating to matters of succession, marriage, divorce, dowry, the rights and authorities of parents, the tenure of land or any other matter, shall, where not repugnant to natural justice, nor incompatible with the principles of the law of England or with any law or Ordinance of the Colony applying **Native laws to remain in force.**

to the Protectorate (whether by virtue of the immediately preceding section hereof or in any other manner), continue and remain in full force and effect, and shall be taken cognizance of and enforced in all Courts of law, whether in the Colony or the Protectorate, in all causes and matters whatsoever arising in or relating to the Protectorate.

Offences punishable summarily by Native Tribunals.

B.—Offences punishable summarily.

XXXI. The criminal jurisdiction of a Native Tribunal, and of the Police Court at Bathurst in dealing with Protectorate cases, shall *inter alia* extend to and include the summary trial and determination of any of the following offences :—

(1) Assaults, including both common and aggravated assaults, indecent assault on any female, assault with intent to rob or commit any felony, and all other the like offences;

(2) The use of threatening, slanderous or defamatory words or songs with intent to intimidate, aggrieve, or annoy any person, challenging or inciting to fight, or any other conduct causing or provoking a breach of the breach.

(3) Being possessed of any poison or other destructive or noxious thing with intent to hurt, aggrieve or annoy any person;

(4) Knowingly doing any act likely to cause the spread of small-pox, or other epidemic or contagious disease;

(5) Causing or allowing the accumulation of rubbish or decaying matter in any street or in the neighbourhood of any house, keeping cattle or other animals in any unsuitable place, obstructing any roadway, or otherwise causing or maintaining any manner of nuisance;

(6) Unlawfully and maliciously setting fire to any dwelling house or other building, or unlawfully and maliciously committing any damage or injury to any lands, buildings, crops, stacks, trees, fences, walls, gates, bridges, fisheries, cattle or other animals, boats, canoes, ships, and generally to or upon any real or personal property whatsoever either of a public or private nature;

(7) Wilfully disobeying or neglecting to comply with or carry out any lawful order of a Commissioner, Head Chief or Headman, including any order given by any Commissioner, or by any Head Chief or Headman in pursuance of the powers and duties hereinabove respectively conferred and imposed on them, or in the discharge of any ministerial duties whatsoever assigned to them by any law or regulation in force in the Protectorate or in any portion thereof, or in pursuance of any reasonable native law or custom;

(8) Insulting, threatening, or endeavouring in any manner to intimidate or overawe a Commissioner, or any

Head Chief or Headman, or behaving in a seditious or turbulent manner, or persuading or inciting, or endeavouring to persuade or incite any person to be guilty of such behaviour;

(9) Seducing or taking away, or instigating, aiding or being in any way concerned in the seduction or taking away of any man's wife, daughter or servant;

(10) Committing theft or any manner of fraudulent practice, including simple larceny, whether after one or more previous convictions or not, all offences declared by any law for the time being in force to be punishable as simple larceny, larceny in a dwelling house, larceny from the person, larceny as a clerk or servant, embezzlement, receiving stolen goods or being unlawfully in possession of any property, including receiving or being in possession of goods stolen or otherwise unlawfully obtained outside the Colony or Protectorate, sacrilege, house-breaking, burglary, or false pretences;

(11) Pretending to exercise any kind of witchcraft or sorcery;

(12) Endangering the life of, or causing actual bodily injury to any person by the reckless discharge of fire-arms, or any other wilful, reckless or negligent act or conduct whatsoever punishable as an offence;

(13) Being drunk and behaving in a disorderly, violent or indecent manner;

(14) Using false weights and measures, or possessing the same in order to use;

(15) Beating any drum, gong, tom-tom, or other similar instrument of music, or otherwise creating noise or disturbance, contrary to the orders of the Commissioner or any Head Chief or Headman;

(16) Committing perjury or subornation of perjury, or fabricating or destroying any evidence, or conspiring to bring any false accusation, or compounding any felony or misdemeanour, or attempting in any way whatsoever to obstruct, prevent, pervert or defeat the course of justice or the administration of the law;

(17) Escaping from lawful custody, or rescuing or aiding the escape of any other person from lawful custody;

(18) Publicly insulting the religion held or professed by any other person, or disturbing any meeting of persons lawfully assembled for any religious worship;

(19) Committing any offence under the Protectorate (Trade Licence) Ordinance 1895, the Protectorate (Public Lands) Ordinance 1896 or any regulations thereunder, or under any law, Ordinance or regulations whatsoever for the time being in force in the Protectorate;

(20) Attempting to commit, or aiding, abetting, counselling or procuring the commission of any such offence:

Only minor offences to be dealt with.

Provided always that only offences of a minor nature, and such as may be adequately punished by the maximum penalty awardable under section thirty-two hereof, or under any regulations for the time being in force limiting the same, shall be so tried and determined by a Native Tribunal:

Governor-in-Council may restrict the jurisdiction.

Provided also that the Governor-in-Council may by regulation under section forty-four hereof restrict the jurisdiction of any Native Tribunal, so as such tribunal may exercise a part only of the criminal jurisdiction herinabove authorised.

Punishment awardable.

XXXII. (1) The punishment to be awarded for any offence mentioned in the last preceding section, shall be subject to such limitation in respect of the amount of any fine, or any period of imprisonment imposable, as may be prescribed whether generally or for any particular tribunal or set of tribunals; and in the absence of any regulation prescribing the same it shall be lawful for a Native Tribunal to award in respect of any such offence whatsoever a fine not exceeding twenty pounds, or in default of payment thereof imprisonment with or without hard labour for any period not exceeding six months.

Peremptory imprisonment, when permissible.

(2) Peremptory imprisonment with or without hard labour for a period not exceeding six months may be awarded without the option of a fine, in respect of a conviction for theft, receiving stolen goods, house-breaking, burglary or any other offence which may be prescribed.

Whipping of juvenile male offenders.

(3) In the case of male offenders under the age of sixteen years whipping may be ordered in addition to any other punishment awarded: provided that no undue cruelty be used and that the number of strokes shall in no case exceed twelve.

Imprisonment to be in common gaol.

(4) Every sentence of imprisonment exceeding fourteen days shall be carried out within the common gaol at Bathurst, the common gaol at McCarthy's Island, or some other building duly appointed under the provisions of the Gaol Ordinance 1891 to be a prison, and not otherwise.

Compensation to aggrieved persons.

XXXIII. (1) The Court may direct any fine, or part thereof, to be paid to the person injured by the act in respect of which such fine has been imposed, on condition that such person, if he shall except the same, shall not have or maintain any suit for the recovery of damages for the loss or injury sustained by him by reason of such act or omission.

Fines to be paid into Colonial Treasury.

(2) Subject to the provision made in sub-section one of this section, all fines imposed by any Native Tribunal, together with all fees or dues of Court, shall be paid into the Colonial Treasury and form part of the Revenue of the Colony and Protectorate. Head Chiefs shall remit all such fines, fees, and dues as aforesaid collected by them to the Commissioner for transmission to the Colonial Treasury.

C.—Procedure in Native Tribunals.

XXXIV. (1) Save so far as may be otherwise prescribed by the Governor-in-Council by any regulation to be made as hereinafter provided, the procedure of any Native Tribunal— **Procedure in Criminal and Civil cases.**

(*a*) in respect of any criminal charge or matter, shall be the same as that for the time being in use in the Police Court;

(*b*) in respect of any Civil action or matter, shall be the same as that for the time being in use in the Court of Requests at Bathurst;

And all Ordinances and Rules regulating the procedure of the said Courts shall extend and apply to any Native Tribunal so far as the same may be conveniently followed.

(2) Nothing herein contained shall be construed as requiring written process for any proceedings before a Native Tribunal, but all summonses, warrants or other process, being served or executed by an authorised messenger of a Head Chief, shall have full validity and the like effect in all respects as though duly drawn up in common form of law. **Written process not required.**

(3) Committals, whether to await trial or in execution of judgment or sentence, may be proved by the oath of any authorised messenger of a Head Chief; and such oath, being made as prescibed by any regulations to be made under section forty-four hereof, shall be sufficient ground and authority for any Commissioner or Justice of the Peace for the Colony to issue a warrant committing the offender to prison in accordance with the terms of such committal so proved as aforesaid. **Committals, when verbal, to be proved by oath.**

Part V.—Miscellaneous.

A.—Removal of Proceedings and Re-hearing by Commissioner.

XXXV. The Commissioner may on the application of any defendant or accused person, or in any case whatsoever where he shall deem it expedient so to do, stop the hearing or further hearing of any civil or criminal case commenced or brought before any Native Tribunal, and himself hear and determine the same summarily; or, if the case be one proper for commitment, he shall commit the offender for trial before the Supreme Court. **Removal of proceedings.**

XXXVI. The Commissioner may, when he shall see reason for so doing, re-hear any civil or criminal case which has been disposed of by any Native Tribunal, and may confirm the decision of such Native Tribunal, or may reverse or vary the same in whole or in part; or, if the case be one proper for commitment, he shall commit the offender for trial before the Supreme Court. **Re-hearing by Commissioner.**

XXXVII. All complaints in respect of any offence cognizable summarily by a Native Tribunal, and all claims of debt or damages or other proceedings, against a Head Chief, shall be heard and determined by the Commissioner or by some Court of law of the Colony having competent jurisdiction, and not otherwise. **Proceedings against Head Chiefs.**

XXXVIII. Where any accused person or litigant shall challenge and take exception to any native member of a tribunal **Challenging of native members.**

on the score of partiality, affinity, interest, ill-will or other the like ground, the tribunal shall inquire into the grounds of such challenge, and on being satisfied as to the sufficiency thereof, may direct such member to abstain from voting, or from taking any part in the proceedings connected with such case.

B.—Appeal to the Supreme Court.

Appeal in all cases.

XXXIX. Appeal to the Supreme Court shall lie from the decision of any Native Tribunal, howsoever constituted, subject to the following conditions:—

(*a*) Appeal shall be taken only when the case has been finally disposed of by the Native Tribunal;

(*b*) Security in a sum not exceeding twenty pounds to meet the costs of the appeal shall be given to the satisfaction of the Commissioner.

C.—Co-operation among Courts and Tribunals.

Courts of Colony and Protectorate to give mutual assistance.

XL. (1) Any Court or Tribunal within the Colony or Protectorate may, and shall so far as may conveniently be done, exercise all or any of the powers and jurisdiction to such Court or Tribunal belonging, in aid of any other Court or Tribunal within the Colony or Protectorate, for—

the detention, investigation, trial and punishment of crimes and offences;

the recovery of stolen property, or any property unlawfully received or in the possession of any person;

the apprehension and detention of offenders and accused persons;

serving summonses on defendants or witnesses, and compelling their attendance before such other Court or Tribunal;

enforcing judgments, decrees, sentences or orders, or executing or facilitating any manner of process; or

any other the like purpose, in connection with any proceedings whatsoever, civil or criminal:

whether by backing or endorsing any warrant or other written process, or, in the case of oral process issued by a Native Tribunal, issuing a written summons or warrant to the like effect, granting search warrants, issuing subpœnas, summonses and warrants, or any lawful means whatsoever.

For the purposes of this section, the expression "*Court*" shall include the Chief Magistrate, or any Justice of the Peace for the Colony, Commissioner or Head Chief, acting alone in the exercise of any ministerial or judicial powers lawfully exercisable in such manner.

Special offences under Protectorate law to be recognised in the Colony, *et vice versa.*

(2) The provisions of this section shall apply to and include any offence committed wholly or in part within the jurisdiction of a court or tribunal having authority to punish the same, notwithstanding that by the law of the place where that court or tribunal is to which application shall be made for assistance as above mentioned, the act or omission complained of is not an offence or not in like manner punishable as in the place wherein the same was committed.

(3) Where the Court or Tribunal to which application shall be made for assistance has itself jurisdiction in respect of the offence or matter concerned, it may in its discretion, in case the same may more conveniently be done, assume the determination of the case, and dispose thereof as it shall deem fit.

Court applied to may assume determination of the case.

D.—Privilege granted to British Subjects, etc.

XLI. (1) Natives born in any portion of the Colony made subject to the Protectorate system, and all persons whatsoever who are British subjects or subjects of any civilised power may, on appearing before any Native Tribunal consisting only of native members, claim to be tried or have the matter adjudged by the Commissioner; and the Native Tribunal shall allow such claim, and forthwith remit the case to the Commissioner accordingly.

Natives born within Colony, etc., may claim trial before the Commissioner.

(2) The Commissioner may, when he shall think fit, remit any such case to the Police Court or Court of Requests at Bathurst, making such order with regard to costs incurred and to be incurred as he shall deem expedient.

E.—Trials before the Supreme Court.

XLII. All actions, causes or matters whatsoever, whether Civil or Criminal, tried before the Supreme Court, shall be tried without a jury, and the Chief Magistrate shall be sole judge of all matters whether of fact or law. The Governor may appoint one or more fit persons to sit as Assessors along with the Chief Magistrate on the trial of any such case, but only for advisory purposes.

Chief Magistrate to be sole judge of matters of fact, etc.

XLIII. (1) Whoever falsely pretends to be a messenger or to hold any office or authority from the Governor, the Commissioner, or any Court of Law of the Colony, or to be the authorised messenger of any Head Chief, or wears any garb or carries any badge or token with the intent that it may be believed, or with the knowledge that it is likely to be believed, that he is such messenger or holds such office or authority, and in such assumed character attempts to do, or procures, or attempts to procure, any person to do or abstain from doing any act whatsoever, shall be guilty of an offence, and may on conviction before the Supreme Court be punished with imprisonment with or without hard labour, which may extend to two years, or with fine which may extend to fifty pounds, or with both.

Falsely pretending to hold office or authority.

(2) Upon the trial of any person charged with an offence under this section, or upon any investigation of such charge, in which it may be necessary for the prosecutor to give evidence of the falsity of the pretences made by the accused person, or any of them, a statement in writing under the hand of the Governor or of a Commissioner or of the Clerk of Courts, as the case may be affirming that the said pretences are false, shall be admitted and taken as sufficient evidence of such falsity, without proof of the signature, unless the Court see reason to doubt its genuineness.

Evidence as to falsity of pretences.

F.—*Making of Regulations, etc.*

Commissioners may hold assemblies of Head Chiefs, etc.

XLIV. It shall be lawful for any Commissioner with the approval of the Governor, at any suitable time and place, to convene all or any of the Head Chiefs and Headmen belonging to the Districts within his territory for the purpose of deliberating together on matters affecting their common interest; and all resolutions passed and adopted at any assembly duly called as aforesaid, shall be submitted to the Governor-in-Council.

Governor-in-Council to make regulations.

XLV. The Governor-in-Council may from time to time make, alter, revoke, amend or vary such regulations, consistent with this Ordinance and subject thereto, as may be suitable or necessary for—

(*a*) Constructing, repairing, clearing, regulating and protecting roads, bridges, wells, springs, water-courses, watering places and bathing places;

(*b*) Making and preserving land marks and fences;

(*c*) Regulating public fisheries;

(*d*) Preventing and abating nuisances;

(*e*) Clearing the outskirts of towns and villages;

(*f*) Providing burial grounds and regulating burials;

(*g*) Preventing discharge of firearms in towns and villages and other dangerous practices;

(*h*) Declaring and giving validity to any reasonable native law or custom existing in the Protectorate;

(*i*) Fixing the maximum punishment awardable in respect of all or any offences whatsoever cognizable before a Native Tribunal;

(*j*) Regulating the holding of Native Tribunals, prescribing the procedure to be followed in civil and in criminal cases, and providing for the reporting and recording of judgments pronounced by the Native Tribunals and for the execution of such judgments;

(*k*) Defining the duties of Head Chiefs, Headmen and members of the Native Tribunals, and fixing the remuneration to be allowed to such members, or to officers or servants employed by or on behalf of such tribunals;

(*l*) Restricting the jurisdiction of any Native Tribunal or Tribunals, so as such Tribunal or Tribunals may exercise only a part of the jurisdiction, civil and criminal, authorised generally by this Ordinance;

(*m*) Defining the duties, both executive and judicial, to be performed by the Commissioners, and the powers exercisable by them, whether within their respective territories or elsewhere in the Protectorate;

(*n*) Regulating the procedure to be followed by Native Tribunals, Commissioners, Head Chiefs or Headmen, in committing offenders for trial before the Supreme Court; and providing for the rectification of any errors and the supplying of any omissions made in connection therewith, whether by a further enquiry to be held before the Commissioner or before the Police Court at Bathurst or in any other manner.

(*o*) Regulating the mode of execution of judgments of any native Tribunal within the Colony, or of judgments of any Court of law of the Colony within the Protectorate, or any other the like purpose;

(*p*) Facilitating and regulating the exercise by any court or tribunal within the Colony or Protectorate of all or any of the powers to such court or tribunal belonging, in aid of any other court or tribunal, as provided in Section forty hereof, and prescribing the forms and procedure to be used in connection therewith; and generally.

(*q*) All such regulations as may be requisite for the further or better carrying out of any of the provisions of this Ordinance.

Every such Regulation shall come into operation upon the publication thereof in the Government Gazette, or at such time thereafter as shall be in such regulation provided, and shall thereupon have the like effect as if made by Ordinance, subject to disallowance by His Majesty.

CAMP OF H.E. THE GOVERNOR (SIR G. C. DENTON) AT SANGAJOR, IN THE JOLAH COUNTRY.

PART VI.

PARTICULARS OF THE DIRECT MARCHES THROUGHOUT THE GAMBIA PROTECTORATE, AND A RETURN OF CHIEFS RECEIVING STIPENDS.

CHAPTER IX.

DIRECT MARCHES AND CHIEFS' STIPENDS.

THE following particulars of the direct marches throughout the protectorate of the Gambia will form, it is hoped, a most important section of this book, and one which may from time to time be found of use to travellers in this portion of His Majesty's dominions.

The line taken is from the town of Essau, on the most western portion of British territory on the north bank of the river; and thence eastward through the countries of Niumi, Jokadu, Baddibu, Salum, Niani, Nianija, Sandu, and Wuli. At this point the River Gambia is crossed, the village of Konia being the most easterly portion of the colony's protectorate, and the country of Kantora on the south bank is reached. Thence the line of marches is taken westward through the districts of Fulladu, Niamina, Jarra, Kiang, Fogni, and Kommbo to Bakau, at the Cape St. Mary, some 7½ miles from Bathurst, the capital of the colony.

Following the details of direct marches particulars are given in this chapter of the stipends received by various chiefs in the Protectorate.

Particulars of the Direct Marches throughout the Gambia Protectorate.

From.	To.	Distance in miles.	Approximate Population.	Denomination.	Trading Stations or Stores in the neighbourhood.	Remarks.
Lower Niumi and Upper Niumi District.						
Essau	Jenkunda	6	320	Mandingo	Barra	Lower Niumi: Between Jenkunda and Duniajo a tidal creek is crossed, which is dry at low water. Essau *via* Jenkunda is the upper road, *via* Bakkendick the lower, by the river. Upper Niumi: Roads good. Between Sami and Jurunku the Sami Creek has to be crossed. The passage takes twenty minutes in canoes.
Jenkunda	Duniajo	2¼	400	Mandingo and Jolloff	—	
Duniajo	Dunku	8½	550	Jolloff	—	
Dunku	Sajuka	7¼	280	do.	—	
Essau	Bakkendick	7	320	Mandingo	—	
Bakkendick	Tubabcolong	7¼	544	do.	—	
Tubabcolong	Albreda	6½	468	do.	Albreda	
Albreda	Sicca	3½	260	do.	Sicca	
Sicca	Sami	5	432	do.	—	
Sami	Jurunku	4	160	do.	—	
Jokadu District.						
Jurunku	Kuntaia	10¼	—	Teucolor	Memene	Cross Memene Creek 600 ft., bridged. The Suarra Kunda Creek has to be crossed on passing into Lower Baddibu, twenty minutes in canoes.
Kuntaia	Dasallami	6½	110	Mandingo	—	
Dasallami	Suarra Kunda Creek	2½	330	—	—	

Lower Baddibu District.

From	To	Miles	Population	Tribe	Wharf	Remarks
Suarra Kunda Wharf	Karawan	1	—	Mandingo	Pannickon	Suarra Kunda Creek.
Karawan	Sabe	$3\frac{3}{4}$	1,208	do.	—	Roads heavy sand.
Sabe	Sallikenni	$6\frac{1}{4}$	1,500	do.	Jammi Kunda	Between No Kunda and Illiassa a swamp has to be crossed. It is bridged in parts.
Sallikenni	Jamma Kunda ...	$6\frac{3}{4}$	3,990	do.	—	
Jamma Kunda ...	No Kunda	$6\frac{1}{2}$	2,000	do.	—	
No Kunda	Illiassa	$5\frac{3}{4}$	1,250	do.	Duntamalong	

Upper Baddibu District.

From	To	Miles	Population	Tribe	Wharf	Remarks
Illiassa	Yalloll	$3\frac{1}{2}$	620	Mandingo	Catchang	Roads good.
Yalloll	Farafenni	$7\frac{3}{4}$	492	Foulah	Jirung	There is a high ironstone ridge between N'Geyn and Ballanghar.
Farafenni	Sokotto	$4\frac{3}{4}$	1020	Mandingo	Beretto	
Sokotto	N'Geyn	8	210	do.	—	
N'Geyn	Ballanghar	$5\frac{3}{4}$	610	Jolloff	—	

Lower Salum District.

From	To	Miles	Population	Tribe	Wharf	Remarks
Ballanghar	Gengi	5	240	Jolloff	Ballanghar Wharf	The roads in the country are good.
Gengi	Ka-uur	$4\frac{3}{4}$	520	Jolloff and Teucolor	—	
Ka-uur	Ka-uur Wharf ...	2	898	Mandingo	Ka-uur Whart	

From.	To.	Distance in miles.	Approximate Population.	Denomination.	Trading Stations or Stores in the neighbourhood.	Remarks.
Eastern Salum District.						
Ka-uur	N'Jau	12	139	Jolloff	None	The roads in Eastern Salum are good and wide. On leaving Panchang proceeding to Nianibantang in Lower Niani, Nianija Creek has to be crossed. This creek is about 125 yards wide. Water exists in it only in the rainy season, July to October, the depth then being 6 ft., but there is a good native bridge. There are no other creeks in Eastern Salum. Government compounds are at Panchang and N'Jau.
N'Jau	Panchang	5	140	do.	Panchang Wharf	
Lower Niani District.						
Panchang	Nianibantang ...	10	40	Mandingo	Nianimaroo Wharf (7 miles from Nianibantang)	Between Kuntaur (4 miles from Gasang) and Wassoo, villages are passed. On the march to Gasang, Panchang Creek has to be crossed. The water is about 3 ft. deep, but there is a good "Crinting" bridge. The roads are sandy. Bamboo here is plentiful. There is fair shooting in this country. Government compounds are at Gasang and Nianibantang.
Nianibantang ...	Gasang	11	67	do.	Gasang Wharf	

UPPER NIANI DISTRICT.

From	To	Miles	Population	Tribe	Nearest wharf	Remarks
Gasang	Sukuta	10	283	Mandingo	Sukuta Wharf	The roads throughout Upper Niani average about 20 ft. in width, and are clear of all obstacles. A few slight gradients exist, but all can be ridden over. The ground is of a somewhat sandy nature, but not inconveniently so. Both sides of the road are covered with low bush, with occasional clear patches where the ground-nut, corn, and rice are grown. Bamboo exists in abundance. There are no creeks or rivers in Upper Niani, and good shooting is to be obtained.
Sukuta	Kai Hai	5	537	do.	Kai Hai Wharf	
Kai Hai	Manna	4	150	do.	McCarthy Island	
Manna	Lamin Koto	6	90	do.	McCarthy Island	
Lamin Koto	Kunting	8	380	do.	Kunting Wharf	
Kunting	Karantaba	9	138	do.	Karantaba Wharf	
Karantaba	Sami	7	133	Teucolor	Sami Wharf	
Sami	Kunchow Creek	2	—			

NIANIJA DISTRICT (EXTRA MARCHES).

From	To	Miles	Population	Tribe	Nearest wharf	Remarks
Ka-uur	N'Jau	12	139	Jolloff	None	In Nianija the roads are fair. The creek of Nianija is crossed between the village of Guijakanka (2 miles from N'Jau) and Nianija. The width here is 40 yards, with deep water all the year round, but a canoe can always be obtained as a ferry. Before the creek is reached there is a swamp ¾ mile wide, but it is under water only in the rainy season.
N'Jau	Nianija	6	90	Teucolor	Carrols Wharf and Nianija Wharf (3 miles distant)	
Nianija	Ker Amadi alieu	5	174	do.	None	
Ker Amadi alieu	Nianibantang	10	40	Mandingo	Nianimaroo Wharf (7 miles distant)	

From.	To.	Distance in miles.	Approximate Population.	Denomination.	Trading Stations or Stores in the neighbourhood.	Remarks.
				SANDU DISTRICT.		
Kunchou Creek ...	... Dembawandeh ...	$\frac{1}{2}$	222	Mohammedan	Dembawandeh Wharf	Road good.
Dembawandeh	... Noudi	$2\frac{3}{4}$	690	do.	Noudi Wharf	do.
Noudi ...	... Korrow	$4\frac{1}{2}$	693	do.	Korrow Wharf	do.
Korrow ..	... Diabuku	$1\frac{3}{4}$	456	do.	Diabuku Wharf	do.
Diabuku ...	... Misera	3	252	do.	Kanube	do.
Misera ...	... Soma Kunda ...	$5\frac{1}{2}$	870	Pagan	Darsilami Wharf	Road fair.
Soma Kunda	... Darsilami	$1\frac{1}{2}$	354	Mohammedan	do.	do.
Darsilami ...	... Yorobywall	5	531	Pagan	Madina	Tuba Kouta Creek to be crossed—really a stream nearly dry during dry season. Road fair.
				WULI DISTRICT.		
Yorobywall ...	... Sambagubudayah ...	$1\frac{3}{4}$	279	Pagan	Madina Kouta Wharf	Very fair road.
Sambagubudayah ...	Kea Kunda	$\frac{1}{4}$	156	do.	do.	do.
Kea Kunda ...	... Chamois	$4\frac{1}{4}$	42	do.	Fattatenda	Good road.
Chamois ...	... Bantonding	$2\frac{1}{2}$	711	do.	do.	do.
Bantonding ...	... Marisuto	2	33	do.	do.	Chamois Creek to be crossed—dry during dry season. Good road.
Marisuto ...	... Sutoko	$2\frac{1}{2}$	1,173	Mohammedan	do.	do.
Sutoko ...	... Berief	5	408	do.	Kwonia	do.
Berief	... Fodi Kunda	$\frac{1}{2}$	261	do.	do.	do.
Fodi Kunda ...	... Kwonia Wharf ...	$2\frac{1}{4}$	42	do.	do.	do.

Kantora District.

Kwonia Wharf ...	... Kwonia Town ...	$2\frac{1}{2}$	330	Mohammedan	Kwonia Wharf	Road bad (marshy).
Kwonia ...	... Keneba	2	60	Pagan	do.	Road good.
Keneba ...	... Jowo Kunda ...	2	51	do.	do.	do.
Jowo Kunda...	... Faringtumbo ...	$1\frac{1}{2}$	120	do.	Yarbutenda	do.
Faringtumbo	... Kassi Kunda ...	$1\frac{1}{4}$	99	Mohammedan	do.	Very fair road.
Kassi Kunda...	... Sunkunda	$\frac{1}{2}$	417	Pagan	do.	Good road.
Sunkunda ...	... Konkuyelle	3	213	do.	do.	do.
Konkuyelle ...	... Konsoon	$2\frac{1}{4}$	105	Mohammedan	Channum	do.
Konsoon ...	... Tuba Kouta	5	300	do.	Peri	do. Tuba Kouta Creek, or stream, has to be crossed. It is bridged, and is 30 yards wide.

Fulladu East District.

Tuba Kouta ...	... Peri	$2\frac{3}{4}$	309	Mohammedan	Peri Wharf	Road very fair.
Peri	... Koulare	$3\frac{1}{4}$	1,335	do.	Findifato Wharf	do.
Koulare ...	... Findifato Wharf ...	$3\frac{1}{4}$	20	do.	do.	—
Findifato Wharf	... Tambasansan ...	4	432	do.	do.	do.
Tambasansan	... Bamfa Kunda ...	$4\frac{1}{2}$	452	do.	Basse Wharf	Road bad.
Bamfa Kunda	... Basse No. 1	$3\frac{1}{2}$	136	do.	do.	Good road.
Basse No. 1 ...	... Basse No. 2	$\frac{3}{4}$	$40\frac{1}{8}$	Pagan	do.	do.
Basse No. 2 ...	... Demba Kunda ...	$5\frac{1}{2}$	738	Mohammedan	Kanube Wharf	do.
Demba Kunda	... Gambasara	$4\frac{1}{4}$	2,343	do.	do.	do. Munchumina Creek, or stream.

From.	To.	Distance in miles.	Approximate Population.	Denomination.	Trading Stations or Stores in the neighbourhood.	Remarks.
			FULLADU WEST DISTRICT.			
Gambasara ...	... Sambell Kunda ...	$5\frac{1}{2}$	36	Pagan	Kossema Wharf	Road good. Mansafa Creek to be crossed.
Sambell Kunda	... Bakadagi	$1\frac{1}{2}$	342	Mohammedan	do.	Road good.
Bakadagi ...	... Kossema	1	162	Pagan	do.	do.
Kossema ...	... Fatako	$2\frac{1}{4}$	192	do.	do.	do.
Fatako ...	... Tabajang	$1\frac{1}{4}$	75	do.	do.	do.
Tabajang ...	... Willinghara ...	$2\frac{3}{4}$	282	do.	Bannatenda	do.
Willinghara	... Korroh No. 1 ...	$1\frac{1}{2}$	108	Mohammedan	do.	do.
Korroh No. 1	.. Korroh No. 2 ...	$1\frac{1}{2}$	252	do.	do.	Fair road.
Korroh No. 2	... Chakunda	$4\frac{1}{2}$	824	Half Pagan and Half Moh.	do.	Very fair road.
Chakunda ...	... Bantanta	9	48	Pagan	Bansang	do.
Bantanta ...	... Sololo No. 1	3	60	do.	do.	Good road.
Sololo No. 1...	... Borroba	7	324	Mohammedan	McCarthy Island	do.
Borroba ...	... Sankuli	$1\frac{1}{2}$	308	do.	do.	Very fair road.
Sankuli ...	... Pachare	$6\frac{1}{2}$	258	do.	Sapu	do.
Pachare ...	... Karawan	$4\frac{1}{2}$	466	Pagan	Walli Kunda	do.
Karawan ...	... Brikama	$3\frac{1}{4}$	336	do.	do.	do.
Brikama ...	... Walli Kunda ...	$2\frac{1}{4}$	30	Christian	do.	Fair road.

Eastern Niamina District.

Ida	... Kununku	4½	200	Mohammedan	Kudang: Trading stations of Messrs. The Bathurst Trading Company and Maurel Frères. Jarrang: Messrs. Waelter & Co.'s store.	Road fairly good and through open country. Wharf at Ida good — steamers drawing 10 ft. can come alongside the wharf at Kudang. Good open road 15 ft. wide. There is a creek at Jarreng about 8 ft. wide, and 3 ft. deep at high water, and it is about ¾ mile long. From Jarreng the main road goes to Kumbani in Western Niamina, a distance of two miles. The population of Jarreng is 200. A road which is only passable during the dry season leads from Jarreng to Sukuta across a ford on the Sofyaniama Creek; the distance is six miles.
Kununku ...	... Kudang	5	550	do.		
Kudang ...	... Sutokoi	3	1,000	do.		
Sutokoi ...	... Bambakolong ...	5	550	do.		
Bambakolong	... Suno Kunda... ...	2	270	do.		
Suno Kunda...	... Jarrang	3	200	do.		

From.	To.	Distance in miles.	Approximate Population.	Denomination.	Trading Stations or Stores in the neighbourhood.	Remarks.
				Western Niamina District.		
Kumbani ...	... Jamara ...	... 1½	210	Mohammedan	Piniai Wharf (called Setokoto): Messrs. Maurel Frères. Dunkunku Wharf: Messrs. The Bathurst Trading Company and Maurel Frères.	The road from Kumbani to Jakoto is not good, being sandy in many places and very narrow. This will be altered in 1905. The wharf at Setokoto is situated on the Sofyaniama Creek, and cutters drawing 6 ft. to 8 ft. can come alongside. The Jakoto Wharf is at the end of the Jakoto Creek, up which only native canoes can proceed. This is the wharf where the people from this bank cross to Ballanghar on the north bank.
Jamara ...	... Choia	... 5½	180	Pagan		
Choia	... Piniai	... 3	40	do.		
Piniai	... Katamina ...	... 1	270	do.		
Katamina ...	... Mali Kunda ...	... 1	290	do.		
Mali Kunda ...	... Dunkunku ...	... 2	350	do.		
Dunkunku ...	... Sami	... 6	700	Mohammedan		
Sami	... Jakoto ...	... 2	40	Pagan		
Jakoto ...	... Jakoto Wharf	... 1½	100	Mohammedan		

EASTERN JARRA DISTRICT.

Piniai (W. Niamina)	Pakalli Ba	4	270	Pagan	PAKALLI BA WHARF: Messrs. Maurel Frères. SUKUTA: Messrs. The Bathurst Trading Company. BURAING WHARF: Messrs. The Bathurst Trading Company. JASSONG WHARF: Messrs. The Bathurst Trading Company.	Road through swamp, bridged in one place, is practically impassable during the rains. Pakalli Ba is on the south of the Sofyaniama Creek; there is no ford and canoes have to be used to cross. Buraing Creek, at the wharf, is 6 ft. wide and 3 ft. deep at high water. The creek is 4 miles long. Cutters come up 2 miles and then canoes are used for the rest of the way. Jassong Creek is practically the same as Buraing as regards depth, width and length.
Pakalli Ba	Sukuta	3½	470	Mohammedan		
Sukuta	Dasallami	5	640	do.		
Dasallami	Buraing	5	330	do.		
Buraing	Jassong	2¼	550	do.		
Jassong	Badumi	4	480	do.		

CENTRAL JARRA DISTRICT.

Badumi	Japinni	3	400	Pagan	BANTANDING WHARF: Messrs. Maurel Frères.	Badumi Creek is only fit for small boats and canoes.
Japinni	Buiba	2½	310	do.		
Buiba	Karantaba	5	240	Mohammedan		

From.	To.	Distance in miles.	Approximate Population.	Denominations.	Trading Stations on Stores in the neighbourhood.	Remarks.
Western Jarra District.						
Karantaba	Soma	2	550	Mohammedan	BAI WHARF: Messrs. The Bathurst Trading Company and Maurel Frères. TONIATTA BA WHARF ON CREEK: Messrs. Waelter & Co., Cie. Francaise, Maurel Frères and Maurel and H. Prom.	Wharf situated at head of creek, 2 miles from river, dry at low water. Boats and canoes only can come up at high water.
Soma	Sekunda	$1\frac{1}{2}$	430	do.		
Sekunda	Toniataba	$1\frac{1}{2}$	390	do.		
Toniataba	Jiffin	2	590	do.		
Jiffin	Kiaff	2	260	do.		
Eastern Kiang District.						
Kaiaff	Massenti	$2\frac{1}{2}$	820	Mohammedan	Wharf at Jossoto three miles from Kolior. Cie. Francaise have a trading station here.	Jossoto Creek is $\frac{1}{2}$-mile from river; boats and canoes only can go up.
Massenti	Kolior	3	190	do.		
Kolior	Mandina	$1\frac{1}{2}$	430	do.		

EAST CENTRAL KIANG DISTRICT.

From	To	Miles	Population	Religion	Wharf/Creek	Remarks
Mandina ...	... Jiroff	2	150	Pagan	MANDINA CREEK: Messrs. Waelter & Co.	Mandina Creek only fit for boats one mile from river.
Jiroff	... Numa Kunda ...	1	170	do.		
Numa Kunda	... Bambako	6	110	Half Pagan and Half Moh.	JIROFF CREEK: Messrs. The Bathurst Trading Company.	Jiroff Creek can be used by cutters both at high and low water.
Bambako ...	... Kwinella	3	150	Pagan		Bambako Creek, $2\frac{1}{3}$ miles long, with wharf at end; it is 20 ft. wide and deep enough for cutters at high water.
Kwinella ...	... Tendaba	3	810	Half Pagan and Half Moh.	BAMBAKO CREEK: Messrs. The Bathurst Trading Company.	
Tendaba ...	... —	—	50	Mohammedan	TENDABA WHARF: Messrs. The Bathurst Trading Company.	Tendaba is on the river, but steamers cannot come within 300 yards of the wharf at low water, or 200 yards at high water. The landing is effected by boats.

WEST CENTRAL KIANG DISTRICT.

From	To	Miles	Population	Religion	Wharf/Creek	Remarks
Jarrol	... Jattaba	$5\frac{1}{2}$	314	Heathen	—	The Vintang Creek, a considerable waterway, has to be crossed between Jarrol and Jattaba, at the straight crossing by Sandeng.
Jattaba ...	... Sannian Kunda ...	6	243	Mohammedan	—	
Sannian Kunda	... Battelling	4	281	do.	—	Between Sannian Kunda and Batelling there are rice fields, flooded in the rains, but bridged in parts. From Batelling on the road to Jali, which is *viâ* Minjan and Boijonjo, there is a swamp and creek, with rice fields up to the town of Mandwa.
Battelling ...	... Jali	$11\frac{1}{2}$	476	do.	—	
Jali	... Mandwa	7	323	do.	—	
Mandwa ...	... Janni Kunda ...	$5\frac{1}{2}$	80	do.	—	
Janni Kunda	... Burrong	5	173	do.	—	

From.	To.	Distance in miles.	Approximate Population.	Denominations.	Trading Stations on Stores in the neighbourhood.	Remarks.
FOGNI DISTRICT.						
Baijana ...	... Bullelai ...	... 15	40	—	—	On leaving Baijana the road to Bulellai goes through a portion of French territory. A creek has to be crossed, fordable at low water. There is also a fresh-water stream. Rice fields (swamp during rains) exist between Bulellai and Kusamai; on leaving this latter town a creek, which is fordable, has to be crossed before reaching Kansalla. Thence to Sangajor there is another fresh-water stream and more rice fields. Between Sangajor and Bondali there is a swamp with plenty of water in the rains, and bad going. On leaving Bondali another swamp, with rice fields, has to be crossed before reaching Jarrol.
Bullelai ...	... Kussamai ...	... 5	162	Heathen	—	
Kussamai ...	... Kansalla ...	... 9	175	do.	—	
Kansalla ...	... Sangajor ...	... $7\frac{1}{4}$	149	Mixed	—	
Sangajor ...	... Bondali ...	... $7\frac{1}{2}$	79	Heathen	—	
Bondali ...	... Jarrol ...	... $4\frac{1}{2}$	106	do.	—	

COAST ROAD—SUKUTA TO GUNJOUR.

From	To	Miles	Population	Religion	Supplies	Remarks
Sukuta	Brufut	$4\frac{1}{4}$	703	Mohammedan	The only permanent stores are at Vintang and Gunjour	Between Sukuta and Brufut there are rice fields with water during the rains. On the road to Tujure a stream and swamp have to be crossed. These are bridged. Another swamp is passed before reaching Sannian. Two fresh-water streams, properly bridged, are met with between Sannian and Gunjour. There is a swamp during the rains between Gunjour and Kartung, as also a fresh-water stream, bridged, near Sifaw. The road *viâ* Kitti is swampy during the rains.
Brufut	Tujure	$5\frac{1}{2}$	153	do.		
Tujure	Sannian	3	137	do.		
Sannian	Gunjour	$6\frac{1}{2}$	91	do.		
Gunjour	Kartung	$6\frac{1}{4}$	1,117	do.		
Kartung	Sifaw	$4\frac{1}{2}$	—	—		
Sifaw	Brikama	$7\frac{1}{2}$	102	—		

ODD MARCHES.

From	To	Miles	Population	Religion	Supplies	Remarks
Vintang	Somita	$8\frac{1}{2}$	298	Mixed	—	Rice fields with water during rain. One creek not fordable at high water.
Somita	Brefet	$7\frac{1}{3}$	153	Heathen	—	

KOMMBO DISTRICT.

From.	To.	Distance in miles.	Approximate Population.	Denomination.	Trading Stations or Stores in the neighbourhood.	Remarks.
Bathurst ...	Bakau... ...	$7\frac{1}{2}$	—	—	—	Between Bathurst and Barkotti there is a fresh-water stream properly bridged. From Bakau to Sukuta there are two roads, one *viâ* Mansa Kunda and one direct which is slightly shorter. There is a swamp with "crinting" bridge; also a stream (in wet season) with rhun bridge. The road from Jambur to Gunjour lies through a cane forest and is *viâ* Kunkujan. There are three fresh-water streams to be crossed, which are bridged. From Gunjour to Brikama, *viâ* Kitti, there is another fresh-water stream, bridged. On the road between Brikama and Farraba Bunta the towns of Mandina Bar, Kembugi, Tunjina and Perang are passed, and a creek properly bridged has to be crossed. There is also a swamp, bridged in parts. From Faraba Bunta the road to Kafuta is *viâ* the town of Faraba Sotu. A creek has to be crossed, over which there is a bridge. There is a direct road newly opened. Between Kafuta and Baijana there is a fresh-water stream and a big creek, which, however, is fordable at low water.
Bakau... ...	Sukuta ...	$5\frac{1}{2}$	392	Mohammedan	—	
Sukuta ...	Busumballa ...	$5\frac{1}{2}$	703	do.	—	
Busumballa ...	Jambur ...	$2\frac{1}{2}$	177	do.	—	
Jambur ...	Gunjour ...	$10\frac{1}{2}$	163	do.	—	
Gunjour ...	Brikama ...	$10\frac{1}{2}$	1,117	do.	—	
Brikama ...	Faraba Bunta ...	$10\frac{1}{2}$	275	do.	—	
Faraba Bunta ...	Kafuta ...	$8\frac{3}{4}$	303	—	—	
Kafuta ...	Baijana ...	7	134	—	—	

A RETURN OF CHIEFS IN THE GAMBIA PROTECTORATE WHO RECEIVE STIPENDS.

From the following return it will be seen that the largest allowances are made to chiefs in the Upper River district, where the annual stipends range from the £500 paid annually to Musa Molloh down to the £20 paid to Manjang. Maranta Sunko, of the North Bank district, receives £83 6s. 8d.; Sunta Koma, of the McCarthy Island district, £20; and the headman of Bakau (British Kommbo), £10. The remaining stipends (with one exception) do not individually exceed £2 per annum.

North Bank District.

Chief Towns.	Name of Chief.	Amount of Stipend (Annual). £	s.	d.
Essau	Maranta Sonko	83	6	8*
Essau	Maranta Sonko	2	0	0
Dasallami	Bulli Forfana	2	0	0
Sallikenni	Arafang Buli Dabu	2	0	0
Sabe	Ansumana Singate	1	0	0
Jabba Kunda	Ansumana Jaiti	1	0	0
No Kunda	Koli Damfa	1	0	0
Illiassa	Jato Silang Jani	2	0	0
Beretto	Sitafa Debacha Ko	1	0	0
Sanchi n'Gur	Amadi Gay	1	0	0
Kekoto Kunda	Arafang Jani	2	0	0
Ka-uur	Macomba Sow	1	0	0
Ka-uur	Jooka Turay	1	0	0

McCarthy Island District.

Chief Towns.	Name of Chief.	£	s.	d.
N'Jau	Sa Wallo Cisi	2	0	0
Nianija	Yura Cham	2	0	0
Nianibantang	N'Garry Saballi	2	0	0
Manna No. 1	Sunta Koma	20	0	0
Sami No. 1	Homar Bake	2	0	0

Upper River District.

Chief Towns.	Name of Chief.	£	s.	d.
Misera	Jimbermang Jowlah	50	0	0
Bantonding	N'Yakadu Walli	40	0	0
Sunkunda	Manjang Sanyan	20	0	0
Tambasansan	Farli Cora	45	0	0
Borroba	Dembo Densa	50	0	0
Kesseli Kunda	Musa Molloh	500	0	0†

South Bank District.

Chief Towns.	Name of Chief.	£	s.	d.
Kwinella	Fodi Brima Saniang	2	0	0
Pakalli Ba	Fodi Dabu	2	0	0
Japinni	Jallali	2	0	0
Sukuta	Arafang Sedi Jali	2	0	0
Katamina	Tambaring Jadama	2	0	0
Kudang	Fodi Sani Ceesay	2	0	0

* Treaty No. 2, June 15th, 1826.
† Treaty dated June 10th, 1901.

Chief Towns.	Name of Chief.	Amount of Stipend (Annual)		
	KOMMBO AND KIANG DISTRICT.			
Sukuta	Kabba Chamm	2	0	0
Katung	Tumani Ture	2	0	0
Brikama	Fodi Musa Bojan	2	0	0
Faraba Bunta ..	Mamady Sannian	2	0	0
Jali	Janko Sammati	2	0	0
Janni Kunda.. ..	Fodi Karum Janni.. ..	1	0	0
Baijana	Lan Sannian	2	0	0
	SUB-CHIEFS.			
Kaiaff	Lamin Dabu Sani	1	0	0
Dunkunku	Brimah N'Boye	1	0	0
	HEADMEN.			
Jassong	Mousa Kani..	1	0	0
Buraing	Infamara Dabu	1	0	0
	FOGNI DISTRICT.			
Vintang	Maserai Sisi	1	0	0
Brefet	Lansaniang	1	0	0
Kansalla	Janko Dahaba	1	0	0
Kangaramba	N'Yanki Baji	1	0	0
	BRITISH KOMMBO.			
Bakau	Alcaide of	2	1	8*
Bakau	Headman of..	10	0	0†

* Treaty No. 1, April 14th, 1823. † Treaty dated December 26th, 1850.

BRIDGE OVER A SMALL CREEK.
Constructed of "Crinting" (interwoven bamboo) on stake piles.

PART VII.

AN ENGLISH-MANDINGO DICTIONARY OF SOME EIGHT HUNDRED WORDS AND PHRASES IN COMMON USE.

CHAPTER X.

A Dictionary of Mandingo Words and Phrases more Commonly Used, with their English Equivalents.

The following is a vocabulary of the more commonly used words and phrases in the Mandingo language, the tongue most universally spoken in the Gambia Protectorate:—

English.	Mandingo.
accident	lanyini
accuse	bulandi
affliction	bataro
afternoon	salli-fanna
age	jelu
agitate	kibirinde
alcaide	alcarli
all	bay
alligator	bambow
alter	altaro
amount	jelu
and	ning
ankle	singo
anoint	mosea
another	doe
answer	danku
ant	mennimennow
apostle	keelar
approach	kattar
arm	bullow
armour	kellidumfing
arrive	futar
arrow	beniow
ashamed	mallou
ashes	serbutow
ask	nyninkar
ass	fallow
assault	leepar
assemble	beng
astonished	kumpata
aunt	binke
awaken	kooni
axe	terango
back	kor
bad	jowiarta
bad smell	nora jowiarta
bag	boto
ball	kesso
bamboo	bongo
bark of tree	eri fatto
basin	bawlow
basket	sing singo
bastard	jankarding
bat	tonsow
bath	coo mirango
bathe	coo
Bathurst	Banjune
be careful	e suma dung
beads (shiny)	malarlar
beans	soso
beard	bora
beat	butai
beautiful	nynnartar
because	kartiko
bed	larungo
bee	combarungo
beef	subo
bee's-wax	kanio
beetle	kubero
before	nearto
beginning	follo

English.	Mandingo.
behind	koma
bell	talango
belt	taysitirango
best	betearta baytee
better	ficiarta
bicycle	toobab suo
big	awarita
biggest	awarita baytee
bird	coonow
biscuit	pongo
bit (bridle)	karafayo
black	fartifing
black man	fartifingo
blacksmith	kodetunkana
blessed	barakatar
blind	finkeetali
blood	yellow
blow	fingaro
blue	boluow
boa constrictor	ninkenanko
boat	kolungo
body	ballow
boil	faggi
book	kitabo
boot	samatto
bosom	ceeso
bottle	cabo
bow	kallo
box	kunayo
brains	kunuow
brother (elder)	koto
brother(young)	domar
brother-in-law	bitangkay
bug	babar
build	low
bullet	kesso
bullock	tura
buried	bardi
bush cat	bangbango
bush hog	woloconosayo
bush turkey	konkoduntango
business	murado
but	barri
butcher	ningsefarla
butter	toolow
butterfly	firriferro
calabash	mirango
camel	yongkomow

English	Mandingo.
candle	candio
cannon	payso
canoe	juano
cap	nafo
cap, gun	pistong kedo
carefully	kookay
carpenter	calfintaro
carrier, a	doonoola
Carrols Wharf	Sitto Kotto
carry	samba
cat	yangkomow
cattle owner	ningse teo
chain	naydulow
chair	serung
change (money)	falling
chanting	sookoo o kay
charms (to wear)	safayo
chat	kacha
cheek	tamo
chewing stick	ningsoosarango
chief	safo
child	ding ding
chin	bombongo
Christian	Miselmo
church	jamango
citizen	satemo
clay	potto
clean	seniarta
cleaning (a farm)	sasarow
climb	selli
cloth	buyo
cloth (a pang)	fanno
clothes	dundiko
cloud	sangkulo
cloudy	sangkoolow
cold	sumiar
cold season	kunchamaro
come in	dung nang
come near	kata na
complaint	koomo
compound	corda
cook, a	tabirilar
cook, to	keeno tabi
corkscrew	caba woterango
corn	neeor
cotton	cottondoe
cotton thread	dulow boro

English.	Mandingo.
cough	toetoe
country	duwow
court fees	keete joe
cover (house only)	teepar
covering	bitterango
cow	yearayo
creek	bolongo
crown bird	kumari
cry	koombo
cursing	nendeera
curtain	sankayo
cut	namma
cut off	cuntoo
cutter	kolungo
damp	monta
dance	donkeelo
day	tilli
daylight	kenno ketta
dead	farta
dead body	foorayo
dead person	bardi
death	siar
debt	julow
deep	dingcata
deer	mimango
devil	ginayo
dig	sing
dirty	anawtali
distance	jam farta
distance, please	jam carah
doctor, English	doctaro
doctor, native	jaralar
dog	woolu
dollar	dalassi
door	da towndango
drink	ming
drinking vessel	mindango
drown	toonen
drunk	sirata
dry	jattar
duck	burro
dust	kangkango
eagle	bibbo
early	juno

English.	Mandingo.
earring	toolto kodo
earth	banco
earthen jar	geebidda
east	tiliboo
easy	aficiarta
eat	dummo
eating	dumoro
ebb tide	ba jar
egg	sisikeelo
elephant	samow
elephant tusk	samanyngo
eleven	tang ningkilling
empty	kenseng
England	Baba, or Tubab Duo
English	Toobab
enter	dung
evening	uraru
every day	lung o lung
every time	toomo o toomo
every town	satay o satay
every year	sang o sang
everywhere	da o da
ewe	sa musu
except	damantang
eye	nea
face	nea da
faint	ketto
fall	boy
family	eela morlu
fan	feenjarango
farm	ballingo, or kunkoto
fat	awarita
feed	domorunde
fence	sortayo
fever	sasa
filthy	notali, or noring
fingers	bullow-kondingo
fire	dimba
fireman	dimbadadala
first	foloto
fish	yayo
fishing	doeling fi
fishing line	doling julow
five	lulu

English.	Mandingo.	English.	Mandingo.
flag	bandeero	ground	banco
flamingo	hello	ground-nut oil	tea toolow
flea	jattakolong	ground-nut seed	tea tura
flint lock	keede bero	grow (person)	sorong
flower	turotura	grow (plant)	fui
fly	seeo	guinea fowl	cammow
fly, to	tee	gum	kambaro
flying	teeta	gun	keedo
fog	kombo	gun cartridge	kedi kesso
food	damafengo	gun fire 8 p.m.	payso fita
fool	morfooring	gun powder	kedi muncko
foolish	fooringo		
foot bracelet	sunto kodo		
forest	alo	hair	kungtoonear
forgot	neenata	hammer	perrirango
fork	subosirango	hand	bullow
fort	tatto	hand bracelet	bulleto kodo
fought	kellata	handkerchief	teeko
four	nani	handle	muterango
fowl	susayo	hang	deng
free man, a	foriarta	happy	jusula, or jusu diartala
Friday	Arjuma		
friend	teari	hat	nafo
frog	tottow	have you	yea soto
fruit	eri dingo	he	ate
funny	saranow	he cannot go	ate ta nola
		he must go	foiarta
gaol	bunjauo	headache	kung dimingo
get	soto	heal	jarrandi
getting close	cattata	heart	sondummo
give	deena	heat	kando
go	ta	heathen	carfeero
go aside	ta jenke	heaven	argenna
go on	awa	heavy	koolia
goat	bar	height	lownearte
God	Alla	hell	jahanama
gold	sanno	herdsman	cantarla
gone out	funtita	hides	ningsekulo
goods	nafulolu	hill	tungo
Governor	Mansa	hippo	mallow
grasp	mutta	his	atela
grass	nyamo	hit	leepa
graveyard	bardadula	hoe	dabbo
great	ba	hog	sayo
green	nyamamoo-lungo	hold a meeting	bengo kayla
green grass	nyama kitingo	hole (in ground)	dinko
grey	barayo	hole (pierced)	sore
gri gri (a charm)	safayo	honest	jicko
		honey	leo

ENGLISH.	MANDINGO.
honeycomb	lee carnio
hoof	warra sore
hook	dolingo
horse	suo
horse boy	su fa
hospital	jarradula
hot	kandita
hot water	gee cando
house	bungo
how many	jelu
how much	jelu
however it may be	kay o kay
hunger	konko
hungry	konkota
hunter	dano
hurry	bang bang
husband	kay ma
hut tax	bungo kodo
hyæna	suluo
I	inte
impertinence	kang-ja
india-rubber	folayo
india-rubber tree	folayero
indigo	karo
infant	dingdingo
interpret	cannasora
interpreter	cannasoralla
iron	nay
iron pot	kalero
ivory	sammanyingo
jealous	kiliar
joists	sibolu
Jolluf	Suruwa
jug	doombow
jump	saun
keep	marbow
kettle	tasalow
keys	kooni dingo
kick	damfo
kidney	kor kilow
kill	fa
king, governor	mansa
kneel	jimmy
knife	muro
know	long

ENGLISH.	MANDINGO.
kola-nut	kuruo
koose	footow
lad	combano
land	banco
language	kango
large	awarita
laugh	jelle
lay	landi
lazy	sembendango
leaf	jambo
leak	soolen
leaked	asolenta
leg	wutow
leopard	sollo
letter	batio
level	temberingo
lid	beetindang
lie	fania
lie down	la
life	neeo
lift	chicka
light	fayar
light (not dark)	malata
light, the lamp	lampo marra
lighten	fayandi
lighting	sangnalasow
lime	lasso
lion	jatto
liquor	dollor
liver	jusow
lizard	basso
load	sosow
load	duno
lock	sorong
lock, a	karriyado
locked	sorongta
locust	kuntingo
locust, native food	toolingo
locust on tree	nettetto
lonesome	keydee
long	jungiar
look	filli
looking glass	fangfaylerango
loose	filita
lost	filitati
loud	awaramarkay

English.	Mandingo.
love	kannu
low	sutia
lungs	nee geo
make	dada
man	kayo
many	ciarta
market place	marseeo
marriage	futuo
mason	karangkayo
mast	kolimow
matter (sores)	feeo
McCarthy Island	Jang Jang Burri
meat	soobow
medicine	boro
meeting, a	bengo
meeting, to hold	bengo kayla
mend	cara
merchant	markeeno
milk, fresh	kekeyo
milk, sour	nonnor
mind	hakelow
mine	intela
mistake	fili
mistaken	filita
Monday	Tenenglungo
money	kodo
monkey	kongo
morning	soma
mosque	jamango
most	ciarta ba
mother	ba
moustache	da teo
mouth	da
mud	potto
murder	fa
murderer	fala
my name is	intemoo
nail	perayo
nail, finger	ngoringo
native bishop	fodi
native minister	arafang
native woman	fartifing mooso
near	kata
neck	kango
needle	bendango
neighbour	kantanyo
net	jallow
new	koota
next year	jarri
niece	barrinding muso
night	suto
no	honey
noise	sara
noon	tilibullow
north	marra
nothing	toos
oar	barrajibbo
oil	tulu
open	yeali
or	fo
order	kuma
ostrich	suntokoonow
ours	intolula
overturned	kupita
owl	kikiango
owner	tamow
pack up	kessung
parrot	joebow
passage, a	da
pen	kala
pencil	safarango
pepper	kano
pick up	tombo
pillow	kung larungo
pin	peeno
plant	fui
play instrument	koosi
poisoned	kunow
poor	dowba
pray	sali
put out	dobeng
rain	sanjayo
rake	korango
ram	sakotong
rat	nyeenow
receive	sotto
remember	mira
replace	seejinde
rest	tenkung

English.	Mandingo.
return	say
rice	mannow
ride	susello
ripe	amortali
rise	wulli
river	bolongo
road	silo
rock stone	bero
root	sulo
rope	dulow
run	bori
sack	botow
saddle	creekayo
sail	bassefano
salt	ko
sand	kaneneo
satisfied	jusula
Saturday	Sibitilungo
save	kisandi
saw	sero
say	fi
scale	peeo
scatter it	jang jang
scent	carabani geo
school	karangdula
school-master	karamow
scissors	tesearo
scorpion	buntalow
sea	geo ba
see	jube
seed	kesso
sell	sang
send	key
serpent	ninkinanko
servant	kunifa
seven	worrowulla
sew	kara
shade	dibengo
shadow	neeka
shake it	kong kong
shame	malundi
shark	patamow
shilling	taranso
shine	mala
shiny beads	mallarla
shoe	samatto
shoemaker	karangkayo
shoot	fi
shop	komfar
short	jungiar
show me	etan na
shut	town
silk	soiow
silver	kodo
silversmith	koditunkana
sing	donkeelo
six	worro
skin	koolow
skin, to	bussa
slave	jungo
slave owner	jung teo
sleep	seeno
sleeping sickness	ceno jankaro
sling	kutokato
small pox	jambarlow
snake	sa
snuff box	foolayo
soap	safano
soft	foya
softly	kookay, or doma doma
sometimes	tumando
soon	sambi, or dombi
sore	telli
sour milk	nonnor
sour tumbler (tree)	timberingo
south	bolloba
spade	darambow
sparrow hawk	canna
spear	tambo
spider	tarlingo
spit	da fi
split	fara
spoil	tiniar
sponge	balasosarango
spoon	cojaro
spread it	fayni
spring (water)	jeenya
sprinkle	jung jung
spur	sembero
squirrel	kerango
stairs	sellerango
stand	wulli
standing	loring
starch	lampowio
stars	lolow
stay	batto

English.	Mandingo.
steal	sunaro
steamer	sisikolungo
steer	senayo
stick	kolimow
stirrup	deelow
stockade	tatto
stomach	connor
stop	um batto
stopper	caba sukarango
straight	tilinde
strange farmer	tea senila
stranger	luntango
stream	wuyo
strength	sembo
stretch	tilindi
string	dulow
strong	bambanta
stump	eri cunto
sugar	sukuro
summer	tili cando
sun	telow
Sunday	Alahadolungo
supper	seemungo
surname	kontong
swallow	conung
swamp	layo
swarm of bees	combarung juramow
sweep	feeta
sweet	diarta
swell	foonoo
swim	nor
swizzler	foroforoango
sword	fango
table	tabullow
tailor	karala
take care of	marra
take off	wura
tall	kjango
teeth	nyngo
teeth, set of	nyng kesso
ten	tang
that's it	woolemu
that's not it	wonti
theirs	itolula
these	ningolu
thief	sungo
thirsty	mindow

English.	Mandingo.
thirty	tang saba
those	wolu
thread	dulow boro
three	saba
throw	fi
thunder	sangfetengo
thundering	koomarla
Thursday	Aramisalungo
tie	siti
to-day	bee
to-morrow	cining
to-night	sutow
tobacco	taba
toes	singkondingo
tongue	nengo
tools	dorango
tornado	toolubardo
tortoise (hard backed)	kootow
tortoise (soft back)	tantow
towel	bulow feetarango
tree	ero
Tuesday	Talatalungo
turn round	moorung
turn up	woolendi
twenty	moang
twist	minning
two	fulla
ugly	mullung jow
unblessed	barrakantang
uncertain	um un koi
uncle	barring
understood	moi
unload	soso bow
upper storey	santofunko
upset	coopita
vaccination	bullow nama
visit	kumpabo
waist beads	joeknow
wait	battu
wake me up	m coonee
walk	tamma
wander	jenke
want	lafi
war	kello

ENGLISH.	MANDINGO.	ENGLISH.	MANDINGO.
wasp	dondola	window	palanteero
watch	watto londango	wine, palm	tanjayo
water	geeo	wing	kampango
water-jar	geebita	witchcraft	boa
we	intelu	witness	sedeo
weak	um mun ban-bang	wolf	soolouo
		woman	muso
Wednesday	Arabulango	wood	low
week	lokung	word	kumo
weep	kombala	work	doko
well	kolongo	world	dunya
west	tilligee	worm	callia
wet	seenunta	wounded	dallama
what	moo	write	safay
when	muntama	writer	saferla
when	toomadgejema		
whip	busso	year	sangee
white	koi	yesterday	coonung
white man	fartakoi	you	ite
who	juma	you only	ite fang fang
wide	fannulati	your	eela
wild cat	bangbango	yours	altolula
wind	fonio	youth	combano

GAMBIAN CATTLE.

PART VIII.

PERSONNEL OF IMPERIAL AND COLONIAL DEPARTMENTS CONCERNED IN THE GOVERNMENT AND ADMINISTRATION OF THE GAMBIA: SERVICE REGULATIONS: GENERAL INFORMATION AS TO COLONIAL APPOINTMENTS: FINANCIAL AND OTHER DETAILS AS TO THE COLONY AND ITS INSTITUTIONS: FISCAL ARRANGEMENTS: LOCAL DIRECTORY.

CHAPTER XI.

PERSONNEL OF IMPERIAL AND COLONIAL DEPARTMENTS: SERVICE REGULATIONS: GENERAL INFORMATION.

Personnel of the Colonial Office—Crown Agents—Members of Executive Council and other Governing Bodies in the Gambia—Justices of the Peace and Commissioners of the Courts of Requests—Personnel of the Official Departments of the Colony — Foreign Consuls — British Consuls — Key Holders of the Vault—Instructions to Travelling Commissioners—Travelling Allowances—Regulations as to Leave of Absence—Vacations and Sick Leave for Native Officers—Family Remittances—Officers Trading—Regulations as to Official Correspondence and Departmental Routine—Table of Returns to be Submitted by Heads of Departments—Transference of Military Officers — Hours of Office Attendance — Public Holidays—Granting Certificates of Character and Service—Return of Pensioners in the Colony—Information as to Colonial Appointments—Hints on Outfit—Precautions against Effects of Sun.

IN the following chapter is given the personnel of the two Imperial Departments in London which are directly concerned with the Government of the Crown Colonies, and the personnel of the civil and military establishments of the Gambia. The author has also included the chief regulations which govern the appointment, duties and conduct of officers of the Colony; and some hints as to desirable outfit for West Africa:—

COLONIAL OFFICE: DOWNING STREET, S.W.

Principal Secretary of State for the Colonies: Right Honourable Alfred Lyttelton, K.C., M.P., £5,000.

Private Secretaries: Bernard H. Holland, C.B., E. H. Marsh, C. Russell.

UNDER-SECRETARIES.

Permanent: Sir Montagu F. Ommanney, G.C.M.G., K.C.B., I.S.O., £2,000.

Parliamentary Under-Secretary: Duke of Marlborough, K.G., £1,500.

Assistant Under-Secretaries: Frederick Graham, C.B., £1,500; Charles Prestwood Lucas, C.B., £1,200; Hugh B. Cox, C.B., (Legal) £1,200; Reginald L. Antrobus, C.B., £1,200.

Chancellor of the Order of Saint Michael and Saint George: Duke of Argyle, K.T.

Chief Clerk: Sir W. A. Baillie-Hamilton, K.C.M.G., C.B., £1,125.

Principal Clerks: Arthur A. Pearson, C.M.G., Francis Richard Round, C.M.G., Hartmann Wolfgang Just, C.B., C.M.G., Chas. Alex. Harris, C.M.G., G. V. Fiddes, C.B., Geo. Wm. Johnson, S. Olivier, C.M.G., £850 to £1,000.

Legal Assistant: John Schuckburgh Risley, £750.

First-Class Clerks: H. J. Read, Charles Strachey, H. C. M. Lambert, A. E. Collins, W. D. Ellis, G. E. A. Grindle, J. F. N. Green, T. C. Macnaghten, £600 to £800.

Second-Class Clerks: E. H. Marsh, C. T. Davis, F. G. A. Butler, W. A. Robinson, A. Fiddian, H. E. Dale, E. R. Darnley, A. B. Keith, R. Geikie, G. G. Robinson, R. E. Stubbs, R. V. Vernon, D. O. Malcolm, W. C. Bottomley, A. J. Harding, H. R. Cowell, R. H. Griffin, E. J. Harding, £200 to £500.

Accountant: A. H. H. Engelbach, I.S.O., £600 to £700.

Librarian: C. Atchley, I.S.O., £540 to £600.

Chief Registrar: W. F. Westbrook, £300 to £450.

Superintendent of Printing: E. D. Rockett, £300 to £450.

Clerk for Legal Instruments: C. H. Niblett, £375 to £450.

Assistant Accountant: W. H. Eggett, £300 to £450.

Assistant to Superintendent of Printing: A. H. Bridgman, £200 to £300.

Supervisor of Copying: S. J. Meaney, £200 to £300.

Second Division Clerks (Higher Grade): M. J. Drayson, W. Scott, T. Wilson, W. E. Hobson, J. A. Smith, £250 to £350.

Medical Adviser: Sir Patrick Manson, M.D., K.C.M.G.

Botanical Adviser: Sir W. T. Thiselton Dyer, K.C.M.G., F.R.S.

Affairs relating to the Gambia are under the special supervision of:—

S. Olivier, C.M.G., H. J. Read, E. R. Darnley, W. C. Bottomley.

THE CROWN AGENTS FOR THE COLONIES, WHITEHALL, S.W., 1 TOKENHOUSE BUILDINGS, E.C.

Crown Agents: Sir E. E. Blake, K.C.M.G., Major M. A. Cameron, C.M.G., R.E., W. H. Mercer, C.M.G.

Secretary: P. H. Ezechial.

Chief Clerk and Accountant: E. G. Antrobus.

Registrar of Inscribed Stocks: T. S. Dunn, I.S.O.

Chief Cashier: L. Adams.

Engineering and Works Branches: Capt. J. F. Carmichael, R.E., A. M. Heath, A.M.I.C.E.

Assistant Head of Works Branch: W. H. Lancaster.
Head of General Stores Branch: H. F. Smith.
Head of Shipping Branch: N. Hardingham, I.S.O.
Head of Correspondence Branch: G. Hodgson.
Head of Appointments Branch: H. Martin.

The Crown Agents are the commercial and financial agents in the United Kingdom for all the colonies except those possessing responsible government, and for the protectorates, which are under the control of the Colonial Office. They are directly responsible to the colonial Governments, but the Secretary of State exercises a general control and supervision over the conduct of their business, and they are from time to time instructed by him on questions of principle and in cases of emergency or of great importance. They are appointed by the Secretary of State for the Colonies, and are paid by fixed salaries settled by him. The charges for the different classes of business transacted by them are fixed by the Secretary of State. The accounts kept by the Crown Agents are audited by the Comptroller and Auditor-General, and an abstract of them is rendered to the Secretary of State.

They now transact business for some forty-four colonies and protectorates.

The Executive Council and other Governing Bodies in the Gambia.

Executive Council.

Governor: Sir George Chardin Denton, K.C.M.G.
Colonial Secretary: H. M. Brandford Griffith, C.M.G.
Treasurer: F. Bisset Archer (by special appointment).
Attorney-General: W. R. Townsend (by special appointment).

Legislative Council.

Governor: Sir George Chardin Denton, K.C.M.G.
Colonial Secretary: H. M. Brandford Griffith, C.M.G.
Chief Magistrate: A. D. Russell.
Treasurer: F. Bisset Archer.
Attorney-General: W. R. Townsend.
Collector of Customs: T. E. Peirce.
Unofficial Members: S. J. Forster, A. L. Bennett.

Official Members hold seats in the Council during their tenure of office in the colony. Unofficial Members are appointed for a term of five years. The Governor is addressed as "His Excellency," other Members of Council as "The Honourable."

BOARD OF EDUCATION.

Governor and Commander-in-Chief: Sir George C. Denton, K.C.M.G.
Colonial Secretary: H. M. Brandford Griffith, C.M.G.
Chief Magistrate: A. D. Russell.
Colonial Treasurer: F. Bisset Archer.
Attorney-General and Inspector of Schools: W. R. Townsend.
Collector of Customs: T. E. Peirce.
Honourables S. J. Forster, A. L. Bennett.
Reverends Arthur Pool, M. A. Wieder, F. J. Nicholas, B.A.

QUARANTINE BOARD.

Senior Medical Officer: R. M. Forde, President.
Superintendent of Police: J. Brown.
Medical Officer acting for the time being as Inspector of Health of Shipping.

PILOTAGE AND NAVIGATION BOARD (Ordinance No. 1 of 1904).

Collector of Customs: Hon. T. E. Peirce, Chairman.
Senior Medical Officer: Dr. R. M. Forde, Superintendent of Police: J. Brown, Esq., The Hon. A. L. Bennett, H. Staub, Esq. } Members.

LIST OF JUSTICES OF THE PEACE AND COMMISSIONERS OF THE COURT OF REQUESTS.

The Honourable H. M. Brandford Griffith, C.M.G.
The Honourable F. Bisset Archer.
The Honourable T. E. Peirce.
The Honourable S. J. Forster.
J. Brown, Esq.
Dr. R. M. Forde.
H. L. Pryce, Esq.
G. H. Sangster, Esq.
W. B. Stanley, Esq.
J. K. McCallum, Esq.
E. Vaughan, Esq.
Captain C. F. O. Graham.
Lieutenant H. Hoskyns.
Dr. F. A. Baldwin.
Dr. E. Hopkinson, D.S.O.
T. B. Bracken, Esq.
Dr. J. C. Franklin.
J. D. Richards, Esq.
E. Thomas, Esq.
S. Horton Jones, Esq.
J. E. Mahoney, Esq.

PERSONNEL OF THE OFFICIAL DEPARTMENTS OF THE COLONY.

CIVIL ESTABLISHMENT.

Governor and Commander-in-Chief: Sir G. C. Denton, K.C.M.G., £1,500 and £600 allowances.

Private Secretary: Captain L. F. Scott, Oxfordshire Light Infantry, £250.
Governor's Clerk and Interpreter: J. P. Joof, £80 to £100.

SECRETARIAT.

Colonial Secretary: H. M. Brandford Griffith, C.M.G., £600 to £700 by £25 per annum, and £100 duty allowance.
Chief Clerk: J. A. Mensah, £200 to £250 by £10 per annum.
Second Clerk: H. G. Fowlis, £120.

TREASURY.

Treasurer: F. Bisset Archer, £600, and £60 duty allowance.
Chief Clerk and Cashier: S. D. A. Coker, £175 to £200, and £20 personal allowance.
First Clerk: P. Sowe, £80 to £100.
Second Clerk: James C. Johnson, £50 to £75.
Third Clerk: J. J. Fowlis, £36.

ATTORNEY-GENERAL'S OFFICE.

Attorney-General: W. R. Townsend, £400 to £450, and private practice.
Clerk: S. A. Peacock, £36.

CUSTOMS.

Collector of Customs: T. E. Peirce, £400 to £500, and £60 duty allowance.
Chief Clerk and Cashier: S. J. Auber, £175 to £200, and £20 personal.
Second Clerk: J. A. Gomez, £60 to £65, and £12 as Magazine Keeper.
Tide Surveyor and Quarantine Officer: S. F. Leigh, £175 to £200, by £5 per annum.
Chief Landing Waiter and Locker: J. C. Chapman, £125 to £150.
First Class Landing Waiters: James E. King and James T. Monday, £50 to £60 each.
Second Class Landing Waiters: S. C. Richards and T. B. Wright, £40 to £50 each.

JUDICIAL DEPARTMENT.

Chief Magistrate: A. D. Russell, M.A., LL.B., £750.
Clerk of Courts: C. W. Thomas, £120 to £150.
Interpreter: F. M. Fye, £60.
Sheriff: Joseph Brown, £50.
Beadle and Bailiff: N. J. Allen, £60.

PROTECTORATE.

Travelling Commissioners: First Class, H. L. Pryce, £500; Second Class, G. H. Sangster, £400; Third Class, W. B. Stanley, J. K. McCallum and one vacancy, £300 each, and 10s. per diem when travelling.

WEST AFRICAN FRONTIER FORCE.

Captain Commanding: C. F. O. Graham, R.M.L.I., £400, command pay, £96.

Lieutenants: H. Hoskyns, £325; C. Morley, £325.

Sergeants: W. Wheatcroft, J. C. Noble, £120.

All officers draw a horse allowance of 2s. 3d. per diem, and a field allowance of 5s. per diem when absent from headquarters.

POLICE FORCE.

Superintendent: Joseph Brown, £350; and £50 duty allowance, £50 personal allowance.

Assistant Superintendent: T. B. Bracken, £250. Both officers have forage allowance of 2s. 3d. per diem.

PRISONS.

Inspector of Prisons: Joseph Brown, £50.

Gaoler: C. C. Johnson, £120.

Chief Warder: T. T. Turner, £50.

MEDICAL.

Senior Medical Officer: R. M. Forde, £600 to £700.

Medical Officers: F. A. Baldwin, J. C. Franklin, E. Hopkinson, £400 to £500.

A forage allowance of 2s. 3d. per diem is drawn by each officer.

Dispenser: W. S. Smart, £75 to £85.

Assistant Dispenser: F. G. Manly, £60.

Clerk: Colin Shaw, £70 to £80.

PRINTING OFFICE.

Government Printer: N. E. Williams, £100 to £125.

First-Class Compositor: J. M. Lawani, £50 to £60, by £2 per annum.

COLONIAL ENGINEER'S DEPARTMENT.

Colonial Engineer: E. Vaughan, £450; forage allowance, 2s. 3d. per diem, and duty allowance £90.

Clerk of Works: W. Pickering, £300; F. W. Mead, £275.

Foreman of Works: G. M. N'Jie, £150.

Accountant: Vacant.

Storekeeper: John C. Fye, £85.

AUDIT DEPARTMENT.

Local Auditor: E. N. Lubbock, £350.
Clerk: S. F. N'Jie, £75.

GOVERNMENT VESSELS.

Chief Engineer and Master: R. F. Batty, £300, and £50 allowance.
Assistant Engineer: T. W. Hart, £200, and £50 allowance.
Purser: Henry Venn, £60.

POST OFFICE.

Postmaster: The Treasurer.
Assistant Postmaster: A. K. Lewis, £150 to £200 by £10 per annum.
Chief Clerk: I. G. McCarthy, £100.
Assistant Clerk: C. M. Savage, £50 to £75 per annum.
Sorter: Thomas Williams, £24 to £36 per annum.

All European officers are provided either with furnished quarters, on which they pay 2½ per cent. on the value of the furniture, or with lodging allowance, calculated at the rate of 10 per cent. of their salary.

FOREIGN CONSULS.

Belgium: Appointment vacant at present.
United States: Appointment vacant at present.
France: F. Orcel, Consular Agent.
Portugal: Hon. A. L. Bennett.
Spain: Appointment vacant at present.

BRITISH CONSULS.

British Consul at Dakar: Captain C. F. Cromie.
British Vice-Consul at Dakar: Horatio G. Mackie.

KEY HOLDERS OF THE VAULT.

The Treasurer: Hon. F. Bisset Archer.
The Attorney-General: Hon. W. R. Townsend.
The Superintendent of Police: J. Brown.

INSTRUCTIONS (dated November 1st, 1899) FOR THE GUIDANCE OF THE TRAVELLING COMMISSIONERS.

1. The commissioner will, on return to duty in November, before proceeding to his district, obtain from the treasurer an advance sufficient to pay the annual stipends allowed to the head chiefs, &c., and properly receipted vouchers for such must be returned to the treasurer before the end of the year in time to be included in the payments of the colony for the year.

2. The commissioner must submit to the Colonial Secretary, for publication in the "Gazette," a list showing the places and dates where he proposes to hold courts up to the end of March. If unable to hold court on the date fixed, the commissioner should adjourn the court to a subsequent date and report it.

3. On first passing through his district after his return in November, the commissioner will obtain full particulars of all cases heard by the native courts, and forward a return of the same, not later than the 31st of December, to the Chief Magistrate, made out for the four months July-October.

4. All other monthly returns required to be prepared when the commissioners are present should be treated similarly in one return for the four months, July-October.

5. All returns should be sent under flying seal through the Colonial Secretary, addressed to the respective heads of departments by whom they are required.

6. In January the commissioner should inspect all the messengers in every town, and should count the number of badges issued and check them to see that none have been lost. The result of this inspection when complete must be submitted by March. If a badge is lost the value, 1s., should be recovered in addition to any other punishment.

7. The commission allowed by the Government to head chiefs and headmen, on yard tax and other items of revenue collected by them, will be payable at the Treasury in January every year on the actual receipts shown by the Treasury books to have been collected in the previous year, due provision being made in the estimates for these disbursements.

8. Each commissioner will receive the total amount payable in his district and distribute it amongst the several head chiefs, &c., as soon as possible, sending all vouchers, when complete, to the treasurer.

9. Court fees, payable to messengers, or for special work approved by the Governor, can be made at the time and charged in the monthly account which the commissioner has to render to the treasurer.

10. The commissioner should be present as often as possible at any native court held in his district, and report the fact of his doing so and how the court was conducted. It is an important part of his duty to explain the practice of the native courts to the head chiefs, &c., and to do all he possibly can to assist in their proper conduct.

11. If a head chief, sub-chief or any other person appointed by the Governor dies or vacates his office, the commissioner

should at once report the fact with his recommendations for filling the vacancy.

12. No new town is to be built without the sanction of the commissioner, who should endeavour to fix upon an appropriate name for it. Towns are not to be built under any circumstances within 100 yards of the Anglo-French boundary line.

13. All correspondence which has a registered number on it should be returned to the Colonial Secretary, with the report of the commissioner, not later than one month after its issue.

14. Any headman who neglects to report any case of slave dealing in his town should be punished, and the fact at once reported.

15. The sale of cap-guns and caps, as well as breech-loaders with their ammunition, has been prohibited for some years. If the commissioner sees any new guns or ammunition of the above description he should confiscate them, as they must have been smuggled into the protectorate.

16. The commissioners should not allow Arabs, Moors and wandering professional beggars to settle in any town in their district.

17. A constable belonging to the Bathurst Police Force is not allowed to arrest any native in the protectorate. All arrests are to be made by the messengers acting under orders of the head chief or headman.

18. If a commissioner on any emergency requires assistance of a Bathurst policeman he should apply to the Colonial Secretary for instructions, who will, if possible, send the required assistance which shall only take action in the presence of the commissioner who is responsible for law and order in his district.

19. The Police Force of Bathurst in any number cannot be employed in the protectorate except with the approval of the Governor.

20. The Governor does not wish the head chiefs or any of the inhabitants of the protectorate to send him "presents." The commissioners should acquaint the people of this, and they should not themselves accept presents nor allow their interpreters to do so. All services rendered by the people as carriers, and the persons who supply the commissioners with wood and water, &c., should be paid *in cash*. This change from the "old custom" can be gradually worked out with tact and discretion, and is not intended to be too rigidly enforced in trifling articles.

21. The commissioner should remit any cash he may have on hand in excess of £25 as soon as possible to the treasurer,

and at the end of every month submit a copy of his cash-book showing the month's transactions.

22. During the tax collecting season the commissioner should employ, when he has a large balance, a messenger as watchman.

23. Specie should be sent on board the *Mansah Kilah* in charge of the interpreter with an escort if necessary, and a receipt obtained from the purser.

24. The alphabetical list of towns in each district should be revised by the commissioner every year in June, and a copy of the list sent to the Governor to be reprinted during the rainy season.

25. Each commissioner is required to submit a monthly diary of his work and report not later than the end of June, showing what work he has done, and other general information relating to his district, and to close up his accounts satisfactorily with the treasurer before going on leave.

26. The commissioner must leave with his interpreter general instructions as to what he is to do during the rainy season, and leave a copy of such instructions with the Colonial Secretary.

27. The commissioner should deposit with the treasurer prior to leaving the colony the abstract-book, cash-book and licence-books. His box and medicine chest with their keys should be left at the Colonial Secretary's office, together with all registered minute papers not dealt with, and a report explaining why the subjects have not been disposed of.

MONTHLY RETURNS.

1. Statement of revenue and expenditure each month.
2. Analysis of ,, ,, ,, ,,
3. Commissioner's court cases each month.
4. Native ,, ,, ,,

RATE OF TRAVELLING ALLOWANCES, Ordinance No. 8 of 1895.

	Per diem.
The Governor	£3 0 0
Officers in receipt of an annual salary of £300 and upwards	1 0 0
Officers in receipt of an annual salary of £150 and upwards, but less than £300	0 10 0
Officers in receipt of an annual salary of £75 and upwards, but less than £150	0 5 0
Officers in receipt of an annual salary of £50 and upwards, but less than £75, and non-commissioned officers of the Police Force	0 1 6
Constables and others (not boatmen)..	0 1 0

Special Rules as to Leave of Absence and Passages for Officers of the Colonies and Protectorates in West Africa.

*424.—(*a*) Subject to the necessities of the Service, European officers, that is to say, officers who were not themselves born in West Africa and neither of whose parents was born there, may, after every tour of twelve consecutive months of residential service, be granted vacation leave with full pay, for two calendar months *plus* the time necessarily taken on the journey to England; and, if specially detained by the Governor or High Commissioner on public grounds after the completion of a tour of service, they may be granted vacation leave for ten days more with full pay in respect of each calendar month that they may have been detained, but no additional leave will be granted in respect of any fraction of a month.

(*b*) In the case of officers who are returning to West Africa, there may be added to their vacation leave a further period of leave with full pay, known as "return leave," for two calendar months *plus* the time necessarily taken on the journey from England. Officers to whom return leave is granted will be required to sign an agreement to the effect that, in the event of their failing to return to the colony or protectorate they will, if called upon to do so, refund the amount of any pay drawn in respect of such leave.

(*c*) No extension of vacation leave will be granted with full pay, but, in exceptional circumstances, such as continued ill-health, officers who are not returning may be granted an extension of leave with half pay, at the discretion of the Secretary of State.

(*d*) Return leave may be extended with half pay on the ground of ill-health for any period not exceeding three calendar months; or with full pay if the officer is detained in England by the Secretary of State on public grounds.

(*e*) Any extension, however short, which may be granted on any other grounds than those mentioned must be without pay.

(*f*) An officer returning to West Africa will be required to embark by the first steamer leaving England after the date on which his leave of absence expires, and will be allowed pay at the rate which he is then drawing for any days which may elapse between the expiration of his leave and the departure of the steamer; provided that, if there is a later steamer which is timed to arrive at his destination before

* The numbers of these paragraphs are the numbers which appear against them in the Colonial Office Rules and Regulations.

the first one, he will be required to proceed by the later one. Extensions of leave will date from the expiration of the original leave, and not from the day on which the officer would have had to embark if his leave had not been extended.

425.—(*a*) Officers invalided before completing a tour of service may be granted sick leave with full pay for the time necessarily taken on the journey to England *plus* five days in respect of each completed calendar month of residential service. In the case of continued ill-health, this leave may be extended by the Secretary of State with half pay for such period not exceeding four months as he may think proper.

(*b*) In addition to the sick leave which may be granted under the foregoing rule, officers returning to West Africa may be granted "return sick leave" for five days more (making ten days in all), in respect of each completed calendar month of residential service *plus* the time necessarily taken on the journey from England, subject to the same conditions with regard to repayment and date of embarkation as return leave. They will be allowed full pay for the period of the voyage from England, and half pay for any days which may elapse between the end of their leave and the departure of the steamer by which they have to return.

(*c*) If invalided out of the colony, but not to Europe, an officer may either draw full pay and pay all his own expenses or draw half pay and have the cost of his passages paid by the Government, as the Governor or High Commissioner may decide; and in such cases (that is to say, if the officer does not visit Europe) he will not be required to begin a new tour of service on his return, but the two periods of service will be regarded as consecutive residential service. Leave granted under this rule should not exceed three months, and must be reported to the Secretary of State.

426. Officers desiring leave, on the ground of "urgent private affairs," before completing a tour of residential service, may, if specially recommended by the Governor or High Commissioner, be allowed leave without pay, or if they have completed six months of residential service, leave with half pay, at the discretion of the Secretary of State; but such leave must in no case exceed four months, inclusive of the time taken on the journeys.

427. Officers to whom the three foregoing regulations apply are required to discharge any duties upon which the Governor or High Commissioner may think it desirable to employ them; and they are not entitled to receive any available half salary under the 107th and 108th regulations, in addition to the

salary of their own office, for performing the duties of an office vacated by the death or removal or temporary absence of the holder, but they will draw the duty allowance when acting in any office to which such an allowance is attached.

They may also be required by the Secretary of State to discharge any duty or to go through any course of instruction which he may think necessary during their leave of absence, and will not be entitled to any additional remuneration or leave of absence in consideration of such employment. Allowances granted to cover necessary out-of-pocket expenses are not regarded as remuneration.

428. Free passages to England and out again will be allowed to all officers under the rank of Governor who may be granted leave of absence under the 424th and 425th regulations; and a free passage out will be allowed on their first appointment of all such officers on their executing the usual agreement under which they will be bound to refund the cost of the passage in the event of their relinquishing their appointment within three years from the date of their arrival in the colony or protectorate for any other reason than bodily or mental infirmity. Passages will not be granted to wives or children under the 153rd regulation.

429. If an officer is transferred while in West Africa from one West African colony or protectorate to another, he will be regarded as having completed a tour of service in the colony or protectorate to which he is transferred when the sum of his service in the two colonies or protectorates amounts to twelve months, and the whole of his salary during leave of absence will be paid from the funds of the last colony or protectorate.

430. The foregoing regulations (424 to 429) do not apply to native officers, that is to say, officers who were themselves born in West Africa or whose parents were either of them born there. All such officers are subject to the general regulations as to leave of absence and passages, with the exception that they are not entitled to any pay under the 107th and 108th regulations when acting in the place of an European officer. They will, however, in lieu of such pay, draw the duty allowance when acting in any office to which a duty allowance is attached; and when they are acting for an European officer and not receiving any duty allowance, the Governor may, if he thinks fit, award a gratuity in respect of such acting service, subject to the approval of the Secretary of State.

Instructions for Officers Proceeding on Leave of Absence.

1. On arriving in England an officer must address a letter to "The Under Secretary of State, Colonial Office, London," as well as to "The Crown Agents for the Colonies, Downing Street, London, S.W.," reporting the date of his arrival and mentioning the place of his residence. Any subsequent change of address must also be notified both to the Under Secretary of State and to the Crown Agents.

2. Officers must apply direct to the Crown Agents for the Colonies, and not to the Colonial Office, for the forms required to enable them to draw their pay. But they must not apply to the Crown Agents until they have received from the Colonial Government a copy of the usual "leave certificate" signed by the Governor which should be furnished to every officer before he leaves the colony. A "last pay certificate" is of no use for this purpose. Officers should not transmit their copy of the leave certificate either to the Crown Agents or to the Colonial Office, unless called upon to do so.

3. If an officer does not receive the usual leave certificate before leaving the colony and it does not reach him by the next mail after his arrival in England, he may ask the Under Secretary of State to authorise the Crown Agents to issue a portion of his pay before the certificate is received; but in that case he must explain why he cannot wait until the certificate has arrived; and must send to the Colonial Office (1) a last pay certificate and (2) the original letter or telegram from the Colonial Government allowing him to leave the colony. If the Secretary of State is satisfied that there are sufficient grounds for making an exception, the necessary authority will be given to the Crown Agents; and on learning from the Colonial Office that this has been done, the officer may then, and not till then, apply to the Crown Agents for his pay.

4. Applications for an advance of salary must be made to the Under Secretary of State and not to the Crown Agents, and *no communication on any other subject should be introduced into such applications.* Advances will only be granted to officers about to return to the colony, and will, except in very special cases, be limited to the amount of one month's salary.

5. An officer seeking an extension of leave must apply to the Under Secretary of State at least one clear month before the time when he ought to embark for the colony under the conditions of his existing leave, and must state the grounds on which he asks for the extension. Any extension, however short, which

may be granted on any other ground than that of ill-health will be without salary.

6. An officer returning to the colony after leave of absence (other than leave on urgent private affairs, in which case he has to provide his own passages) must apply by letter, at least twenty-one days before he has to leave England, to the Under Secretary of State, and not to the Crown Agents, to have his passage taken, naming the date of the departure of the steamer by which he proposes to go, and the address to which the passage ticket should be sent. The Crown Agents will then be instructed to take the passage, and to send the ticket direct to the officer. *No communications on any other subject should be introduced into a letter applying for a passage.*

7. The attention of officers is called to the following extract from the Colonial Regulations, No. 424 (*f*):—"An officer returning to West Africa will be required to embark by the first steamer leaving England after the date on which his leave of absence expires, and will be allowed pay at the rate which he is then drawing for any days which may elapse between the expiration of his leave and the departure of the steamer; provided that, if there is a later steamer which is timed to arrive at his destination before the first one, he will be required to proceed by the later one. Extensions of leave will date from the expiration of the original leave, and not from the day on which the officer would have had to embark if this leave had not been extended."

It is the duty of the officer himself to see that the steamer which he names in his application for a passage is the correct one under the rules quoted, and an officer who fails to return to the colony in proper time is liable to be treated as having forfeited his appointment.

8. The foregoing directions apply to all officers, whether they were originally selected for appointment by the Secretary of State or by the Crown Agents for the Colonies.

9. It should be clearly understood that, in the absence of any recommendation from the Governor, increments will not be sanctioned by the Secretary of State, and that officers on leave of absence whose increments have not been sanctioned on their leave certificates should apply to the colony and NOT to the Colonial Office or to the Crown Agents for the Colonies for permission to draw such increments.

10. (*a*) Every officer before applying for permission to proceed on leave of absence will obtain from the medical officer of his station a certificate as to his state of health, and, in case he is not in good health, the certificate must contain a recommendation as to the course he should pursue on his arrival in the

United Kingdom, and must be accompanied by the notes of the case. He will forward these papers to the Governor or High Commissioner through the proper channel when applying for leave of absence, and they will be enclosed in the despatch notifying to the Secretary of State the leave of absence which has been granted.

(*b*) When the officer arrives in the United Kingdom he will receive instructions to present himself to one of the medical advisers of the Colonial Office if that course is recommended by the local medical officer, and in any case he will be required to show that the recommendations of the local medical officer are being carried out.

(*c*) If an officer falls ill, so as to require medical attendance, during the voyage home or during his leave of absence, and remains ill for a week, he will report the fact to the Colonial Office and will send a fortnightly report from his medical attendant as long as he remains under his care.

(*d*) Unless these rules are observed, an officer will not be entitled to pay during any extension of leave which it may be necessary to grant him on the ground of ill-health.

11. In order to avoid delay in obtaining salary on arrival in the colony officers who are returning from leave should at least a fortnight before sailing inform the Crown Agents of the day up to which they desire to draw their pay in England.

Rules for Granting Vacation and Sick Leave to Native Officers of the Gambia Colony.

Vacation Leave.

The rules given below are those in force relating to the granting of vacation leave to native officers:—

1. The following vacation leave may be granted to native officers by the Governor, provided the exigencies of the service so allow:—

Officers in receipt of salaries at the rate of £150 per annum and upwards: Three months in any two years.

Officers in receipt of salaries at the rate of £100 and under £150 per annum: Two months in any two years.

Officers in receipt of salaries at the rate of £50 and under £100 per annum: One month in any two years.

Officers with salaries under £50 per annum: Twenty days in any two years.

2. There will be no abatement of salary during leave; but the officer absenting himself must, with the concurrence and sanction of the Governor, have made such arrangements as may be necessary for the adequate discharge of his duties without cost to the public.

No accumulation of leave will be permitted unless under very special circumstances.

3. All periods of leave of one day and upwards, except on medical certificate, are to be entered in a book to be kept for the purpose at the secretariat, and must be taken into account when calculating the vacation leave to which an officer is entitled.

4. A record of all vacation leave granted to native officers will be kept at the secretariat and the chief clerk will be responsible for the correctness of such record.

Sick Leave.

1. An officer not subject to the provisions of Chapter XVIII. of the Colonial Office regulations may, in case of illness, be absent on full pay without forfeiting vacation leave for a period not exceeding ten days at any one time or twenty-eight days in the space of one calendar year, provided his illness is duly certified by a medical officer within twenty-four hours of his first absenting himself. Failing such certificate he will be considered absent without leave, and will not receive salary for any period he may be so absent, unless on field duty or in an outstation where it is impossible to obtain a medical certificate and the head of his department is satisfied of its being a *bonâ-fide* case of illness.

2. If at the end of such time the medical officer certifies the officer's continued inability through illness to perform the duties of his office, he may remain absent on full pay for the full period of any vacation leave he may be entitled to. Such further absence should be reported to the Colonial Secretary in order that the period of vacation leave claimable may be decided.

3. Upon the return of an officer, the period of absence should be reported to the Colonial Secretary in due course. All absences from duty on account of ill-health in excess of twenty-eight days in one year or in excess of ten days at a time must be deducted from vacation leave to the extent to which vacation leave is due. Absence on medical certificate beyond the period for which vacation can be claimed must be on half pay.

4. Where there is a Government medical officer within reach his certificate only should be accepted by heads of departments as evidence of the inability of any officer to attend office on account of ill-health.

Family Remittances.

The privilege of remitting through the Crown Agents is only intended to apply to cases where officers desire to make regular and periodical provisions for insurance purposes, or for the support of their wives or other members of their family, and it is not to be used for occasional remittances to discharge debts, or to pay for goods ordered in England, or other matters of a similar nature.

The amount to be remitted by an officer through the Crown Agents must not, except in cases specially authorised by the Secretary of State, exceed the half of his salary in any one year, and it will be the duty of the Colonial Treasurer to take care that drafts beyond this amount are not issued.

The remittances should be made in equal monthly instalments.

The applications for such remittances are to be sent in to the Treasury at or before the time fixed for sending in the Schedule of Personal Emoluments.

Public Officers Trading.

All salaried public officers are prohibited from engaging in trade or connecting themselves with any commercial undertaking without leave from the Governor approved by the Secretary of State. As a general rule this prohibition will be made absolute in the case of officers whose remuneration is fixed on the assumption that their whole time is at the disposal of the Government. No officer on leave of absence or on vacation leave is permitted to accept any employment without previously obtaining the express sanction of the Governor or of the Secretary of State.

No paid officer under the government of a colony can be permitted to be the editor of a newspaper, or to take any active part in the management of it. He may furnish articles signed with his name upon subjects of general interest, abstaining from writing on questions which can properly be called political, or discussing the measures of the Government, or the official proceedings of its officers and from furnishing any articles whatever to a newspaper which, in commenting on the measures of the Government, should habitually exceed the bounds of fair and temperate discussion. If the authorship of anonymous articles should be brought home to any officer, or if, in articles bearing his signature, he should discuss any political subject, or the measures of the Government, or the official proceedings of its officers, he will be liable to be removed from office.

General Regulations laying down the Method of Correspondence to be observed in the Government.

Colony of Gambia.

1. All communications for the Governor, or between the different departments of the Government, will pass through the secretariat.

2. It is at times desirable in the interests of the public service, and economical in the matter of time, that the Governor should convey his instructions direct to public officers, verbally or otherwise, instead of through the usual channel, the secretariat; but in all such cases His Excellency wishes it to be distinctly understood that it is the duty of the officer receiving such instructions to at once forward the same in writing to the Colonial Secretary in order that they may be duly confirmed and recorded.

Letters.

3. All letters sent on official matters by departments of the Government are to be dated and numbered and must be entered in a letter book, to be kept for the purpose, before they leave the office from which they emanate. They should be confined to a single subject and the number and date of previous correspondence, if any, should be quoted in the left hand top corner under the index number.

4. All fair copies of letters sent out must bear the initials (very small in left hand bottom corner) of the officer who checked the correspondence with the copying clerk.

5. When officers are addressed by letter it is their duty to convey their reply in the same form.

6. All letters received by a department, from other than official sources, are to be at once transmitted to the secretariat and a report on their contents by the head of the department should invariably accompany them. Copies of the entire correspondence must be recorded in the department to which the original letters were in the first instance addressed.

7. When the initiation of any subject matter is with a department it will be the duty of the head of that department to address the Colonial Secretary by letter.

Minutes.

8. A minute paper is of the ordinary blue foolscap, and forms a jacket to enclosed correspondence.

9. When any correspondence has been covered by a minute paper it is to be continued by minutes.

10. Communications marked "Confidential" should be kept separate and under lock and key and dealt with by the head of department himself. They should not be entered in the general register of the office but in a confidential register.

11. A full and complete report on the subject brought to notice should always be sent in by heads of departments when they submit any question for the Governor's decision.

12. Applications to incur expenditure under the estimates

should invariably state the vote from which the charge is proposed to be met, and the balance available. Applications to incur expenditure not covered by vote must be accompanied by the fullest information, and will not be sanctioned except under very special circumstances.

13. Any local information which may be required is to be furnished within forty-eight hours. Should detention, however, be unavoidable the minute paper must not be kept back under any circumstances for more than six days. If a coloured slip be placed on a minute paper, pinned at the top, it denotes that the subject must receive immediate attention and that the directions contained in it are to be complied with at once; it is to be returned to the secretariat at the earliest hour possible.

14. Every minute paper will be numbered and the subject of it will be entered in a register to be kept for that purpose at the secretariat.

15. All minutes in connection with a single document or set of documents should follow consecutively the original minute written on the minute paper by the officer who first transmitted it. Special reports of considerable length may be written separately and enclosed with the documents in the minute paper. In this case the forwarding officer should write in due order on the minute paper the words "Report submitted herewith."

16. Minutes should never be written on original documents, only on the front sheet of the jacket and enclosed continuation sheets in consecutive order. Nor should they on any account be written on the last sheet of foolscap forming the jacket.

17. The usual blank quarter margin should be preserved on the continuation sheets. They should be endorsed with the reference number of the minute paper, which will be the same as that of its first or principal enclosure and they should also bear on them the page number of the correspondence. Each document enclosed in a minute paper should also bear the reference number of the minute paper. By this means documents accidentally separated can be replaced together in their proper "jacket."

18. Documents relating to correspondence already jacketted, and in the receiving office should, on receipt, be placed and forwarded with such correspondence, and not in a fresh minute paper. This will avoid the needless multiplication of minute papers.

19. The minute papers in which documents are jacketted are for the use of the departments of Government only, and should not be communicated to others than officers of the Colonial Government.

20. Original documents, unless there is special reason, should

not be allowed to pass beyond the departments of the Government. In the event of its being necessary to communicate their contents to persons not in the Government service, certified copies must be prepared for the purpose.

21. Heads of departments will forward to the secretariat every Monday morning a return, duly signed in the form provided for the purpose, showing what minute papers are in their possession and the reason why such minute papers have not been dealt with in accordance with the instructions which are inserted at the head of the minute form.

In the event of there being no minute papers with a department the usual form of returns, duly signed, will be sent in with the word "Nil" inserted in the blank spaces.

22. All communications and representations from subordinate officers will be forwarded through the head of the department to which they belong. It will be the duty of the head of the department to furnish with every such communication or representation a full report on the circumstances of the case.

Returns.

23. A full statement of the returns to be supplied by the different departments throughout the colony is to be hung up in the secretariat.

24. A statement showing the returns to be furnished by a department is to be hung up in the office of that department.

25. In every case the statements mentioned should contain the date on which the returns therein referred to are to be rendered.

General.

26. The chief clerk of every department will keep a diary, to be written up day by day, in which a record is to be made of all noticeable occurrences; notes are also to be made in it of matters for future consideration.

27. In no case are knife erasures to be made in any official account, document or record. When errors occur in any accounts, documents or records, a line should be drawn through them, and the corrections distinctly inserted over or under the original entry in red ink. Any such alteration should always be attested by the initials of the officer responsible for the accounts, documents or records in question.

28. Requisitions for stationery are to be rendered to the Colonial Secretary on the first Monday of each half-year, and are to be made out on the requisition forms supplied, and which have the following headings:—

1. Articles.
2. On hand at end of previous half-year.
3. Received for last half-year.
4. Total.
5. Expended during the half-year.
6. Remaining on hand.
7. Quantity now required.
8. Quantity received.
9. Remarks.

29. All gazettes, ordinances or other printed matter that are issued from time to time to heads of departments must be regularly guarded and treated as official records.

30. A statement giving the names and addresses of all employés of a department must be hung up in the department to which such employés belong.

Procedure to be Followed as Regards Bills of Lading, Crown Agents' Invoices and Crown Agents' Accounts Current.

31. Requisitions from the colony are made on the Crown Agents, with the approval in writing of the Governor.

32. When such requisitions are complied with stamped bills of lading and the usual invoices are received by the Colonial Secretary.

33. The Colonial Secretary will in each case furnish heads of departments with the stamped bills of lading, which must not be given up until all the packages enumerated upon them have been delivered in good condition, or otherwise satisfactorily accounted for. If any package appears to be so damaged as to render it probable that its contents have suffered exceptionally in transit, a report of the circumstance is to be made to the Colonial Secretary, who will cause a Board of Survey to assemble at which the agent of the steamship company is to be invited to be present. Failure in the above directed duties will render the head of the department concerned primarily responsible for any deficiency.

34. Invoices are to be compared in the secretariat with original requisitions in order that the Colonial Secretary may see whether they agree or differ. Any difference in the supply must at once be brought to the notice of the Governor and communicated to the Treasurer.

35. Invoices are to be referred from the secretariat to the head of department concerned, who will check the articles received and report their condition and full or short delivery. All such stores are to be entered in the detail shown in the

invoice in the store ledger o the department, and the fact of such entry reported to the secretariat. A copy of the invoice is to be made and posted in a guard book for reference.

36. Invoices are to be referred from the secretariat to the Treasurer, who will note the authority and the amount expended, and will see that the Crown Agents have sufficient balance to meet the current expenses of the Government.

37. The Crown Agents' monthly accounts current are to be submitted to the Governor. They must then be referred to the Treasurer, whose duty it is to satisfy himself that they are fully supported by vouchers. The Treasurer will also have the items properly classified, will deal with the accounts as laid down under authority, and report compliance with these instructions to the secretariat.

38. The monthly accounts current are to be kept in the Treasury and bound at the close of each year.

Franking of Correspondence.

No postage shall be payable for the transmission by the Postal Department of any postal matter sent or received by the Governor, or any postal matter sent or received by any public department in connection with the business of such department.

Provided that any postal matter sent by a public department shall be liable to postage unless franked by the signature of the head of such department or by a commissioner in charge of a district, or by some officer authorised to frank by the Governor, such authorisation having first been published in the *Gazette*.

RETURNS AND REPORTS FURNISHED BY GOVERNMENT OFFICES.

A list of returns and reports furnished by the various government offices is given at the end of this chapter.

RULES RELATING TO OFFICERS TRANSFERRED FROM MILITARY TO CIVIL APPOINTMENTS.

1. The officer transferred receives on appointment the minimum salary of his new post, and his increments date from the date of his new appointment. Exceptions to this rule will only be made on the recommendation of the Governor or High Commissioner and when approved by the Secretary of State, and only in cases where it is shown that the officer will lose pecuniarily by the change, or when some special circumstances justify exceptional treatment.

2. The seniority of the officer in his civil employment would, similarly, not be affected by previous service in the West African Frontier Force. It should be borne in mind

that an officer who applies to be transferred from the West African Frontier Force to a civil employment does so because he considers that his prospects of advancement will be improved by a transfer, and that in the case of officers of the Militia the advantages of obtaining civil employment are very great, although no immediate pecuniary benefit may accrue on transfer.

The passages of Government officers who are transferred on promotion from one West African colony to another will in future be governed by the following rule (Clause 428) Colonial Office Rules and Regulations:—

"Free passages home and out again will be allowed to all officers under the rank of Governor who may be granted leave of absence under the 424th and 425th regulations, and a free passage to the West Coast will be allowed on their first appointment to all subordinate officers whose salaries do not exceed £600 per annum, but passages will not be granted to wives or children under the 153rd regulation."

The Hours of Attendance at the Following Offices, viz.:—

The Governor's office, Colonial Secretary's office, Printing office, Treasury department, Customs (indoor branch), Post office, Judicial department, Attorney-General's office, Registrar's office, Superintendent's of Police office, Medical department (clerical staff), Local Auditor's office and the Colonial Engineer's office, are:—

On week days, other than Saturdays, 8 to 11 a.m., and 1 to 4 p.m. On Saturdays 8 to 11 a.m.

The Customs Out-Door Branch.

On week days, other than Saturdays, 6.30 to 10 a.m., and 11.30 a.m. to 5 p.m. On Saturdays 6.30 to 10 a.m., and 11.30 to 3 p.m.

Colonial Engineer's Office (Mechanics, Labourers, &c.).

On week days, other than Saturdays, 6 to 11 a.m., and 12.30 to 5 p.m. On Saturdays 6 to 11 a.m.

Days to be Observed as Public Holidays.

New Year's day, Good Friday, Easter Monday, Empire day, to wit the 24th day of May, being the anniversary of the birthday of Her late Majesty Queen Victoria of glorious memory; the 3rd day of June, being the anniversary of the birthday of His Royal Highness the Prince of Wales; the 9th day of November, being the anniversary of the birthday of His Majesty the King; Christmas day and Boxing day.

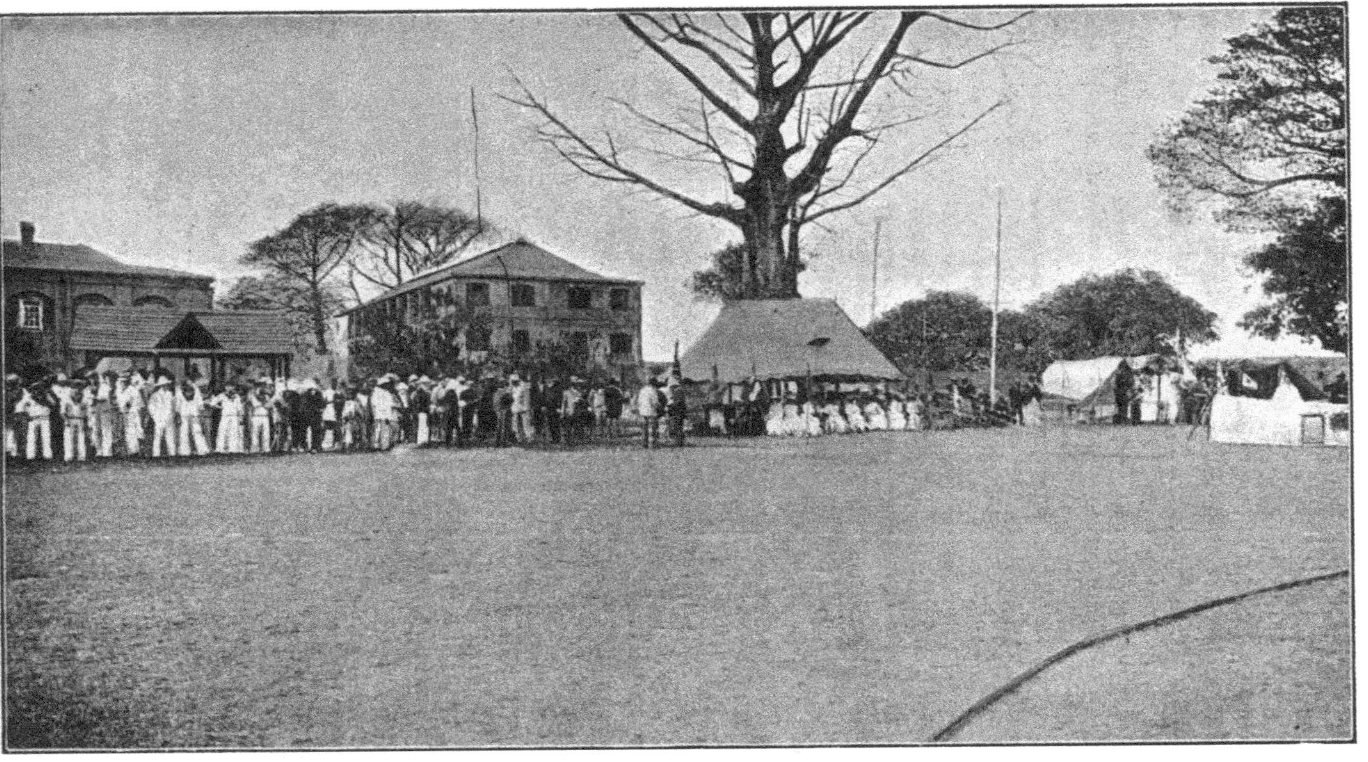

The first Gymkhana held at Bathurst.

Rules to be Observed before Certificates are Granted to Employees Resigning.

Officers have to observe the following regulations as regards the granting of certificates of character and service:—

(*a*) No officer in the Government service will give a certificate of character or of service or of both to anyone who is or has been in the Government service without obtaining previous sanction.

(*b*) In obtaining such sanction the certificate proposed to be given will be forwarded to the Colonial Secretary for his approval and counter signature.

Return of Pensioners in the Colony of the Gambia.

Names.	Amount of Pension. £	s.	d.	Names.	Amount of Pension. £	s.	d.
J. H. Montserrat ..	50	0	0	N. D. Thomas ..	12	15	6
Edwin Adolpus ..	15	19	4	R. J. Williams ..	39	0	0
T. L. Ingram ..	133	6	8	J. W. Davis.. ..	5	11	0
W. J. Davis.. ..	34	1	7	M. J. W. Rocks ..	15	8	0
W. J. Mercer ..	10	0	0	W. Haydon.. ..	28	2	6
J. Maxwell	18	0	0	G. B. Dick	10	19	0
J. C. Bauer	107	18	4	A. John	13	19	10
J. A. Davis	18	8	0	J. T. Coker	47	18	0
G. C. Nicol.. ..	180	0	0	G. J. Thomas ..	62	10	0
S. B. Rose	20	5	0	G. A. B. Artley ..	17	5	8
					£841	8	5

Information as to Colonial Appointments.

The patronage of the Secretary of State for the Colonies is confined to those colonies and countries which are administered under his directions.

As a general rule each colony has its own public service distinct from that of every other colony; and it is only the higher officers who are transferred by the Secretary of State from one colony to another.

Offices of which the emoluments do not exceed £100 a year are invariably filled by the appointment of local candidates selected by the Governor, who has the absolute disposal of all such appointments.

When a vacancy occurs in an office of which the emoluments exceed £100 and do not exceed £200 a year, the Governor reports it to the Secretary of State, together with the name and qualification of the person whom he has appointed to fill it provisionally, and this recommendation is almost uniformly followed.

When a vacancy occurs in an office of which the emoluments exceed £200 a year, the Governor follows the same course as to reporting the vacancy and provisional appointment, and he is at liberty to recommend a candidate for the final appointment; but it is distinctly understood that the Secretary of State has the power of nominating another instead.

This power is, however, seldom exercised in favour of persons not already in the public service. Vacancies are usually filled by promotion; and, as a general rule, it is only in the case of the highest offices, and those requiring professional or other special qualifications not to be found in the colonies themselves, that appointments are made by the Secretary of State from the home country.

The following administrative and political appointments in the Gambia are usually filled from the home country as vacancies occur:—

Travelling commissioners, salary £300 (with 10s. a day while travelling).

Engineers, surveyors, and foremen of works, when required for the Gambia, are usually obtained through the Crown Agents for the Colonies. The Crown Agents have in their hands the selection of such officers for public works (railways, &c.) carried out through them, and they also select for clerical and medical appointments in connection with the works.

Offices for which solicitors are required are almost always filled by the appointment of local candidates. But there are a few appointments, such as minor registrarships, for which solicitors, as well as barristers, are regarded as eligible.

Barristers are required as registrars, law officers, judges, in some instances as magistrates.

Supervisors of customs and assistant treasurers or accountants are required from time to time in the West African colonies and protectorates, with salaries ranging from £250 to £350, according to colony. Only candidates with the necessary experience are selected.

For military officers there are appointments of two classes, Civil Police (including prison appointments) and Military Police. Of the former posts there are few, and no precise qualifications have been laid down, but a knowledge of Civil Police work is in all cases essential. Military Police appointments are described in a separate memorandum. All candidates should be between twenty-two and thirty and unmarried, must hold commissions in the Army or Militia, should hold an officer's certificate from the School of Musketry at Hythe, and (if Militia officers) must have served three trainings with their battalion, and be in possession of a *P.S.* certificate or a certificate for promotion to the rank of captain. Higher military posts are filled by promotion. Appointments in the West African Frontier Force are made by the Secretary of State for the Colonies on the recommendation of the Secretary of State for War, and applications should be addressed to the War Office and not to the Colonial Office.

The salaries attached to appointments in West Africa are higher than those attached to similar appointments elsewhere, and West African service also carries with it special privileges in respect of leave of absence and pension. These advantages are granted on account of the unhealthiness of the climate, and any officer desiring to be transferred must be prepared to take less pay in another colony. It should also be clearly understood that it is impossible for more than a very small proportion of all the officers serving in West Africa to be transferred, and that no applications for transfer can be entertained until an officer has served five years in West Africa.

Medical officers are from time to time selected by the Secretary of State for service in the colonies. A large proportion of these appointments are on the West Coast of Africa, and the proportion has greatly increased during the past few years, owing to considerable extensions of the staff in West Africa and to the general reduction in West Indian establishments. Applicants must be between the ages of twenty-three and thirty (twenty-five and thirty-five in the case of West African appointments), and doubly qualified; preference will be given to unmarried candidates, and to those who have held hospital appointments as house physicians and house surgeons. Selected candidates may be required to undergo a course of training, before taking up appointments, at the School of Tropical Medicine in London or Liverpool. Appointments in the West African Medical Staff carry with them certain privileges (*e.g.*, gratuities on retirement after nine years' service or more), details as to which, with other information, are contained in a pamphlet which will be furnished on application to the Colonial Office. The higher posts are filled by promotion or transfer, but the headships of medical departments in the larger colonies, which are posts requiring administrative as well as professional qualifications, are sometimes filled from outside the service, and there are occasional, though very rare, vacancies for which specialists are required—*e.g.*, the charge of a lunatic asylum. Surgeons-superintendent of vessels carrying coolie emigrants from India are selected by the Crown Agents for the Colonies, who are also entrusted with the selection of medical officers required in connection with public works carried out through them.

All applications for appointments described above as being filled by selection of the Secretary of State must be addressed to the Secretary of State for the Colonies, Downing-street, S.W. Forms are supplied by the Private Secretary, which the candidate must fill with full particulars regarding his career and qualifications, and the employment he desires; he must name on the form two referees who will answer from personal knowledge for his character and capacity, and he must return it to the Private Secretary with originals and copies of testimonials (not more than six), which must be sent in all together. The originals will be inspected and returned to the candidate, and the copies retained for record in the Colonial Office. If the candidate is considered suitable his name will be noted in the list, and will be considered with those of other candidates as vacancies from time to time occur; but no promise can in any case be made, and no definite prospect whatever can be held out, that the Secretary of State will be in a position to offer employment to any particular candidate. If a candidate is offered an appointment, he can usually be allowed sufficient time to make preparations and to terminate the employment in which he may be engaged.

HINTS ON OUTFIT FOR THE WEST COAST OF AFRICA.

Clothing.

1. Europeans wear on the West Coast of Africa the same clothing as in England in the height of summer, but the waistcoat is generally discarded in favour of a cummerbund. Flannel trousers and suits of dark blue serge, or of the thin tweeds which are specially made for the tropics, are much used. In the rainy season an ordinary English summer suit will not be too thick. A suit of evening dress clothes, and a thin black morning coat and waistcoat, should be taken out. A light overcoat will also be found useful.

2. White shirts, with turned down collars, and thin woollen underclothing, are usually worn at headquarters. Merino socks are recommended. Flannel shirts are required for use while travelling. Woollen pyjamas should be worn at night. A couple of cholera belts and a flannel dressing gown should be taken out.

3. Shoes are cooler than boots, and are therefore considered by some to be more comfortable for general use, but others

recommend boots as affording more protection against mosquitoes and sand-flies. Shoes or boots of brown leather or of white canvas are recommended for the dry season; but black ones are better in the rains. A pair of evening shoes or boots should be taken out, and a pair of slippers. Officers whose duties may require them to travel, or whose work is out of doors, should provide themselves with one pair, at least, of lace boots, which should be stout but not too heavy, and a pair of gamekeeper's leggings. For crossings swamps, &c., a pair of high india-rubber rain boots would be useful.

4. A complete set of winter clothes and winter underclothing, and a thick overcoat or ulster, should be taken out by every officer, as his leave of absence may take him to England in the cold weather, and warm clothing is required on board ship. Many officers have had their worst attacks of fever on the homeward voyage through not being provided with warm clothing.

5. Good watches, jewellery, silver flasks and cigar cases, should not be taken out. Waterbury watches keep good time on the coast. A small clock will be found useful.

6. Bullock trunks are better than portmanteaux or wooden boxes. Strong tin boxes of medium size are best for officers who are not resident at headquarters or who may be required to travel—*e.g.*, constabulary officers, district commissioners, and supervisors of customs—as transport is effected by means of native carriers, whose average load is 50 lb. each. It is important to recollect this.

7. Saddlery is required.

8. The following articles should be taken by all officers:—

Helmet: light, pith, coming well over temples and back of neck. (Constabulary officers are required to wear the regulation helmet, which is part of the outfit referred to under the head of "uniform.")

Umbrella: either a white linen one with green lining, or an ordinary black one with a white cover.

Waterproof mackintosh coat, suitable for tropical wear. The seams should be sewn throughout, as those fastened only with composition fall to pieces after a few weeks.

Uniform.

9. Constabulary and police officers must provide themselves with the prescribed uniform. They should also take out with them the following articles: a prismatic compass, a field note book, and a water bottle with vulcanite felt cover. Copies of the dress regulations of each colony can be obtained on ap-

plication at the Colonial Office. Sealed patterns are kept by the Crown Agents for the Colonies, and can be seen in their office.

Quarters.

In the Gambia all officers are granted free *furnished* quarters or an allowance in lieu of quarters. The quarters provided by the Government consist, as a general rule, of two rooms (bed-room and sitting-room) and kitchen accommodation.

The following are the articles of furniture which are generally supplied by the Government of the Gambia to officers' quarters in that colony.

Sitting-room.—One sideboard, one table, three chairs, one Madeira sofa, one Madeira chair.

Bed-room.—One bedstead, one palliasse, one mattress, one bolster, one pillow, one washstand, one toilet set, one towel horse, one press, one small table, two chairs, one bath tub.

Miscellaneous.—One meat safe, one filter and stand, one cooking stove, one bucket, one water drum, one latrine pan and curb, one sand box and scoop.

Household Requisites.

The following list has been compiled for their convenience. They are not required to take out all or any of the articles specified in it, but they are advised to take out those marked with an asterisk. Most of the others can be purchased locally, but the prices are very much higher than in England. As a general rule, it is advisable for officers to take out as little as possible with them; but circumstances vary, and a newly appointed officer should always consult someone who has recently been to the Gambia before deciding how much or how little he will take out with him. If he applies to the Colonial Office, he will be placed in communication with some officer at home on leave of absence who will be able to advise him what to do.

Sitting-room.—Small dinner service, knives (large and small), forks (large and small), spoons (table, dessert and tea), carving knife and fork, tumblers, decanters, wine glasses, cruet stand (travelling recommended), tea pot, coffee pot, milk jug, hot-water jug, cups and saucers, table lamp (with punkah fittings) for kerosine oil, hurricane lantern for kerosine oil (spare chimneys and wicks should be taken for any lamps or lanterns brought out from England), lounge chair (obtainable at Madeira or Grand Canary), spirit lamp and kettle—price 2s. 6d., or nourishment warmer, with kettle and small saucepan—4s. to 6s., table cloths*, napkins*, glass cloths*, dusters*.

Bed-room.—Sheets, if used (some officers think it best to sleep between blankets)*, blankets*, towels (bath and ordinary)*, looking-glass—small, with cover for travelling*, pillows*, pillow cases*, candlesticks (one or two) with small punkah fittings.

Kitchen.—One large kettle (hot water is generally required for baths), one small ditto, one small enamel-lined saucepan, three ordinary saucepans (various sizes), one frying pan, kitchen towelling.

PRECAUTIONS SUGGESTED TO OFFICERS WHO HAVE TO GO OUT IN THE SUN TO PERFORM THEIR DUTIES.

1. Before going to work in the morning an officer should take a fairly substantial breakfast of tea, cocoa or coffee, with eggs, potted meats, or ham and eggs, and fruit.

2. Regularity of the bowels is of prime importance and should be attended to as much as eating and sleeping. The author strongly recommends all officers to take, at about 6 a.m., a glass of water and 5 grains of quinine. It must be remembered that quinine is a preventative and also a tonic, but not a reducer of temperature, in cases of fever. The author has observed the above practice almost regularly since he first came to the West African Coast and has enjoyed excellent health.

3. Exercise, to those who have been in the habit of taking it, is an excellent thing which must never be indulged in when tired or with the head improperly covered. Some men cannot take exercise in this climate without suffering from fever and exhaustion.

4. When arriving at home for meals, or after exercise, all clothes soaked with perspiration should be changed, care being taken that the body is not exposed to any draught.

5. As regards the bath, it is most refreshing after working hours and should be tepid, the body being well soaped all over with carbolic soap. In the morning a sponge down with tepid water is most refreshing.

6. Great care should be exercised in protecting the head from the sun. A helmet which completely shades the forehead, temples, back of the head and nape of the neck, should be worn; and in obtaining one it should be seen that it is ventilated effectively. An umbrella of the tropical kind should always be used, and a large silk handkerchief tied loosely about the neck is of great protection to the neck, especially in stooping.

245–268

List of
RETURNS AND REPORTS
FURNISHED BY
Government Offices

The Royal Instructions of November 28th, 1888, and the Additional Royal Instructions of October 31st 1898, and March 15th, 1902, will be found after the Index (Pages 353 to 364).

LIST OF RETURNS AND REPORTS FURNISHED BY GOVERNMENT OFFICES.

Returns.	Authority.	Furnished. By whom.	Furnished. To whom.	For whom Required.	Number of copies to be furnished.	Remarks.
	TRIENNIALLY.					
Post Office Statistical Returns	Vienna Post Office Convention	Postmaster	G.P.O., London	—	2	
	ANNUALLY.					
Treasury Department.						
Return of Revenue and Expenditure with explanation of Increases and Decreases	Financial Instructions	Treasurer	Colonial Secretary	Governor	3	One copy for Comptroller and Auditor-Gen
" Assets and Liabilities	" "	"	" "	"	3	" " " "
" Investments	" "	"	" "	"	3	
" Excesses of Expenditure under Sub-Heads of Votes	" "	"	" "	"	3	" " " "
" Expenditure for Supplementary Appropriation Ord.	" "	"	" "	"	3	" " " "
" Blue Books Statistics	Sec. of State, Circular Despatch, 31/1/1899	"	" "	"	3	
" Savings Bank, Deposits and withdrawals	Ordinance No. 5 of 1885	"	" "	"	2	
" Family Remittances	M.P. 608, 11/6/1890	"	" "	"	3	One copy to be laid before Legislative Cou[ncil] one copy for Comptroller and Auditor-Gen
" Advances and Repayment of Advances	Financial Instructions	"	" "	"	2	
" Deposits and Repayment of Deposits	" "	"	" "	"	1	
" Overpayments recovered	" "	"	" "	"	1	
" Licenses Issued	" "	"	" "	"	1	
" Ground Rents	" "	"	C. & A. General	"	1	
" Grants to Schools	Education Ordinance No. 2, 1882	"	" "	—	1	
Blue Book Return	Colonial Regulations	"	Colonial Secretary	"	1	For Legislative Council.
Annual Financial Report	" "	"	" "	—	1	
Return of Trees	Public Lands Regulations 1897 Amendment	Travelling Commissioners	" "	"	1	To be laid before Legislative Council as [soon] after end of year as possible.
Customs Department.						
Return showing colony's capacity of supply of Coal, Fuel, Provisions, &c., for the Admiralty	M.P. 1332/1903	Collector of Customs	" "	Admiralty	1	To be sent to the Admiralty in January each y[ear]
Blue Book Return, Imports, Exports, Shipping and Manufactures	M.P. 978/92	" "	" "	"	3	One copy for Imperial Institute.
Return of Comparative Statement of principal articles, of Imports and Exports, 2 years	S. of S. Cir. Desp. 31/1/99 Gov. M.P. 13/3/99	" "	" "	"	2	
" Tonnage and Nationality of Vessels, 2 years	" "	" "	" "	"	2	
" Imports and Exports, last 5 years	" "	" "	" "	"	2	
" Shipping Inwards and Outwards, last 5 years	" "	" "	" "	"	4	
" Strengths of Spirits in centesimal degrees	Secretary of State Despatch No. 45 of August 11/99 and M.P. 452/99	" "	" "	"	2	
" Local Shipping	Instructions to Registrars of Shipping, 1901	" "	Board of Trade	—	2	
Blue Book Return	Colonial Regulations	" "	Colonial Secretary	"	1	
Post Office.						
Blue Book Return		Postmaster		"	1	
Return to International Bureau	Postal Regulations	"	International Bureau, Berne	—	1	
Travelling Commissioners.						
Population of each Town or Village at end of tour	M.P. 690/1902	Travelling Commissioners	Colonial Secretary	"	1	
Report on inspection of Boundary Pillars at end of tour	M.P. 405/1902	" "	" "	"	1	
Annual Report on District	—	" "	" "	"	1	
Instructions to Interpreters during Rains	—	" "	" "	"	1	
Report on District after first tour	—	" "	" "	"	1	
Messengers' Badges, List of	—	" "	" "	"	1	
Revised List of Towns and Villages	—	" "	" "	"	1	
Report and Maps of Road Surveys	—	" "	" "	"	1	
Judicial Department.						
Criminal Statistics	Colonial Regulation 268	Chief Magistrate	" "	"	2	For Blue Book.
Inspection of Registrar's Books, &c.	Registration Ordinance No. 5 of 1880	" "	" "	"	1	
Annual Report on Crime	Colonial Regulations	" "	" "	"	2	
Attorney-General's Department.						
Report on Registers of Births, Deaths, Marriages, Aliens and Friendly Societies		Colonial Registrar	" "	"	1	
Return of Accounts, &c.	Ordinance No. 6 of 1890	Curator of Intest. Estates	Colonial Treasurer	—	1	
Blue Book Return	Colonial Regulations	Colonial Registrar	Colonial Secretary	—	1	
Medical Department.						
Return of Diseases	Standing Orders	Senior Medical Officer	" "	"	1	
" Meteorology	" "	" "	" "	"	1	
Annual Medical Report	" "	" "	" "	"	1	
Report on Vaccination	M.P. 121/1902	" "	" "	"	1	To be rendered on 31st December.
Blue Book Return	Colonial Regulations	" "	" "	—	1	
West African Frontier Force.						
Annual Report on the Force	Correspondence Rules	O.C., G.C., W.A.F.F.	" "	"	1	
Police Department.						
Report on Arms of Precision	Ordinance No. 4 of 1902	Superintendent of Police	" "	—	1	
" Sale of Flint-lock Guns and Trade gunpowder	" "	" "	" "	"	1	
Blue Book Return	Colonial Regulations	" "	" "	"	1	
Annual Report on Civil Police	Correspondence Rules	" "	" "	"	1	
Prisons Department.						
Flogging Return	Sec. of State's Despatch, September, 1897	Inspector of Prisons	" "	"	2	For Secretary of State.
Blue Book Return	Colonial Regulations	" "	" "	"	1	
	HALF-YEARLY.					
Customs Department.						
Return of Traffic in Arms and Ammunition in the Colony and Protectorate	His Excellency the Governor	Collector of Customs	" "	"	2	For transmission to Secretary of State
Attorney-General's Department.						
Return of Marriages		Colonial Registrar	" "	—	1	For Gazette.
" Accounts	Ordinance No. 6 of 1890	Curator of Intest. Estates	Treasurer	—	2	One copy for publication in Gazette. One for Treasury.
Medical Department.						
Report on Hospital	Rules under Ordinance No. 13 of 1901	Senior Medical Officer	Colonial Secretary	"	1	
West African Frontier Force.						
Race classification Return Form 4/W.A.F.F.	—	O.C., G.C., W.A.F.F.	Inspector-General	—	—	
Clerk of Councils.						
Executive and Legislative Councils—Minutes of	Standing Orders	Clerk of Councils	Governor	Secretary of State	—	
	QUARTERLY.					
Secretariat.						
Return of all changes in the holders of existing offices and appointments	M.P. 182/1902	Colonial Secretary	" "	"	2	
Return of all new offices and appointments created	" "	" "	" "	"	2	
" " additions to Salaries and Allowances under settled Regulations for length of service	Colonial Regulations	" "	" "	"	1	To be furnished within five days after the [end] of the quarter and to be telegraphed to Secretary of State.
Treasury Department.						
Return of Revenue	Secretary of State	Colonial Treasurer	Colonial Secretary	Governor	3	
" Revenue and Expenditure	Colonial Regulations	" "	C. & A. General	"	3	" " " "
" of all additions to Salaries and Allowances not provided for by settled Regulations	" "	" "	" "	"		
" Payments of an unusual or special description and payments amounting to £200 incurred without authority from the Secretary of State	" "	" "	" "	"	3	For Secretary of State.
" Receipts and Payments of Board of Health	" "	" "	" "	"	1	Gazette.
" W.A.F.F. Reward Fund	Frontier Force Regulations of 23rd May, 1905, under Ordinance No. 3 of 1902	" "	O.C., G.C., W.A.F.F.	Colonial Secretary	1	
Customs Department.						
Account current—Receipts and Disbursements of Seamen Board of Trade	His Excellency the Governor	Collector of Customs	Board of Trade	—	1	To be furnished within five days after the [end] of the quarter and to be telegraphed to Secretary of State.
Return of value of Imports and Exports	" "	" "	Colonial Secretary	Governor	2	
" Stock and issue of Gunpowder in Magazine	—	" "	" "	"	1	
Medical Department.						
Medical Officer's Report on Prisons	Prisons Regulations 1891, Par. 139	Senior Medical Officer	" "	"	1	
Police Department.						
Return of Crimes	M.P. No. 55 of 1895	Superintendent of Police	" "	"	1	
Prisons Department.						
Return of Prisoners awaiting trial at Supreme Court	Gaol Ordinance No. 12 of 1891, Section 18	Inspector of Prisons	C. M. & Crown Prosecutor	—	1	
Report on Prisons	" Sub-Section " 15	" "	Colonial Secretary	"	1	
West African Frontier Force.						
Distribution Return Form 1/W.A.F.F.; Ordnance and Small Arms 2/W.A.F.F.; Ammunition Return Form 3/W.A.F.F.	—	O.C., G.C., W.A.F.F.	" "	Inspector-General	—	To be forwarded through Governor under fl[ying] seal.
Post Office.						
Dead Letter Return	Post Office Regulations	Postmaster	U. K. Colonial Post Office	—	1	
	MONTHLY.					
Travelling Commissioners.						
List of Courts to be held in Districts	—	Travelling Commissioners	Colonial Secretary	"	—	For publication in the Gazette.
Governor's Office.						
Return of Presents sold	—	Private Secretary	Treasurer and Audit Dept.	—	—	One copy to each Department.
Secretariat.						
Return of Ordinances and Gazettes sold	—	Second Clerk C. S. Office	" "	—	2	" " "
Treasury Department.						
Return of Revenue and Expenditure	M.P. No. 591/98	Colonial Treasurer	Colonial Secretary	—	1	For Gazette.
" Advances to various Governments	—	" "	" "	—	—	
Customs Department.						
Imports, Exports, Shipping and Statement of Revenue	His Excellency the Governor	Collector of Customs	" "	—	1	
Return of Fees	—	" "	Local Auditor	—	2	" "
Travelling Commissioners.						
Statement of Revenue collected	—	Travelling Commissioners	Treasurer			
Travelling Commissioner in account with Treasurer	—	" "	"			
Petty Cash Account	—	" "	"	—	1	To be forwarded under flying seal thro' Colonial Secretary.
Return of Commissioners Courts	—	" "	Chief Magistrate			
" Native Tribunals	—	" "	" "			
Judicial Department.						
Return of Offences	His Excellency the Governor	Clerk of Courts	Colonial Secretary	Printing Department	1	For Gazette.
Court Fees	" "	" "	Local Auditor	" "	1	
Attorney-General's Department.						
Return of Births and Deaths registered in the previous month	—	Colonial Registrar	Colonial Secretary	"	1	"
" number of Aliens registered or removed during previous month	—	" "	" "	"	1	"
" Colonial Registrar's Fees	—	" "	Local Auditor	—	1	
Medical Department.						
Return of Diseases	—	Senior Medical Officer	Colonial Secretary	—	1	"
" Meteorology	—	" "	" "	—	1	"
Maintenance of Sick and Sale of Medicines	—	" "	Treasurer and Auditor	—	2	
Return of Patients treated at Colonial Hospital	His Excellency the Governor	" "	Colonial Secretary	Governor	1	One copy to each Department.
" Visits of Medical Officers to pauper patients	" "	" "	" "	"	1	
Police Department.						
Return of Fines	Ordinance No. 9 of 1899, Section 37	Superintendent of Police	Local Auditor	—	1	
" Sale of Government Property	—	" "	" "	—	1	
" Pigs shot	Ordinance No. 9 of 1891, Sec. 6, S. S. 3	" "	" "	—	1	
" Stray dogs	" " 4 of 1890, " 30	" "	Treasurer	—	1	
Prisons Department.						
Return of Prisoners in the Gaol	Gaol Ordinance No. 12 of 1891, Section 19	Inspector of Prisons	Colonial Secretary	—	1	For Gazette.
" " received and discharged	His Excellency the Governor	" "	" "	—	1	" "
Fines inflicted upon Warders	—	" "	Treasurer	—	1	
West African Frontier Force.						
Progress Report	—	O.C., G.C., W.A.F.F.	Inspector-General	—	1	To be forwarded through Governor under flying seal.
Post Office Department.						
P. O. General Account	Post Office Regulations	Postmaster	G.P.O., London, Treasurer and Local Auditor	—	3	G.P.O., one; Treasurer, one; Local Auditor.
Statement of Intercolonial Parcel Mails received	" "	"	General Post Office	—	1	
Abstract of Parcel Mails	" "	"	" "	—	2	
Money Order List of lapsed and void Orders	—	"	" "	—	1	
Gazette Returns	Colonial Regulations	"	Colonial Secretary	—	1	
Copy of Cash Book	" "	"	Local Auditor	—	1	
Public Works Department.						
Return of payments into Treasury	—	Colonial Engineer	" "	—	—	
" Works in hand during previous month	M.P. 1083/1902	" "	Colonial Secretary	Governor	1	To be rendered by 15th of each month.
Government Vessels.						
Fines stopped from Crew	Rules by Administrator, 29th January, 1896	Master of Mansah Kilah	Treasurer & Local Auditor	—	2	One copy to each Department.
	WEEKLY.					
All Departments.						
Attendance Roll	—	All Departments	Colonial Secretary	—	1	
Return of Minute Papers	M.P. 97/1902	" "	" "	—	1	
Police Department.						
Return of Surprise Visits to Constables on beat duty	M.P. 815/1901	Superintendent of Police	" "	—	1	
Mansah Kilah.						
Voyages of Mansah Kilah	—	Master of Mansah Kilah	" "	—	1	
	DAILY.					
Medical Department.						
Morning Health Report	—	Senior Medical Officer	" "	—	1	
Police Department.						
Morning State	—	Superintendent of Police	" "	—	1	
Police Report	—	" "	" "	—	1	
Prisons Department.						
Daily occupation of Prisoners	Gaol Form 104	Inspector of Prisons	" "	—	1	
	OCCASIONALLY.					
Judicial Department.						
Report on sentences of more than 12 months hard labour	Ordinance 4/1899	Chief Magistrate	" "	—	—	To be sent in after each assize.
Medical Department.						
Sick Report of Officials	His Excellency the Governor	Senior Medical Officer	Heads of Departments	—	—	
Police Department.						
Morning Sick Report	—	Superintendent of Police	Senior Medical Officer	—	1	
Prisoners Charge Sheet	—	" "	C. M. and Clerk of Courts	—	2	
Statement of Ration money issued to Native Chiefs, Messengers and Witnesses	M.P. P./401/98	" "	Colonial Treasurer	—	1	
Prisons Department.						
Fines paid by Prisoners	Committal Form	Inspector of Prisons	Clerk of Courts	—	—	
Officers Sick Report	—	" "	Senior Medical Officer	—	—	

CHAPTER XII.

Receipts and Expenditure for 1903—Invested Capital—Savings Bank Statistics—Banking Arrangements—Rate of Exchange of Five-Franc Pieces—The Supreme Court of the Colony—Court Fees—Solicitors' Charges—Fees as to Alien Children, Friendly Societies, and Births, Deaths and Marriages—Postal Guide—Telegraphic Arrangements—Hospital Rules—Rules for Guidance of European Nurses.

FOLLOWING a detailed statement of the receipts and expenditure of the colony for the year 1903, and particulars of its invested capital, there will be found grouped in this chapter various other details as to the internal arrangements of the colony, such as banking, legal administration, and postal and telegraphic service. The hospital regulations in force have also been included here.

COLONY OF GAMBIA.

Statement showing the Total Receipts and Expenditure in the Year 1903.

RECEIPTS.	Amount estimated.	Amount received in the colony as per monthly abstracts.	Amount received by the Crown Agents in England.	Total Receipts.	More than estimated.	Less than estimated.
	£ s. d.	£ s. d.	£ s. d.	£ s. d.	£ s. d.	£ s. d.
Balance on 1st January, 1903	—	1,455 2 4	483 5 6	1,938 7 10	—	—
Customs	38,555 0 0	41,628 12 7	—	41,628 12 7	3,073 12 7	—
Port dues...	925 0 0	714 0 0	300 0 0	1,014 0 0	89 0 0	—
Licenses, excise and internal revenue, not otherwise classified	585 0 0	1,108 0 0	—	1,108 0 0	523 0 0	—
Fees of court or office, payments for specific services, and reimbursements in aid ...	715 0 0	738 13 9	1 13 0	740 6 9	25 6 9	—
Post Office	725 0 0	553 3 3	—	553 3 3	—	171 16 9
Government vessels	800 0 0	433 18 6	—	433 18 6	—	366 1 6
Rents of Government property	460 0 0	381 9 0	1 0 0	382 9 0	—	77 11 0
Interest	1,500 0 0	—	1,793 11 4	1,793 11 4	293 11 4	—
Miscellaneous receipts	203 0 0	1,464 13 9	76 3 5	1,540 17 2	1,337 17 2	—
Protectorate	4,275 0 0	6,349 2 4	—	6,349 2 4	2,074 2 4	—
	48,743 0 0	53,371 13 2	2,172 7 9	55,544 0 11	7,416 10 2	615 9 3
Land sales	—	20 0 0	—	20 0 0	20 0 0	—
Total	48,743 0 0	53,391 13 2	2,172 7 9	55,564 0 11	7,436 10 2	615 9 3
Steamer Depreciation Fund		18 0 0	250 0 0	268 0 0		
Surplus Funds withdrawn from investments...		—	—	—		
Advances repaid		8,552 12 2	9,662 16 8	18,215 8 10		
Deposits received		12,406 11 3	34 6 6	12,440 17 9		
Remittances received by Crown Agents		—	10,500 0 0	10,500 0 0		
		74,368 16 7	22,619 10 11	96,988 7 6		
Amount owing to Crown Agents on overpayments...		—	4,111 15 5	4,111 15 5		
Total		75,823 18 11	27,214 11 10	103,038 10 9		

PAYMENTS.	Amount estimated.	Amount paid in the colony as per monthly abstracts.	Amount paid by the Crown Agents in England.	Total Payments.	More than estimated.	Less than estimated.
	£ s. d.	£ s. d.	£ s. d.	£ s. d.	£ s. d.	£ s. d.
Pensions	886 8 6	51 18 3	697 0 7	748 18 10	—	137 9 8
The Governor	2,864 1 3	2,723 19 10	171 14 11	2,895 14 9	31 13 6	—
The Colonial Secretary	1,176 0 0	857 2 1	310 3 4	1,167 5 5	—	8 14 7
Printing Department	636 0 0	274 13 1	346 17 6	621 10 7	—	14 9 5
The Protectorate	5,034 19 7	5,332 0 9	447 2 11	5,779 3 8	744 4 1	—
Treasury	1,002 10 0	808 5 0	202 11 2	1,010 16 2	8 6 2	—
Customs Department	2,076 5 10	1,623 14 10	303 6 5	1,927 1 3	—	149 4 7
Post Office	666 5 0	604 19 5	15 6 5	620 5 10	—	45 19 2
Audit Department	556 10 0	324 6 0	180 6 9	504 12 9	—	51 17 3
Judicial Departments	1,228 18 9	920 19 5	303 19 4	1,224 18 9	—	4 0 0
Education	1,200 0 0	848 18 6	—	848 18 6	—	351 1 6
Frontier Force	6,651 8 10	4,413 8 6	1,331 0 6	5,744 9 0	—	906 19 10
Police	4,512 15 11	3,379 15 10	943 17 4	4,323 13 2	—	189 2 9
Prisons	799 4 7	635 8 8	70 18 5	706 7 1	—	92 17 6
Medical Department...	2,332 1 8	1,899 17 11	301 0 1	2,200 18 0	—	131 3 8
Hospitals and dispensaries...	886 0 0	508 1 8	309 19 3	818 0 11	—	67 19 1
Government vessels	2,257 2 6	1,984 14 3	287 8 10	2,272 3 1	15 0 7	—
Charitable allowances	100 0 0	89 19 0	1 0 0	90 19 0	—	9 1 0
Transport	500 0 0	796 15 3	100 13 6	397 8 9	397 8 9	—
Miscellaneous services	2,278 10 0	1,137 19 1	1,363 4 1	2,501 3 2	222 13 2	—
Drawback and refund of duties	50 0 0	32 15 7	—	32 15 7	—	17 4 5
Agriculture	711 0 0	439 3 2	147 12 6	586 15 8	—	124 4 4
Colonial Engineer's Department	1,593 17 11	1,296 8 2	235 9 9	1,531 17 11	—	62 0 0
Public works, recurrent	3,955 0 0	4,364 8 8	859 1 10	5,223 10 6	1,268 10 6	—
Public works, extraordinary	11,617 0 0	7,676 5 4	4,933 17 1	11,710 2 5	93 2 5	—
Special services	—	1,285 16 6	9,716 11 5	11,002 7 11	11,002 7 11	—
Attorney-General	487 0 0	376 12 8	135 14 1	512 6 9	25 6 9	—
TOTAL	56,059 0 4	44,688 7 5	22,815 18 0	67,504 5 5	13,808 13 10	2,363 8 9
Steamer Depreciation Fund		18 0 0	250 0 0	268 0 0	STATEMENT OF BALANCE.	
Investments		—	—	—		
Advances		9,748 8 4	1,376 7 2	11,124 15 6		
Repayment of deposits		9,144 2 8	2,772 6 8	11,916 9 4		
Remittances to Crown Agents		10,500 0 0	—	10,500 0 0		
		74,098 18 5	27,214 11 10	101,313 10 3		
Balance on 31st December, 1903		1,725 0 6	—	1,725 0 6		
TOTAL		75,823 18 11	27,214 11 10	103,038 10 9		

F. BISSET ARCHER,
Treasurer.

STATEMENT OF INVESTMENTS AT DECEMBER 31ST, 1903.

Description of Stock.		Amount of Stock. £ s. d.	Actual Price. £ s. d.
GENERAL:—			
New Zealand Inscribed Stock		5,003 18 9	5,000 0 0
Jamaica "		3,015 0 6	3,000 0 0
British Guiana "		2,056 10 1	2,000 0 0
West Australia "		6,254 4 0	5,992 9 0
Trinidad "		5,032 19 9	4,800 5 8
Natal "		4,428 9 9	4,500 0 0
Queensland "		4,376 7 2	4,584 10 0
South Australia "		7,242 8 3	7,007 11 0
Cape of Good Hope "		3,567 4 0	3,500 0 0
Victoria "		4,665 5 3	4,415 10 0
Gold Coast "		3,000 0 0	2,688 6 11
Reading Corporation "		4,000 0 0	3,807 14 7
STEAMER DEPRECIATION FUND:—			
Grenada Inscribed Stock		211 7 6	250 0 0
West Australia "		1,082 9 4	1,031 19 10
Trinidad "		287 19 9	285 5 7
South Australia "		306 6 6	289 6 10
General	£51,296 7 2		
Steamer Depreciation ...	1,856 12 3		
	£53,152 19 5		
		£54,530 10 7	£53,152 19 5

SAVINGS BANK.

The Treasury Savings Bank was established on January 1st, 1886, by authority of Ordinance No. 11 of 1884, and is under the management of the Colonial Treasurer.

To meet the requirements of depositors, sums of 1s. and upwards are received; the total amount, however, lodged by any one depositor must not exceed £500, inclusive of interest, which is 2½ per cent. per annum, or ½d. in the £1 for every complete calendar month.

The moneys paid into the bank by depositors are invested by the Crown Agents in England in securities estimated to yield not less than 3 per cent., and the amount realised is applied to the payment of interest due locally.

The following is the statement of the Savings Bank transactions for the five years from 1899 to 1903:—

Year.	Number of depositors.	Amount.
1899	203	£2,456
1900	219	1,856
1901	238	2,038
1902	275	2,057
1903	349	2,290

BANK OF BRITISH WEST AFRICA, LIMITED.

There is a branch of this bank at Bathurst, with premises in Buckle-street.

Under an agreement entered into on September 8th, 1902, with the Colonial Government, through the medium of the Crown Agents, all the banking business of the colony is transacted by the bank, without charge, except in certain specified cases, such as remittances, overdrafts if desired, and a deficiency of the current account below £400, in the last two cases the interest permissible being at the lowest rate the bank would charge its most favoured customers.

Overdrafts on behalf of the Government are guaranteed up to £5,000, and the interest thereon is debited against the current account half-yearly.

The security given by the bank for the due performance of its agreement is £2,500 East India Government Stock, and this amount is lodged with the trustees, the Crown Agents for the Colonies.

The head office of the bank is at 14 Castle-street, Liverpool, and its London office at 17 Leadenhall-street, E.C. There are branches at Hamburg, Axim, Sekondi, Cape Coast, Accra and Lagos, with agencies at Madeira, Teneriffe, Grand Canary, Fernando Po and Tarkwa.

The capital is £250,000, in 25,000 shares of £10 each, of which 15,000 shares have been issued, with a paid-up capital of £60,000.

TABLE OF FIVE-FRANC PIECES, SHOWING EQUIVALENT IN STERLING.

No.	Equal to			No.	Equal to			No.	Equal to			No.	Equal to		
	£	s.	d.		£	s.	d.		£	s.	d.		£	s.	d.
1	0	3	10½	32	6	4	0	63	12	4	1½	94	18	4	3
2	0	7	9	33	6	7	10½	64	12	8	0	95	18	8	1½
3	0	11	7½	34	6	11	9	65	12	11	10½	96	18	12	0
4	0	15	6	35	6	15	7½	66	12	15	9	97	18	15	10½
5	0	19	4½	36	6	19	6	67	12	19	7½	98	18	19	9
6	1	3	3	37	7	3	4½	68	13	3	6	99	19	3	7½
7	1	7	1½	38	7	7	3	69	13	7	4½	100	19	7	6
8	1	11	0	39	7	11	1½	70	13	11	3	110	21	6	3
9	1	14	10½	40	7	15	0	71	13	15	1½	120	23	5	0
10	1	18	9	41	7	18	10½	72	13	19	0	130	25	3	9
11	2	2	7½	42	8	2	9	73	14	2	10½	140	27	2	6
12	2	6	6	43	8	6	7½	74	14	6	9	150	29	1	3
13	2	10	4½	44	8	10	6	75	14	10	7½	160	31	0	0
14	2	14	3	45	8	14	4½	76	14	14	6	170	32	18	9
15	2	18	1½	46	8	18	3	77	14	18	4½	180	34	17	6
16	3	2	0	47	9	2	1½	78	15	2	3	190	36	16	3
17	3	5	10½	48	9	6	0	79	15	6	1½	200	38	15	0
18	3	9	9	49	9	9	10½	80	15	10	0	300	58	2	6
19	3	13	7½	50	9	13	9	81	15	13	10½	400	77	10	0
20	3	17	6	51	9	17	7½	82	15	17	9	500	96	17	6
21	4	1	4½	52	10	1	6	83	16	1	7½	600	116	5	0
22	4	5	3	53	10	5	4½	84	16	5	6	700	135	12	6
23	4	9	1½	54	10	9	3	85	16	9	4½	800	155	0	0
24	4	13	0	55	10	13	1½	86	16	13	3	900	174	7	6
25	4	16	10½	56	10	17	0	87	16	17	1½	1,000	193	15	0
26	5	0	9	57	11	0	10½	88	17	1	0	2,000	387	10	0
27	5	4	7½	58	11	4	9	89	17	4	10½	3,000	581	5	0
28	5	8	6	59	11	8	7½	90	17	8	9	4,000	775	0	0
29	5	12	4½	60	11	12	6	91	17	12	7½	5,000	968	15	0
30	5	16	3	61	11	16	4½	92	17	16	6	6,000	1,162	10	0
31	6	0	1½	62	12	0	3	93	18	0	4½	7,000	1,356	5	0

THE SUPREME COURT OF THE COLONY.

Constitution.

The Supreme Court of Judicature for the Colony of the Gambia consists of and is holden by and before a chief magistrate named and appointed by His Majesty the King.

Sessions.

There are three sessions each year — namely, the spring session, during the first week in March; the summer session, during the first week in July; and the autumn session, during the third week in November. The Court continues to sit so long as there is any business before it—civil and criminal—and it is lawful for the chief magistrate to appoint and hold a special sitting or sittings of the Court when he deems it expedient so to do for the despatch of any civil causes upon such notice to the parties and also such public notification (if any) as seems reasonable and necessary (*vide* Ordinance No. 11 of 1903).

Vacation.

The vacation of the Court commences on the 10th of August and terminates on the 24th of October each year (*vide* Ordinance No. 4 of 1889). During vacation no pleading shall be delivered or amended unless directed by the chief magistrate. Vacation time is not to be reckoned in the computation of the times appointed or allowed by any rule of Court for filing, amending, or delivering any pleading unless otherwise ordered by the chief magistrate. The chief magistrate hears and disposes of all applications which may require to be immediately or promptly heard.

Jurisdiction.

The Supreme Court exercises all the jurisdiction, powers and authorities which are vested in or are capable of being exercised by His Majesty's High Court of Justice in England, save and except the jurisdiction possessed and exercised by the High Court of Admiralty, unless or so far as such jurisdiction may become exercisable by the said Court by virtue of any Act of the Imperial Parliament. The Supreme Court has jurisdiction in probate and divorce matters, which is exercised by it in conformity with the law and practice for the time being in force in England.

Laws.

The statutes of general application which were in force in England on 1st November, 1888, are in force in the colony.

SCHEDULE OF FEES TO BE TAKEN BY THE CLERK OF COURTS.

Police Court.

	s.	d.
Summonses	2	0
Subpœnas	1	0
Warrant to apprehend persons for disobeying summonses	4	0
Bail bond	3	6
Copy of depositions, per folio	0	1½

Court of Requests.

	s.	d.
Filing every plaint and issuing summonses where the amount does not exceed £1	0	6
Where it exeeds £1 and does not exceed £2	1	0
,, £2 ,, ,, £3	1	6
,, £3 ,, ,, £4	2	0
,, £4 ,, ,, £5	2	6
,, £5 ,, ,, £6	3	0
,, £6 ,, ,, £7	3	6
,, £7 ,, ,, £8	4	0
,, £8 ,, ,, £9	4	6
,, £9 ,, ,, £10	5	0
,, £10 ,, ,, £11	5	6
,, £11 ,, ,, £12	6	0
,, £12 ,, ,, £13	6	6
,, £13 ,, ,, £14	7	0
,, £14 ,, ,, £15	7	6
,, £15 ,, ,, £16	8	0
,, £16 ,, ,, £17	8	6
,, £17 ,, ,, £18	9	0
,, £18 ,, ,, £19	9	6
,, £19 ,, ,, £20	10	0
Every amount exceeding £30	15	0
For every warrant to levy goods and chattels (in the £1) ...	1	6
,, ,, of commitment for persons disobeying orders of Court	4	0

FEES RECEIVED IN THE COURT OF REQUESTS UNDER THE COURT OF REQUESTS RULES, 1890.

SCHEDULE.

For every plaint, counter claim or petition, sixpence in the pound.

Where in any case the number of defendants shall exceed three, an additional fee of one shilling for each defendant above three.

For entering judgment by consent, sixpence in the pound on the amount claimed in the summons.

For every hearing, sixpence in the pound; to be charged once only in an action.

In all cases where the defendant shall, either personally or by his solicitor or agent, admit the claim, one-half of the fee paid by the plaintiff for the hearing of the plaint shall be returned to the plaintiff by the Clerk of Courts, although the Court may have been required to decide upon the terms and conditions upon which the claim is to be paid.

For issuing every warrant, eighteenpence in the pound.

For every judgment summons under the Debtor's Ordinance, 1893, threepence in the pound on so much of the amount of the original demand as in obedience to the order of the Court should have been paid at the time of the issue of the summons.

For every hearing of the matters mentioned in such judgment summons, sixpence in the pound on the amount upon which the fee on the summons is calculated.

	s.	*d.*
For every subpœna, to be served by the beadle if served within two miles of court house	1	0
For every mile beyond two	0	6
For filing every affidavit or other document not being a document annexed to an affidavit	1	0
For every application for a search and searching	2	0
For giving notice required by an order of law	2	0
For every official copy, per folio	0	4
For every taxation of costs	4	0
Where it is necessary for the beadle to place a man in possession of property seized, for every day	1	6

Costs to be Paid to Solicitors in Actions or Matters as well between Party and Party as between Solicitor and Client, where the Subject Matter or the Sum recovered exceeds £10.

——	Where the subject matter or the sum recovered exceeds £10 and does not exceed £30.	£30 and over.
Plaints, Particulars, Summons and Notices.	£ s. d.	£ s. d.
1. Preparing particulars of claim or counter claim, including necessary copies where the claim is a liquidated demand, provided that such particulars and copies are signed by the solicitor	0 4 0	0 7 0
2. The like in all other claims	0 6 0	0 12 0
3. Preparing further particulars when same required by defendant, including copy to file when signed by the solicitor	0 2 0	0 3 0
Or per folio	0 0 8	0 0 8
Notices.		
4. For preparing any necessary or proper notice or demand, including copies to file and serve	0 1 6	0 1 6
5. Or if special, and necessarily exceed three folios, for each folio beyond three, including copy to file	0 1 0	0 1 0
Instructions.		
6. To sue or defend, or for a petition	0 3 4	0 6 8
7. For counter claim	0 3 4	0 6 8
8. If exceeding six folios, for each additional folio	0 0 6	0 1 0
9. In special cases, in addition, for preparing or making copies of any account or other document, not being notes or observations relating to the evidence of the witnesses only, which the Clerk of Courts may think necessary for solicitor's use at the trial, such sum as he may consider reasonable, not exceeding	—	0 10 0
Drawing.		
10. Notice and particulars of special defence or admission of facts, including necessary copies	0 3 0	0 5 0
11. Affidavit of personal service of a notice or document, including engrossing, attending to be sworn, and filing	0 3 4	0 5 0
Copy to leave, per folio	0 0 8	0 0 8
12. Bill of costs for taxation, including copy for Clerk of Courts	—	—

—	Where the subject matter or the sum recovered exceeds £10 and does not exceed £30.	£30 and over.
	£ s. d.	£ s. d.
COPIES.		
13. Of documents, and where no provision is made herein that the fee for preparing or drawing any document is to include copies thereof, for each copy the Clerk of Courts may consider necessary, per folio... ...	—	o o 4
PERUSALS.		
14. Of particulars of claim or counter claim, further particulars or special defence by the solicitor of the party to whom the same are delivered	—	o 3 4
15. Of notice to produce by the solicitor of the party served	—	o 5 o
16. Of special affidavits by the solicitor of the party against whom the same can be read, per folio	—	o o 4
ATTENDANCES.		
17. To enter plaint or file petition, including filing of *precipe*, obtaining any unnecessary leave from the Clerk of Courts, or giving any proper undertaking prior to each entry or filing	o 3 4	o 6 8
18. To deliver or file any counter claim, special defence and further particulars	—	o 3 4
19. To lodge order and when action or matter remitted or transferred to Court of Requests, including preparing all necessary documents and copies	—	o 13 4
20. To inspect or produce for inspection documents pursuant to any order or a notice under any rule	o 3 4	o 6 8
Or per hour	—	o 6 8
21. To obtain or give any necessary or proper consent...	—	o 3 4
22. On examination of a witness under sec. 7 of Ordinance No. 6 of 1882, per hour ...	—	o 6 8
23. On deponents being sworn or by a solicitor or his clerk to be sworn to any special affidavits	—	o 3 4
24. To enter a judgment by default	o 3 4	o 3 4
25. Any other attendance upon the Clerk of Courts or at his office, or upon the opposite party not otherwise provided for, which the Clerk of Courts may deem necessary	—	o 3 4
26. Where by any proceeding taken by the opposite party it becomes necessary to advise or receive instructions from a client in the progress of an action or matter, for each attendance the Clerk of Courts may deem necessary	—	o 6 8

----	Where the subject matter or the sum recovered exceeds £10 and does not exceed £30.	£30 and over.
	£ s. d.	£ s. d.
27. At court conducting case where no counsel employed	0 15 0	1 1 0
28. Or if specially allowed at trial or hearing by the Chief Magistrate (Items 27 and 28 to be allowed only once in an action or matter)...	1 1 0	2 2 0
29. Where the trial lasts more than one whole day, or is adjourned for want of time, or upon payment of the cost of the day in lieu of the fee for attendance, there may be allowed	0 10 0	0 15 0
30. To make or oppose any application or motion before the Chief Magistrate in Chambers when no counsel employed ...	0 5 0	0 6 0
The like of in court	0 10 0	0 13 4
31. To hear a deferred judgment	—	0 6 8
32. On taxation of the costs of the action or matter after trial or hearing	0 3 4	0 6 8
33. On taxation of any costs allowed by order of Chief Magistrate, where such taxation necessarily takes place at some time other than at the time the order giving the costs sought to be taxed was made, to include drawing bill, copies, notice and service	—	0 4 0
FEES TO COUNSEL.		
34. For conducting case in court	1 1 0	2 2 0
35. On conference, when allowed by Chief Magistrate	—	2 2 0
36. Where the trial lasts more than one whole day, or is adjourned for want of time, further consideration, or upon payment of the costs of the day, a refresher may be allowed by order of Chief Magistrate not exceeding...	1 3 6	1 3 6
37. To make or oppose any application or motion in court, if Chief Magistrate certifies for counsel	—	1 3 6
LETTERS.		
38. Letters before action	0 3 6	0 3 6
39. Letters to be allowed once only in an action or matter	—	0 5 0
40. Circular-letters	—	0 5 0
Costs for searches for certificates of births, marriages, and deaths, which the Clerk of Courts may upon taxation think necessary, such sum as the Clerk of Courts shall deem necessary	—	—
41. Oaths, sum paid	—	—

COURT OF REQUESTS.

Beadle's Fees.

	£	s.	d.
Serving every summons beyond 1 and within 2 miles of Court House ...	0	0	9
,, beyond 2 miles and within 3 miles ...	0	1	3
,, ,, 3 ,, ,, 4 ,, ...	0	1	10
,, ,, 4 ,, ,, 5 ,, ...	0	2	6
,, ,, 5 ,, ,, 6 ,, ...	0	3	3
,, ,, 6 ,, ,, 7 ,, ...	0	4	0
,, ,, 8 miles, 1s. extra for every mile.			

Mileage fee for executing warrants is twice the fee for the service of summonses.

SUPREME COURT FEES.

		£	s.	d.
1.	Issuing writs of summons:—			
	(A) Where amount claimed is under £50, in every case ...	0	5	0
	,, ,, ,, ,, ,, if filled in by Clerk of Court ...	0	16	6
	(B) Where amount claimed—£50 and upwards	½ per cent. claim, but not exceeding £3.		
	(C) In actions for recovery of land ...	2	0	0
2.	Issuing writ of *Fi. Fa.* or other writ or warrant of execution against property ...	0	10	6
3.	,, ,, *Capias ad respondendum* ...	1	2	6
4.	,, ,, *Ca. Sa.* or any writ or warrant of execution against the person ...	0	10	6
5.	Seal fee on the above and for each and every document ...	0	5	0
6.	Entering every appearance ...	0	3	6
7.	Filing every document ...	0	2	6
8.	Reading every deed or other exhibit ...	0	1	6
9.	Attending in chambers before Chief Magistrate ...	0	10	6
10.	Attending in court, per diem ...	0	10	6
11.	For every satisfaction of a judgment ...	0	5	0
12.	For certifying a record upon a writ of error or appeal...	0	10	6
13.	For office copies of all records and proceedings, per folio ...	0	0	9
14.	For every copy transcript or extract, per folio ...	0	0	9
15.	Rule ...	0	10	6
16.	Summons in chambers ...	0	5	0
17.	Motion on application in court ...	0	10	0
17a.	Order in chambers ...	0	5	0
18.	Order or motion on application in court ...	0	10	0
18a.	Order for adjournment of hearing, rendered necessary by default of either party (to be paid by defaulter), 5s. to 10s., as may be ordered by the Court.			
18b.	Writ, summons, motion, application, or other matter specifically charged, the like fee as is payable in the High Court of Justice in England, or in the event of there being no such fee ...	0	5	0

18c. Hearing fee:—

On entering or setting down cause for trial—

		£ s. d.
(A)	Where amount claimed is under £50	0 5 0
(B)	Where amount claimed is £50 and upwards	½ per cent. on claim, but not exceeding £3
(C)	In actions for the recovery of land	1 0 0

		£ s. d.
19.	Divorce matters, the fees taken in the Divorce Division of the High Court of Justice in England	—
19a.	For every report or determination on special reference from Court ... ... 10s. 6d. to	1 1 0
20.	For every examination *viva voce* or on written interrogatories on special reference from Court	0 10 6
21.	For taxing bills of costs, if under 6 folioes	0 6 8
22.	If bill exceeds 6 folios, for every additional folio besides the fee above mentioned	0 0 4
23.	Signing judgment and entering same	0 15 0
24.	Subpœna	0 5 0
25.	Searching records	0 2 6
26.	For money paid into court, sums under £100, per cent. ...	1 0 0
27.	For money paid into court, sums above £100, per cent. ...	0 10 0
28.	Drawing every recognizance, bail bond, or other writing, per folio	0 1 0
29.	Copy of Chief Magistrate's notes, affidavits or writing, per folio	0 0 9
30.	Fiat for Habeas Corpus	0 2 0

SUPREME COURT FEES.

By the Sheriffs, Bailiffs and others the officers of the Sheriff of the Colony.

	£ s. d.
For every warrant which shall be granted by the Sheriff to his officers upon writ process	0 2 0
For an arrest	0 10 6
For conveying the defendant to gaol from the place of arrest, per mile	0 1 0
For a bail bond	0 10 6
For receiving money upon deposit for arrest and paying same into court	0 6 8
Assignment of bail or other bond...	0 5 0
For the return of any writ of Habeas Corpus	0 8 0
To the bailiffs for serving writs of summons or for executing warrants of *Fi. Fa.*, *Ca. Sa.*, for each, if the distance from the Sheriff's office does not exceed 5 miles	0 5 0
If beyond that distance, per mile additional	0 0 6
For every man left in possession on writ of *Fi. Fa.*, when absolutely necessary, per diem	0 1 0
For every sale by auction, notwithstanding the defendant may become bankrupt or insolvent, where the property sold does not exceed £300	5 per cent.
Where it produces £300 and does not exceed £500	3 per cent.
And when it exceeds £500	2½ per cent.

For any duty not herein provided for, such sum as the Court may direct the Clerk of Courts to allow.

Ordinance, 14*th February*, 1878.

In addition to the fees receivable for the Sheriff in respect of himself and his officers under the authority of any schedule of fees in force, the Sheriff shall demand and receive the fees in the schedule set forth :—

Table of Fees.

	£	s.	d.
Upon every *Fi. Fa.*, where the amount levied does not exceed £100, a poundage for every pound of	0	1	0
Where the amount exceeds £100, a poundage for every pound over and above the sum, of	0	0	6
Upon every writ of possession, where the whole yearly value of the land does not exceed £100, a poundage in every pound of ...	0	1	0
Where the value of the lands delivered exceeds £100, a poundage for every pound above the sum of	0	0	6
The bond of indemnity	0	10	6
Sheriff attending civil trials, per diem	0	10	6
Sheriff's bailiffs (not exceeding two) attending court, per diem ...	0	2	6
Sheriff's bailiffs (not exceeding two) attending sale by auction, per diem	0	3	0

Removing goods seized under *Fi. Fa.* to place of security, such expenses as the Chief Magistrate shall allow.

Upon orders to arrest, the same fee as were payable upon a *Capias.*

Ordinance, 31st December, 1883.

TABLE OF FEES TO BE TAKEN AT THE COURT OF REQUESTS.

By the Court.

	£	s.	d.
Each undertaking to sue by next friend	0	4	0
Order appointing guardian	0	2	0
Summons for ejectment, where the value of the land is under £20,	0	10	0
Above £20	0	10	0
Warrant for execution in ejectment	0	4	0
Every judgment in ejectment	0	3	0

Beadle's Fees.

The same as is allowed for serving summonses, executing warrants, under the Court Fees Ordinance, 1878.

Order in Council, dated 18th August, 1884.

SCHEDULE OF FEES RECEIVABLE BY REGISTRAR OF DEEDS UNDER ORDINANCE DATED 14TH JULY, 1880.

	£	s.	d.
For every acknowledgment or proof of an instrument	0	2	6
The registration and recording of an instrument other than memorial executed before the Registrar, for every 72 words ...	0	0	9
Verifying every memorial and recording same	0	5	0
Depositing every will or other instrument	0	2	6
Taking out same	0	2	6
Every search in the records, for half-an-hour or under	0	2	6
Every additional half-an-hour or under...	0	2	6

	£	s.	d.
An attested copy or extract from any recorded instrument or memorial, for every folio of 72 words	0	1	0
Comparing, if required, any instrument with the register thereof, for every 72 words	0	0	6
Every other certificate or extract	0	2	6

FEES TAKEN AT THE REGISTRY FOR ALIEN AFRICAN CHILDREN, UNDER ORDINANCE 4 OF 1893.

For registering every alien African child	0	4	0

FEES TAKEN AT THE REGISTRY OF FRIENDLY SOCIETIES UNDER ORDINANCE 3 OF 1865.

Registering approved copy of rules	0	5	0
Notice of change of place of meeting	0	2	0
Filing annual statement of society's funds	0	2	0

REGISTERING BIRTHS, DEATHS AND MARRIAGES, UNDER ORDINANCE 11 OF 1886.

There is no fee for registering any birth or death.

For every marriage licence	3	3	0
Searching for births, deaths and marriages, for each name within ten years	0	1	0
Every year beyond	0	0	6
For certified extract from the registry of births, deaths or marriages	0	2	6
Registering birth of child after the time fixed by ordinance ...	0	1	0

A Gambian Harness Antelope.

THE GAMBIA POSTAL GUIDE.

The General Post Office, Bathurst, is open daily for transaction of postal business with the public between 8 a.m. and 11 a.m. and between 1 p.m. and 4 p.m. (Sundays and Public Holidays excepted).

On the arrival of a mail steamer in port on Sundays and Holidays, the Post Office is opened for the receipt and despatch of mails.

The only District Post Office as yet established is that at McCarthy Island, in the Protectorate of the Gambia.

INLAND MAILS.

There is no house-to-house delivery either at Bathurst or McCarthy Island, for which place mails are made up weekly by the "Mansah Kilah," and by other conveyances when obtainable.

PILLAR OR WALL BOXES.

The are no pillar or wall boxes in the colony and protectorate.

RATES OF POSTAGE.

The rates of postage are given on page 288.

MONEY ORDERS.

Foreign Money Orders are issued and paid. The rates of commission at which orders are issued are as follows:—

For sums	Not exceeding £2.	Above £2 not exceeding £5.	Above £5 not exceeding £7.	Above £7 not exceeding £10.
	s. d.	s. d.	s. d.	s. d.
If payable in the United Kingdom ...	0 6	1 0	1 6	2 0
In Sierra Leone	0 9	1 6	2 0	3 0
In Foreign Countries	0 9	1 6	£5 to £6 2 0	£6 to £10 2 9
In Lagos, Gold Coast, and the two Nigeria Protectorates	2d. on every 10s. or part thereof.			

There is a proposal, that will shortly be adopted, to extend the issue of Money Orders to £40.

PARCEL POST.

The rates of postage of Foreign and Colonial Parcels for such places as have adopted the three scales, are:—

	s. d.
Up to 3 lb.	1 0
Over 3 lb. „ 7 lb.	2 0
Over 7 lb. „ 11 lb.	3 0

The rates of postage for foreign countries and other colonies differ, as extra transit fees become payable from the United Kingdom to destination.

The postage on inland parcels is 3d. per lb. or fraction thereof.

The dimensions permitted for parcels are restricted to 3 ft. 6 in., with length and girth combined of 6 ft.

The Parcel Post business hitherto done by the Customs was transferred entirely to the Post Office during 1903.

PRIVATE LETTER BOXES.

There are private letter boxes of three sizes placed in the General Post Office of the colony for the convenience of the public and for the safe custody of their letters, *viz.*:—

		Annually.		
		£	*s.*	*d.*
Size 1, to be used by	two persons	0	5	0
,, 2, ,,	five persons same family, ..	0	15	0
,, 3, ,,	firms, hotels, schools, &c. ..	2	0	0

STAMPS, POST CARDS, REGISTRATION ENVELOPES.

Postage Stamps, Post Cards, and Registration Envelopes, are obtainable at the General Post Office, Bathurst, and at the District Office at McCarthy Island.

The values are as follows:—

Postage Stamps—½d., 1d., 2d., 2½d., 3d., 4d., 5d., 6d., 7½d., 10d., 1s., 1s. 6d., 2s., 2s. 6d., 3s.

Post Cards—Single, 1d; Reply, 2d.

Registration Envelopes—Size F, 2½d. each; size G, 2½d. each; size H, 3d. each.

INFORMATION RESPECTING THE GENERAL POSTAL SYSTEM.

Letters.—Letters posted unpaid are chargeable with double postage on delivery; if insufficiently paid, with double the deficiency.

Letters with the declared value of the contents outside cannot be transmitted by post to places abroad unless insured.

Printed Papers.—This description includes the undermentioned articles wholly printed—*viz.*, Newspapers, books of any description, periodical works, pamphlets, sheets of music, visiting cards, address cards, proofs of printing, plans, maps, catalogues, prospectuses, announcements, circulars, notices, engravings, photographs and designs; but the articles which are entitled to be sent at the rate applicable to printed papers are mostly impressions or copies obtained upon paper, parchment, or cardboard, by means of printing, lithography, engraving, photograph, or any other mechanical process easy to recognise. Besides these articles, there are others which are admitted, though not really printed matter, as, for instance, manuscript intended for the press (when sent with the proofs of the same), papers impressed for the use of the blind, albums containing photographs, and cardboard drawing models stamped in relief, and packages of a like nature. Postage stamps, whether obliterated or not, and in general all printed articles constituting the sign of monetary value, are excluded from transmission. at the reduced rate of postage to countries of the Postal Union.

Commercial Papers.—Comprise all papers or documents written or drawn wholly or partly by hand (except letters or communications in the nature of letters, or other papers or documents having the character of an actual and personal correspondence), documents of legal procedure, documents drawn up by public functionaries, copies of or extracts from deeds under private seal written on stamped or unstamped paper, way bills, bills of lading, invoices, and other documents of a mercantile character, documents of insurance or other public companies, all kinds of manuscript music, the manuscript of books and other literary works, and pupils' exercises with corrections but without any comment on the work, and other papers of a similar description.

Books.—Printed papers and commercial papers may be sent by Book Post, in which case they should be posted with a cover not fastened by gum, wafer or sealing wax, or in an ordinary letter envelope left wholly unfastened, or a cover entirely opened at both ends; but for security of the contents the packets may be tied with a string, but the string must be easy to unfasten so as to admit of the contents being easily withdrawn for examination.

Samples.—It is intended that the use of the Sample Post to and from foreign countries and colonies be restricted to (*a*) *bona-fide* trade samples of merchandise without saleable value, and (*b*) natural history specimens and plants, geological specimens, and scientific specimens generally when sent for no commercial purpose. Packets containing goods for sale, or articles sent by the private individual to another, which are not actually trade samples or scientific specimens cannot be sent by Sample Post.

Registration.—There are few countries where no arrangements for registration exists. The fee chargeable for registration is 2d.; registration is applicable equally to letters, post cards, newspapers, book packets and patterns, addressed to places abroad. An acknowledgment of delivery may be obtained by the sender of a registered letter or package on payment, either at the time of posting or any time after, of a fee of 2½d. The name and address of the sender as well as of the addressee are recorded in the Post Office at which the packet is registered. A registered article must not be posted in a letter box, it must be given to an agent of the Post Office, and a receipt obtained, except in cases beyond control (*e.g.*, tempest, shipwreck, earthquake, war, etc.). This Government undertakes to give compensation of not more than £2 when it is satisfactorily proved that the registered article was lost whilst in the custody of the Post Office.

Money Orders.—No single money order can be issued for more than £40. The Post Office can stop or transfer payment, according to the direction of the remitter. Payment can be refused if the remitter's name be not correctly furnished. An order may be made payable through a bank by being crossed by the holder of the order. In all cases where an order is issued the surname and at least the initial of one Christian name of the payee should be given by the remitter. After once paying a money order, by whomsoever presented, the Post Office is not responsible for any further claim, nor can any application for compensation for loss or injury arising out of the delay of a money order, or out of any other irregularity in connection therewith, be entertained. Money orders can not be issued on Sundays.

Postal Orders.—In accordance with Circular Despatch from the Secretary of State dated 18th August, 1903, a postal order system has been introduced between this colony and the United Kingdom, and also with other places in the Empire which have adopted the postal order system of remitting small sums. The scheme came into operation on the 1st October, 1904. The following are the denominations issued in the colony—*viz.*, 6d., 1s., 2s., 2s. 6d., 3s., 5s., 7s. 6d., 10s., 15s., and 20s. The poundage is—for sums up to 1s., 1d.; above 1s. and not exceeding 10s., 2d.; above 10s. and not exceeding 20s., 3d.

Insurance.—Letters with declared value, as well as parcels, can be insured to any place which has adopted the insurance system.

Work Done in 1903-04.

The number of letters, post cards, books, newspapers, and sample packets, dealt with was 94,365; parcels, 1,532. Money orders issued, £2,410 9s. 3d.; paid, £159 17s. 2d. During 1904 the letters, etc., dealt with were 94,358; parcels, 1,677. There was a decided falling off in the number of money orders issued, due to the increased Bills of Exchange through the Bank of British West Africa. The Post Office revenue during 1904 was, however, £63 4s. 6d. more than that for 1903.

RATES OF POSTAGE.

PAYMENT MUST BE EFFECTED BY MEANS OF POSTAGE STAMPS.

TO	For a letter, per ½ oz.	For a single postcard.	For a reply postcard.	For newspaper or other printed paper, per 2 oz.	Registration fee.	Registration fee for commercial papers.	Registration fee for samples.
The undermentioned British Possessions and Protectorate—*viz.*, Aden (including Perim), Ascension, Bahamas, Barbados, Bermudas, British Central Africa Protectorate, British East Africa Protectorate, British Guiana, British Honduras, British North Borneo, Canada, Cape Colony, Cayman Islands, Ceylon, China (places at which British post offices are maintained—*viz.*, Amoy, Canton, Chefoo, Foochow, Hanhow, Holhow, Lin-Kung-Tan (Wei-Hai-Wei), Ningpo, Shanghai, Swatow), Cyprus, Falkland Islands, Fanning Island, Fiji, Gambia, Gibraltar, Gold Coast, Hong Kong, India, Jamaica, Johore, Labuan, Lagos, Leeward Islands (*viz.*, Antigua, St. Kitts, Nevis, Dominica, Montserrat, and the Virgin Islands), Malay States, (Federated—*viz.*, Perak, Selangor, Negri-Sembilan, and Pahang), Malta, Mauritius, Natal (including Zululand), Newfoundland, New Zealand (including Cook Islands), Nigeria (Northern), Nigeria (Southern), Orange River Colony, St. Helena, Sarawak, Seychelles, Sierra Leone.	1d.	1d.	2d.	½d.	2d.	Same as for printed papers, except that the lowest charge is 2½d.	Same as for printed papers, except that the lowest charge is 1d.
All other places in the Postal Union ...	2½d.	1d.	2d.	½d.	2d.	—	—

AFRICAN DIRECT TELEGRAPH COMPANY, LIMITED.

The following are the charges for Cablegrams between Bathurst, Gambia, and the following places:—

	Per word. s.	d.
Great Britain and Ireland	3	6
Ascension	2	0
Bissao and Bolama ..	1	7
Cameroons	3	0
Canaries	2	5
Dahomey—Kotonou, etc.	2	5
French Congo — Libreville, etc.	3	10
French Guinea—Conakry	1	8
,, ,, Other places	1	9
Gold Coast—Accra and Sekondi ..	2	2
,, Other stations	2	4
Ivory Coast—Grand Bassam ..	2	2
,, Other stations	2	4
Madeira, *viâ* Teneriffe ..	2	8
Nigeria—		
Bonny	2	10
Brass	2	10
Lagos	2	10
Government Stations *viâ* Bonny	3	0
,, ,, Lagos	3	0
St. Helena	3	0
St. Iago	1	1
St. Thome'	3	7
St. Vincent	3	11
Senegal	1	9
Sierra Leone	1	0
,, Railway stations	1	1
Togoland..	2	6

Telegrams for Transmission.

Attention is called to the great importance of legible writing.

The name of the place, time, and date of origin, and the number of words charged for, are transmitted free; everything else written by the sender on the telegram form for transmission is charged for.

Code telegrams must consist of words or pronounceable combinations of letters not exceeding ten letters.

Plain language telegrams.—Words containing more than fifteen letters and not exceeding thirty letters are charged for as two words.

Combinations or alterations of words contrary to the usage of the language cannot be accepted.

The sender of a telegram is responsible for the consequences arising from incorrect or insufficient address.

The sender of a message must sign his name at the foot of the message, adding his address for purpose of reference.

The company will give a receipt for the payment of every message handed in at their stations.

All important telegrams should be repeated. An additional charge, equal to one-quarter of the ordinary rate, is made for this extra service.

Telegrams delivered.

An abbreviated telegraphic address will be registered free of charge.

Application should be made at once to the telegraph office if the message is mutilated. The charges paid for official rectification of the mutilated words will be refunded if the telegraph service has been at fault. No claims for rectifications obtained direct between sender and receiver will be entertained.

HOSPITAL RULES

MADE UNDER SECTION XXV. OF THE HOSPITALS AND DISPENSARIES ORDINANCE No. 13 OF 1901.

GENERAL HOSPITAL AT BATHURST.

1.—Accommodation for Female Patients.

I. The general hospital at Bathurst contains a separate ward, bath-room, and latrine, for the use of female patients.

2.—The Admission of Persons as In-Patients.

II. Upon or over every patient's bed a bed-ticket is hung, whereon is entered as soon as possible after the admission of the patient full particulars, as follows:—

(*a*) Patient's name, sex, age (so far as ascertainable), occupation and place of residence;
(*b*) Number of bed;
(*c*) Number in medical register;
(*d*) Folio in case book;
(*e*) Date of admission;
(*f*) Disease from which suffering;
(*g*) Prescriptions and directions as to treatment.
(*h*) Extra diet ordered.

III. Patients are admitted to hospital as in-patients daily: in ordinary cases between 6 a.m. and noon, and in urgent cases at any hour.

IV. Every person admitted or to be admitted as an in-patient is, as soon as possible after having been seen by one of the medical officers, either given a bath or washed, unless the medical officer otherwise directs.

3.—Care and Treatment of In-Patients.

V. The beds in each ward are numbered consecutively; and every bed is furnished with a mattress, a pillow, a pillow-case, a sheet, a blanket, and a coverlet.

VI. Every in-patient is provided with a night-shirt and (when prescribed by one of the medical officers) a dressing-gown and a pair of slippers.

VII. Every patient's bed clothes and clothing is exchanged for clean ones once a week or as much more frequently as one of the medical officers may order.

VIII. Subject in any individual case to any order to the contrary of one of the medical officers, every patient shall wash himself or be washed every morning and evening, and shall take a bath at least twice weekly.

THE INTRODUCTION OF VACCINATION INTO THE GAMBIA PROTECTORATE.*

IX. Meal times of patients are as follows:—

(*a*) For Europeans, early tea at 7 a.m., breakfast at 10 a.m., dinner at 2 p.m., and tea at 6 p.m.

(*b*) For Natives, morning drink at 6.30 a.m., breakfast at 10 a.m., dinner at 4 p.m.

These hours are not to be departed from without special orders from one of the medical officers. Half-an-hour is allowed for each meal. No food shall be allowed to remain on or near the beds after meals.

X. The diets are according to the diet table given in Schedule A to these Rules, or such as any of the medical officers shall in particular cases specially order.

* And see Page 109 *ante*.

XI. All orders for extras—such as brandy, port, champagne, meat extracts, etc.—shall be written by the medical officer making the same on the bed-head ticket of the patients for whom such extras are prescribed. In orders of extras the terms included in the first column of Schedule B to these Rules shall have the respective denotations attached to them in the second column of that schedule.

XII. Relatives and friends of patients are permitted to visit the latter in hospital on Sundays, Tuesdays and Thursdays, between the hours of 2 and 4 p.m., provided that any of the medical officers may at any time prohibit any such visit if he be of opinion that the same would be injurious to any patient; provided also that any of the medical officers may authorise any person to visit any patient at any time.

XIII. Clergymen of any denomination, or their accredited representatives, may visit patients of their own religious persuasion at any reasonable hour, provided that such visits be not prohibited by any of the medical officers on medical grounds.

XIV. No visitor shall give to any patient, or bring into the hospital for such purpose, any food, drink, or tobacco, without having first obtained leave for the purpose from one of the medical officers.

XV. The use of tobacco in the wards, and gambling, quarrelling, swearing, the use of abusive or indecent language, and every kind of unnecessary noise, in any hospital building or in any part of the hospital or hospital compounds are strictly prohibited.

XVI. No patient shall leave the hospital, even temporarily, without the permission in writing of one of the medical officers.

XVII. The discharge of patients from the hospital shall in general be subject to the control of the senior medical officer; and no in-patient shall be discharged except upon a written order of the senior medical officer, or in his absence of a medical officer, to be written on the bed-head ticket of such patient.

XVIII. No indigent and infirm patient not known to have friends ready to receive him are discharged from the hospital without the directions of the Governor having first been taken with regard to such discharge.

4.—Scale of Charges for Paying In-Patients.

XIX. The following sums are paid by way of fees and charges for accommodation, treatment, and maintenance, in the hospital by patients able to pay the same:—

	s.	d.
Government officers (including native clerks in the Government service who may wish for the same accommodation and treatment as Europeans) whose salaries amount to £300 per annum and upwards, per day	4	0
Ditto, ditto, whose salaries do not amount to £300 per annum, per day	2	6
Native clerks and employees whose salaries are £150 and do not exceed £300 per annum, and who do not require the same treatment and accommodation as Europeans, per day.. ..	1	6

H.E. THE GOVERNOR. Dr. E. HOPKINSON (Protectorate Medical Officer).

THE INTRODUCTION OF VACCINATION INTO THE GAMBIA PROTECTORATE.

Native clerks and employees whose salaries are £100 and under £150, a day	1	0
Ditto, ditto, are £50 and under £100, a day	0	9
Ditto, ditto, are under £50 per annum, a day	0	6
Privates of the West African Frontier Force and of the Civil Police, per day	0	3
For patients other than those specified below and not in the Government service, the above charges to be doubled.		
Artizans, labourers, servants, etc., per day.. ..	0	6
Women to be charged according to their station or that of their husbands, parents or guardians, etc.		

Children under fourteen years of age are charged for at half the rates of non-officials, according to the station of their parents or guardians.

Paupers .. .. Free

All wine, spirits, mineral waters, and special appliances provided for patients, shall be charged and paid for by them to the steward.

No proceedings are taken for the recovery of any sum payable under this rule without the consent of the Governor having first been obtained for the purpose; provided that the senior medical officer may, with the approval of the Governor, require a written guarantee for the payment of any fees or charges, to be given by the patient himself, his employer, or some fit and responsible person, prior to the admission of the patient.

The Governor may, for any reason which he shall deem sufficient, remit altogether or in part any sum payable under this rule.

Patients are placed in such wards and receive such diet treatment as the senior medical officer or the medical officer attending the same in each case direct.

5.—The Attendance of "Out-Patients."

XX. "Out-patients" shall include all persons attending regularly for treatment at the "out-patient" department.

"Casualties" shall be such out-patients as attend once for some injury or slight ailment.

The hours of attendance for such patients shall be from 8 till 9 every morning, and patients attending after 9 o'clock shall on demand be admitted by the dispenser, but except in cases of urgency shall not be entitled to receive medical attention until the next visit of a medical officer.

6.—Hours of Attendance of the Medical Officer at the Out-Patient Department of the Colonial Hospital.

XXI. The medical officer shall attend daily at the out-patient department from 8 till 10 a.m. on week days and from 8.30 to 9 a.m. on Sundays until further notice.

7.—Regulations for the Information of Visitors to the Colonial Hospital.

XXII. The days and hours for visitors shall be Sundays, Tuesdays and Thursdays, from 2 to 4 p.m. Special permission may be given at other times by the medical officer in certain cases.

XXIII. Not more than four visitors shall be allowed in any ward at the same time. Children are not permitted to enter the wards as visitors.

XXIV. Visitors shall on no account give to any patient articles of food, drink, or tobacco, etc., without the permission of a medical officer.

XXV. No visitor shall be permitted to remain for a longer period than ten minutes in the ward except when special permission has been given by the medical officer.

XXVI. Visitors shall await their turn to enter the wards in the entrance hall of the hospital; they must not wander about the hospital buildings or compounds.

10.—Scale of Diets at the Bathurst Hospital.

SCHEDULE A.

EUROPEAN.

FULL.	LOW.
1 lb. beef or mutton, or 1 chicken	1 lb. beef or mutton, or 1 chicken
½ „ fish	½ „ fish
1 „ bread	1 „ bread
¼ „ rice	¼ „ sugar
⅛ „ sugar	⅛ „ butter
⅛ „ butter	½ „ milk
¼ „ milk	¼ „ flour
½ „ potatoes	2 dr. onions
¼ „ pumpkin, tomatoes or cassada	3 „ salt
¼ „ flour	1 „ pepper
2 dr. onions	4 „ tea
3 „ salt	
1 „ black pepper	
4 „ tea or 2 oz. cocoa	
8 „ lard	
4 eggs	

NATIVE.

FARINA OR AGIDI.	RICE.
1½ lb. of bread or 1 lb. agidi	¼ lb. meat
4 oz. fish	1 „ rice
5 „ greens	2 dr. onions or tomatoes
2 dr. of onions or tomatoes	5 oz. greens
2 „ pepper	2 dr. pepper
1 oz. ground nut oil	1 pint milk
1 pint of milk	1 „ soup
1 „ beef tea	1 oz. ground nut oil
3 dr. salt	1 lb. bread
	3 dr. salt

11.—Meaning of Certain Terms in Orders for Extras.

SCHEDULE B.

A pint of Tea.—¼ oz. tea, 1½ oz. sugar, 2 dr. condensed milk.

Lime Drink.—1½ oz. sugar and 1 lime.

Barley Water.—½ oz. barley, ½ oz. sugar.

Gruel.—1 oz. oatmeal, 1 oz. sugar, 2 oz. condensed milk.

Rice Pudding.—2 eggs, 2 oz. rice, ½ oz. sugar, 2 oz. condensed milk.

Benger's Food.—2 oz. Benger's food, 4 oz. milk.

Custard Pudding.—3 eggs, ½ oz. sugar, 1 oz. condensed milk.

RULES FOR THE GUIDANCE OF EUROPEAN NURSES.

I. The staff of European nurses shall consist of a matron or senior nurse, and such other nurses as may from time to time be appointed.

II. The matron shall be the head of the general staff of the hospital, and shall be responsible for the discipline of the institution to the medical officer.

III. The other nurses shall obey the orders of the matron or senior nurse, and perform whatever duties she may detail them for in addition to their duties as prescribed by the senior medical officer.

IV. All nurses shall obey such orders as may be given them by the senior medical officer or by any medical officer on duty in the hospital.

V. It shall be the duty of the senior medical officer to issue all necessary orders affecting nurses with regard to hours of duty, meals, temporary leave of absence, and special duty.

VI. There shall always be one nurse on duty in the hospital. A nurse when off duty may be absent from the hospital between the hours of 4 and 9 p.m. No nurse shall be absent at any other time except with the written permission of the senior medical officer. All special leaves shall be entered in a book kept for that purpose.

VII. The native nurses shall be under the supervision and orders of the nurses in charge in all matters appertaining to attendance on patients and the cleanliness of the wards.

VIII. The nurses shall report at once to the senior medical

officer, through the matron, any misconduct or neglect of duty on the part of the native nurses, or any damage to furniture or appliances which may have occurred through their carelessness.

IX. The matron or senior nurse shall take charge of all garments, linen, furniture and appliances, in the European ward, and the other nurses shall be responsible for similar articles in the wards in their charge. An inventory of such articles shall be taken at least once in every three months by the nurse in whose charge they are, all deficiencies, etc., being brought to the notice of the senior medical officer or medical officer in charge.

X. These rules shall be read as forming part of Hospital Rules 1902, made under section xxv. of the Hospital and Dispensaries Ordinance No. 13 of 1901.

OSTRICH, GIVEN BY MOUSA MOLLAH TO H.E. THE GOVERNOR, SIR G. C. DENTON, ON ITS WAY HOME TO ENGLAND FOR PRESENTATION TO THE ROYAL ZOOLOGICAL SOCIETY.

CHAPTER XIII.

Miscellaneous Information.

Days and Hours of Attendance of Customs Officials and Fees Chargeable—Customs Tariff—Charges for Depositing Goods in the King's Warehouses—Tariff for Licences—Buoyage Dues—Licensing of Pilots—Licensing of Inland Water Craft—Rates for Use of Government Wharf—Slaughter-House Regulations and Fees—Charges for Animals Impounded—Market Regulations—Rules as to Importation of Arms and Ammunition—Local Directory.

Fiscal arrangements, the conditions and tariffs affecting various licenses, slaughter-house and market regulations, and the rules in force as to the importation of arms and ammunition, are the main features of the following chapter. It concludes with a local directory which, though at present of limited dimensions, may be of use to many who have relations with the colony.

CUSTOMS DEPARTMENT.

DAYS AND HOURS OF, AND FEES FOR, ATTENDANCE OF CUSTOMS OFFICIALS.

I. The days of general attendance of all officers and persons in the service of the Customs are all days in the year, with the exception of Sundays and of public holidays; and the hours of general attendance during such days are as follows, *viz* :—

A.—*Out-door Officers.*

(1) In general, from 6.30 a.m. till 11 a.m., and from 1 p.m. till 5 p.m.

(2) On half-holidays, from 6.30 a.m. till 11 a.m., and from 1 p.m. till 3 p.m.*

* The hours of attendance for the Customs Out-Door Branch as given here vary slightly from those given on page 236, which are incorrect.

B.—*In-door Officers.*

(1) In general, from 8 a.m. till 11 a.m., and from 1 p.m. till 4 p.m.

(2) On half-holidays, from 8 a.m. till 11 a.m.

Subject to the exigencies of the service, every Saturday is observed as a half-holiday, provided always as follows: That where the exigencies of the service render it necessary to require the attendance of the officers of the in-door branch of the Customs on a Saturday or Public Holiday, the said in-door branch is, subject to such exigencies as aforesaid, closed upon the following Wednesday for the whole day, or the half or any part thereof equivalent to the time the same was opened on such preceding Saturday or Public Holiday.

II. For the attendance of any officer or officers of the Customs on Sundays or Public Holidays, or during any hours on any day whatsoever in the year other than the hours of general attendance above expressed, there is payable by the importer or person on whose behalf, or by the owners, charterers, or master, or by the agent of the owners, charterers, or master of the vessel in respect whereof such attendance is given, the following fees and charges:—

(*a*) For the attendance of all or any of the in-door officers (to be charged in respect of the attendance of such officers collectively, and irrespective of the number whose services are required)—

	£	s.	d.
(1) Between the hours of 6 a.m. and 8 p.m.			
For the first hour or fraction thereof ..	1	0	0
For every subsequent hour or fraction thereof	0	10	0
(2) Between 8 p.m. and midnight.			
For the first hour or fraction thereof ..	3	0	0
For every subsequent hour or fraction thereof	2	0	0
(3) Between midnight and 6 a.m.			
For the first hour or fraction thereof ..	4	0	0
For every subsequent hour or fraction thereof	2	0	0
(4) On Sundays and Public Holidays, at any hour.			
For the first hour or fraction thereof ..	4	0	0
For every subsequent hour or fraction thereof	2	0	0

In no case are the fees payable under this scale to exceed the sum of £10 for any one day of twenty-four hours, to be reckoned from 6 a.m. to 6 a.m.

(*b*) For the attendance of every one or more out-door officers (to be charged only in respect of such officers individually as may be required for the services to be rendered to the said person or vessel)—

	Tide Surveyor. s. d.	Other Officers, each. s. d.
(1) Between 6 a.m. and 8 p.m.		
For the first hour or fraction thereof ..	6 0	3 0
For every subsequent hour or fraction thereof	3 0	2 0
(2) Between 8 p.m. and midnight.		
For the first hour or fraction thereof ..	8 0	4 0
For every subsequent hour or fraction thereof	4 0	3 0
(3) Between midnight and 6 a.m.		
For the first hour or fraction thereof ..	10 0	5 0
For every subsequent hour or fraction thereof	5 0	4 0
(4) On Sundays and Public Holidays, at any hour.		
For the first hour or fraction thereof ..	8 0	4 0
For every subsequent hour or fraction thereof	4 0	3 0

In no case do the fees payable under this scale exceed £2 in respect of the services of the Tide Surveyor, and £1 in respect of the services of any other officer, for any one day of twenty-four hours, to be reckoned from 6 a.m. to 6 a.m.

III. All such fees are payable to the Collector of Customs, who pays the same into the Treasury as portion of the revenue of the colony.

Note.—The above regulations apply, not only to the port of Bathurst, but to all loading ports on the river Gambia.

Dog Race at a Gymkhana in Bathurst.

GAMBIA CUSTOMS TARIFF IN FORCE.

IMPORTS.

Under Ordinance No. 1 of 14th January, 1905.

Article.	Rates of Duty.	Authority.
Coffee, raw	5s. per 100 lb.	Imposed by Ordinance No. 1 of 14th Jan., 1905.
Gunpowder	1d. per lb.	
Guns and Rifles (breech-loading) ...	20s. each	
Other Firearms	4s. each	
Kola Nuts	2d. per lb.	
Malt Liquor	1s. per gallon	
Oils, cooking and edible, in bulk in packages of not less than 1 gallon ...	6d. per gallon	
Oils, Paint and Turps, Kerosine and other burning oils not being edible	3d. per gallon	
Rice	6d. per cwt.	
Salt	5s. per ton	
Brandy and Whisky of or under the strength of $12\frac{1}{2}$ per cent. under proof by Sykes' hydrometer, and so in proportion for any greater strength	4s. per imperial gallon or part thereof	Ordinance No. 5 of 25th April, 1905.
Upon other Spirits, except perfumes, of the strength of $12\frac{1}{2}$ per cent. under proof by Sykes' hydrometer, and so in proportion for any greater or lesser strength	4s. per imperial gallon or part thereof	
Upon all kind of Spirits sweetened so that the degree of strength cannot be ascertained by Sykes' hydrometer	4s. per imperial gallon or part thereof	
Sugar	1d. per lb.	Imposed by Ordinance No. 1 of 14th Jan., 1905.
Tobacco, manufactured...	1s. 6d. per lb.	
Cigars and Cigarettes	2s. per lb.	
Tobacco, unmanufactured	3d. per lb.	
Wines, Claret, in bulk, not less than 20 gallons	1s. per gallon	
Claret, in bottles or other packages, less than 20 gallons	2s. per gallon	
Other Wines	2s. per gallon	
Ad valorem duty on all other goods other than free goods...	5 per cent.	

TABLE OF EXEMPTIONS.

Animals—all sorts.

Birds—including poultry.

Boats—canoes, lighters, steam launches, etc.

Books—printed, including maps and all printed matter except ruled books or forms.

Bullion.

Carts and Wagons—used for agricultural purposes.

Coals—coke and patent fuel.

Coin—current in the colony.

Drawings, paintings, engravings, lithographs and photographs.

Fish—fresh.

Fruit—fresh.

Hay and Straw.

Ice—and all fresh provisions on ice.

Meat—fresh.

Machines—[not bicycles] set in motion by hand or any power.

Mills—for grinding, sawing, raising water, or any such as are set in motion by electricity, steam, horse, wind or water power, and all parts of the said mills.

Manures—all sorts.

Oil Cake—and other prepared food for cattle and animals.

Packages—in which goods are ordinarily imported.

Pipes—for conveying fluids.

Plants—growing, and seeds for planting.

Ploughs—harrows, cultivators, clod-crushers, and other farming implements.

Pumps—for raising water.

Scientific and surgical instruments and apparatus.

Specimens—illustrative of natural history, mineralogy, botany, etc.

Steam Engines—or any part of a steam engine.

Tombstones.

Turtle.

Vegetables—fresh.

Wire Fencing—iron fencing, standards for the same, tomb railings.

Passenger's baggage, consisting of wearing apparel and personal effects, such as jewellery, brushes and combs, intended for the personal use of such passenger, but not spirits, wines, liqueurs, tobacco, provisions, scent, and other articles included in such baggage. Provided always that duty shall not be charged on any spirits or scent not exceeding one half-pint of either, or on any cigars, cigarettes or tobacco not exceeding in the aggregate 1 lb. in weight included in a passenger's baggage. Deck chairs and bedding used by the passenger during the voyage.

Articles of every description imported for the use of the Colonial Government.

Articles of every description imported by the officer administering the Government for his personal use.

War Department and Admiralty: All non-consumable articles, such as furniture, plate, glass, or cutlery, for the sole use of any mess or canteen belonging to officers or sergeants of His Majesty's army, when certified by the officer commanding the corps having such mess or canteen, and such certificate is countersigned by the officer commanding the troops that the same are imported solely for the use of any such mess or canteen, on an understanding that none of the articles shall be sold in the colony.

Arms, accoutrements, and uniforms the property of officers of His Majesty's army, navy or civil service, imported by such officers for their personal use on duty as required by the regulations of their respective services.

Articles of every description imported for the sole use of any mess or officer or any of the crew of any of the ships of His Majesty's squadron on the coast of Africa, upon proof being made to the satisfaction of the Governor that the same are *bonâ fide* imported for the sole use of any such mess, officer or crew, and on an undertaking that none of the articles shall be sold in the colony.

Telegraph materials: All *bonâ fide* telegraph materials landed for the use of the African Direct Telegraph Company.

Educational appliances: Copy books, ruled books, stationery, school furniture and appliances, when imported by the manager of a school and certified by him as being solely intended for educational purposes.

Consulates: Official goods imported for the use of Consulates.

The following manufactured and unmanufactured articles of African produce—*viz.*, Aggidi, foofoo, shea butter, palm oil, kernel oil, corn, melon seed, raw ginger, dried pepper, raw cotton, beni-seed, gum copal, gum arabic, palm kernels, ivory.

The following rates of rent are payable in respect of goods deposited or secured in the King's warehouses, after an entry made for that purpose (under Governor's order dated March 29, 1901), *viz.*:—

ARTICLES.	RATE. s.	d.	
Wines, Malt Liquours or Spirits, in bottles, per imperial gallon	0	½	Per month, or fractional part of a month.
,, ,, ,, in bulk, per gallon	0	½	
Tobacco, per 100 lb.		2	
Crockery, per crate	2	0	
Other goods, per barrel	0	3	
,, ,, puncheon	0	8	
,, ,, larger casks	1	0	
,, per bale, package or case, not exceeding 3 cubic feet	0	1	
And larger packages in proportion.			

Large consignments of goods, in cases similar in size and description, may, in the option of the Collector of Customs, be charged at the rate of ½d. per cubic foot of the space occupied by such goods, in lieu of the above rates.

In respect of goods deposited or secured in the King's Warehouses without entry made for that purpose, rent shall be chargeable at four times the above rates. Kolas shall be chargeable at the rate of 6d. per 50 lb. weight thereof per week.

In case of goods entered to be warehoused, the rent shall run and become chargeable as from the date of such entry.

On other goods rent shall become chargeable when the same have remained in the King's warehouse forty-eight hours, or in the case of kolas one week.

GROUND-NUT STORE IN BATHURST.

Picking the best nuts for the English Market, where they are sold for decorating Cakes and for other purposes.

TARIFF FOR LICENSES.

	(a) Retail Licenses.	(a) Wholesale Licenses.	Authority.
(a) Where the premises in respect of which the license is granted are situate in the town of Bathurst or elsewhere in the Island of St. Mary—			Ordinance No. 13 of 1903.
For an annual license	£50	£15	
For a half-yearly license ...	£30	£8	
(b) Where the premises in respect of which the license is granted are situate in the Protectorate			
For an annual license	£10	£10	
For a half-yearly license ...	£6	£6	

License.	£	s.	d.	Authority.
Auctioneer's Licenses as follows:—				Ordinance 28th June, 1901.
1. For the Colony of the Gambia and the Protectorate—				
Every License of the Form A., for one year ...	20	0	0	
,, ,, for a half-year ...	15	0	0	
,, ,, Form B., for one year ...	25	0	0	
,, ,, for a half-year ...	18	0	0	
,, ,, Form C., for one year ...	2	0	0	
,, ,, for a half-year ...	1	0	0	
2. For the Protectorate, including McCarthy's Island and other portions of the colony whereto the Protectorate ordinance has been or may hereafter be extended—				
Every License of the Form A., for one year ...	5	0	0	
,, ,, for a half-year ...	3	0	0	
,, ,, Form B., for one year ...	6	0	0	
,, ,, for a half-year ...	4	0	0	
,, ,, Form C., for one year ...	2	0	0	
,, ,, for a half-year ...	1	4	0	
Hawkers' Licenses—a year	1	10	0	Ordinance 21st Dec., 1897.
Boats and Canoes ,, ,, ...	0	10	0	Ordinance 20th June, 1862.
Marriage ,, ...	3	3	0	Ordinance 24th July, 1890.
Dog ,, a year	0	5	0	
To sell arms and ammunition in Bathurst ...	20	0	0	
,, ,, ,, up the river ...	2	0	0	
Traders in Protectorate	10	0	0	
,, ,, ...	3	0	0	Ordinance 13th July, 1895.
,, ,, ...	2	0	0	
Petty Traders in Protectorate	0	10	0	
,, ,, ,, ...	0	8	0	
,, ,, ,, ...	0	4	0	

THE FOLLOWING RULES (DUES FOR BUOYAGE) ARE IMPOSED UNDER ORDINANCE No. 1 OF 1904, AND ARE COLLECTED BY THE NAVIGATION AND PILOTAGE BOARD.

BUOYAGE DUES.

All ships or vessels entering at or clearing from the port of Bathurst from or for ports beyond the sea, shall, subject to the exemptions and modifications hereinafter expressed, pay to the Harbour Master, or to the Clerk of the Board, or any other officer authorised by the Board to receive the same, the following charges in the name of Buoyage Dues, *viz.*:—

(1.) (*a*) Vessels of or under 20 tons gross register, 10s.

(*b*) Vessels over 20 and less than 50 tons gross register, 20s.

Such charges of 10s. and 20s. respectively, payable on entry, to be in full of all buoyage dues payable by any vessel in respect of both—

(i.) her entry into port, and

(ii.) her subsequent clearance therefrom, provided always such clearance shall be within six months from the date of entry; but in case clearance shall not be made within six months from the date of entry, as aforesaid, a further and additional sum of 10s. or 20s. respectively shall be due and exigible in respect of such clearance.

(2) Vessels of over 50 tons gross register, a sum to be calculated at the rate of 5s. for each and every foot or fraction of a foot which the said vessel may draw at the time of entering the said port, payable on entry; and a like sum, similarly calculated, on clearance from the said port, whether within six months from entry or otherwise.

Vessels registered at the port of Bathurst under the provisions of the Merchant Shipping Acts shall not in any case be liable in more than a single payment, according to the rate imposed in the last preceding section in the name of buoyage dues, during the currency of any one year; the year for the purpose of this section to be reckoned from the 1st day of January to the 31st day of December inclusive.

Steamers of or belonging to—

(*a*) The British and African Steam Navigation Company (1900), Limited,

(*b*) The African Steamship Company, Limited,

(*c*) Any other mail company approved of and recognised by the Governor as mail steamers for the carriage of His Majesty's mails,

(*d*) Ships of war, pleasure yachts and telegraph steamers, shall be exempted from the dues imposed by this Ordinance.

LICENSING OF PILOTS.

Persons applying to be licensed as pilots must be of the full age of twenty-one years, and must be of good character, and have had five years' experience of the navigation of the River Gambia.

All applications shall be submitted to the Collector of Customs as chairman of the Licensing Board, and no pilot's license shall be granted except with the approval of the board.

Every license shall expire on the 31st day of December in the year in or in respect of which the same is issued; but may be renewed from year to year at the discretion of the Harbour Master. Every renewal shall be endorsed on the license under the hand of the Harbour Master.

Licenses may be issued and renewals granted not earlier than the 1st day of October of any year in respect of the year then next ensuing.

A fee of 10s. shall be paid in advance in respect of every application made or license issued or renewal granted.

All fees for licenses and renewals shall be received by the Clerk of the Board, who shall forthwith pay the same into the Treasury, into a separate account to be kept for that purpose.

The employment of a qualified pilot shall be compulsory for all vessels over 100 tons navigating any part of the River Gambia between the port of Bathurst and McCarthy's Island.

The rates payable to pilots in respect of services rendered by them shall be such as may be agreed between the parties, but shall not in any case exceed the following amounts:—

PILOTAGE ABOVE THE PORT OF BATHURST.

For piloting vessels from Bathurst to	Ballangar.	Kuntawur.	McCarthy's Island or above.
Steamers over 500 tons ..	£4	£6	£8
Vessels below	£2	£3	£4

These rates include the return voyage.

PILOTAGE BELOW THE PORT OF BATHURST.

For piloting vessels of any description to the fairway buoy, 8s. per foot of the vessel's draught.

Pilots employed on vessels outward bound and landed at ports beyond the sea shall further be entitled to receive a sum sufficient to cover the expenses of their passage back to Bathurst.

All pilots shall report themselves to the Clerk of the Board when about to leave the port of Bathurst and immediately on their return to the port.

Any pilot refusing to accept service without reasonable cause within two hours after notice has been given that his services are required by the owner, consignee, or master of a vessel, shall be liable to suspension or have his license cancelled by the Board.

LICENSING OF INLAND WATER CRAFT.

1. The following classes of inland water craft shall be licensed in manner hereinafter in these bye-laws provided, *viz*:—

(*a*) British ships registered at the port of Bathurst under the provisions of the Merchant Shipping Acts (but with exemption from payment of any fee on first licensing thereof, as provided below in Rule 3);

(*b*) Schooners, cutters, and other decked vessels;

(*c*) Canoes constructed on European principles;

(*d*) Lighters;

(*e*) Steamers and all craft propelled by machinery.

The following are exempt from licensing—

(i) Un-decked boats, and "dug-outs" or other canoes constructed on native principles;

(ii) Schooners and other vessels engaged in the direct export of ground-nuts, and not employed for any other purpose in the colonial waters;

2. It shall be the duty of the Harbour Master to survey, and on being satisfied as to their sea-worthiness to license inland water craft falling to be licensed as above provided.

3. The following fees shall be payable for annual licenses—

Vessels under 10 tons gross register	5s.
Over 10 tons and not exceeding 20 tons ..	10s.
Over 20 tons and not exceeding 30 tons ..	20s.
Over 30 tons and upwards	30s.

Registered British ships shall be exempt from payment of any fee on the first licensing thereof, but shall pay the yearly fee as prescribed above.

All fees shall be paid to the Clerk of the Board prior to the issue of the license. The Clerk of the Board shall forthwith pay such fees into the Treasury, into a separate account to be kept for that purpose.

The Harbour Master and the Clerk of the Board shall be entitled to receive such monthly salaries or fees from the Treasury as may be fixed by the Governor.

4. All licenses shall expire on the 31st day of December in the year in or in respect of which the same have been issued.

5. Licenses may be issued not earlier than the 1st day of October of any year in respect of the year then next ensuing.

THE FOLLOWING RATES ARE PAYABLE TO THE COLLECTORS OF CUSTOMS FOR THE USE OF THE GOVERNMENT WHARF.

Steamers or vessels of any description lying alongside the wharf for any day, or part of a day, ending at 6 p.m., as follows :—

Over 1,000 tons gross register, for the first day ..	£10
,, ,, ,, ,, ,, for each subsequent day	£5
,, 500 tons and not exceeding 1,000 tons, half the above rates	
,, 150 ,, and not exceeding 500 tons, quarter the above rates	
,, 50 ,, and not exceeding 150 tons, one-eighth of the above rates	
Under 50 ,, ...per diem.	10s.

SLAUGHTER-HOUSE REGULATIONS AND FEES.

SECTIONS 34 AND 35 OF ORDINANCE NO. 4 OF 1887.

No cattle to be slaughtered except in licensed slaughter-house.

34. Whosoever shall slaughter or cause to be slaughtered any cattle, except sheep or goats, in any part of the Island of St. Mary except in the public slaughter-house, or in such other slaughter-houses as may from time to time be licensed and proclaimed by the officer administering the Government, shall be liable to a penalty not exceeding 10s., and in default of payment to imprisonment, with or without hard labour, for a period not exceeding one week.

Board may make by-laws for management of slaughter-house.

35. It shall be lawful for the Board of Health from time to time to make, alter, and amend, rules for all or any of the following purposes :—

(1.) With respect to the management of slaughter-houses ;

(2.) For preventing cruelty in slaughter-houses ;

(3.) For keeping slaughter-houses in a cleanly and proper state, and providing them with a sufficient supply of water ;

(1897-17-3)

(3*a*.) For prescribing the manner in which fees payable for the slaughter of cattle or other live stock slaughtered in the public slaughter-house shall be collected or accounted for, and imposing a penalty on any person whose duty it is to collect or account for such fees refusing or neglecting to do so ;

(4.) For the inspection of slaughter-houses by the Inspector of Nuisances, Colonial or Assistant Colonial Surgeon, or by any officer acting in either capacity ;

and to annex and appoint penalties on persons contravening any of such rules, or wilfully obstructing any person acting in the execution thereof, not

(1867-17-3)

exceeding for any one offence the sum of 40s., and in the case of continuing breaches or offences, not exceeding the sum of 10s. for every day on which such breach or offence is continued after a conviction thereof: Provided that in the case of a contravention of a rule made under sub-section (3*a*.) the penalty may exceed 40s., but shall not exceed £25.

Tariff of Slaughter-House charges fixed by the Governor-in-Council under the Provisions of the foregoing Ordinance.

Any person slaughtering cattle in the public slaughter-house shall pay in advance the following fees, that is to say—

	s.	*d.*
For every head ot cattle	1	6
For every sheep or goat	0	9
For every pig	1	0

Schedule of Charges to be made on Impounded Animals under the Provisions of Sections 102, 103 and 104 of Ordinance No. 4 of 1887.

Penalty for each head of cattle impounded, 2s.

Charge for feeding and detaining the above animals per diem—

	s.	*d.*
For every bull, cow, or ox ..	1	0
For every heifer or calf	1	0
For every horse, mare, gelding, or foal	1	0
For every ass or mule	1	0
For every pig	0	6
For every sheep	0	6
For every goat	0	6

REGULATIONS MADE BY THE GOVERNOR-IN-COUNCIL ON FEBRUARY 20TH, 1903, UNDER SEC. 3 OF THE MARKET ORDINANCE No. 16, 1897.*

1. These Regulations may be cited as the Market Regulations, 1903.

2. The Clerk of the Market shall allot stands and places to any person applying therefor for the sale of goods; and shall, previous to any such allotment, collect the necessary fee set out in the schedule hereto.

3. The Clerk shall not allot any stand or place to more than one person for any one period of time.

4. No person shall sell or offer goods for sale at any place within the market except at the stand or place so allotted to such person, and without having previously paid the necessary fee as set out in the schedule hereto.

5. No person shall sell or offer goods for sale at any stand or place within the market other than the person to whom such stand or place has been allotted.

6. The tariff of market fees fixed by the Administrator-in-Council on 3rd January, 1898, under sec. 3 of the Market Ordinance 1897, is hereby repealed.

* The draft of a more comprehensive set of Market Regulations is now under consideration.

7. Any person wilfully or negligently contravening the provisions of these regulations shall be liable on conviction to a penalty not exceeding 4s.

SCHEDULE.

	s.	d.
For every allotment, stand, or place, per day or part thereof	0	1
For every allotment, stand, or place, per calendar month or part thereof, terminating on the last day of the month	1	6
For every stand or place on which any table, stall, booth, or other erection is placed	Three times the above charges.	

IMPORTATION OF ARMS AND AMMUNITION.

All firearms, ammunition and gunpowder imported into the colony must be deposited at the cost, risk, etc., of the person or persons importing, and must be placed in buildings that are provided for storing such goods as the Government may direct.

It is not lawful to introduce by land any firearms, ammunition or gunpowder from neighbouring countries; but the Governor may, on special request, grant licenses for such introduction into the colony on the following conditions:—

1. To persons affording sufficient guarantee that the firearms, ammunition or gunpowder in question wiil not be given, assigned, or sold, to third persons.

2. To travellers provided with a declaration of their Government stating that the firearms, ammunition or gunpowder are destined exclusively for their personal defence.

Any person contravening the above conditions are liable to summary conviction, with forfeiture of goods imported and a penalty, not exceeding £100, or imprisonment, with or without hard labour, for any period not exceeding twelve months.

No firearms, ammunition or gunpowder can be withdrawn from a public warehouse without the express authority of the Governor, under penalties similar to those above quoted, and the authority for withdrawal applies only to firearms with unrifled barrels and trade powder; moreover, the number of guns and the quantity of powder withdrawn must be specially mentioned in the authority given, and the destination of the stores also stated, as well as the quantities remaining in store.

Other important conditions as to the importation and disposal of arms, ammunition and gunpowder, with penalties for contravening such rules, will be found in Ordinance Nos. 4 and 7 of 1902, and No. 5 of 1903, which provides for forfeiture of goods remaining in the custody of the Government over twelve months without payment of warehouse rents.

LOCAL DIRECTORY

CLERGY.

Rev. Pierre Wieder, Roman Catholic, Superior.
Rev. Miestermann, Roman Catholic.
Rev. Brother Healy, Roman Catholic.
Rev. F. J. Nicholas, B.A., Anglican Chaplain.
Rev. Arthur Pool, Wesleyan.
Rev. J. L. Davis, Wesleyan.
Rev. J. W. King, Wesleyan.
Mari N'Jie, Mohammedan, The Almami.

LAWYERS.

W. R. Townsend, Attorney - General, Marine Parade. Permitted private practice.
S. J. Forster, Jr., B.A., B.C.L.(Oxon.), Wellington Street.
I. J. Roberts, Solicitor, Buckle Street.
Z. T. Gibson, Solicitor, Buckle Street.

DOCTORS.

R. M. Forde, L.R.C.S., etc., Buckle Street.
F. A. Baldwin, M.R.C.S., etc., Government Quarters.
J. C. Franklin, L.R.C.S., etc., Government Quarters.
E. Hopkinson, M.B., D.S.O., Gambia Protectorate.
(Government Medical Officers, permitted private practice.)
T. Bishop, M.R.C.S.

DRUGGISTS.

W. S. Smart, Colonial Dispenser, Colonial Hospital.
J. Hart Deigh, Dobson Street.

MERCHANTS (EUROPEAN).

Bathurst Trading Company, Limited, liquor, haberdashery, cotton goods, millinery, provisions, etc., Wellington Street.

Compagnie Francaise, hardware, liquor, provisions, cotton goods, millinery, coal, etc., Wellington Street.

Maurel Freres, cotton goods, liquor, hardware, provisions, haberdashery, etc., Wellington Street.

Maurel & H. Prom, provisions, cotton goods, liquor, hardware, millinery, etc., Wellington Street.

T. Waelter & Co., hardware, cotton goods, provisions, liquor, etc., Wellington Street.

Solomon Lasry, cotton goods, millinery, provisions, etc., Wellington Street.

MERCHANTS (NATIVE).

S. Horton Jones, cotton goods, provisions, etc., Russell Street.
H. R. Carrol, cotton goods, provisions, etc., Wellington Street.
S. J. Forster, cotton goods, provisions, etc., Wellington Street.
J. D. Richards, cotton goods, provisions, etc., Wellington Street.
E. Thomas, provisions, hardware, etc., McCarthy Square.
J. E. Mahoney, cotton goods, provisions, etc., Buckle Street.
A. W. Carrol, cotton goods, provisions, etc., Buckle Street.
Job Beigh, cotton goods, provisions, etc., Picton Street.
Charles Goddard, cotton goods, provisions, etc., Fitzgerald Street.
J. W. Sawyerr, cotton goods, provisions, etc., Primet Street.
H. S. Williams, cotton goods, provisions, etc., Buckle Street.

In addition to the above, there are numerous Syrian and Native petty traders.

PRINCIPAL ARTIZANS.

Lattry Geo. Joof, carpenter, Anglesea Street.
Samuel Tebbs, carpenter, Pignard Street.
Zachaeus Ease, mason, Pignard Street.
Albert R. F. Andrews, mason, Clarkson Street.
William B. Bright, mason, Allen Street.
S. E. J. Thomas, tailor, Buckle Street.
J. W. Small, tailor, Blucher Street.
F. J. Chow, tailor, Lemon Street.
David A. Thomas, shoemaker, Fitzgerald Street.
Samuel Thomas, gold- and silver-smith, Fitzgerald Street.
Samuel T. Roberts, gold- and silver-smith, Clarkson Street.
J. Hall, blacksmith, Lancaster Street.
Mbye Cham, blacksmith, Clarkson Street.

PART IX.

A RECORD OF OFFICERS' SERVICES.

CHAPTER XIV.

A List of Officers, with Records of their Services: Administrators of the Gambia.

In this—the final—chapter is given a list of the officers of the Colony, with the titles ot their substantive appointments, the dates of their first appointments in the public service, the dates of their appointments in the Colony, the titles of their present acting appointments, the amounts of their salaries and allowances, details of their service in the Colony, and a record of the services generally of all officers. The author has also added a list of the Administrators of the Gambia since it became a·separate Colony in 1843.

Name.	Substantive appointment.	Date of first appointment in the public service.	Date of appointment in the Colony.	Present acting appointment.	Amount of annual salary and allowance, if any.
DENTON, Sir Geo. Chardin, K.C.M.G.	Governor	Ensign, 57th Regiment, October, 1869; Chief of Police, St. Vincent, April, 1880	Administrator, November, 1900; Governor, March, 1901	—	£1,500 per annum; £600 duty allowance
ARCHER, Francis Bisset	Treasurer and Postmaster	March 29, 1894	January 1, 1903	Acting Colonial Secretary	£600, and £60 per annum duty allowance; £100 per annum duty allowance when acting Colonial Secretary
AUBER, Steven Jeremie	Chief Clerk and Cashier of Customs	'une, 1878	March 31, 1883	Measuring Surveyor of Shipping (Fees only), November 13, 1902	Salary, £200; personal allowance, £20
BAILEY, Jeremiah Collingwood	Sergeant-Major of Police	November 1, 1876	November 1, 1876	—	£100; moiety of poundage, £10

Service in the Colony.	General Remarks, Record of Service, etc.
As Governor from 1900 ...	Ensign, 57th Regiment, October, 1869; Lieutenant, May, 1871; Adjutant, August, 1876; Captain, January, 1878; retired, 1879; Chief of Police, St. Vincent, April, 1880; appointed a Commissioner to inquire into the Police Force, Barbadoes, October, 1880; member of Executive and Legislative Councils, October, 1881; represented St. Vincent at the Telegraphic Conference at Barbadoes, May, 1882; administered Government, St. Vincent, May to July, 1885, and during 1886-7-8; Acting Colonial Secretary, 1886-8; Colonial Secretary, Lagos, March, 1888; administered Government on many occasions, 1889-1900; appointed Lieutenant-Governor of Lagos, 1900; C.M.G., 1891; K.C.M.G., 1900.
Acted as Colonial Secretary, February to August, 1903, and again from July, 1904, to May 12, 1905; Acting as Deputy Governor, March-May, 1905; J.P. and Commissioner of the Court of Requests; Treasurer and Postmaster; member of Executive and Legislative Councils; Manager, Savings Bank	Principal Clerk, Colonial Secretary's office, Gold Coast, March, 1894; Chief Clerk, January, 1896; Acting Assistant Colonial Secretary, August, 1896; Clerk of Council, September, 1896; Lieutenant, Gold Coast R.V., 1895; Acting Adjutant, June to October, 1896; Field Officer's certificate, Wellington Barracks, 1897; Assistant Colonial Secretary, Lagos, June, 1897; compiled Lagos Official Hand-book; in charge of the Secretariat on many occasions, 1898-1902; Acting Treasurer, January to May, 1901; and member of Executive and Legislative Councils.
Acting Measuring Surveyor of Shipping, March to June, 1886; Clerk in Charge of Customs Department from November 14 to 24, 1902; Secretary of Navigation Board	Temporary Outdoor Officer of Customs, Sierra Leone, June, 1878; Tide Waiter, August, 1879; Landing Waiter, September, 1880; Senior Acting Measuring Surveyor of Shipping, Sierra Leone, August, 1882; Clerk of Customs, Gambia, 1883; Chief Clerk and Cashier, 1892; had temporary charge of the Customs Department for twelve days during the absence of the Collector of Customs on sick leave at the Cape in November, 1902.
27 years and 5 months ...	Punitive Expedition to Bondali, Fogni, 1878; marched from the Gambia to Sierra Leone with Administrator Gouldsbury, 1881; accompanied Sir Alfred Maloney, Sir James Shaw Hay and Sir Gilbert Carter, on several missions in the hinterland as Interpreter and in charge of police escort; Punitive Expedition to the north and south bank of the River Gambia, under Sir Samuel Rowe, 1887; in command of police escort which accompanied the Anglo-French Boundary Commissioners to the hinterland under Captain Kenny, R.E., 1891; Gambia Expedition, 1891-2; granted medal and clasp; in command of the police stationed in foreign Kombo for about a year after the close of the war with Chief Fody Silah, 1894; Punitive Expedition to Karrenai, Fogni, when that town was shelled and destroyed by the police in November, 1898.

Name.	Substantive appointment.	Date of first appointment in the public service.	Date of appointment in the Colony.	Present acting appointment.	Amount of annual salary and allowance, if any.
BALDWIN, Francis J. A., M.R.C.S., L.R.C.P., L.S.A., London Hospital; diploma of London School of Tropical Medicine by examination	Colonial Medical Officer	April 1, 1902	April 1, 1902	Acting Senior Medical Officer	£440; and £50 per annum duty allowance when acting as Senior Medical Officer; free quarters.
BATTY, R. Fenwick	Master and Chief Engineer, Government Vessels	March 30, 1901	March 30, 1901	—	£300, and allowance £50
BRACKEN, Thomas B.	Assistant Superintendent of Police	January 29, 1903	January 29, 1903	—	£250 a year, with horse allowance of 2s. 3d. per diem; free quarters.
BROWN, Joseph	Superintendent of Police, October 29, 1894; Inspector of Prisons, March 9, 1895; Sheriff, January 1, 1903	February 21, 1878	February 6, 1892	—	£400 a year, with duty allowance £50 a year, and horse allowance of 2s. 3d. per diem; £50 a year personal allowance; £50 a year as Sheriff; free quarters.

Service in the Colony.	General Remarks, Record of Service, etc.
Acting Protectorate Medical Officer and Medical Officer to W.A.F.F.; Acting Senior Medical Officer	Medical Officer to St. Saviour's Union, London, 1894-8; Public Vaccinator, St. Saviour's Union, 1896-8; Surgeon, Elder Dempster & Co.'s s.s. "Teneriffe"; lecturer on Ambulance Work to Walthamstow Urban Council, 1898; publications in *British Medical Journal* in 1894 and 1900, *Lancet*, 1904.
As Second Engineer from April 20 to May 8, 1901; acted as Master, Government vessels on several occasions; and finally appointed Master, Government vessels, on January 2, 1902	Apprentice engineer, from February, 1888, till 1893 (Locomotive, Mining and Mechanical); Assistant Marine Engineer, from October, 1893; Senior Assistant Marine Engineer, from 1895 to 1900; Student at Dr. Ever's Engineering Academy, Leith; obtained Assistant Certificate and also first Certificate, and was a student at the Ruthford College for Science and Art.
2 years and 6 months ...	Assistant Superintendent of Police, Gambia, 1903; Acting Superintendent of Police, Inspector of Prisons and Sheriff, from February, 1903, to January, 1904. Served in South African War, 1900-1902; medal with clasps.
12 years and 2 months ...	Served in the Royal Horse Artillery; embarked for India in 1880; passed in the native languages of that country; passed long course Artillery College, Woolwich, 1891-2; specially mentioned on two occasions out of three in the manufacturing branches of the Royal Arsenal; awarded a certificate; Sub-Inspector of Police, Gambia, 1892; Acting Superintendent of Police, from July, 1892, to January, 1893; Justice of the Peace and Commissioner of the Court of Requests, Gambia, 1892; Acting Superintendent of Police and Sheriff from March to September, 1893; Acting Inspector of Prisons from March to September, 1893; member of the Quarantine Board. May, 1893; member of the Board of Health, July, 1893; Acting Superintendent of Police, from March to October, 1894; Acting Colonial Engineer, from April to December, 1894; Inspector of Prisons, March, 1895; Inspector of Weights and Measures, December, 1895; Acting Colonial Engineer, from July to November, 1896; successfully commanded a Punitive Expedition in Fogni against two Jolah chiefs—Wawo and Jaja—in 1898, mentioned in despatches and thanked for services; commanded the Artillery with the Gambia Field Force, 1901, mentioned in despatches, granted medal and clasp; Officer in charge of Secretariat, Gambia, from July to December, 1902; Sheriff, January, 1903; Acting Treasurer, &c., from February to July, 1903.

Name.	Substantive appointment.	Date of first appointment in the public service.	Date of appointment in the Colony.	Present acting appointment.	Amount of annual salary and allowance, if any.
CHAPMAN, J. C.	Chief Landing Waiter and Locker	March 1, 1890	March 1, 1890	—	£125 to £150
COKER, S. D. A.	Chief Clerk and Cashier, Treasury	January 1, 1872	January 1, 1872	—	£220
FORDE, Robert Michael, L.R.C.P., L.R.C.S., etc.	Senior Medical Officer	November, 1891	February, 1895	—	£600 to £700; 2s. 3d. a day horse allowance and free quarters

Service in the Colony.	General Remarks, Record of Service, etc.
Second Clerk of Customs, from March 1, 1890, to September 30, 1891; Second Landing Waiter, from October 1, 1891, to August 31, 1892; Second Clerk of Customs, from September 1, 1892, to August 31, 1897; Senior Landing Waiter and Locker, from September 1, 1897, to February 28, 1898; Second Clerk of Customs and Acting Magazine Keeper, from March 1, 1898, to July 7, 1903; Chief Landing Waiter and Locker, from July 8, 1903.	
Messenger, Treasury, Gambia, January, 1872, to May, 1873; Assistant Clerk, Treasury, May, 1873, to August, 1875; Second Landing Waiter, Customs, August, 1875, to February, 1879; Assistant Clerk, Treasury, February, 1879, to March, 1883; Chief Clerk, Treasury and Post Office, March, 1883, to December, 1888; Chief Clerk, Treasury, January, 1889; Acting Governor's Clerk, Clerk of the Legislative Council, and Deputy Coroner, June to November, 1889; Cashier, January, 1892; in charge of the Treasury, June to November, 1892, July to September, 1893, April to August, 1896, June to September, 1898, October, 1902	
Nine years in the Colony, first as Colonial Surgeon and then as Senior Medical Officer under new regulations; is Chairman of the Board of Health and of the Quarantine Board; Health Officer of the Port; J.P. and Commissioner of the Court of Requests	Assistant Colonial Surgeon, November, 1891, Gold Coast Colony; Acting Commissioner of the same colony; Medical Officer, Special Expedition, Anglo-French Boundary Commission, January to June, 1892; Medical Officer attached to Special Mission to Kumasi, December, 1894, to February, 1895; Medical Officer at the base, Gambia Expedition, 1901, medal with clasp; discovered the "Trypanosomiasis" in the blood of a European, April 15, 1901.

Name.	Substantive appointment.	Date of first appointment in the public service.	Date of appointment in the Colony.	Present acting appointment.	Amount of annual salary and allowance, if any.
FOWLIS, Henry George	Second Clerk, Colonial Secretary's Office	July 5, 1890	July 5, 1890	—	£125 per annum
FRANKLIN, J. C., L.R.C.S.&P.Ed., L.F.P.&S.Glas.	Medical Officer and Public Vaccinator	December, 1902	December, 1902	Acting Senior Medical Officer and Chairman of Board of Health, March, 1904	£400 to £500; 2s. 3d. a day horse allowance and free quarters
GRAHAM, Charles Frederick Oliver	O.C. W.A.F.F.	January 1, 1896	November 30, 1901	O.C. W.A.F.F.	£400; £96; 2s. 3d. a day horse allowance, 5s. when absent from headquarters
GRIFFITH, Horace Major Brandford	Colonial Secretary	October, 1880	October, 1894	—	Salary, £700; allowance, £100; free quarters
HART, Thomas Wood	Second Engineer of Government Yatch "Mansah Kilah,"	March 13, 1903	April 9, 1903	Master and Engineer. of Government Yacht "Mansah Kilah"	Salary, £200; allowance, £50
HOPKINSON, Dr. Emilius	Protectorate Medical Officer	—	December, 1901	—	£400 to £500 per annum; and 10s. per diem whilst travelling

Service in the Colony.	General Remarks, Record of Service, etc.
Messenger and Copyist, Judicial Dept., 1890; Messenger and Copyist, Administrator's office, 1893; promoted Second Clerk, 1898; transferred to Colonial Sec.'s office as Second Clerk, Registrar of Correspondence and Stationery Storekeeper, Jan. 1, 1902; appointed Clerk to the Board of Education, March, 1898.	Judicial Department, 1890-2; Acted as Confidential Clerk to the late Hon. J. R. Maxwell; acted as Clerk of the Police Court and Court of Requests; Administrator's office, 1893-1901; acted as Confidential Clerk to His Excellency Sir Robert Llewelyn, K.C.M.G., and Clerk of Legislative Council, March to October, 1899; acted as Chief Clerk and Cashier, Customs Department, in June, 1900; acted as Clerk of Legislative Council at different times in 1901.
April 9 to July 1, 1903, Medical Officer to W.A.F.F. at Salikeni; Medical Officer and Acting Commissioner of McCarthy's Island District, August to December, 1903	Medical Officer to H.M. Forces at Home and in South Africa, from December, 1899, to September, 1902; passed Tropical School of Medicine, London, 1903.
December 10, 1901, to date; J.P.; acted as Treasurer, Collector of Customs; Postmaster, 10 days, 1902	Joined the Marines as Second Lieutenant, January 1, 1896; promoted Lieutenant, January 1, 1897; Channel Squadron, December 12, 1897; appointed W.A.F.F. as Lieutenant, June 3, 1899; served in several minor expeditions, Borgu, North Nigeria, 1899 and 1900; Temporary Captain, January 17, 1901; commanded company under General Kemball, in Kontajora Bida expedition, 1901; special mention in despatches; medal and clasp; formed Gambia Company; Local Captain, November 30, 1901; Captain R.M.L.I., March 29, 1903; passed in the Mandingo language.
Treasurer, 1894; Colonial Secretary, 1902; has administered the Government on numerous occasions and also acted as Collector of Customs and Postmaster; is a J.P. and a Commissioner of the Court of Requests	Confidential Clerk to Administrator, Lagos, 1880; Chief Clerk, Customs Department, 1883; Private Secretary to Governor of the Gold Coast, 1885-6; Collector of Customs, Lagos, 1889; Treasurer, 1891; Acting Colonial Secretary, 1894; when transferred to the Gambia as Treasurer.
From April 9, 1903	First joined the Keyham Dockyard, 1893, serving up to 1895 on H.M. ships, principally afloat and steam trials; entered Woolwich Arsenal as a Mechanical Engineer, War Department, Field Gun Section, April 13, 1896, to March, 1903, working principally with breech mechanism; transferred to Colonial Service, March 13, 1903.
Medical Officer, W.A.F.F., 1901-02; Protectorate Medical Officer, January, 1904	M.A., M.B., B.Ch. (Oxon), M.R.C.S., L.R.C.P., Surg.-Capt., 15th Batt. 1st Yeo., South Africa (mentioned in desp. and D.S.O.); late Surg.-Lt. (Oxf. Yeo.); late Opht. House Surg. and Clin. Asst., Ear Dept., St. Thomas's Hosp.; Clin. Asst., Royal London Opht. Hosp., Moorfields; House Surg., Radcliffe Infirmary, Oxford.

Name.	Substantive appointment.	Date of first appointment in the public service.	Date of appointment in the Colony.	Present acting appointment.	Amount of annual salary and allowance, if any.
HOSKYNS, Henry Charles Walter	Lieutenant, Lincolnshire Regiment	September 21, 1898	November 30, 1901	Lieutenant, Gambia Company W.A.F.F.	£325; 2s. 3d. a day horse allowance; 5s. a day when absent from headquarters
JOHNSON, Charles Claudius	Gaoler	January 19, 1885	January 19, 1885	—	Salary, £120; allowance £12
JOOF, John P. ...	Governor's Clerk and Interpreter	December, 1892	—	—	£100 per annum, and 5s. a day when on duty in the Protectorate with His Excellency the Governor
LEIGH, Solomon Frederick	Tide Surveyor	January 1, 1884	November 1, 1902	—	£180

Service in the Colony.	General Remarks, Record of Service, etc.
From December 10, 1901 ...	South African War, January 4, 1900, to January 7, 1901, South African medal with clasps, Cape Colony, Paardeburg, Johannesburg; Royal Humane Society Bronze Medal; commanded Gambia Company, W.A.F.F., May 4 to November 11, 1903; B.A., Cambridge.
19 years and 2 months ...	Staff-Sergeant, Gambia Police Force; transferred to the Gambia Frontier Force as Sergeant-Major, February to October, 1895, when Force was disbanded; special service to the Upper River with the Lake Expedition, December, 1895, to March, 1896; appointed First-Class Sergeant, Gambia Police Force, April to December, 1896; appointed Pay and Quartermaster-Sergeant, January, 1897, to January, 1899; appointed Gaoler, February 1, 1899.
Apprenticed, Customs Out-door Branch, December, 1892, to December, 1893 (performed duties of Landing Officer on several occasions); appointed Third Landing Waiter, January, 1894; Acting Purser, H.M.C.S. "Mansah Kilah," April to May, 1897; Acting Junior Clerk, Treasury Department, July, 1897, to February, 1898; appointed Interpreter, Messenger and Copyist, Administrator's office, March, 1898; Acting Chief Landing Waiter, Customs Department, December, 1898, to July, 1899; appointed First-Class Landing Waiter, August, 1899; appointed Governor's Clerk and Interpreter, January, 1902	During this period performed the duties of Second Clerk, Chief Clerk and Tide Surveyor on officers' leave of absence.
——	Educated C.M.S. Collegiate Institute, Lagos; Messenger, Custom and Treasury, January 1, 1884; Out-door Officer of Customs, 1885-8; Assistant Examining Officer, 1889-90; Acting First Clerk and Statistician, Customs, on different occasions, 1887 and 1891 Assistant Examining Officer of Customs and Deputy Registrar of Courts, Badagry, W.D., 1891-2; acted on one occasion as Coroner; Queen's Warehouse Keeper, Customs, 1893-8; District Examining Officer of Customs, 1899-1901; Station Master, Lagos Government Railway, Lagos Terminus, 1901-2.

Name.	Substantive appointment.	Date of first appointment in the public service.	Date of appointment in the Colony.	Present acting appointment.	Amount of annual salary and allowance, if any.
LEWIS, Arthur Kennedy	Assistant Postmaster	April 3, 1893	February 3, 1903	—	£150 to £200
LUBBOCK, E. N. ...	Local Auditor	February 3, 1902	June 1, 1903	—	£350 per annum; no allowance, free quarters
MCCALLUM, John Keltie	Travelling Commissioner	October 19, 1901	November 5, 1901	Private Secretary to Acting Governor	£300 per annum and 10s. paid when travelling
MCCARTHY, I. G.	Chief Clerk, Post Office	October 1, 1891	October 1, 1891	—	Salary £100
MEAD, Frederick W.	Clerk of Works	August, 1891	September 11, 1901	Clerk of Works	£250; no allowance
MENSAH, Joseph Anthony	Chief Clerk, Colonial Secretary's Office	March 17, 1887	July 5, 1901	—	£200 to £250 by £10
MORLEY, Cecil ...	Lieutenant	February 17, 1900	November 30, 1901	—	£325 per annum; 2s. 3d. per day horse allowance; 5s. per day when away from headquarters
N'JIE, G. M. ...	Foreman of Works	November 23, 1891	November 23, 1891	Foreman of Works	£120
N'JIE, S. F. ...	Audit Clerk	October, 1884	October, 1894	Audit Clerk	£75

Service in the Colony.	General Remarks, Record of Service, etc.
Assistant Postmaster, February, 1903	Educated Wesleyan High School and Grammar School, Sierra Leone; Medical Dresser attached to Anglo-French Boundary Commission, December, 1891, to April, 1892; Clerk to D. C. and Registrar of Births and Deaths, etc., Western District, Sierra Leone, April, 1893, to October, 1895; Third Clerk, Registrar-General's Department, 1895-7; Second Clerk, Attorney-General's office, 1898; travelled as Clerk to Attorney-General during the trial of insurgents by Judge Bonner in the Sierra Leone Protectorate, 1898; Transport Clerk, 1899 (June), to August, 1901; accompanied Governors Sir F. Cardew, M. Nathan and C. A. King-Harman, as O.C. of Transport on various tours to the Protectorate; Registration Officer, G.P.O., Sierra Leone, August, 1901, to January, 1903.
June 1 to September 8, 1903	Clerk, Head Office, Audit and Exchequer Department, February 3, 1902; appointed Assistant Auditor, Lagos, July 26, 1902; present position June 1, 1903.
Travelling Commissioner, McCarthy Island District	Passed in the Mandingo language
Chief Clerk, Post Office ...	Appointed Customs Apprentice, January, 1891; Sorter, Post Office, October 1, 1891; transferred to Customs as Third Landing Waiter, February 1, 1893; transferred to post as Clerk, January, 1894.
4 years	Served 6 years Gold Coast Public Works Department.
Appointed to the Gambia as Chief Clerk, Secretariat, July 5, 1901	Gold Coast Service, March 17, 1887, to January 31, 1898, Lagos Service, February 1, 1898, to July 4, 1901
3 years and 10 months ...	Gazetted to Manchester Regiment, February 17, 1900; Seconded to West African Frontier Force, November 30, 1901.
November 23, 1891, to date	
October, 1884, to date ...	Apprentice, Governor's Office, 1884-6; Messenger and Copyist, Governor's Office, 1886-92; Assistant Clerk, Treasury, 1892-7; Clerk, Audit Office, 1897.

Name.	Substantive appointment.	Date of first appointment in the public service.	Date of appointment in the Colony.	Present acting appointment.	Amount of annual salary and allowance, if any.
PEIRCE, T. Estwick	Collector of Customs and Harbour Master	October, 1880	August 11, 1896	—	£480; £60 duty allowance; free quarters
PICKERING, William	Clerk of Works	March 22, 1899	March 22, 1899	Clerk of Works	£300
PRYCE, Howard Lloyd	Travelling Commissioner	October, 1897	November, 1897	—	£500, and 10s. per day travelling allowance
RUSSELL, Alexander David	Chief Magistrate	October, 1898	November, 1898	—	£750, and quarters or allowance in lieu thereof
SANGSTER, Guy Henry	Travelling Commissioner, Kommbo and Fogni	Assistant Superindent of Police, Gambia, February 5, 1897	December 17, 1900 (re appointed to the Gambia)	—	£400 per annum, and 10s. per day travelling allowance
SCOTT, Captain Lionel Folliott	A.D.C. and Private Secretary	November 22, 1902	November 22, 1902	—	£250

Service in the Colony.	General Remarks, Record of Service, etc.
Collector of Customs, 1896; Acting Treasurer, August to December, 1902, and several times subsequently; member of Legislative Council; Commissioner of Court of Requests; J.P.; acted as Colonial Post-master on many occasion.	Educated at Harrison College, Barbadoes; Clerk, Colonial Secretary, Barbadoes, 1880; Fifth Clerk, Colonial Secretary's Office, January, 1881; Fourth Clerk, Auditor General's Office, March, 1881; Excise Officer, St. Lucia, 1882; Special Clerk, Audit General's Office, Barbadoes, 1884; Officer of Customs, 1887; Acting Harbour Master, 1888; Supervisor of Customs, Gold Coast, 1892; Acting Travelling and Inspecting Supervisor, May to August, 1892; Cashier, Treasury, 1893; Assistant Treasurer, February, 1894; Assistant Comptroller of Customs, November, 1895; in charge of Chest, Ashanti Expedition, 1895-6, and received the thanks of the General Commanding.
From March 22, 1899 ...	Acting Colonial Engineer from May to July 20, 1901; and again from October 3, 1902, to February 13, 1903.
From November, 1897. ...	Acting Chief Magistrate, August to October, 1903.
From November 18, 1898. Compiled Mohammedan Laws.	Born August 29, 1864; educated Dr. Deigh's School, near Aberdeen; Master of Arts, Aberdeen University, 1885; Bachelor of Laws (LL.B.), University of Edinburgh, 1889; Member of the Faculty of Advocates, Edinburgh, 1889.
Assistant Superintendent of Police, 1897-98; Acting Superintendent of Police, 1897; Inspector of Prisons, 1897; Private Secretary to Acting Governor, 1901; Field Treasurer, Gambia Field Force, 1901; Special mention despatch, Gambia, 1901; *London Gazette*, September 10, 1901	Served in 2nd Dragoons and 91st Argyll and Sutherland Highlanders; appointed from Gambia as Assistant Inspector Frontier Force, Sierra Leone, 1898; Inspector Frontier Force, 1899; Acting Commissioner Karene District, 1899; Assistant Commissioner Karene District, 1899; Sierra Leone medal, 1897-8 clasp; Royal Humane Society bronze medal, 1898; West African General Service medal and clasp "Gambia"; mentioned in despatches, Mendi rising, Sierra Leone, 1898; Hythe School of Musketry certificate; Chatham School of Military engineering certificate.
2 years and 10 months ...	Second Lieutenant, Oxfordshire Light Infantry, April 23, 1893; Lieutenant, March 25, 1897; Captain, September 27, 1900; served with W.A.F.F., Northern Nigeria, March, 1898, to March, 1899; West African medal and clasp; served with 1st Battalion of Oxfordshire Light Infantry in South African War, December, 1899, to June, 1902; present at engagements of Klip Drift, Paardeburg, Poplar Grove, Driefontein; South African medal and clasps; King's South African medal and clasps.

Name.	Substantive appointment.	Date of first appointment in the public service.	Date of appointment in the Colony.	Present acting appointment.	Amount of annual salary and allowance, if any.
SHAW, Colin	Steward, Clerk, and Store-keeper	May 4, 1896	May 4, 1896	—	Medical Department, £70-£80; Board of Health Department, £12
SMART, William S.	Dispenser, Dresser, and Keeper of Meteorological Registrar	1896	August 3, 1899	—	Salary, £85, £6; and £12 in lieu of house
SOWE, P. C.	First Clerk, Treasury	June 1, 1898	June 1, 1898	—	£80
STANLEY, W. B.	Travelling Commissioner	August 27, 1901	September, 1901	—	£300, and 10s. per diem travelling allowance
THOMAS, Charles Whitfield	Clerk of Courts	1884	1884	—	£120 to £150
TOWNSEND, William Richard	Attorney-General	May 1, 1902	May 1, 1902	—	£400 to £450 and Private Practice
VAUGHAN, Edward	Colonial Engineer	May 5, 1895	September, 1901	—	£450, duty allce. £90, and horse allce. 2s. 3d. per diem; free quarters
VENN, Henry O. ...	Purser	July 22, 1903	July 22, 1903	Purser	£60

Service in the Colony.	General Remarks, Record of Service, etc.
9 years	Appointed First-Class Warder, Prison Department, May 4, 1896; promoted Chief Warder, Prison Department, January 1, 1897; appointed Market Clerk, May 1, 1898; appointed Senior First-Class Landing Waiter, Customs Department, February 1, 1902; promoted Second Clerk, Indoor Branch Customs, July 1, 1903; Steward, Clerk and Storekeeper, Medical Department, October 1, 1903, as also Clerk to the Board of Health.
Clerk, Board of Health, 1899-1902; Dispenser to W.A.F.F., 1902	Appointed Ward Master, Colonial Hospital, Sierra Leone, 1896; Dispenser and Dresser to the Anglo-French Boundary Commission, Sierra Leone, 1896; appointed Third-Class Clerk, Treasury Department, Accra, 1897; appointed Third-Class Dispenser, Accra, 1899; promoted Dispenser, Clerk, and Clerk to Board of Health, Bathurst, Gambia, 1899.
Junior Clerk, Treasury, June, 1898, to October, 1899; Assistant Clerk, November, 1899, to December, 1903; First Clerk, January, 1904	—
During Expedition, 1901, as an Adjutant to half battalion West Indian Regiment; Acting Travelling Commissioner, May 21 to July 1, 1901; Travelling Commissioner, August 27, 1901	Lieutenant, West Indian Regiment.
20 years	Educated at the Wesleyan High School, Bathurst, Gambia; Assistant Government Printer, 1884-91; Junior Clerk and Bailiff, Police Court, 1891-4; Inspector of Nuisances, 1894-1902; Clerk of Courts, 1902; Acting Colonial Registrar, 1903; appointed Secretary to the Collision Commission in 1903.
From May 15, 1902.	Government Inspector of Schools; Colonial Registrar; Curator of Intestate Estates; Member of Executive Council; Member of Legislative Council; educated at Trinity College, Dublin, B.A., called to the Bar, King's Inns, Dublin, 1894.
As Colonial Engineer; and has carried out a considerable amount of work since his arrival in the Colony	Foreman of Works, Lagos, 1895; First-Class Foreman, 1898.
—	Appointed Purser, Government vessels, July 22, 1903

Name.	Substantive appointment.	Date of first appointment in the public service.	Date of appointment in the Colony.	Present acting appointment.	Amount of annual salary and allowance, if any.
WEBB, Percy L. ...	Sergeant, R.M.L.I.; Sergeant, 1st Rating of Infantry	October 24, 1894	February 25, 1904	—	£120, and allowance, 2s. 6d. per diem whilst serving in Colony
WHEATCROFT, Arthur Henry	Colour-Sergeant	Worcestershire Regiment, April 20, 1887	November 30, 1901	Armourer	£120, £24, £12; with 2s. 6d. per day local allowance while serving in the Colony
WILLIAMS, Nicholas Emine	Government Printer	April 29, 1897	March 22, 1904	—	£100-£120; no allowance
WOODS, Thomas...	Band-master to Civil and Military Forces	May 12, 1873	March 27, 1903	—	£225, with an increment of £25 to £250; if travelling on duty an allowance will be paid as the Government may seem fit
Mother Joseph Mary	Matron	January 1, 1903	January, 1903	—	£100 per annum } with quarters
Sister Mary Alix	Sister	January 1, 1903	January, 1903	—	£100 per annum } with quarters
Sister Mary Veronica	Sister	January 1, 1903	January, 1903	—	£100 per annum } with quarters

Service in the Colony.	General Remarks, Record of Service, etc.
W. A. F. F.; Promotions: Lance-Corporal, August 3, 1896; Corporal, June 17, 1899; Sergeant, August 22, 1901	Passed for Corporal (First Class), March 11, 1899; Sergeant (Special), December 2, 1901; Instructor Life-saving, September 8, 1902; Musketry Instructor, Hythe (Distinguished), July 7, 1903; Education, First-Class Army (Distinguished), July 10, 1901; Armourer Class (Volunteer and Auxiliary Forces), Birmingham, February, 1904.
W. A. F. F. 2 years; length of service Northern Nigeria, 15 months; Ashanti, 5 months. Corporal, November, 1891; passed Sergeant, April, 1893; Third-Class Education, August 16, 1888; Second-Class November 24, 1891; Mounted Infantry, March 12, 1890; Indian Transport and Supply, May 14, 1894; Military Engineering, August 19, 1898; Amourer's Class Volunteer, February 27, 1903.	Portsmouth, April, 1887; Pembroke Dock, September, 1888; Limerick, April, 1889; Curragh, April, 1891; Kamptu, India, January, 1893; Rangoon, Burma, September, 1894; Aden, October, 1895; Plymouth, December, 1896; Northern Nigeria, February, 1899; Ashanti, May, 1900; Tipperary, June, 1901; Bathurst, W.A., December, 1901; Ashanti medal, 1900, with clasp Kumasi; charge of escort, Anglo-French Boundary Commission, Northern Nigeria, January to May, 1900.
Government Printer, March 22, 1904	Educated at the C.M.S. Grammar School, Freetown, Sierra Leone; entered in January, 1890; left in April, 1897; Sierra Leone Government Printing Office as an apprentice for a period of three years, April 29, 1897, to April 29, 1900; Third-Class Compositor, June, 1900; Second-Class, December, 1900, to March 7, 1904; transferred to the Gambia Government, 1904.
—	Enlisted on May 12, 1873; embarked for East India, September 26, 1878; arrived Bombay, October 26, 1878; completed fourteen years in India at different stations,—*viz.*, Cawnpore, Calcutta, Jubbulpore and Mooltan; then proceeded to Colombo (Ceylon), remaining a little over two years, thus completing sixteen years thirty-two days abroad; in possession of medal for long service and good conduct; discharged on pension, November 7, 1894, after serving twenty-one years and 180 days; engaged as acting band-master to 3rd battalion Suffolk Regiment until December 31, 1902.
—	Are Sisters of the Convent of St. Joseph of Cluny, Paris.
—	
—	

ADMINISTRATORS OF THE GAMBIA.

1843. H. P. Seagram.
1843. E. Norcott.
1844. Commander G. Fitzgerald, R.N.
1847. R. G. Macdonnell.
1852. A. E. Kennedy.
1852. Col. L. S. O'Connor.
1859. Col. G. A. K. D'Arcy.
1866. Admiral C. G. E. Patey, C.M.G.
1871. T. F. Callaghan, C.M.G.
1873. C. H. Kortright, C.M.G.
1875. Samuel Rowe, C.M.G.
1877. V. S. Gouldsbury, C.M.G.
1884. C. A. Moloney, C.M.G. (now Sir C. A. Moloney, K.C.M.G.).
1886. J. S. Hay, C.M.G. (now Sir J. S. Hay, K.C.M.G.).
1888. Gilbert T. Carter, C.M.G. (now Sir G. T. Carter, K.C.M.G.).
1891. R. B. Llewelyn, C.M.G. (now Sir R. B. Llewelyn, K.C.M.G.).
1900. Sir G. C. Denton, K.C.M.G. (Governor).

INDEX.

APPENDIX.

(1) The Royal Instructions of November 28th, 1888. (2) The Additional Royal Instructions of October 31st, 1898; and (3) The Additional Royal Instructions of March 15th, 1902.

(1) INSTRUCTIONS passed under the Royal Sign Manual and Signet to the Governor and Commander-in-Chief of the Colony of the Gambia.

VICTORIA R.

Instructions to Our Governor and Commander-in-Chief in and over Our Colony of the Gambia, and to Our Lieutenant Governor or other Officer for the time being administering the Government of our said Colony. Dated 28th November 1888.

Given at Our Court at Windsor, this Twenty-eighth day of November 1888, in the Fifty-second year of Our Reign.

WHEREAS by certain Letters Patent under the Great Seal of Our United Kingdom of Great Britain and Ireland, bearing even date herewith, We have erected Our Settlement on the Gambia, lately forming part of the Government in Chief of Our West Africa Settlements, into a separate Colony, and have ordered, and declared that there shall be a Governor and Commander-in-Chief, or a Lieutenant Governor, or an Adminstrator, as we shall from time to time direct (each of whom is therein and herein-after called the Governor) in and over Our Colony of the Gambia (therein and herein-after called the Colony): Preamble. Recites Letters Patent constituting the office of Governor.

And whereas We have thereby authorized and commanded the Governor to do and execute all things that belong to his said Office, according to the tenor of Our said Letters Patent and of such Commission as may be issued to him under Our Sign Manual and Signet, and according to such Instructions as may from time to time be given to him under our Sign Manual and Signet, or by Our Order in Our Privy Council, or through one of Our Principal Secretaries of State, and to such Laws as are now or shall hereafter be in force in the Colony:

And whereas We are minded to issue these Our Instructions under Our Sign Manual and Signet for the Guidance of the Governor, Lieutenant Governor or other officer administering the Government of the Colony:

We do hereby direct and enjoin and declare Our will and pleasure, as follows:—

Governor to administer Oaths.

I. The Governor may, whenever he thinks fit, require any person in the public Service of the Colony to take the Oath of Allegiance, in the form prescribed by the Act mentioned in Our said Letters Patent, together with such Oath or Oaths as may from time to time be prescribed by any Laws in force in the Colony. The Governor is to administer such Oaths, or to cause them to be administered by some Public Officer of the Colony.

Instructions to be observed by Deputies.

II. During the absence of the Governor from the Colony these Instructions, so far as they apply to any matter or thing to be done, or to any power or authority to be exercised by a Deputy acting for the Governor, shall be deemed to be addressed to and shall be observed by such Deputy.

Deputies may correspond direct with Secretary of State in urgent cases.

III. If in any emergency arising in the Colony during the absence of the Governor it is necessary that instructions should be obtained from Us without delay, the Deputy (if any) acting for the Governor may apply to Us, through one of Our Principal Secretaries of State, for instructions in the matter; but every such Deputy shall forthwith transmit to the Governor a copy of every despatch or communication which he has so addressed to Us.

Constitution of Executive Council.

IV. The Executive Council of the Colony shall consist of the following Members, that is to say: the Lieutenant Governor of of the Colony (if any), the person for the time being lawfully discharging the functions of Treasurer, Chief Magistrate, and Collector of Customs, and such persons as We may from time to time appoint by any Instruction or Warrant under Our Sign Manual and Signet.

Extraordinary Members.

Whenever upon any special occasion the Governor desires to obtain the advice of any person within the Colony touching Our affairs therein, he may, by an Instrument under the Public Seal of the Colony, summon for such special occasion any such person as an Extraordinary Member of the Executive Council.

Precedence.

V. The Members of the Executive Council shall have seniority and precedence as We may specially assign, and, in default thereof, the above-mentioned Officers in the Order in which their offices are above mentioned, and other Members according to the priority of their respective appointments, or if appointed by the same Instrument according to the order in which they are named therein.

Governor to communicate Instructions to Executive Council.

VI. The Governor shall forthwith communicate these Our Instructions to the Executive Council, and likewise all such others, from time to time, as We may direct, or as he shall find convenient for Our Service to impart to them.

Executive Council not to proceed to business unless summoned by Governor's authority.

Quorum.

VII. The Executive Council shall not proceed to the despatch of business unless duly summoned by authority of the Governor, nor unless two Members at the least (exclusive of himself or of the Member presiding) be present and assisting throughout the whole of the meetings at which any such business shall be despatched.

Governor to preside.

VIII. The Governor shall attend and preside at all meetings of the Executive Council, unless when prevented by illness or other grave cause, and in his absence such Member as the Governor may appoint, or in the absence of such Member the senior Member of the Council actually present, shall preside.

IX. A full and exact Journal or Minute shall be kept of all the proceedings of the Executive Council; and at each meeting of the Council the Minutes of the last preceding meeting shall be read over and confirmed or amended as the case may require, before proceeding to the despatch of any other business.

Journals or Minutes of Executive Council to be kept.

Twice in each year a full and exact copy of all Minutes for the preceding half year shall be transmitted to Us through one of Our Principal Secretaries of State.

To be transmitted home twice a year.

X. In the execution of the powers and authorities granted to the Governor by Our said Letters Patent, he shall in all cases consult with the Executive Council, excepting only in cases which may be of such a nature that, in his judgment, Our service would sustain material prejudice by consulting the Council thereupon, or when the matters to be decided shall be too unimportant to require their advice, or too urgent to admit of their advice being given by the time within which it may be necessary for him to act in respect of any such matters. In all such urgent cases he shall, at the earliest practicable period, communicate to the Executive Council the measures which he may so have adopted, with the reasons thereof.

Governor to consult Executive Council.

Proviso: Urgent cases.

XI. The Governor alone shall be entitled to submit questions to the Executive Council for their advice or decision; but if the Governor decline to submit any question to the Council when requested in writing by any Member so to do, it shall be competent to such Member to require that there be recorded upon the Minutes his written application, together with the answer returned by the Governor to the same.

Governor to propose questions.

No Member to propose a question, but may record application for so doing.

XII. The Governor may act, in the exercise of the powers and authorities granted to him by Our said Letters Patent, in opposition to the advice given to him by the Members of the Executive Council, if he shall in any case deem it right to do so; but in any such case he shall fully report the matter to Us by the first convenient opportunity, with the grounds and reasons of his action. In every such case it shall be competent to any Member of the Council to require that there be recorded at length on the Minutes the grounds of any advice or opinion he may give upon the question.

Governor may act in opposition to Executive Council.

Reporting grounds for so doing.

Members may record on Minutes their adverse opinions.

XIII. The Legislative Council of the Colony shall consist of the Governor, the Lieutenant Governor (if any), the person for the time being lawfully discharging the functions of Treasurer, Chief Magistrate, and Collector of Customs, and such other persons holding offices in the Colony as We may from time to time appoint by any Instructions or Warrants under Our Sign Manual and Signet, and all such persons shall be styled Official Members of the Legislative Council; and further of such persons not holding offices in the Colony as the Governor, in pursuance of any Instructions from Us, through one of Our Principal Secretaries of State may from time to time appoint by any Instrument under the Public Seal of the Colony, and all such persons shall be styled Unofficial Members of the Legislative Council.

Constitution of Legislative Council.

Official Members.

Unofficial Members.

Provisional appointments of Unofficial Members.

XIV. If any Unofficial Member of the Legislative Council shall die, or become incapable, or be suspended or removed from his seat in the Council, or be absent from the Colony, or if he resign his seat by writing under his hand, or if his seat become vacant, the Governor may, by an Instrument under the Public Seal, appoint in his place a fit person, to be provisionally a Member of the said Council.

Such person shall forthwith cease to be a Member if his appointment is disallowed by Us, or if the Member in whose place he was appointed shall return to the Colony, or as the case may be, shall be released from suspension, or shall be declared by the Governor capable of again discharging his functions in the said Council.

Provisional appointments to be immediately reported.

Revocation of such appointments.

The Governor shall, without delay, report to Us, for Our confirmation or disallowance, through one of Our Principal Secretaries of State, every provisional appointment of any person as an Unofficial Member of the Legislative Council. Every such person shall hold his place in the Council during Our pleasure, and the Governor may by any Instrument under the Public Seal revoke any such appointment.

Extraordinary Member.

XV. Whenever upon any special occasion the Governor wishes to obtain the advice of any person within the Colony, touching any matters about to be brought before the Legislative Council, he may by an Instrument under the Public Seal of the Colony appoint any such person to be for such occasion an Extraordinary Member of the Legislative Council.

Council may transact business notwithstanding vacancies.

Quorum.

XVI. The Legislative Council shall not be disqualified from the transaction of business on account of any vacancies among the Members thereof; but the said Council shall not be competent to act in any case unless (including the Governor or the Member presiding) there be present at and throughout the meetings of the Council three Members at the least.

Precedence of Members.

XVII. The Official Members of the Legislative Council shall take precedence of the Unofficial Members; and among themselves shall take precedence as We may specially assign, and, in default thereof, first the above-mentioned Officers in the order in which their respective offices are mentioned; then other Official Members and all Unofficial Members according to the priority of their respective appointments, or if appointed by the same Instrument according to the order in which they are named therein.

Governor to preside in Council, or in his absence the Senior Member.

XVIII. The Governor shall attend and preside in the Legislative Council, unless prevented by illness or other grave cause; and in his absence that Member shall preside who is first in precedence of those present.

Questions to be decided by a majority.

Governor to have an original and casting vote.

XIX. All questions proposed for debate in the Legislative Council shall be decided by the majority of votes, and the Governor or the Member presiding shall have an original vote in common with the other Members of the Council, as also a casting vote, if upon any question the votes shall be equal.

XX. The Governor shall frame and propose to the Legislative Council from time to time for their adoption such standing rules and orders as may be necessary to ensure punctuality of attendance of the Members of the Council, and to prevent meetings of the Council being holden without convenient notice to the several Members thereof, and to maintain order and method in the despatch of business, and in the conduct of debates in the Council, and to secure due deliberation in the passing of ordinances, and to provide that before the passing of any ordinance intended to affect the interests of private persons due notice of the same is given to all persons concerned therein. Rules and Orders to be made for ensuring punctuality of attendance.

All such rules and orders not being repugnant to Our said Letters Patent, or to these Our Instructions, or to any other Instructions which the Governor may receive from Us, shall at all times be followed and observed, and shall be binding upon the said Council, unless the same or any of them shall be disallowed by Us.

XXI. It shall be competent for any Member of the Legislative Council to propose any question for debate therein; and such question, if seconded by any other Member, shall be debated and disposed of according to the standing Rules and Orders. Provided always, that every ordinance, vote, resolution, or question, the object or effect of which may be to dispose of or charge any part of Our revenue arising within the Colony, shall be proposed by the Governor, unless the proposal of the same shall have been expressly allowed or directed by him. Questions, &c., for debate.

XXII. In the making of Ordinances the Governor and the Council shall observe, as far as practicable, the following Rules:— Rules and Regulations under which Ordinances are to be enacted.

1. All Laws shall be styled "Ordinances," and the enacting words shall be, "enacted by the Governor (Lieutenant Governor, "or Adminstrator) of the Colony of the Gambia, with the advice "and consent of the Legislative Council thereof." Form of enacting Ordinances.

2. All Ordinances shall be distinguished by titles, and shall be divided into successive clauses or paragraphs, numbered consecutively, and to every such clause there shall be annexed in the margin a short summary of its contents. The Ordinances of each year shall be distinguished by consecutive numbers, commencing in each year with the number one. Ordinances to be numbered and methodically arranged.

3. Each different matter shall be provided for by a different Ordinance, without intermixing into one and the same Ordinance such things as have no proper relation to each other; and no clause is to be inserted in or annexed to any Ordinance which shall be foreign to what the title of such Ordinance imports, and no perpetual clause shall be part of any temporary Ordinance. Different subjects not to be mixed in same Ordinance. No clause to be introduced foreign to what title of Ordinance imports. Temporary Ordinances.

XXIII. The Governor shall not, except in the cases hereunder mentioned, assent in Our Name to any Ordinance of any of the following classes:— Description of Ordinances not to be assented to.

1. Any Ordinance for the divorce of persons joined together in holy matrimony.

2. Any Ordinance whereby any grant of land or money, or other donation or gratuity, may be made to himself.

3. Any Ordinance whereby any increase or diminution may be made in the number, salary, or allowances of the public officers.

4. Any Ordinance affecting the Currency of the Colony or relating to the issue of Bank notes.

5. Any Ordinance establishing any Banking Association, or amending or altering the constitution, powers, or privileges of any Banking Association.

6. Any Ordinance imposing differential duties.

7. Any Ordinance the provisions of which shall appear inconsistent with obligations imposed upon Us by treaty.

8. Any Ordinance interfering with the discipline or control of Our forces by land or sea.

9. Any Ordinance of an extraordinary nature and importance, whereby Our prerogative or the rights and property of Our subjects not residing in the Colony, or the trade and shipping of Our United Kingdom and its dependencies, may be prejudiced.

10. Any Ordinance whereby persons not of European birth or descent may be subjected or made liable to any disabilities or restrictions to which persons of European birth or descent are not also subjected or made liable.

11. Any Ordinance containing provisions to which Our assent has been once refused, or which have been disallowed by Us.

Proviso in cases of emergency for immediate operation of an Ordinance.

Unless such Ordinance shall contain a clause suspending the operation of such Ordinance until the signification of Our pleasure thereupon, or unless the Governor shall have satisfied himself that an urgent necessity exists requiring that such Ordinance be brought into immediate operation, in which case he is authorized to assent in Our name to such Ordinance, unless the same shall be repugnant to the law of England, or inconsistent with any obligations imposed on Us by treaty. But he is to transmit to Us, by the earliest opportunity, the Ordinance so assented to, together with his reasons for assenting thereto.

Private Ordinances

XXIV. No private Ordinance shall be passed whereby the property of any private person may be affected in which there is not a saving of the rights of Us, Our heirs and successors, and of all bodies, politic and corporate, and of all other persons except such as are mentioned in the said Ordinance, and those claiming by, from, and under them. The Governor shall not assent in Our Name to any private Ordinance until proof be made before him that adequate and timely notification, by public advertisement or otherwise, was made of the parties' intention to apply for such Ordinance before the same was brought into the Legislative Council; and a certificate under his hand shall be transmitted with and annexed to every such private Ordinance, signifying that such notification has been given, and declaring the manner of giving the same.

Ordinances to be sent home duly authenticated

XXV. When any Ordinance shall have been passed in the Legislative Council, the Governor shall transmit to Us, through One of Our Principal Secretaries of State, for Our final approval, disallowance, or other direction thereupon, a full and exact copy in duplicate of the same, and of the marginal summary thereof, duly authenticated under the Public Seal of the Colony, and by his own signature. Such copy shall be accompanied by such explanatory observations as may be required to exhibit the reasons and occasion for passing such Ordinance.

XXVI. At the earliest practicable period at the commencement of each year, the Governor shall cause a complete collection to be published, for general information, of all Ordinances enacted during the preceding year. Collection of Ordinances to be published every year.

XXVII. Minutes shall be regularly kept of all the proceedings of the Legislative Council; and at each meeting of the said Council, the Minutes of the last preceding meeting shall be read over, and confirmed or amended, as the case may require, before proceeding to the despatch of any other business. Minutes of proceeedings to be kept.

Twice in each year, the Governor shall transmit to Us, through one of Our Principal Secretaries of State, a full and exact copy of the said Minutes for the preceding half year. Minutes to be sent home twice a year.

XXVIII. Before disposing of any vacant or waste land to Us belonging, the Governor shall cause such reservations to be made thereout as he may think necessary for roads or other public purposes. Reservations to be made before waste lands are disposed of. The Governor shall not, directly or indirectly, purchase for himself any of such lands without Our special permission given through one of Our Principal Secretaries of State. Governor not to purchase lands.

XXIX. All Commissions to be granted by the Governor to any person or persons for exercising any office or employment shall, unless otherwise provided by law, be granted during pleasure only; and whenever the Governor shall appoint to any vacant office or employment any person not by Us specially directed to be appointed thereto, he shall, at the same time, expressly apprise such person that such appointment is to be considered only as temporary and provisional until Our allowance or disallowance thereof be signified. Appointments to be provisional and during pleasure

XXX. Before suspending from the exercise of his office any public Officer who has been appointed by virtue of a Commission or Warrant from Us, or whose emoluments exceed 100*l*. a year, the Governor shall signify to such Officer, by a statement in writing, the grounds of the intended suspension, and shall call upon him to state in writing the grounds upon which he desires to exculpate himself. The Governor shall lay both statements before the Executive Council, and, having consulted them thereon, shall cause to be recorded on the Minutes whether the Council or the majority thereof does or does not assent to the suspension, and if the Governor thereupon proceed to such suspension, he shall transmit both of the said statements, together with the Minutes of the Executive Council, to Us through One of Our Principal Secretaries of State by the earliest opportunity. But if in any case the interests of Our service shall appear to the Governor to demand that a person shall cease to exercise the powers and functions of his office instantly, or before there shall be time to take the proceedings herein-before directed, he shall then interdict such person from the exercise of the powers and functions of his office. Suspension of Officers.

Governor to promote Religion and Education amongst the Natives.

Protection of persons and property.

XXXI. The Governor is to the utmost of his power to promote religion and education among the native inhabitants of the Colony, and he is especially to take care to protect them in their persons and in the free enjoyment of their possessions, and by all lawful means to prevent and restrain all violence and injustice which may in any manner be practised or attempted against them.

Regulation of power of pardon in capital cases.

Judge's report to be laid before the Executive Council.

XXXII. Whenever any offender shall have been condemned to suffer death by the sentence of any Court in the Colony, the Governor shall call upon the Judge who presided at the trial to make to him a written report of the case of such offender, and shall cause such report to be taken into consideration at the first meeting thereafter which may be conveniently held of the Executive Council, and he may cause the said Judge to be specially summoned to attend at such meeting and to produce his notes thereat. The Governor shall not pardon or reprieve any such offender unless it shall appear to him expedient so to do, after receiving the advice of the Executive Council thereon; but in all such cases he is to decide either to extend or to withold a pardon or reprieve according to his own deliberate judgment, whether the Members of the Executive Council concur therein or otherwise, entering, nevertheless, on the Minutes of the Executive Council a Minute of his reasons at length, in case he should decide any such question in opposition to the judgment of the majority of the Members thereof.

Governor to take advice of Executive Council in such cases.

May exercise his own judgment.

Entering his reasons on Council Minutes.

Blue Book.

XXXIII. The Governor shall punctually forward to Us from year to year, through one of Our Principal Secretaries of State, the annual book of returns for the said Colony, commonly called the Blue Book, relating to the Revenue and Expenditure, Defence, Public Works, Legislation, Civil Establishments, Pensions, Population, Schools, Course of Exchange, Imports and Exports, Agriculture, Produce, Manufactures, and other matters in the said Blue Book more particularly specified, with reference to the state and condition of the Colony.

Governor's absence.

XXXIV. The Governor shall not upon any pretence whatever quit the Colony without having first obtained leave from Us for so doing under Our Sign Manual and Signet, or through one of Our Principal Secretaries of State, except during his passage by sea to or from any part of the Colony.

Limits of Government explained.

The Governor during any such passage, or when in discharge of his duties he is in any territories adjacent to the Colony, shall not be considered absent from the Colony within the meaning of Our said Letters Patent.

Term "the Governor" explained.

XXXV. In these Our Instructions the term "the Governor" shall, unless inconsistent with the context, include every person for the time being administering the Government of the Colony.

V. R.

(2) ADDITIONAL INSTRUCTIONS passed under the Royal Sign Manual and Signet to the Governor and Commander-in-Chief of the Colony of the Gambia, providing that the duration of the appointment of Unofficial Members of the Legislative Council shall be for five years, and that persons re-appointed immediately on the termination of their appointments shall take precedence in the said Council according to the date of their first appointment.

VICTORIA R.

ADDITIONAL INSTRUCTIONS to Our Governor and Commander-in-Chief in and over Our Colony of the Gambia, and to Our Lieutenant Governor or other Officer for the time being administering the Government of Our said Colony.

Dated 31st October 1898.

Given at Our Court at St. James's, this Thirty-first day of October 1898, in the Sixty-second year of Our Reign.

Preamble.

WHEREAS by certain Letters Patent under the Great Seal of Our United Kingdom of Great Britain and Ireland bearing date at Westminster the Twenty-eighth day of November 1888, constituting the office of Governor and Commander-in-Chief in and over Our Colony of the Gambia, We did amongst other things declare that there should be a Legislative Council in Our said Colony, which should be constituted of such persons as We should direct by any Instructions from Us under our Sign Manual and Signet, and that all such persons should hold their places in the said Council during Our pleasure:

Recites Letters Patent of 28th November 1888.

And whereas by Our Instructions under Our Sign Manual and Signet, bearing date the Twenty-eighth day of November 1888, accompanying Our said Letters Patent, We did constitute Our said Legislative Council as therein is set forth:

Recites Instructions of 28th November 1888.

And whereas We are minded to make further provisions respecting the Unofficial members of Our said Legislative Council:

Now, therefore, We do by these Our Additional Instructions, under Our Sign Manual and Signet declare as follows:—

Vacation of Seats by Unofficial Members of the Legislative Council.

I. Every person who at the date of the receipt of these Instructions in Our said Colony is an Unofficial Member of the Legislative Council may retain his seat until the end of five years from the date of the Instrument by which he was appointed, and every Unofficial Member appointed or to be appointed after the date of the receipt of these Instructions shall vacate his seat at the end of five years from the date of the Instrument by which he is appointed.

Unofficial Members eligible for re-appointment

Every such Unofficial Member shall be eligible to be re-appointed by Our said Governor for the like period of five years.

Precedence of Unofficial Members re-appointed.

II. Every Unofficial Member of Our said Legislative Council re-appointed immediately on the termination of his term of Office shall take precedence according to the date of his first appointment to the said Council.

V. R.

(3) ADDITIONAL INSTRUCTIONS passed under the Royal Sign Manual and Signet, to the Governor and Commander-in-Chief of the Colony of the Gambia, respecting the Executive and Legislative Council.

EDWARD R.

Dated 15th March 1902.

ADDITIONAL INSTRUCTIONS to Our Governor and Commander-in-Chief, in and over Our Colony of the Gambia, and to Our Lieutenant Governor or other Officer for the time being administering the Government of Our said Colony.

Given at Our Court at St. James's, this Fifteenth day of March 1902, in the Second Year of Our Reign.

Preamble.

Recites Letters Patent of 28th November 1888.

WHEREAS by certain Letters Patent under the Great Seal of Our United Kingdom of Great Britain and Ireland bearing date at Westminster, the Twenty-eighth day of November 1888, constituting the office of Governor and Commander-in-Chief in and over Our Colony of the Gambia, provision was made, amongst other things, for the constitution of an Executive Council and a Legislative Council in Our said Colony:

Recites Instructions of 28th November 1888.

And whereas Her late Majesty Queen Victoria did, by certain Instructions under Her Royal Sign Manual and Signet, dated the said Twenty-eighth day of November 1888, direct and appoint that the said Executive Council and the said Legislative Council respectively should consist of such officers and persons as in the said Instructions are more particularly described:

Recites additional Instructions of 31st October 1898.

And whereas by certain Additional Instructions under Her Royal Sign Manual and Signet bearing date the Thirty-first day of October 1898 Her late Majesty Queen Victoria did define the duration of the appointment of Unofficial Members of the said Legislative Council and provide for the precedence of such Unofficial Members of the said Council as might be re-appointed immediately on the termination of their term of Office:

And whereas We are minded to substitute fresh clauses for Clauses Four, Thirteen, and Seventeen of the aforesaid Instructions of the Twenty-eighth day of November 1888;

Revokes Clauses 4, 13, and 17 of Instructions of 28th November 1888, and substitutes other clauses.

1. Now know you that We have thought fit to revoke the aforesaid Fourth, Thirteenth, and Seventeenth Clauses of the aforesaid Instructions of the Twenty-eighth day of November 1888, and the same are hereby revoked and determined accordingly without prejudice to anything lawfully done thereunder; and instead thereof We do by these Our Additional Instructions under Our Sign Manual and Signet direct and enjoin and declare Our will and pleasure as follows:—

The aforesaid Instructions of the Twenty-eighth day of November 1888 shall hereafter be read as though the following clauses had been inserted therein in place of the Fourth, Thirteenth, and Seventeenth Clauses thereof respectively:—

Constitution of Executive Council.

"IV. The Executive Council of the Colony shall consist of the following Members, that is to say: the Lieutenant-Governor of the Colony (if any), the person for the time being lawfully discharging the functions of Colonial Secretary, who shall be styled *ex-officio* Members of the Executive Council, and such persons as We may from time to time appoint by any Instructions or Warrants under Our Sign Manual and Signet, or through one of Our Principal Secretaries of State, or as the Governor may provisionally appoint in the manner hereafter provided."

"Whenever upon any special occasion the Governor desires to obtain the advice of any person within the Colony touching Our affairs therein he may, by an Instrument under the Public Seal of the Colony, summon for such special occasion any such person as an Extraordinary Member of the Executive Council." Extraordinary Members.

"Whenever any person appointed by Us shall, by writing under his hand, resign his seat in the Executive Council, or shall die, or be suspended from the exercise of his functions as a member of the Executive Council, or be declared by the Governor by an Instrument under the Public Seal to be incapable of exercising his functions as a Member of the Council, or be absent from the Colony, or shall either permanently or temporarily become an *ex-officio* Member of the Council, the Governor may, by an Instrument under the Public Seal, appoint some person to be provisionally a Member of the Council in the place of the Member so resigning or dying, or being suspended or declared incapable, or being absent, or becoming either permanently or temporarily an *ex-officio* Member. Provisional appointments.

"Every such provisional appointment may be disallowed by Us through one of Our Principal Secretaries of State, or may be revoked by the Governor by any such Instrument as aforesaid."

"XIII. The Legislative Council of the Colony shall consist of the Governor, the Lieutenant Governor (if any), the persons for the time being lawfully discharging the functions of Colonial Secretary and Chief Magistrate, who shall be styled *ex-officio* Members of the Legislative Council, and such other persons holding office in the Colony as We may from time to time appoint by any Instructions or Warrants under Our Sign Manual and Signet, or through one of Our Principal Secretaries of State, or as the Governor may provisionally appoint in the manner hereinafter provided, who shall be styled Official Members of the Legislative Council; and further of such persons, not holding office in the Colony as the Governor, in pursuance of any Instructions from Us, through one of Our Principal Secretaries of State may from time to time appoint by any Instrument under the Public Seal of the Colony, who shall be styled Unofficial Members of the Legislative Council." Constitution of Legislative Council. Official Members. Unofficial Members.

"Whenever any Official Member shall, by writing under his hand, resign his seat in the Council, or shall die, or be suspended from the exercise of his functions as a Member of the Council, or be declared by the Governor by an Instrument under the Public Seal to be incapable of exercising his functions as a Member of the Council, or be absent from the Colony, or shall either permanently or temporarily become an *ex-officio* Member of the Council, the Governor may, by an Instrument under the Public

Provisional appointment of Official Members.

Seal, appoint some person to be provisionally a Member of the Council in the place of the Member so resigning or dying, or being suspended or declared incapable, or being absent, or becoming either permanently or temporarily an *ex-officio* Member.

"Every such provisional appointment may be disallowed by Us through one of Our Principal Secretaries of State, or may be revoked by the Governor by any such Instrument as aforesaid."

Precedence of Members.

"XVII. The *ex-officio* and Official Members of the Legislative Council shall take precedence of the Unofficial Members; and among themselves shall take precedence as We may specially assign, and, in default therof, first the *ex-officio* Members in the order in which their respective offices are mentioned; then the Official Members; and after them the Unofficial Members; and the Official Members and Unofficial Members shall among themselves take precedence according to the priority of their respective appointments, or if appointed by the same instrument, according to the order in which they are named therein."

2. These Our Additional Instructions shall take effect so soon as they shall have been received in the Colony by the Governor.

E. R.

For Product Safety Concerns and Information please contact our EU representative GPSR@taylorandfrancis.com
Taylor & Francis Verlag GmbH, Kaufingerstraße 24, 80331 München, Germany

www.ingramcontent.com/pod-product-compliance
Lightning Source LLC
Chambersburg PA
CBHW052140300426
44115CB00011B/1462

* 9 7 8 1 0 3 2 4 2 1 7 4 2 *